Coping with Chronic Stress

The Plenum Series on Stress and Coping

Series Editor:
Donald Meichenbaum, *University of Waterloo, Waterloo, Ontario, Canada*

Editorial Board: Bruce P. Dohrenwend, *Columbia University* •Marianne Frankenhauser, *University of Stockholm* • Norman Garmezy, *University of Minnesota* • Mardi J. Horowitz, *University of California Medical School, San Francisco* • Richard S. Lazarus, *University of California, Berkeley* • Michael Rutter, *University of London*• Dennis C. Turk, *University of Pittsburgh* • John P. Wilson, *Cleveland State University* • Camille Wortman, *University of Michigan*

Current Volumes in the Series:

BEYOND TRAUMA
Cultural and Societal Dynamics
Edited by Rolf J. Kleber, Charles R. Figley, and Berthold P. R. Gersons

COMMUTING STRESS
Causes, Effects, and Methods of Coping
Meni Koslowsky, Avraham N. Kluger, and Mordechai Reich

COPING WITH CHRONIC STRESS
Edited by Benjamin H. Gottlieb

COPING WITH WAR-INDUCED STRESS
The Gulf War and the Israeli Response
Zahava Solomon

HANDBOOK OF SOCIAL SUPPORT AND THE FAMILY
Edited by Gregory R. Pierce, Barbara R. Sarason, and Irwin G. Sarason

PSYCHOTRAUMATOLOGY
Key Papers and Core Concepts in Post-Traumatic Stress
Edited by George S. Everly, Jr. and Jeffrey M. Lating

STRESS AND MENTAL HEALTH
Contemporary Issues and Prospects for the Future
Edited by William R. Avison and Ian H. Gotlib

TRAUMATIC STRESS
From Theory to Practice
Edited by John R. Freedy and Stevan E. Hobfoll

THE UNNOTICED MAJORITY IN PSYCHIATRIC INPATIENT CARE
Charles A. Kiesler and Celeste G. Simpkins

A Continuation Order Plan is available for this series. A continuation order will bring delivery of each new volume immediately upon publication. Volumes are billed only upon actual shipment. For further information please contact the publisher.

Coping with Chronic Stress

Edited by
Benjamin H. Gottlieb
University of Guelph
Guelph, Ontario, Canada

PLENUM PRESS • NEW YORK AND LONDON

Library of Congress Cataloging-in-Publication Data

Coping with chronic stress / edited by Benjamin H. Gottlieb.
       p.   cm. -- (The Plenum series on stress and coping)
    Includes bibliographical references and index.
    ISBN 0-306-45470-X
    1. Adaptability (Psychology) 2. Adjustment (Psychology)
 3. Stress (Psychology)   I. Gottlieb, Benjamin H. II. Series.
 BF335.C588 1997
 155.9'042--dc21   96-51879
                                                               CIP

ISBN 0-306-45470-X

© 1997 Plenum Press, New York
A Division of Plenum Publishing Corporation
233 Spring Street, New York, N. Y. 10013

http://www.plenum.com

All rights reserved

10 9 8 7 6 5 4 3 2 1

No part of this book may be reproduced, stored in a retrieval system, or transmitted in any form or by any means, electronic, mechanical, photocopying, microfilming, recording, or otherwise, without written permission from the Publisher

Printed in the United States of America

For Barbara

Contributors

Carolyn M. Aldwin, Department of Human and Community Development, University of California, Davis, Davis, California 95616

Julian Barling, School of Business, Queen's University, Kingston, Ontario, Canada K7L 3N6

Jennifer Brustrom, Department of Human and Community Development, University of California, Davis, Davis, California 95616

Sarah L. Clark, Department of Psychology, Kent State University, Kent, Ohio 44242-0001

Bruce E. Compas, Department of Psychology, University of Vermont, Burlington, Vermont 05405-0134

Jennifer Connor, Department of Psychology, University of Vermont, Burlington, Vermont 05405-0134

Anita DeLongis, Department of Psychology, University of British Columbia, Vancouver, British Columbia, Canada V6T 1Z4

Susan Folkman, Center for AIDS Prevention Studies, University of California, San Francisco, San Francisco, California 94105

Monique A. M. Gignac, Arthritis Community Research and Evaluation Unit, The Wellesley Hospital Research Institute, Toronto, Ontario, Canada M4Y 1J3

Benjamin H. Gottlieb, Department of Psychology, University of Guelph, Guelph, Ontario, Canada N1G 2W1

Zev Harel, School of Social Work, Cleveland State University, Cleveland, Ohio 44115

C. Gail Hepburn, Department of Psychology, Queen's University, Kingston, Ontario, Canada K7L 3N6

Jeanne M. Hoffman, Department of Psychology, Arizona State University, Tempe, Arizona 85287-1104

Lani Holland, Department of Sociology, Case Western Reserve University, Cleveland, Ohio 44106-7124

Boaz Kahana, Department of Psychology, Cleveland State University, Cleveland, Ohio 44115

Eva Kahana, Department of Sociology, Case Western Reserve University, Cleveland, Ohio 44106-7124

Kathy Kelly, Department of Sociology, Case Western Reserve University, Cleveland, Ohio 44106-7124

Stephen J. Lepore, Department of Psychology, Carnegie Mellon University, Pittsburgh, Pennsylvania 15213-3890

Catherine A. Loughlin, Department of Psychology, Queen's University, Kingston, Ontario, Canada K7L 3N6

Pam Monaghan, Department of Sociology, Case Western Reserve University, Cleveland, Ohio 44106-7124

Judith Tedlie Moskowitz, Center for AIDS Prevention Studies, University of California, San Francisco, San Francisco, California 94105

Tess Byrd O'Brien, Department of Psychology, University of British Columbia, Vancouver, British Columbia, Canada V6T 1Z4

Dana Osowiecki, Department of Psychology, University of Vermont, Burlington, Vermont 05405-0134

Elizabeth M. Ozer, Division of Adolescent Medicine, University of California, San Francisco, San Francisco, California 94105

Crystal L. Park, Department of Psychology, Miami University, Oxford, Ohio 45056

John W. Reich, Department of Psychology, Arizona State University, Tempe, Arizona 85287-1104

Rena L. Repetti, Department of Psychology, University of California, Los Angeles, Los Angeles, California 90095-1563

CONTRIBUTORS

Mary Ann Parris Stephens, Department of Psychology, Kent State University, Kent, Ohio 44242-0001

Amy Welch, Department of Psychology, University of Vermont, Burlington, Vermont 05405-0134

Blair Wheaton, Department of Sociology, University of Toronto, Toronto, Ontario, Canada M5T 1P9

Jenifer Wood, Department of Psychology, University of California, Los Angeles, Los Angeles, California 90095-1563

Alex J. Zautra, Department of Psychology, Arizona State University, Tempe, Arizona 85287-1104

Preface

Much of what we know about the subject of coping is based on human behavior and cognition during times of crisis and transition. Yet the alarms and major upheavals of life comprise only a portion of those experiences that call for adaptive efforts. There remains a vast array of life situations and conditions that pose continuing hardship and threat and do not promise resolution. These chronic stressors issue in part from persistently difficult life circumstances, roles, and burdens, and in part from the conversion of traumatic events into persisting adjustment challenges. Indeed, there is growing recognition of the fact that many traumatic experiences leave a long-lasting emotional residue. Whether or not coping with chronic problems differs in form, emphasis, or function from the ways people handle acute life events and transitions is one of the central issues taken up in these pages.

This volume explores the varied circumstances and experiences that give rise to chronic stress, as well as the ways in which individuals adapt to and accommodate them. It addresses a number of substantive and methodological questions that have been largely overlooked or sidelined in previous inquiries on the stress and coping process. Do relatively enduring problems, conflicts, and threats elicit mainly palliative responses because so little can be done to manage or resolve these difficulties? When persistent demands are not eventful in nature, but form much of the fabric of everyday life, how can coping responses be distinguished from ordinary behavior? How is it possible to gauge coping when neither objective events nor subjective stress can be used to anchor respondents' reports? How much of coping is intentional and volitional, how much is automatic and overlearned, and how much do these two kinds of responses cycle back and forth? Are certain modes of coping implicated in the genesis or persistence of stress because of the social conflict produced by interpersonal clashes in coping or because some coping devices magnify or prolong distress? Does coping become more flexible and effective over time as a result of trial and error learning, or does its effectiveness decrease due to the narrowing or depletion of personal and social resources? More generally, how do people gauge the progress and efficacy of their coping responses when it is apparent that the stressful conditions or demands they face cannot be mastered?

The contributors to this volume were invited to address these and other important questions about the subject of chronic stress. They were chosen because of their considerable knowledge of the stress and coping literature and their pioneering research on particular aspects or contexts of chronic stress. The authors were requested not only to highlight the features of chronic stressors that shape particular coping responses, but also to set out an agenda for future inquiries on the subject. By formulating testable hypotheses that link coping tasks and goals to the persons and contexts under study, investigators will spur theoretical advances in this field. At present, few empirical investigations of coping are based on such theoretically derived propositions. Finally, the contributors were asked to discuss the varied effects of chronic stressors. In addition to their implications for personal mental health and role functioning, chronic life difficulties may exert an influence on social relations, including the availability of social support, and aggravate the impact of acute life events.

I offer thanks to all the authors for their cooperation and for the intellectual vigor of their contributions. I am especially grateful to Carolyn Aldwin, Barbara Morrongiello, and Bob Weiss for their insightful comments and sage advice regarding the introductory chapter. In addition, my thanks go to the series editor, Donald Meichenbaum, and to Plenum's Executive Editor, Eliot Werner, for their guidance and forebearance during the course of this project. Most of all, I am indebted to Barbara Morrongiello. Her unswerving support and love made one of the most trying periods of my life renascent and joyful.

Contents

I: INTRODUCTION

1. Conceptual and Measurement Issues in the Study of Coping with Chronic Stress 3

Benjamin H. Gottlieb

Introduction 3
Acute and Chronic Stressors: Fluid Boundaries
  and Interactive Effects 5
The Challenges of Assessing Coping with Chronic Stress 10
  Determining the Focus of Coping 10
  Documenting Coping without Relying on Eventful or Stressful
    Markers 12
Temporal Changes in Coping with Chronic Stressors 16
Prominent Modes of Coping with Chronic Stress 19
  Vigilance and Respite 20
  Future Outlook 24
  Making Meaning through Cognitive Reinterpretation 25
  Acceptance, Resignation, and Religiosity 27
  Instrumental Coping 28
The Bases of Efficacy 29
Organization and Overview of the Volume 32
References 37

II: THEORY AND PERSPECTIVES

2. The Nature of Chronic Stress 43

Blair Wheaton

Prefatory Note	43
Introduction	44
Of Stressors, Stress, and Stress Outcomes	44
Defining Stress	45
Elaborating the Stress Domain	48
Models of the Stress Concept—Reconsidered	49
Events versus Chronic Stressors	52
Forms of Chronic Stress	57
Threats	57
Demands	58
Structural Constraints	59
Underreward	60
Complexity	61
Uncertainty	62
Conflict	63
Restriction of Choice	63
Resource Deprivation	64
Measuring Chronic Stress	65
Conclusions	68
Appendix: Classification of the Chronic Stress Items from the Stress Measurement Survey	69
References	72

3. Theories of Coping with Chronic Stress: Illustrations from the Health Psychology and Aging Literatures 75

Carolyn M. Aldwin and Jennifer Brustrom

Theoretical Models of Coping	76
Coping with Acute Stress	76
Critique	80
Application of Current Models of Chronic Stress	81
Models of Coping with Chronic Stress	82
Patterns of Coping with Chronic Illness	85
Predictors of Coping Patterns	85

CONTENTS

Outcomes of Coping Efforts 87
Limitations of Studies 90
Aging as a Paradigm for Coping with Chronic Stress 92
A Deviation Amplification Model of Coping
  with Chronic Stress 95
Future Research 98
References 99

4. Effortful and Involuntary Responses to Stress: Implications for Coping with Chronic Stress 105

Bruce E. Compas, Jennifer Connor, Dana Osowiecki, and Amy Welch

Acute and Chronic Stress 107
Responses to Stress: Effortful and Involuntary Processes 109
  Coping as an Effortful Process: Try and Try Again 109
  Involuntary Responses to Stress: Unwanted Effects
    of Unintended Reactions 110
  Engagement and Disengagement Responses to Stress 115
  Rumination, Avoidance, and Distraction 116
  A Framework for Distinguishing Responses to Stress 117
Understanding Responses to Chronic Stress 121
  Involuntary Processes Contribute to Chronic Stress 121
  Affective and Physical Consequences of Avoidant
    Coping Efforts 123
  Involuntary Thoughts, Avoidance, and Effortful
    Engagement Coping 125
Future Directions 126
References 128

III: THE SOCIAL CONTEXT OF COPING WITH CHRONIC STRESS

5. Social–Environmental Influences on the Chronic Stress Process 133

Stephen J. Lepore

Overview 133
Social Origins of Chronic Stress 133

Loneliness 135
Social Stimulus Overload 136
Stressful Life Events 137
Social Roles 137
Stigma 139
Migration 139
Summary 140
Social Environment as a Modifier of Chronic Stress 141
Chronic Stress Buffer 141
Chronic Stress Amplification 144
Summary 149
Social Environment as a Mediator of Chronic Stress 150
Support Deterioration 150
Stress Transmission 152
Summary 153
Conclusion 154
References 156

6. Coping with Chronic Stress: An Interpersonal Perspective .. 161

Tess Byrd O'Brien and Anita DeLongis

The Interpersonal Context of Coping 162
Sources of Strain in Chronic Stress Contexts 162
Dyadic Patterns of Coping and Their Significance
    for Well-Being 164
The Role of Close Relationships in Coping and Well-Being ... 169
The Role of Coping in Disrupting Relationships
    and Diminishing Support 171
Relationship-Focused Coping: Sustaining Social Relationships during
    Periods of Chronic Stress 173
Empathic Coping 174
Other Forms of Relationship-Focused Coping 183
Conclusion 184
References 185

7. Families Accommodating to Chronic Stress: Unintended and Unnoticed Processes 191

Rena L. Repetti and Jenifer Wood

Coping as an Interpersonal Process 192
The Unintentional Involvement of Others in Coping 192

The Daycare Study	198
Long-Term Implications of Coping as an Interpersonal Process	208
What Can Short-Term Responses to Stress Tell Us about Coping with Chronic Stress?	208
Family Accommodation to Chronic Stress	211
Implications for Coping Assessment	213
Accommodation to Poverty and Community Violence	216
Summary	218
References	219

8. Reciprocity in the Expression of Emotional Support among Later-Life Couples with Stroke 221

Mary Ann Parris Stephens and Sarah L. Clark

Stroke as a Chronic Stressor for Married Couples	221
Emotional Support in the Context of Chronic Illness	222
A Dyadic Study of Couples Coping with Stroke	225
Sample Characteristics	227
Measures of Interpersonal Communication and Distress	228
Supportive and Unsupportive Communications	230
Comparing Partners on Psychological Distress and Communications	232
Reciprocity in Communications	232
Some Observations on Couples Coping with Stroke	235
Concluding Comments	239
References	240

IV: CONSIDERATIONS OF EFFICACY IN COPING WITH CHRONIC STRESS

9. Changes in Coping with Chronic Stress: The Role of Caregivers' Appraisals of Coping Efficacy 245

Monique A. M. Gignac and Benjamin H. Gottlieb

Introduction	245
Coping with the Chronic Demands of Caregiving	246
Appraisals of Coping Efficacy	248

The Relationship between Coping and Appraisals
  of Coping Efficacy 254
The Stability of Coping Appraisals 258
The Impact of Efficacy Appraisals on Coping 260
Summary and Conclusions 263
References 266

10. The Role of Two Kinds of Efficacy Beliefs in Maintaining the Well-Being of Chronically Stressed Older Adults 269

Alex J. Zautra, Jeanne M. Hoffman, and John W. Reich

Origins of Research on Efficacy Beliefs 270
The Life Event and Aging Project 273
Assessment of Efficacy Beliefs for Positive and Negative
  Events: Development of Two Efficacy Measures 274
  Factor Analysis of Control Beliefs 275
  Stability of Efficacy Ratings 276
The Relationship of Efficacy Beliefs to Adjustment 277
  Efficacy Effects on Well-Being over Time 278
  Correlates of Efficacy Beliefs with Clinical Outcomes:
    The Arthritis Project 279
Examining the Antecedents of Efficacy Beliefs 281
  Social Influences on Efficacy Beliefs 282
  Social Encouragement of Self-Reliance versus Dependency ... 283
Implications for Understanding Coping
  with Chronic Stressors 286
References 289

V: ILLUSTRATIONS OF COPING WITH PERVASIVE LIFE DIFFICULTIES

11. Positive Meaningful Events and Coping in the Context of HIV/AIDS 293

Susan Folkman, Judith Tedlie Moskowitz, Elizabeth M. Ozer, and Crystal L. Park

Introduction 293

Positive Meaningful Events: Relevant Findings and Theoretical Issues	295
Goals of This Chapter	297
Background: The UCSF Coping Project	298
Method: Coding Scheme	299
Coding Process	304
Findings	304
Mood	305
The Context of Meaningful Events	305
Source of Meaning	306
Self-Agency	307
Discussion	308
Theoretical Implications	309
Clinical Implications	311
Conclusion	312
References	313

12. A Framework for Understanding the Chronic Stress of Holocaust Survivors 315

Boaz Kahana, Eva Kahana, Zev Harel, Kathy Kelly, Pam Monaghan, and Lani Holland

Chronic Stressors Faced by Elderly Holocaust Survivors	317
Sample and Methods	318
Trauma-Related Stressors	321
Prewar Stressors	321
Holocaust Traumatic Stressors	321
Postwar Stressors	322
Coping with Chronic Posttraumatic Stressors	322
Coping with Intrusive Memories of Trauma	323
Coping with Fear and Mistrust	326
Coping with the Chronic Stress of Social and Psychological Isolation	328
Coping with Stigma	330
Normative Chronic Life Stressors: Characteristics and Coping Efforts	332
Childhood Life Stressors	333
Adult Life Stressors	333
Chronic Stressors of Aging	337
Conclusion	339
References	340

13. Coping with Chronic Work Stress 343

C. Gail Hepburn, Catherine A. Loughlin, and Julian Barling

Introduction	343
Chronic Work Stressors	344
Sources of Chronic Stress in the Workplace	344
Contemporary Sources of Chronic Work Stress	346
Perceptions of Workplace Stressors	348
Outcomes of Workplace Stressors	349
Methodological Problems in Connecting Chronic Stressors to Specific Effects	350
Coping with Chronic Work Stress	351
The Measurement of Coping	351
Workplace Stressors and Coping	353
Strain and Coping	354
Coping as a Moderator	356
Further Methodological Problems in the Study of Coping	357
Workplace Interventions for Chronic Work Stress	358
Tertiary Preventive Interventions	359
Secondary Preventive Interventions	359
Primary Prevention	360
Conclusion	361
References	363

Index 367

I

Introduction

1

Conceptual and Measurement Issues in the Study of Coping with Chronic Stress

BENJAMIN H. GOTTLIEB

INTRODUCTION

Systematic research on the subject of coping with chronic stress is long overdue. Compared to the voluminous literature that examines responses to acute or short-term stressful events and transitions that have clearly demarcated time spans, the behavioral and emotional regulatory processes that unfold in circumstances of unremitting demand have been understudied. For example, how do people deal with the ongoing threat of neighborhood violence or crime? How do family members come to terms with and learn to manage the long-term disability that results from a spinal cord injury or the uncertainty that arises in the wake of a heart attack or stroke? Are there certain psychological devices that assist recently divorced partners to preserve or restore their sense of self-worth? Are there daily routines and patterns of social interaction that help people maintain their equilibrium in the face of persistent life strains that involve balancing multiple and frequently conflicting social roles?

BENJAMIN H. GOTTLIEB • Department of Psychology, University of Guelph, Guelph, Ontario, Canada N1G 2W1

Coping with Chronic Stress, edited by Benjamin H. Gottlieb. Plenum Press, New York, 1997.

These examples comprise an abbreviated subset of chronic stressors, defined by Wheaton (1994) as " . . . problems and issues that are either so regular in the enactment of daily roles and activities, or so defined by the nature of daily role enactments or activities, that they behave as if they are continuous for the individual" (p. 82). The study of coping with chronic stress promises to enrich theory and enlarge our understanding of human adaptation and development. It can offer insights into our capacity to accommodate to circumstances of continuing hardship and to persevere in the face of unremitting demands. It can also illuminate the extent to which human thought, emotion, and perception are flexible enough to foster adjustment under conditions of continuing and even intensifying difficulty. The study of coping with chronic adversity can also reveal how the routines of ordinary life and everyday patterns of social interaction ward off threat and sustain morale. From this perspective, coping is not conceptualized as a special set of behaviors and cognitions that are activated by alarming events or excessive demands. Instead, it is viewed more broadly as part of the ongoing lifecourse process of adapting and accommodating to transitions, discontinuities, and other destabilizing and threatening experiences.

There is a vast array of relatively enduring and open-ended life difficulties and conditions that fall under the rubric of chronic stress. They vary in terms of their prominence, some standing out in the foreground of daily life and bombarding the individual with blasts of noxious stimuli. Examples include hectic and complex jobs and exposure to family members with disordered functioning, such as those suffering from later stage Alzheimer's disease. In contrast, the background of daily life may be characterized by chronically stressful conditions, such as living in poverty, feeling underrewarded by one's employer, and living apart from the people or places to whom one is most attached. Additional forms of chronic stressors include long-term illness and disability, as well as the frustration and disappointment that attend one's inability to attain life goals, such as career advancement, conception of a child, and involvement in a satisfying romantic relationship. Beyond these forms of chronic stressors, there are ongoing role strains and volcanic situations that threaten to erupt at any moment, such as social climates characterized by tension and competition, and physical environments that pose immediate or long-term danger due to circumstances of crime, pollution, disease, or starvation. Finally, the harshest and most persistently challenging circumstances of chronic stress are epitomized by the experience of imprisonment, terrorism, captivity, and war.

CONCEPTUAL AND MEASUREMENT ISSUES 5

Given the many forms and varied salience of chronic stressors, ranging from disappointments and deprivations that negatively color daily existence for years to immersion in physically or socially noxious environments, it is uncertain whether any but the most general propositions can be advanced about how people cope with them. To address this question with precision, it is necessary first to classify chronic stressors along a common set of dimensions, and then to investigate possible similarities and differences in response patterns as a function of these dimensions. More generally, a systematic approach to the study of coping with chronic stress should properly lay out the boundaries and scope of the subject, identify appropriate parameters for comparing various contexts of chronic stress, and explore the nature and effects of the coping responses of those inhabiting these contexts. Ideally, inquiry should culminate in theoretically derived propositions that link human cognition and behavior to the coping tasks and goals that are relevant to the persons and contexts under study (Coyne & Gottlieb, 1996).

The chapters in this volume begin to address this investigative cycle by distinguishing further among various conceptions and contexts of chronic stress, examining the diverse responses that are elicited by prolonged exposure to life difficulties, and discussing the social and psychological ramifications of these strivings to adjust and accommodate to ongoing challenges. Since many of the contributors have reviewed various portions of the literature on coping with chronic stress, I will not do so in this chapter. Instead, I will touch on the challenges to theory and methodology that arise from the study of chronic stress. These challenges revolve around five topics: the relationship between chronic and acute stressors, techniques for measuring coping with stressors that are not eventful in nature, changes in coping over time, prominent modes of coping with chronic stress, and the bases for assessing the efficacy of these ways of coping. The chapter concludes with an overview of the volume's organization and contents.

ACUTE AND CHRONIC STRESSORS: FLUID BOUNDARIES AND INTERACTIVE EFFECTS

Recent efforts to categorize the full range of chronic stressors divide them in somewhat different ways but share a common recognition of their continuing problematic nature and extended duration. In his chapter in this volume, Wheaton identifies nine fundamental forms of chronic stress, which he organizes into a fourfold classification. He includes stressors arising from both ongoing role occupancy (e.g., role ambiguity on the job) and role inoccupancy (e.g., not being in a desired relationship), as well as stressors that launch new but unwanted social roles, such as single parenthood and job loss leading to prolonged exclusion from the workforce and the receipt of social assistance. His fourth category is more general in nature, consisting of disadvantageous life circumstances, such as overcrowding, poverty, living in substandard and unsafe housing, and repeated experiences of personal discrimination.

McLean and Link (1994) present a similar scheme for classifying chronic stressors, organizing them into four classes that include persistent life difficulties, role strains, and the chronic strain of discrimination. However, their typology uniquely introduces community strains, such as technological and natural disasters, as a fourth category of chronic stressors. One might question why such disasters are considered to be chronic in nature, given that floods, toxic spills, tornadoes, earthquakes, and nuclear accidents are relatively short-lived events. If chronic stressors are defined solely in terms of the duration of exposure, then these natural disasters would not qualify. However, as Baum, O'Keefe, and Davidson (1990) point out, if acute and chronic stressors are distinguished on the basis of the persistence of threat and the duration of the stress and coping responses they elicit, then natural disasters and many other traumatic experiences could be deemed to be chronic stressors.

This conceptualization is certainly consistent with clinical evidence revealing that posttraumatic stress is a disorder that has long-term implications for adjustment. Although many victims of traumatic events, such as rape, sexual abuse in childhood, and criminal victimization, continue to relive these experiences for months, if not years, not all individuals experience such chronic stress. The ways people appraise and cope with traumatic stressors may therefore partially determine whether or not they subsequently experience chronic stress. Hence, to some extent, stressor chronicity is a function of individual differences in the psychological scope of the original event's impact, the continuing threat and sense of vulnerability it arouses, and the ensuing persistence of efforts to manage these sequelae. For some types of stressors then, dispositional, social, and circumstantial factors may be implicated in converting acute adversity into chronic hardship (Baum et al., 1990; Figley, 1985; Herman, 1992).

Generally, the more closely one examines the circumstances and trajectories of the stress process, the more fluid and evanescent are the boundaries between acute and chronic stress. For example, although marital separation, the death of a loved one, and job loss can be conceived as strictly point-in-time events, there is a huge volume of evidence testifying to the extended course of stress that often precedes and follows these events. Job loss can be followed by numerous crises involving failed job interviews and arguments at home, as well as by a prolonged period of financial strain and difficulty in establishing satisfying daily routines. The converse is true as well; the chronic stress of juggling work and family roles is periodically punctuated by acutely stressful events, such as crises in childcare arrangements, accidents and illness diagnoses of elderly relatives, and special projects and time-sensitive assignments at work. Similarly, many chronic illnesses are characterized by unpredictable symptom flare-ups, as in the case of multiple sclerosis and arthritis, or by episodic losses of metabolic control, as in the case of diabetes.

Equally important, the dynamic relations among time-limited stressors that occur only once, recurrent time-limited stressors, and ongoing, open-ended stressors have not been explored. Yet multiple and interacting stressful experiences tend to be the rule rather than the exception in many circumstances of chronic hardship. For example, family caregivers of persons with dementia have to grapple with the specific demands of daily care; manage the disturbing, recurrent cognitive and behavioral problems brought on by the disease; and come to terms with the dislocations and deprivations occasioned by their captivity in the caregiving role (Gottlieb, 1989; Pearlin, Mullan, Semple, & Skaff, 1990). At the same time, they must come to terms with the long-term threat of deterioration, not only in their relative's functioning, but also in their relationship with him or her. In addition, since caregiving tends to be a long-term responsibility, a variety of fateful life events can intercede along the way, further challenging the caregivers' adaptive resources.

Recently, Redinbaugh, MacCallum, and Kiecolt-Glaser (1995) reported that a higher annual frequency of stressful life events was one of the strongest factors differentiating caregivers who had recurrent syndromal depression over a 3-year period from those who had never been depressed and those who had been episodically depressed only once or twice. These findings are consistent with Monroe and Simons' (1991) formulation of diathesis-stress theory, which maintains that the risk of recurrent depression stems from life events being superimposed upon chronic difficulties. It is also noteworthy that the chronically depressed group was also further distinguished from the other two groups by virtue of their exposure to episodes of upsetting interaction with network members at times when they needed emotional or practical aid from them. Hence, prolonged exposure to stress, in combination with depressive affect, can undermine people's social resources and amplify their distress just when they most need the support and help of others. This latter subject is addressed in greater detail by both O'Brien and DeLongis and by Lepore in their respective chapters in this volume.

One factor that deters research on the unique and interactive effects of chronic and acute stressors is the difficulty of determining whether stressful experiences are chronic or acute in nature. For example, McGonagle and Kessler's (1990) method of resolving this quandary was to use a temporal criterion: (1) Chronic stressors were occurrences that had begun at least 12 months before the research interview and ongoing difficulties created by acute events that had taken place more than 12 months earlier; (2) acute stressors were events that had begun in the last 12 months or that qualified as point-in-time stressors. They also coded ongoing difficulties that had significantly changed for the worse as two stressors, one chronic and one acute. However, the authors do not offer any conceptual or empirical justification for choosing the 12-month cutoff, nor do they provide any information about inter-rater reliability in coding life stressors in this way, including the number of items that could not be assigned to one category or the other due to insufficient or ambiguous information. They do, however, acknowledge the bias that may inflate reports of chronic stress, namely that prior mental health problems can increase the duration of stress.

Despite the ambiguity surrounding their classification of stressors, McGonagle and Kessler (1990) found that chronic stressors were stronger predictors of depression than acute stressors, a result they interpreted in two ways. One interpretation is that vulnerability to depression is predicated more strongly on continuing threat, rather than change. The other is that the more recent acute stressors are more likely to have been resolved than the chronic, longer-term stressors. Hence, it is the continuing, open-ended demands that have the stronger ability to undermine equilibrium. This finding echoes but does not replicate Brown and Harris' (1978, 1989) inquiries into the etiology of depression, in which they carefully documented the role that ongoing life difficulties played in concert with acute life events. Specifically, they found that when recent life events were matched in their meaning with a long-term life difficulty, predictive power increased threefold, Thus, there were interactive effects of the two types of stress in predicting depressive symptoms. Consistent with this, other studies have shown that ongoing stressors have the power to amplify the impact of acute life events and must therefore be taken into account in models of risk and vulnerability. For example, there is evidence that environmental stressors exert a stronger adverse impact on people who occupy a lower rung on the socioeconomic ladder compared to those with higher incomes (Kessler & Essex, 1982; Turner & Noh, 1983).

Additional evidence of interaction between acute and chronic stressors comes from studies revealing that stress issuing from ongoing problems in one sphere of life can spill over into other spheres of life (Eckenrode & Gore, 1990; Moen, 1992). For example, hectic and complicated jobs cast a long shadow on home life through the moods that carry over to interactions with family members, the distracting thoughts and preoccupations, and even the expression of patterns of behavior that are normative at work but maladaptive at home (Greenhaus & Beutell, 1985). Moreover, distress is not only transmitted from one context to another; so, too, are the ways of managing it. Coping responses that are employed to moderate the impact of pressures and demands at work can intrude at home. This process is illustrated in Repetti and Wood's chapter in this volume. They show that the ways mothers deal with tensions at work have far-reaching effects on their subsequent interactions with their preschoolers, and that these effects can have adverse relational consequences in the long run.

Coping, including the mobilization of social support, is also likely to be affected by interactions between chronic and acute stressful experiences. If people are preoccupied by ongoing adaptive challenges at a time when they are suddenly exposed to a severe short-term stressor, they may have more difficulty responding effectively because their psychological energy or physical stamina is depleted. Alternatively, efficiency may improve when one only has to shift vigilance, among other coping efforts, from one focus to another. Similarly, it may be easier to mobilize supporters around a new stressor once one has already involved them in ongoing difficulties unless they are so drained by or resentful toward the ongoing demands being made of them that they cannot afford to become involved in yet another stressful episode, regardless of its brevity.

In sum, acute and chronically stressful experiences may shade into one another and interact in a variety of ways. The study of chronic life difficulties presents the opportunity to formulate and test models of the stress process that give full recognition to the interrelationships among acute life disturbances and ongoing life strains. At the least, these models must reflect the facts that the impact of life events differs according to the stressfulness of the ongoing life circumstances and that continuing life difficulties expose people to stressful events that can further deplete their coping resources. Finally, it is important to recognize that the interactive effects of acute and chronic stressors can also decrease stress. Wheaton (1990) points to instances when an acute event can terminate long-term difficulties, such as when marital separation brings conflict to an end and when adoption provides relief from the strain of a protracted, costly, and disappointing process of trying to conceive a child (Stanton & Dunkel-Schetter, 1991).

THE CHALLENGES OF ASSESSING COPING WITH CHRONIC STRESS

Particularly vexing conceptual and methodological problems attend the task of gauging coping with persistent demands and difficulties that are built into the fabric of everyday life. How is it possible to determine the focus of coping when fear of crime or job loss is a fact of life, or when complexity and uncertainty combine over long periods of time, as in the case of a protracted legal battle? What is the most apposite focus and timing of coping measures among people living in overcrowded, dilapidated housing; among couples who have been unsuccessfully attempting to conceive a child; or among families caring for a child who has a serious chronic illness or disability? In these and many other contexts of persistent adversity, characterized by a variable course and an uncertain point of termination, there are few if any signposts to guide the task of measuring coping efforts.

Determining the Focus of Coping

When persistent demands are woven into the tapestry of life, it is virtually impossible to bracket off coping from all the other thoughts and behaviors that people employ to maintain their equilibrium and stay productively engaged in their role repertoires. In these circumstances, it is not meaningful to point to one set of behaviors and cognitions and say that they constitute coping, whereas all the rest is ordinary living. Moreover, depending on the point in time when questions are asked, coping with recurrent or persistent life difficulties may be more effortful or more automatic in nature. For example, what began as an effortful cognitive response designed to be reassuring, such as telling oneself that things could be worse, may later become an automatic habit of mind that is no longer grounded in the particular stress context. Nevertheless, it is employed even more consistently than when it originally emerged as a deliberate response to novel stress. Similarly, behavioral efforts to distract oneself from demoralizing thoughts about one's inability to make career advances, by working out or playing squash for instance, can eventually become incorporated in one's daily life routines and can come to serve other desirable personal and social functions as well. In time, their link to the original stress-moderating function they served will no longer be discerned by the respondent because they have become part of the organization of daily life.

These observations bring into question some basic assumptions of the transactional model of coping that dominates present theorizing in the stress field (Lazarus & Folkman, 1984). This model maintains that coping is effortful, situationally focused, and accessible to consciousiousness so that it can be reported. But if the source of chronic stress resides in the relatively enduring circumstances of life, such as living in poverty or being the target of discrimination, then it may not be possible for the respondent to identify a specific stressful transaction. Even if it were possible for respondents to punctuate their experience of chronic stress by focusing on particularly stressful occurrences, why should these occasions be deemed to be representative of all the stressful components of this life experience? Similarly, why should the coping efforts that are elicited at these times necessarily epitomize the respondent's way of dealing with the experience? For example, in studies of ways of coping with chronic illnesses, researchers typically inquire about junctures of heightened demand and threat, such as the time of initial diagnosis and the occasions when flare-ups and setbacks occurred. However, coping with illness during these acute episodes, when one's life may be threatened, is likely to be quite different than coping with the disease when one's condition is stable.

Human conduct and cognition during times of turbulence and extra pressure are not necessarily continuous with actions and thoughts under steady-state conditions. Furthermore, in chronically stressful contexts, steady-state does not necessarily mean stress-free conditions, but conditions of usual or normative demand that nevertheless require adaptive responses. It is likely that the coping profiles that characterize periods of alarm will differ from those that characterize periods of relative calm by virtue of the predominance of emotion-focused responses to heightened threat and more flexible and more broadly distributed responses in periods of relative calm. Perhaps the functions rather than the modes of coping will differ on these contrasting occasions. For example, whereas supporters may be called on for emotional security and validation during episodes of intense threat, at times of less intense demand they may be enlisted to provide advice, information, and practical assistance. It is also possible that the ways of coping with normative versus heightened demand do not differ, but have different patterns of relationships with outcomes during these contrasting periods. When crises erupt, coping will restore emotional equilibrium; in periods of relative calm, coping will contribute to positive affect and a sense of well-being.

The point is that there is no single optimal moment, stressful occasion, or stage when the most accurate picture of coping with chronic stress is likely to be gained. In fact, because coping changes over time in response to fluctuating personal and environmental conditions, it is necessary to sample the coping process as broadly as possible. Hence, techniques should be employed to capture thoughts and behaviors at times of extraordinary and everyday demand, without exclusive reliance on eventful markers and stressful ratings of life experiences. By superimposing a life event framework on the experience of chronic stress, people's efforts to come to terms with ongoing conditions of uncertainty, complexity, novelty, conflict, or disappointment will be artificially constrained to mirror the coping efforts they make during times of crisis. Moreover, as Coyne and Gottlieb (1996) suggest, differences in respondents' ratings of the stressfulness of a given event may signify differences in their ability to absorb its impact through routinely and naturally deploying their resources. Reports of modest or no stress may be due to the respondent's ability to take the demand in stride through adopting certain attitudes, engaging in certain daily routines, and affiliating with particular people. Some individuals may possess the skills and resources to smoothly integrate adversity, whereas others may experience continuous disruption and distress.

In sum, many contexts of chronic stress do not lend themselves to an event-centered strategy of measuring coping, and much of coping with chronic stress will be missed if attention is focused only on effortful responses to perceived stress on those occasions when acute events punctuate the chronic stress process. To gain a comprehensive understanding of the coping process, it is necessary also to sample people's responses to the demands they face during periods when they absorb them more and less smoothly and with more and less subjective distress.

Documenting Coping without Relying on Eventful or Stressful Markers

How then is it possible to gauge the ways people cope with repeated external and internal messages that communicate to them that they are underachieving at work? How is it possible to document the ways people deal with continuing unhappiness in a close relationship or with the restriction on their freedom that results from caring for a relative with dementia? In these instances, it is not possible to identify a discrete stressor because the adaptive challenge is created by basic structural arrangements, role responsibilities, deprivations, or the press of living.

Recent developments in the measurement of daily stress, coping, mood, and physiological states are particularly well suited to the study of responses to chronic hardships. However, virtually all of these techniques attempt to capture the day's stressful demands by relying on self-report event checklists or by obtaining a global rating of stress and then having the respondent circle back to the events that produced the rating (Stone, Neale, & Shiffman, 1993). Therefore, they cannot gauge the chronic stressors that are built into daily role enactment, environmental demands, or the daily pressures that people place on themselves via expectations of themselves or the discomfiting messages they communicate to themselves. These latter sources of stress are likely to be so deeply embedded in the fabric of life and so well ingrained as habits of mind as to be inaccessible to the respondent who is asked to account for elevated stress ratings or to represent the days' difficulties by endorsing even minor daily hassles. Moreover, if the day's stress is not related to the events that occurred or if the day's stress was smoothly handled or preempted by employing certain habits and routines (Coyne & Gottlieb, 1996), then much of the stress of life and much of how it is managed or contained will be missed. For instance, for the experienced commuter, the daily after-work ride in a jammed, noisy, and filthy subway car probably does not register as a stressful experience because the newspaper or radio headphones offers the necessary diversion. If questioned explicitly about the stress of the subway ride, the respondent would probably acknowledge its unpleasantness but not its stressfulness because of the shielding function of the newspaper habit.

This example also points to the subtle and unnoticed way in which a chronic "foreground stressor" can become a "background stressor" over time. This transformation does not simply reflect stress habituation; diminished arousal following repeated exposure occurs only in part because the novelty of the stressor wears off. Rather, the salience of chronic stressors diminishes partly because adaptive coping responses are eventually found and then routinely and effortlessly employed. What began as intentional efforts to moderate or blunt the stressful aspects of the subway ride are eventually incorporated into daily routines. In their chapter in this volume, Aldwin and Brustrom refer to these routines as "generalized management skills" and propose that these skills often play a critical function in preventing stress. Once developed, these skills are abandoned or modified when they prove maladaptive, insufficient, or too costly or when they interfere with competing personal needs, social pressures, or environmental constraints. Hence, coping also shifts from foreground activity involving effort to reduce or manage salient demands to background activity constituting only a tiny fraction of a well-rehearsed pattern of daily life.

By extension, when it comes to the measurement of coping with chronic background stress, the challenge is to sample all those thoughts and behaviors that are related to the subject of special interest to the researcher, but to do so without asking the respondent to link them explicitly to perceived stress levels or to the occurrence of daily events. This conceptual approach is strikingly different from the conventional strategy of assessing coping, which presents the respondent with a checklist of many different ways of coping or inquires about a broad type of coping to determine whether the respondent thought or did anything *with the intention* of managing certain identified stressful demands. In short, if coping evanesces into ordinary routines and mental habits, then it is the researcher, not the respondent, who must gather the empirical evidence linking acts and cognitions to the chronic background stress of interest.

The tools that are presently available to accomplish this task include thought-sampling techniques (Kendall & Hollon, 1981; Wegner, Schneider, Carter, & White, 1987), daily diaries (Eckenrode & Bolger, 1995) and within-day recordings (Stone & Shiffman, 1992) as well as *in situ* monitoring devices, including surveillance reports by trained observers who record certain target behaviors (Suls & Martin, 1993). As several authors have noted, daily and within-day techniques of naturalistic monitoring can be recorded on an interval-contingent, signal-contingent, or event-contingent basis (Wheeler & Reis, 1991). Interval-contingent recording involves the respondents reporting their thoughts and behaviors at predetermined times, either in an open-ended way or by selecting the responses that apply to them from a checklist. For example, to study conflict between work and family roles, researchers may wish to sample behaviors, cognitions, and affective states at strategic times: at home before the workday commences, during the commute to work, at the lunch hour, at the time of day when the children are expected to return home, during the commute back home, at the time when the two parents are reunited, during dinner preparation, and after the children have gone to bed. As its name implies, signal-contingent recording has respondents complete a structured questionnaire or checklist whenever they receive a message—by phone, pager, or signal watch—to do so. Fixed, random, or both types of signal intervals can be used, depending on the researcher's aims. Finally, when event-contingent recording is used, respondents complete a report whenever a predetermined event occurs, such as an argument with their spouse or an asthma attack.

CONCEPTUAL AND MEASUREMENT ISSUES

Since chronic background stress is not eventful in nature, however, event-contingent recording cannot be used. Although there may be environmental stimuli that occasionally make this background stress more prominent, they are not necessary or sufficient triggers of coping responses. Hence, instead of employing an event-contingent recording schedule, a thought-contingent technique may be more appropriate. For example, to capture the chronic background stress that attends the performance of work and family roles, respondents could be asked to record their cognitive and behavioral reactions each time they have thoughts about the cross-pressures between these two spheres of life. They could be provided with a sample list of these thoughts that might include items touching on their performance in each domain, their children's well-being, the quality of the time they spend with their family, and the ways in which their mood and worries spill over from one domain to the other. They could then either complete a checklist or a structured questionnaire to record their feelings and their cognitive and behavioral responses to these thoughts.

One objection to this strategy might be based on the potential confounding of the stressor and the coping response since those who are dealing with such role conflict by monitoring or sensitizing modes will be overrepresented relative to those who employ cognitive avoidance and denial. However, according to the empirical evidence reviewed by Compas and his colleagues in this volume, because of its prolonged or recurrent character, chronic stress is likely to arouse automatic or involuntary cognitions that act as internal mechanisms for re-experiencing stress. Hence, relatively early in a chronic stressor's course, most individuals experience these intrusive thoughts, and they constitute an internal representation of the stress to which they feel subjected. The key factor that distinguishes those who are more and less vulnerable to the adverse effects of these automatic thoughts is their ability to assert control in ways that preempt or disrupt the thoughts. Adjustment is therefore predicated on the ways individuals learn to respond to these thoughts. On the basis of both laboratory and field data, Compas concludes that if these individuals come to rely on avoiding or suppressing the intrusive thoughts, then they are at greater risk of prolonged distress and associated adverse health effects, whereas if they employ distraction and other forms of actively disengaging from the thoughts, ameliorative effects are more likely to follow. Hence, the measurement strategy of choice is to assess the sequence of thoughts and responses as early as possible in the course of chronic stress, gauging changes both in their frequency or persistence and in the pattern of coping responses they elicit. In this way, it may be possible to discern how people cycle between automatic reactions and effortful responses, and how the kinds of coping they employ affect their current and future adaptation.

TEMPORAL CHANGES IN COPING WITH CHRONIC STRESSORS

Chronic stressors offer a vantage point for examining human adaptation because repeated or prolonged exposure to similar demands provides opportunities for learning through trial and error. Certain ways of coping may fall by the wayside because they are ineffective or because, cumulatively, they are too costly. Other ways of coping may be retained, and new efforts may be introduced to replace those that have been discarded. For example, although withdrawal may be effective in the short term as a way of handling marital conflict, in the long run this strategy may alienate the parties even further, forcing them either to abandon these tactics for the sake of their relationship or to consider separation.

The fact that chronically stressful experiences and circumstances are open-ended and extended in duration does not mean that they do not change. With the passage of time, stressors can change in their nature, frequency, and intensity. For some types of chronic stressors, it is likely that periods of relative stability and predictability alternate with periods of upheaval, novelty, and uncertainty. Consequently, prospective investigations may reveal cycles of effortful and routinized coping. This pattern is well exemplified by reports of people who are striving to adjust to chronic illnesses that have variable courses. For example, in their study of temporal changes in patterns of diabetes symptom and regimen management, Peyrot, McMurray, and Hedges (1987) cite numerous instances of patients and their family members oscillating between efforts to adhere strictly to the regimen set out for them and a more relaxed and natural style of handling their illness. At times when they experienced complications, crises, and flare-ups, they responded to the threat by exercising tight control over their regimen, whereas during periods of relative stability they relaxed their control, integrating the management of their disease in day-to-day routines.

Coping responses can also shift in relation to changes in the individual's commerce with the environment. After all, since coping is in part determined by the use and perception of available resources in the individual's social, institutional, and physical surroundings, the trajectory of coping can be powerfully shaped by changes in these circumstances. When people move from one geographic community to another, they may experience vast changes in both their social networks and in the institutional resources to which they have access. But even when people stay in the same community, they can experience changes in their household composition and in their neighborhood and workplace associates, as well as in their own health, attitudes, and values. Both these social and developmental changes can powerfully alter the resources they can employ as well as the meaning and impact of the life difficulties they continue to face.

Changes in the external environment can affect coping both directly and indirectly. They can have a direct effect by improving or blocking individuals' access to valued social and material resources, whereas they can exercise an indirect effect on several forms of psychological coping. For example, Viney and Westbrook (1984) asked coronary patients about their reliance on different modes of coping while they were in the hospital immediately after an acute health event, and 7 months later at home. The patients believed they were using more optimistic coping in the hospital and more fatalistic coping at home. In addition to an interpretation based on differences in the ways people cope with acute versus long-term effects of illness, the authors suggest that the greater safety and expertise that is provided in hospital produces more optimistic expectancies. In addition, the hospital may contribute to optimism by offering opportunities for downward social comparisons and by actively involving the patients in a regimen that promises to speed their recovery from the acute episode.

As a result of prolonged mobilization, both personal and social resources can also deteriorate or improve over time. For example, the fund of support can become depleted or it may be construed in more threatening ways. Coyne, Wortman, and Lehman (1988) have reported on the ways in which a protracted sequence of interpersonal helping can miscarry and even compound the stress that provided the initial occasion for the mobilization of support. In their chapters in this volume, Lepore and O'Brien and DeLongis discuss the many ways in which close relationships can be adversely affected when patterns of coping clash, when the parties' coping goals diverge, and when they arrive at different conclusions about the progress of their coping, using different criteria. Especially when intense support is required for an extended period of time, as opposed to a brief crisis episode, the support providers can come to resent the burden that has been placed on them rather than gaining a sense of pride and satisfaction from the helpful role they have assumed. Naturally, this depends a great deal on their relationship with the recipient, on their interpretations of their role responsibilities, and on the responses they receive from both the recipient and other reference group members. For example, in the field of gerontology, despite some acknowledgement of the satisfactions and rewards of caregiving, the weight of the evidence testifies to the strain, subjective burden, and adverse health consequences it engenders (for a review, see Schulz, O'Brien, Bookwala, & Fleissner, 1995).

Chronic stress can place enormous strain on the fund of support, especially if the source of continuing demand and pressure is unchangeable or poses a similar threat to others. When long-term stress and threat are posed by medical illnesses, disability, financial strain, and impaired cognitive or emotional functioning, the support process is particularly delicate and susceptible to deterioration. This is not only because sustained support can drain the providers' energy and overtax their good will, but also because it can undermine the recipient's autonomy and sense of efficacy. For example, in their chapter in this volume, Zautra, Hoffman, and Reich show that support that encourages disabled persons to be self-reliant has different effects depending on the extent to which the recipients' activities are limited by the disability. In examining the course of disability among a sample of elderly persons, they found that when there was little activity limitation, encouragement of self-reliance bolstered a sense of self-efficacy. However, once activity limitation was more extensive, such encouragement undermined the respondents' self-efficacy because it suggested that they could not cope by calling on assistance from others. That is, when support was not perceived to be available to cope with existing disability, it undermined confidence in one's ability to respond effectively to present demands.

These findings are echoed by Krause (1995), who found that high levels of support amplified rather than buffered the effects of the chronic financial strain experienced by a sample of elderly persons. Whether this occurred because of the emotional overinvolvement of others or because of declines in self-efficacy is unknown. In any case, accumulating evidence suggests that, as hardship persists, the support process must be carefully managed, especially in terms of the extent of reciprocity, autonomy, and empathy that is communicated between the parties.

Intriguing questions are posed by the longitudinal study of coping with chronic stressors. Do chronic stressors have cumulative adverse effects on mental health or morale, or do they lose their sting over time because they can be anticipated and because past experience has taught that they can be managed? In a fascinating and important study, Erdal and Zautra (1995) compared the distress experienced by elderly persons who experienced at least two health "downturns" stemming from chronic arthritis and vision problems with elderly persons who were newly diagnosed with these two health problems. They found that the downturn group, especially those with arthritis, experienced greater distress than the newly diagnosed group, even when pain reports were statistically controlled. Hence, in this instance, familiarity with health stressors and their consequences did not cushion their impact, a finding that suggests that coping does not improve after repeated exposure to the same stressor. Of course, if the downturn group actually experienced new rather than recurrent signs of worsening health, they may not have been able to predict the kind of health event that would occur and to engage in anticipatory coping. It is therefore essential for future studies of this sort to verify that coping and health outcomes are examined in relation to a truly recurrent stressor in the sense that it approximates the intensity or severity of earlier stressful episodes.

Finally, as Aldwin and Brustrom point out in their chapter in this volume, there have been few longitudinal studies of coping with chronic stressors, and therefore little is known about the extent of flexibility and variability in human coping. Do people actually gain new insights about ways of managing or tolerating recurrent or persistent stressors? Can they translate these insights into action, channeling their thoughts in new ways and changing their behavioral patterns? To the extent that people learn from and can redirect their responses, coping can be seen as a truly strategic enterprise rather than as a set of reflexes, strongly ingrained habits, and dominant responses that are dictated by the force of personality (Costa, Somerfield, & McCrae, 1996). Moreover, if personality characteristics are revealed most strongly in responses to novel, unpredictable, and uncertain circumstances (Caspi & Moffitt, 1993), then perhaps familiar circumstances of stress potentiate more deliberate and planful responses that are calculated to deal with situational demands and constraints. To the extent that some chronic stressors recur with the same form and intensity, whether they involve crowding, traffic congestion, or exposure to the daily grind at work, they allow for a slower, more measured series of responses that may incrementally improve the fit between demands and resources.

PROMINENT MODES OF COPING WITH CHRONIC STRESS

Are some modes of coping more likely to be elicited by chronic stressors than others? Obviously, the answer depends on the character of the chronic stressor and the point in time when measurement is taken. Nevertheless, in analyzing how people deal with repeated or prolonged adversity, it should be possible to recognize some modes of coping that are more likely to be employed. Although the process of coping is inherently complex and dialectical in nature, and despite the fact that no single trajectory necessarily conforms to a theoretically derived profile, the characteristic features of chronic stressors are likely to evoke several modes of coping.

Vigilance and Respite

When people are continuously challenged to respond to immediate, specific, and repeated biological, environmental, or psychosocial demands, or when they reexperience traumatic events internally through intrusive thoughts, sensations, or images, they tend to employ two modes of coping: They adopt a vigilant stance that assists them to prepare for, detect, and respond rapidly to fluctuations that can affect their well-being, and they employ various strategies of gaining respite or relief that help them return to baseline levels of arousal and regain their energy.

Intense watchfulness or vigilance is likely to characterize responses to relatively enduring conflicts, problems, and threats. By definition, many forms of chronic stress are menacing in nature, characterized by the possibility of repeated harm, loss, deterioration, and even death (Lazarus & Folkman, 1984). Examples include fear of a recrudescence of the symptoms of mental illness, anxiety about the threat of relapse or further setbacks in the course of a chronic illness like multiple sclerosis, fear of further biological damage from technological disasters such as nuclear power plant accidents, and fear of crime or discrimination. Vigilance can be highly adaptive in managing chronic illnesses such as asthma, diabetes, and cancer because proper diagnosis and treatment require careful monitoring of symptoms and the side effects of medication.

Although vigilance is employed in most circumstances involving danger and threat, it is sharply magnified when people believe in or have objective evidence of their vulnerability to future adversity, but cannot predict its timing, form, or intensity. People who suffer from multiple sclerosis, arthritis, and other diseases that have a variable course involving periodic flare-ups are constantly watchful for signs and symptoms of an imminent attack. In their study of 55 seropositive gay men, Siegel and Krauss (1991) report that virtually all their respondents adopted a hypervigilant posture toward their symptoms, carefully monitoring and investigating even common and minor symptoms that most uninfected people would dismiss. Similarly, in developing an instrument to measure how patients with chronic fatigue syndrome manage their illness, Ray,

Weir, Stewart, Miller, and Hyde (1993) identified a factor that they labeled "Focusing on Symptoms." It included such items as "My symptoms are always at the back of my mind," "I think a great deal about my symptoms," and "I pay close attention to how well or badly I am feeling." The constant presence of uncertainty, excessive demand, complexity, or novelty means that the individual must be poised to respond at any moment. This constant state of alertness is exhausting because it takes a toll on both physical and mental energy. The literature on traumatic stress disorders carefully documents this state of hyperarousal. The traumatized individual startles easily, reacts irritably to the slightest provocation, and sleeps fitfully. Hilberman (1980) describes how this state of intense vigilance is manifested among battered women: "There was chronic apprehension of imminent doom, of something terrible always about to happen. Any symbolic or actual sign of potential danger resulted in increased activity, agitation, pacing, screaming, and crying. The women remained vigilant, unable to relax or to sleep" (p. 1341). Similarly, Herman (1992) presents the following account of the vigilant posture that is adopted by children who are chronically abused:

> Adaptation to this climate of constant danger requires a state of constant alertness. Children in an abusive environment develop extraordinary abilities to scan for warning signs of attack. They become minutely attuned to their abusers' inner states. They learn to recognize subtle changes in facial expression, voice, and body language as signals of anger, sexual arousal, intoxication, or dissociation. (p. 99)

Similar but less extreme depictions of anticipatory anxiety have been applied to women who have been raped (Burgess & Holmstrom, 1979), homicide survivors, and victims of crime (Bard & Sangrey, 1979). On the latter score, there is evidence that being a victim of crime and even knowing someone who has been robbed or attacked creates fear and dread that can last well beyond the initial event. Once the assumption of safety is violated, it is replaced by a more enduring sense of vulnerability that is reflected in a heightened state of self-protective vigilance.

In instances of more severe trauma that usher in lengthy periods of continuing adaptation, precautionary measures more typically involve avoidance of settings and experiences that may even be remotely associated with the original trauma. To this effect, Kilpatrick, Veronen, and Best (1985) report that for rape victims there may be so many cues that remind them of the original trauma that many become chronically avoidant and their behavior becomes quite restricted. Moreover, they found that most of their sample of rape victims met one of the major diagnostic criteria for posttraumatic stress disorder (PTSD), namely high levels of event-related intrusive thoughts, feelings, and images as well as high levels of avoidance of certain ideas, feelings, and situations. The chronicity of these reactions is powerfully established by evidence that they remain elevated several years after the original trauma (Kilpatrick & Veronen, 1984).

Even when events are not traumatic but still raise the specter of future harm, hyperarousal and its manifestations in intrusive imagery and avoidant behaviors have been documented. For example, Davidson, Fleming, and Baum (1986) maintain that the chronic stress occasioned by technological accidents maps onto the PTSD symptom complex. They show that, despite the fact that residents living near the Three Mile Island nuclear facility had no tangible evidence of danger or harm, the uncertainty and ambiguity surrounding the future impact of these toxic accidents left them with the same symptoms of hyperarousal, withdrawal, and avoidance as are found among trauma victims (Baum, Singer, & Baum, 1981).

Vigilance can cycle back and forth between the two forms of coping that offer temporary relief, namely respite and relaxation. In fact, rather than being mutually exclusive modes of coping, these approach and avoidance responses can rapidly alternate (Roth & Cohen, 1986). Horowitz (1979, 1986) and Herman (1992) both propose that approach and avoidance processes oscillate in the wake of traumatic experiences and other severe life events. In an effort to come to terms with the stressful event, selective inattention and thought restriction alternate with perceptual vigilance until a more or less stable equilibrium is reached. Over the course of this accommodative process, individuals experience intrusive thoughts and episodes of denial.

Research we have conducted among the family caregivers of persons with dementia spotlights the many forms that respite can take. It can involve short-term physical withdrawal from the aversive stimulus, as illustrated in the following remarks of a daughter who was besieged by her mother's constant harping on the same subject:

> When she's fixed on something, she goes on about it over and over. It's very frustrating. I find myself sometimes having to leave the room because, you know, she just won't stop. (Gottlieb & Gignac, 1996; p. 147)

Family caregivers can gain longer, regularly scheduled periods of respite by using day programs, volunteer visitors, or home attendants. Reports from those who have used these respite services suggest that, in taking the pressure off, the services foster a return to a state of emotional equilibrium, allowing the caregivers to be more patient and compassionate toward their relatives. In the words of one caregiver: "Because of the day program I feel more relaxed. There's a release of tension in the relationship. I need to relax. We can have more enjoyment in each other after the break" (Gottlieb & Johnson, 1994, p. 7).

In addition, respite can involve a number of cognitive devices, such as ignoring the offending stimulus, distracting oneself from it by turning one's attention to music or reading material, using artificial means of dulling the stressful experience, or using imaginative techniques, such as fantasy. For example, to escape the tensions associated with managing her demented husband's stubborn refusal to take a bath, one wife in our study reported that she often imagined that she was flying away in her magic saucer. Another caregiver fantasized riding off on her trusty steed whenever her husband began to complain about a daughter-in-law who he suspected of stealing valuable jewelry (Gottlieb & Gignac, 1996).

In other contexts of chronic stress, respite can be gained in many different ways. The daily automobile commuter uses the radio or tape player to take his mind off the trek and relieve the tension of high-volume traffic, whereas the train commuter may doze, read, or entertain himself with a portable cassette player. In the workplace, stress may be relieved by taking time out to chat around the coffee pot, and norms develop that proscribe "shop talk." In some workplaces, employees take every opportunity to escape the daily grind, celebrating birthdays, anniversaries, and all the major civic holidays. Where permissible, music is piped into the office, its purpose sometimes being to relieve the tension that accompanies boring or montonous jobs, and sometimes to relax the individuals who have come to the office to receive anxiety-provoking treatment, such as dental work. In fact, in a recent study that inquired into the techniques that individuals use to try to change a bad mood, almost half the respondents stated that they listened to music, and an equal percentage (47%) mentioned taking steps to avoid the source of their bad mood (Thayer, Newman, & McClain, 1994).

Strategies of stressor avoidance that temporarily remove or mask the stressor—or distance the individual from it—are especially likely to be elicited in circumstances where individuals are regularly bombarded by noxious stressors. For example, family caregivers of persons with dementia are constantly called upon to steer their relative's behavior, while also being confronted with evidence of their relative's deteriorating cognitive and personality functioning. The work of caregiving is so emotionally and physically taxing that the caregiver must withdraw in order to regain composure and perspective on his or her circumstances. Repetti (1989) has documented this process of withdrawal in her studies of coping among air traffic controllers, whose jobs require constant perceptual vigilance, mental alertness, and careful judgment.

Respite strategies can eventually become incorporated into daily patterns of life. Television viewing is the prototypical respite strategy that can become a habitual means of dividing one's attention and thereby softening somewhat the impact of harsh realities. Eventually, the television may be left on permanently, providing easy escape from unpleasant, intrusive thoughts, interactions, or other stressful demands.

Whereas respite functions to reduce tension in more passive ways that involve avoidance of and withdrawal from the stressor, relaxation represents a more active way of temporarily altering one's circumstances and regaining emotional stability. By initiating an exercise regimen or a daily walk or by working on a home improvement project, gardening, or serving as a volunteer in a local civic organization, there is the possibility of gaining a greater sense of control over one's circumstances. These activities are intended less to distance oneself from the stressful context than to demonstrate to oneself that the stressful context does not define all of one's life because other valued roles can be assumed that provide pleasure and self-satisfaction. Relaxing activities that involve effort devoted to refreshing or entertaining oneself represent one way of disproving one's helplessness in the face of adversity and of demonstrating one's ability to create positive and rewarding alternative experiences. Moreover, many of these active forms of relaxation not only accomplish the function of tension reduction but also restore and enhance the energy needed to cope effectively with ongoing life pressures. Hence, while distraction and relaxation both serve the function of temporarily distancing oneself from and dulling awareness of one's stressful circumstances, relaxation has the added benefit of replenishing both physical and psychological energy through immersing oneself in pleasurable activities.

Future Outlook

Whereas vigilance is one way of preparing for or rapidly managing the unpredictability and uncertainty of the stressful demands that may occur in the future, another way of dealing with threat and reducing its uncertainty is to adopt a particular outlook on the future. Optimistic or pessimistic expectancies, as well as hope and a sense of coherence (Antonovsky, 1987) represent coping orientations that can be psychologically beneficial. By evaluating one's own behavior and future outcomes in favorable terms, the stressor's implications can be at least temporarily reconstrued in ways that increase motivation to continue to engage one's circumstances. Moreover, even if they are transient, the positive emotions that accompany a sanguine outlook can make individuals more attractive recipients of social support. That is, given evidence that negative moods alienate would-be helpers, in part because of the threat of contagion, people who are able to communicate a more hopeful outlook are likely to be more welcomed recipients of support. Even if there is little objective basis for believing that the future holds promise of improvement, positive thoughts about certain aspects of the future, such as believing that a remission in one's illness or a new treatment is around the corner, can elicit positive emotional responses. In turn, these responses can lead the individual and network members to adopt more favorable perceptions of well-being (Goodhart, 1985).

In their content analysis of the coping responses reported by the family caregivers of persons with dementia, Gottlieb and Gignac (1996) identified a set of "Future Expectancies" that included optimistic and pessimistic statements about two kinds of future eventualities: (1) expectancies regarding improvement or deterioration in the stressfulness of their situation and (2) expectancies regarding their ability to continue coping with the demands they face. Thus, whereas some respondents were uplifted by thoughts that the day was fast approaching when their burdens would lighten or cease, others only expected further aggravation and deterioration of their circumstances. Similarly, in contemplating the future progress and achievements of their own coping, some caregivers stated that they were confident that in time they would improve their coping skills and gain greater insight into how to manage their relative with less emotional upset, whereas others were pessimistic about their future ability to tolerate or manage their circumstances. Moreover, the stances people adopt toward the future are fluid and mutable, changing as a function of feedback from the environment. Hence, these variable outlooks differ from the relatively stable, dispositional characteristics of optimism and pessimism (Scheier, Weintraub, & Carver, 1986).

Making Meaning through Cognitive Reinterpretation

Just as the victims of serious life crises face the challenge of making sense of their plight, those who experience chronic disorders and life difficulties must also come to terms with the larger meaning and significance of their continuing adversity. Particularly in circumstances where individuals must expend considerable energy responding to ongoing demands, when the stressor intrudes in a way that causes major dislocations and lifestyle changes, or when stigma of some sort attaches to the individual, the need to place experience in a meaningful framework will be accentuated. Moreover, the process of reinterpretation is further abetted as time passes and the individual enters settings and accumulates experiences that cast a new light on the stressful circumstances. What underlies the familiar notion that time casts a different light on events is the effect that new experiences and new social contacts can have on one's values, priorities, and self-concept.

Although there are several ways of coping that can be conceived as part of the work of making meaning, such as social comparisons, positive framing, and the employment of humor, they all revolve around the adoption of a perspective that, at least temporarily, answers questions about the causes, the extent of hardship, and the purposes served by one's continuing stressful experiences. For example, in the context of the chronic stress of caring for a relative with dementia, Pearlin et al. (1990) assess the management of meaning in terms of three dimensions:

1. the construction of a larger sense of the illness, which corresponds to the search for the causes of the stressors to which the caregivers are exposed
2. making positive comparisons, which reflects the need to place one's hardship in perspective
3. the reduction of expectations, which relates to the purpose of one's hardship, in this case to learn to be content with present circumstances.

In contexts marked by illnesses or constitutional vulnerabilities that are permanently disabling or limiting in important ways, it is beneficial for individuals to take perspectives that facilitate the normalization of their experience rather than constructing it in terms that suggest they are being held back by their disabilities.

Cognitive reinterpretation also involves changing attributions about the causes of one's adversity and the factors that control its course. It is noteworthy that less exaggerated reactions to stressors may result from cognitive reinterpretation of their causes. For example, when caregivers of persons with dementia are taught that the symptoms are not volitional expressions of hostility, but are largely uncontrollable symptoms of a biological disease process, their emotional significance and impact are appreciably reduced (Zarit & Zarit, 1982). Similarly, there is evidence that the emotional intensity of reactions to chronic stressors such as noise and pain can be reduced by altering the psychological meaning attributed to them (Gil, Wilson, Edens, Webster, Abrams, Orringer, 1996; Staples, 1996). In fact, interventions for pain patients have recently incorporated instruction in cognitive coping, such as reinterpreting pain sensations, and have shown considerable promise in their ability to lower pain reports, at least in the laboratory setting (Gil et al., 1996).

More generally, Cohen, Evans, Stokols, and Krantz (1986) observe that more research is needed on the effects of cognitive control on responses to chronic environmental stressors that resist more instrumental coping efforts.

Acceptance, Resignation, and Religiosity

If, by definition, chronic stressors do not promise resolution, then an additional way of responding to them is to endure them. However, acceptance and resignation are not necessarily passive modes of adaptation that involve surrender and defeat. Instead, they involve both the realistic recognition that certain aspects of one's self or one's circumstances cannot be altered and an accompanying emotional calm. If the latter affective state is not present, then coping is more likely to be expressed in ways that reflect angry defiance. This is why it is necessary to gauge both the affective and the cognitive dimensions of acceptance. In addition, it is important to distinguish among the aspects of chronically stressful circumstances to which people may resign themselves. For example, the father of a child born with severe disabilities may come to accept the permanence of the disability but may be unable to resign himself to the permanence of the caregiving role. Similarly, individuals with end-stage cancer may resign themselves to the prospect of imminent death but nevertheless be incapable of coming to terms with the loss of their control over basic biological functions.

Perhaps because of the dearth of longitudinal studies, little is known about the adaptive value of acceptance and resignation at different points in time and in relation to different aspects of the long-term difficulties people face. For example, even though realistic acceptance was found to be a significant predictor of *decreased* survival time among men who were diagnosed seropositive (Reed, Kemeny, Taylor, Wang, & Visscher, 1994), it is conceivable that this mode of coping aided their present adaptation. It may have allowed the men to avail themselves of AIDS-related services and support groups and to make decisions and preparations for later disease stages. In short, acceptance of the permanence of certain aspects of personal or environmental hardship may free the energy needed to deal with other demands or stressful conditions that are changeable.

In a recent review of research exploring the relationship between religiosity and health outcomes, there is the suggestion that prayer, spirituality, and faith in God correlate highly with acceptance and resignation (Koenig & Fetterman, 1995). One possible underlying model of religion's effects on health is that stress causes an increase in religious behaviors (e.g., prayer, scripture reading) and cognitions (e.g., trust in a divine plan), which leads to peaceful acceptance of certain stressful conditions and in turn to lower distress and maladjustment. In light of evidence revealing that very large proportions of older adults rely heavily on prayer and faith in God as ways of coping with chronic health problems and other ongoing life difficulties (Koenig, Kvale, & Ferrel, 1988; Krause, 1991), more attention should be given to improving the measurement and investigating the stress-moderating functions of religious beliefs and behaviors.

Instrumental Coping

Finally, there is a misconception that efforts to cope with chronic stressors defy or are not aided by problem-focused or instrumental responses. This fallacy may stem from the frequent assertion in the literature that problem-focused coping decreases psychological symptoms in situations appraised as controllable, whereas emotion-focused coping decreases symptom levels in situations that are appraised as uncontrollable (Lazarus & Folkman, 1984). Since chronic stress implies repeated or continuous exposure to demands that do not promise resolution, this is interpreted to mean that these demands are uncontrollable, that avenues toward resolution of the stressful demands are apparently closed, and that, therefore, problem-focused efforts aimed to remove or even modulate these demands are precluded or will prove ineffective. For example, since nothing can be done to halt the course of dementia or to remove its behavioral symptoms, problem-focused coping efforts are assumed to be closed off, or if employed, are expected to be damaging to the caregivers' morale and to their relationship with their relatives.

This line of reasoning confuses actions oriented to removing or resolving the stressful demands with actions directed to their management. In addition, it does not take into account the ingenious ways people assert control by identifying stressful aspects of their situations that they are able to eliminate or soften or by taking concrete steps to alter their exposure to the stressful demands they cannot change or remove. Consider further the example of caring for a relative with dementia. Although little can be done in practical terms to prevent the expression of dementia symptoms, the caregivers can take steps to extinguish the behavior quickly or to reduce the danger it poses. They can also alter their physical surroundings in order to reduce the risk of their relative sustaining an accident or injury or wandering away from home. They can register their relative with the police in case they do wander away, and they can change some behaviors of their own that have been reliable triggers of conflict in the past. Similarly, people living in crime-infested neighborhoods can reduce the threat of harm or loss by installing lighting and security systems, taking special precautions when they go out, forming or joining a neighborhood watch organization, and even arming themselves.

A second strategy of asserting behavioral control in the face of immutable and persistent stressors is to fall back on a goal that can be achieved through problem-focused efforts. For example, in developing a measure of instrumental coping relevant to persons suffering from chronic fatigue syndrome, Ray et al. (1993) identified a factor called "Maintaining Activity" that included such items as, "I deliberately break the rules to give my spirits a lift," "I organize my life to avoid overdoing things," and "I plan my day so that there are times when I am active and times when I can rest." Similarly, in the context of AIDS, Siegel and Krauss (1991) report that the vast majority of the seropositive gay men they interviewed strongly asserted that they could take action to influence the course of their infection. Some even believed that these actions could return them to seronegativity. Practical strategies included seeking out medical treatment, gaining information about new treatments, and adopting a healthy lifestyle by avoiding alcohol, tobacco, and drugs, getting rest, and eating nutritionally balanced meals. In their intriguing chapter in this volume, Folkman and her colleagues also identify ways in which seropositive men actively create events that have positive meaning and instill in them a sense of control over their affective lives.

THE BASES OF EFFICACY

If, by definition, chronic stress is characterized by its open-ended nature, then the goals of coping are likely to revolve around accommodation to rather than resolution or termination of the stressor. Accommodation involves a process of learning to live with one's lot in life, improving the compatibility between one's own needs and one's circumstances, and making certain adjustments that harmonize one's inner and outer experience. It is a process of eventually reconciling oneself to conditions that are challenging without wholly giving into them or wholly resisting them. In his classic paper on strategies of adaptation, White (1974) described adaptation through the use of military metaphors: " . . . adaptation often calls for delay, strategic retreat, regrouping of forces, abandonment of untenable positions, seeking fresh intelligence, and deploying new weapons" (p. 50). Moreover, adaptation lies neither in victory nor defeat, but in " . . . a striving toward acceptable compromise" (White, 1974, p. 52).

The process of accommodation to chronically stressful life conditions involves the goals of keeping distress within manageable limits, preserving or regaining a sense of personal worth, maintaining or restoring relations with valued associates, working out a personally meaningful understanding of one's situation, and developing a measure of confidence that progress is being made toward a more desirable future despite the persistence of stressful circumstances. Some of these goals apply with equal force to situations of acute stress, whereas others are more relevant to or salient in conditions of enduring hardship. For example, virtually all experiences that are appraised in stressful terms call for responses geared to regulating emotional distress. However, chronic stressors accentuate concerns about the future course of events and their implications for one's well-being. For this reason, evaluations of coping efficacy may depend as much on one's ability to face threat with a greater measure of confidence and equanimity as they do on one's ability to modulate present affect. Similarly, whereas crises and acute life events are occasions for gauging one's ability to rapidly mobilize and capitalize on the support of one's associates, chronically stressful circumstances pose a far more severe test; they gauge the grace, reciprocity, and emotional control that are needed to maintain others' long-term involvement as supporters.

The efficacy of coping with chronic stressors may also hinge more strongly on one's ability to experience positive emotions than on one's ability to avoid or diminish distress. The latter subject has been largely overlooked in the stress literature because coping is seen exclusively as a way of mitigating adversity rather than as a way of promoting an improved emotional state or a better quality of life despite adversity. This point is convincingly demonstrated by a recent investigation conducted by Zautra, Burleson, Smith, Blalock, Wallston, DeVellis, et al. (1995). Based on data gathered from two independent samples of arthritis patients, they marshal strong empirical evidence showing that those who cope with their pain by making positive self-statements and employing more active forms of coping, such as engaging in physical exercise, experience more positive affect *even though these ways of coping do not reduce negative affect*. A similar point is made by Register (1987) in her poignant account of the challenges and adjustments that are made by people who live with a chronic illness. She quotes one interviewee who proclaimed: "The first day I ever realized you could be happy and still be sick was a real red-letter day" (pp. xiv–xv).

Two chapters in this volume, one authored by Folkman and colleagues and one by Zautra and colleagues, also call attention to the contribution of positive events to the well-being of those who live with

AIDS and those who experience the chronic stress of disability. Considered together, both chapters reveal that valued activities that seem to be unrelated to the primary difficulties of life, especially activities that are self-initiated, may in fact serve the indirect function of augmenting a sense of control, placing those difficulties in a broader perspective, and offsetting the distress occasioned by them with positive experiences and emotional states. When people can make positive events happen in their lives and find pleasure amidst pain, they learn that life is worth the struggle. This lesson, in turn, can sustain their morale and shore up continued coping. The larger point is that the ability to create positive events and experience even transient positive emotions may be a particularly important basis for judging efficacy in the context of chronic stress.

More generally, although people experiencing chronic stress still search for evidence that they can productively engage their circumstances, their recognition that they cannot turn off the source of continuing hardship may prompt them to rely on other indicators of forward movement. What are some of these alternative sources of feedback about one's coping progress?

A recent study of family members who had been caring for a relative with dementia for an average of $2^1/_2$ years points to several bases for evaluating the efficacy of coping with chronic stress (Gignac & Gottlieb, 1996). Many caregivers observed that they had learned to react less strongly to symptoms that had previously upset them immensely. They registered pride in their present ability to respond with a greater measure of equanimity. A second, related achievement was that they had learned to respond to these noxious symptoms in ways that required them to expend less energy. Some caregivers had learned to manage their relatives' behavior more efficiently, and others had discovered ways of quickly extinguishing undesirable behaviors. Third, the majority of caregivers observed that they had identified ways of responding to their relative that avoided or minimized interpersonal conflict. For example, some described changing behaviors of their own that had previously served as reliable cues for conflict, whereas others reported that they had learned to ignore rather than criticize irritating behaviors. This was a major triumph and signal of progress for them because it precluded the guilt they experienced after emotional outbursts.

Two additional bases for efficacy judgements concerned their own personal development, particularly improvements in their self-knowledge and coping skills and desirable changes in their ability to anticipate and regulate the consequences of alternative ways of coping. Both reflect the unique opportunities provided in chronically stressful situations to learn by trial and error how to enlarge or specialize one's coping repertoire, how to modulate or suppress responses that are too psychologically costly, and how to identify more realistic coping goals. These efficacy judgments also spotlight the ways coping may enhance personal growth and development. The process led to insights about one's strengths and foibles as well as one's values and commitments.

ORGANIZATION AND OVERVIEW OF THE VOLUME

Part Two of this volume explores a number of conceptual issues that surround the topic of coping with chronic stress. It begins with Wheaton's adept reexamination and critical analysis of some of the basic premises and concepts of the stress literature. He reviews many of the classic formulations of the nature and meaning of stress, and then elucidates several defining features of chronic stress by invoking the stress model that is adopted in the field of engineering, a model that he maintains has greater applicability to psychosocial stress than Seyle's (1956) biological model. For example, he shows that the engineering model accounts for different processes that take place when continuous and long-term forces act on material than when the material is subjected to a single acute shock or physical challenge. By analogy, coping with relatively enduring hardship may bring into play more stable resources, whereas acute life events call for the more rapid mobilization and deployment of resources for a brief period. Following a more extended discussion of the distinctions between eventlike stressors and chronic stressors, Wheaton presents a framework that comprises four sources and nine forms of chronic stress. In addition, he presents a new measure that includes 60 chronic stress items organized into several life domains. The chapter concludes with a discussion of selected measurement issues, with special attention to the vexing problems that surround the adoption of subjective versus objective stress indicators.

Aldwin and Brustrom follow with a parallel chapter on the subject of coping with chronic stress. They too begin with a brief review of classic contributions, including the models of coping that fall into the psychodynamic, coping styles, and coping processes traditions, commenting on their strengths and shortcomings as well as the empirical support that each model has garnered. Then, in order to generate new insight into patterns of coping with chronic stress, they undertake a careful review of relevant findings in the fields of aging and chronic medical illness. In both fields, they identify numerous determinants of coping responses and several consistent relations between ways of coping and selected outcomes. Not only do they offer important ideas about the methodological challenges that attend investigations of these two contexts of chronic stress, but they also spotlight the ingenious ways that people adjust to chronic hardship. For example, over time, elderly people who suffer from disabilities compensate for decrements in their performance in both cognitive and instrumental ways; they lower their expectations and develop routines that allow them to avoid stressors and to accomplish tasks without overexerting themselves. In closing, Aldwin and Brustrom underscore the important role played by three types of coping resources in reducing the effort needed to cope with daily stress.

The third chapter in Part Two, by Compas, Connor, Osowiecki, and Welch, challenges conventional thinking about the very definition of coping as an exclusively effortful enterprise. In contrasting effortful and involuntary responses to stress, the authors observe that there is a bidirectional interplay between the two coping responses, the automatic responses precluding or interfering with the deliberate responses, and the deliberate responses preempting the reflexive or overlearned responses. Equally important, they show that research on automatic responses to stress can vastly enrich coping theory and help to explain the paradoxical effects of various expressions of approach and avoidance modes of coping, which tend to be more prevalent in contexts of chronic stress. The authors then propose an integrative framework for understanding stress responses that is based on three dimensions that yield eight categories of coping responses. Drawing on this scheme, they conclude the chapter with several intriguing hypotheses about the kinds of responses to chronic stress that are likely to be most and least effective. They also suggest four additional topics for research that arise from the theoretical distinctions they have made.

In Part Three, four chapters address the diverse ways in which chronic stressors affect and are created by social relationships, beginning with Lepore's incisive analysis of the social environment's role in precipitating, moderating, and mediating chronic stress. For example, he explains how social relationships can both cushion and intensify the impact of life events on personal health and well-being. However, he also brings to bear data revealing that the buffering effects of social ties dissipate in the face of longer-lasting stressors such as crowding and disabling illnesses. Similarly, he shows that temporal considerations help to explain the social mechanisms that are implicated in the adverse impacts of certain stressors. For instance, the undesirable emotional effects of job loss may stem in part from the eventual loss of significant sources of social support, and the psychological distress occasioned by natural disasters may be amplified by the loss of valued social roles and the burdens added to existing social roles.

Focusing on the processual aspects of social relationships, O'Brien and DeLongis address in the following chapter the complex interpersonal dynamics that unfold in chronic stress contexts. They explain how differences in people's ways of coping can erupt into outright conflict that damages close relationships and augments the negative impact of relatively minor stressors. In addition, in their analysis of relationship-focused coping, they show how unresolved struggles around issues of autonomy and interdependence can derail the support process and how the expression of empathy can restore emotional solidarity and lead to more cooperative coping efforts. Their chapter carefully considers numerous barriers to the expression of empathy in close relationships that are besieged by stress and concludes with suggestions for further investigation of the adaptational outcomes that result from varied interpersonal patterns of coping with chronic stress.

The next two chapters in Part Three present original data that illuminate the subtle effects of the social environment on coping with ongoing, long-term difficulties. Repetti and Wood's thesis is that there are many indirect and unintended ways that our coping efforts are constrained and guided by others and that our responses to stress can have a variety of social ramifications that, in turn, can trigger counteracting responses. Calling on their observations of mothers' interactions with their preschoolers in a daycare setting, they document a chain of daily interpersonal dynamics that commences with the mothers' efforts to recover from the tensions they experienced on the job, proceeds to their children's reactions to these maternal behaviors, and concludes with changes in the mothers' short-term coping efforts. More generally, the authors suggest that the cumulative social impact of repeated patterns of coping with relatively minor daily stressors can either strengthen or weaken close relationships, depending on the kind of coping responses that are expressed and the kinds of opposing or accommodating reactions they receive. The theoretical yield of this work suggests not only that stress issuing from one domain affects social relations in another domain, but also that coping can cross life domains, transmitting a range of social messages and provoking a range of social responses.

Stroke and its aftermath provide the focus for Stephens and Clark's analysis of distress in relation to congruence and incongruence in the supportive character of couples' communications. On the basis of equity theory, they hypothesize that couples whose communications were more reciprocal—defined as relatively equal in the amount of supportive or unsupportive interaction—would experience less distress than those who were mismatched in the amount and character of their interaction. In addition, they examine the affective consequences of communicative disparity when couples were classified in terms of the source (caregiver or spouse) and nature (supportive and unsupportive) of the disparity. The importance of their findings lies in the evidence they marshal that the partners' distress does not depend on how supportive or unsupportive each is toward the other, but on the extent of equivalence in the partners' styles of responding to one another. Like other long-term stressors that test the strength of close relationships, chronic illness requires extended periods of interpersonal negotiation and accommodation, the partners' needing to be constantly attuned to one another's needs and coping efforts. The more general lesson of the authors' research is that personal and relational adjustment appears to depend more on how similarly the partners behave toward one another than on how each behaves toward the other.

Part Four is devoted to research on efficacy issues in the context of chronic stress. Because many chronic stressors are impervious to instrumental coping efforts aimed at terminating or reducing exposure to their demands, they are less likely to elicit certain outcome expectancies or they may violate people's expectations that they can bring about certain outcomes. However, both chapters in this part reveal that chronic stress may shift the focus of efficacy expectations, create additional bases for assessing one's coping efficacy, and alter efficacy judgments over time. For example, for our chapter on coping efficacy, Gignac and I developed a scheme for classifying the evaluations of coping efficacy made by family caregivers of persons with dementia. We discovered that caregivers judge their progress in handling the diverse practical and emotional demands they face in terms of changes in the toll their coping efforts were taking on their physical endurance and psychological tolerance and on their relationship with their relative. They also evaluated the strategic value of their coping responses, gaining greater confidence in their ability to modulate and plan their reactions rather than reacting impulsively and thereby compounding their difficulties. Our empirical findings also suggest that appraisals of coping efficacy may determine the trajectory of coping and affect distress.

Zautra, Hoffman, and Reich then examine the role of two facets of self-efficacy beliefs in the maintenance of well-being among elderly persons who suffer a loss of autonomy due to disabling illnesses. They also investigate the determinants and stability of these beliefs, weighing the possibility that they are determined by personality characteristics against the possibility that they change as a function of the perceived outcomes of situationally based coping efforts. Their findings are of vast theoretical importance because they reveal that the two different kinds of expectations—one touching on the individual's ability to improve present conditions and one touching on the individual's ability to produce positive events in the future—fulfill different psychological functions. Moreover, their analysis of the social influences that tend to undermine and shore up beliefs in one's ability to cope effectively represents an equally important contribution to the social support literature.

Part Five examines three compelling circumstances of chronic stress: caring for a loved one with AIDS, surviving the Holocaust, and coping with occupational stress. The chapter by Folkman, Moskowitz, Ozer, and Park presents original data revealing that positive life events and other auspicious experiences carry meaning that help the caregivers of persons with AIDS to withstand the horrific threats and losses that otherwise characterize daily life. Echoing Zautra, Hoffman, and Reich's thesis that the ability to create positive events represents a facet of self-efficacy, the authors show that some of these events are actually initiated by the caregivers themselves and serve several important mental health functions in relation to the stress of life with AIDS. Moreover, the theoretical significance of their research is to enlarge the domain of coping to include activities and routines that on the surface appear to have little to do with the challenges imposed by the disease, but that actually make life at least more bearable if not pleasurable for a time.

Boaz, Kahana, and associates offer a far broader and more trenchant analysis of the stress of Holocaust survivorship than has been presented in previous accounts. Placing this experience in a lifecourse perspective, they explain how the trauma endured by survivors overshadows their subsequent experiences, coloring their appraisals of later life stressors and rendering them more capable in some ways and less capable in other ways of coping with the demands of immigration and acculturation. Drawing on data obtained from survivor and comparison groups in both the United States and Israel, they tease out the aspects of the traumatic experience that reverberate most strongly in later life: in family and social relationships, in attitudes toward health, and in the ways survivors construe their own personal identities.

The concluding chapter in Part Five offers a kaleidoscopic view of the challenges of coping with the varied sources of occupational stress that attend modern life, as well as with the more ubiquitous demands that have always faced the labor force. Hepburn, Loughlin, and Barling wrestle with the analytic complications that surround the tasks of specifying the unique adverse outcomes of job stressors and untangling the effects of acute and chronic stressors. In addition, they address problems of establishing the temporal ordering of stressor impacts and suggest several ways of strengthening the design of research and increasing the precision of measurement in this area. In addition to searching for evidence of consistency among various reports of coping with job stressors, they review strategies of preventing and counteracting the harmful effects of chronic stress in the workplace.

REFERENCES

ANTONOVSKY, A. (1987). *Unraveling the mystery of health.* San Francisco: Jossey-Bass.
BARD, M., & SANGREY, D. (1979). *The crime victim's book.* New York: Basic Books.
BAUM, A., O'KEEFE, M. K., & DAVIDSON, L. M. (1990). Acute stressors and chronic response: The case of traumatic stress. *Journal of Applied Social Psychology, 20,* 1643–1654.
BAUM, A., SINGER, J., & BAUM, C. (1981). Stress and the environment. *Journal of Social Issues, 37,* 4–34.
BROWN, G. W., & HARRIS, T. O. (1978). *Social origins of depression: A study of psychiatric disorder in women.* New York: Free Press.
BROWN, G. W., & HARRIS, T. O. (1989). *Life events and illness.* New York: Guilford.
BURGESS, A., & HOLMSTROM, L. (1979). Adaptive strategies and recovery from rape. *American Journal of Psychiatry, 136,* 1278–1282.
CASPI, A., & MOFFITT, T. E. (1993). When do individual differences matter? A paradoxical theory of personality coherence. *Psychological Inquiry, 4,* 247–271.
COHEN, S., EVANS, G., STOKOLS, D., & KRANTZ, D. S. (1986). *Behavior, health, and environmental stress.* New York: Plenum.
COSTA, P. T., SOMERFIELD, M. R., & MCCRAE, R. R. (1996). Personality and coping: A reconceptualization. In M. Zeidner & N. Endler (Eds.), *Handbook of coping* (pp. 444–61). New York: Wiley.
COYNE, J. C., & GOTTLIEB, B. H. (1996). The mismeasure of coping by checklist. *Journal of Personality, 64,* 173–202.
COYNE, J. C., WORTMAN, C. B., & LEHMAN, D. R. (1988). The other side of support: Emotional overinvolvement and miscarried helping. In B. H. Gottlieb (Ed.), *Marshaling social support* (pp. 305–330). Newbury Parks, CA: Sage.
DAVIDSON, L. M., FLEMING, I., & BAUM, A. (1986). Post-traumatic stress as a function of chronic stress and toxic exposure. In C. R. Figley (Ed.), *Trauma and its wake: Vol. II* (pp. 57–77). New York: Brunner/Mazel.
DAVIS, R. C., & FRIEDMAN, L. N. (1985). The emotional aftermath of crime and violence. In C. R. Figley (Ed.), *Trauma and its wake: The study and treatment of post-traumatic stress disorder* (pp. 90–112). New York: Brunner/Mazel.
ECKENRODE, J., & BOLGER, N. (1995). Daily and within day event measurement. In S. Cohen, R. C. Kessler, & L. U. Gordon (Eds.), *Measuring stress* (pp. 80–101). New York: Oxford University Press.
ECKENRODE, J., & GORE, S. (Eds.). (1990). *Stress between work and family.* New York: Plenum.
ERDAL, K. J., & ZAUTRA, A. J. (1995). Psychological impact of illness downturns: A comparison of new and chronic conditions. *Psychology and Aging, 10,* 570–577.
FIGLEY, C. R. (Ed.). (1985). *Trauma and its wake: The study and treatment of post-traumatic stress disorder.* New York: Brunner/Mazel.
GIGNAC, M. A., & GOTTLIEB, B. H. (1996). Caregivers' appraisals of efficacy in coping with dementia. *Psychology and Aging, 11,* 214–225.
GIL, K. M., WILSON, J. J., EDENS, J. L., WEBSTER, D. A., ABRAMS, M. A., ORRINGER, E., GRANT, M., CLARK, W. C., & JANAL, M. N. (1996). Effects of cognitive coping skills training on coping strategies and experimental pain sensitivity in African-American adults with sickle cell disease. *Health Psychology, 15,* 3–10.

GOODHART, D. E. (1985). Some psychological effects associated with positive and negative thinking about stressful event outcomes: Was Pollyana right? *Journal of Personality and Social Psychology, 48,* 216–232.

GOTTLIEB, B. H. (1989). A contextual perspective on stress in family care of the elderly. *Canadian Psychology, 30,* 596–607.

GOTTLIEB, B. H., & GIGNAC, M. A. (1996). Content and domain specificity of coping among family caregivers of persons with dementia. *Journal of Aging Studies, 10,* 137–155.

GOTTLIEB, B. H., & JOHNSON, J. (1994). *Impact of day programs on family caregivers of persons with dementia.* Guelph, Ontario, Canada: University of Guelph.

GREENHAUS, J. H., & BEUTELL, N. J. (1985). Sources of conflict between work and family. *Academy of Management Review, 10,* 76–88.

HERMAN, J. L. (1992). *Trauma and recovery.* New York: Basic Books.

HILBERMAN, E. (1980). The wife beater's wife reconsidered. *American Journal of Psychiatry, 137,* 1336–1347.

HOROWITZ, M. J. (1979). Psychological response to serious life events. In V. Hamilton & D. M. Warburton (Eds.), *Human stress and cognition.* New York: Wiley.

HOROWITZ, M. J. (1986). *Stress response syndromes.* Northvale, NJ: Jason Aronson.

JANOFF-BULMAN, R. (1992). *Shattered assumptions.* New York: Free Press.

KENDALL, P. C., & HOLLON, S. D. (1981). Assessing self-referent speech: Methods in the measurement of self-statements. In P. C. Kendall & S. D. Hollon (Eds.), *Assessment strategies for cognitive–behavioral intervention.* New York: Academic Press.

KESSLER, R., & ESSEX, M. (1982). Marital status and depression: The importance of coping resources. *Social Forces, 61,* 484–507.

KILPATRICK, D. G., & VERONEN, L. J. (1984, December). *The aftermath of rape: A three year follow-up.* Paper presented at the meeting of the Association for Advancement of Behavior Therapy, Washington, DC.

KILPATRICK, D. G., VERONEN, L. J., & BEST, C. L. (1985). Factors predicting psychological distress among rape victims. In C. R. Figley (Ed.), *Trauma and its wake: The study and treatment of post-traumatic stress disorder* (pp. 113–141). New York: Brunner/Mazel.

KOENIG, H. G., & FETTERMAN, A. (1995). *Religion and health outcomes.* Unpublished manuscript available from the Fetzer Institute, 9392 West KL Avenue, Kalamazoo, MI 49009-9398.

KOENIG, H. G., KVALE, J. N., & FERREL, C. (1988). Religion and well-being in later life. *The Gerontologist, 28,* 18–28.

KRAUSE, N. (1991). Stress, religiosity, and abstinence from alcohol. *Psychology and Aging, 6,* 134–144.

KRAUSE, N. (1995). Assessing stress buffering effects: A cautionary note. *Psychology and Aging, 10,* 518–526.

LAZARUS, R. S., & FOLKMAN, S. (1984). *Stress, appraisal, and coping.* New York: Springer.

MCGONAGLE, K. A., & KESSLER, R. C. (1990). Chronic stress, acute stress, and depressive symptoms. *American Journal of Community Psychology, 18,* 681–706.

MCLEAN, D. E., & LINK, B. G. (1994). Unraveling complexity. In W. R. Avison & I. H. Gotlib (Eds.), *Stress and mental health* (pp. 15–42). New York: Plenum.

MOEN, P. (1992). *Women's two roles.* New York: Auburn House.

MONROE, S. M., & SIMONS, A. D. (1991). Diathesis-stress theory in the context of life stress research: Implications for depressive disorders. *Psychological Bulletin, 110,* 406–425.

PEARLIN, L. I., MULLAN, J. T., SEMPLE, S. J., & SKAFF, M. M. (1990). Caregiving and the stress process: An overview of concepts and their measures. *The Gerontologist, 30,* 583–594.

PEYROT, M., MCMURRAY, J. F., & HEDGES, R. (1987). Living with diabetes: The role of personal and professional knowledge in symptom and regimen management. *Research in the Sociology of Health Care, 6,* 107–146.

RAY, C., WEIR, W., STEWART, D., MILLER, P., & HYDE, G. (1993). Ways of coping with chronic fatigue syndrome: Development of an illness management questionnaire. *Social Science and Medicine, 37*(3), 385–391.

REDINBAUGH, E. M., MACCALLUM, R. C., & KIECOLT-GLASER, J. K. (1995). Recurrent syndromal depression in caregivers. *Psychology and Aging, 10,* 358–368.

REED, G. M., KEMENY, M. E., TAYLOR, S. E., WANG, H. J., & VISSCHER, B. R. (1994). Realistic acceptance as a predictor of decreased survival time in gay men with AIDS. *Health Psychology, 13,* 299–307.

REGISTER, C. (1987). *Living with chronic illness.* New York: Harper Collins.

REPETTI, R. L. (1989). Effects of daily workload on subsequent behavior during marital interaction: The roles of social withdrawal and spouse support. *Journal of Personality and Social Psychology, 57,* 651–659.

ROTH, S., & COHEN, L. J. (1986). Approach, avoidance, and coping with stress. *American Psychologist, 41,* 813–819.

SCHEIER, M. F., WEINTRAUB, J. K., & CARVER, C. S. (1986). Coping with stress: Divergent strategies of optimists and pessimists. *Journal of Personality and Social Psychology, 51,* 1257–1264.

SCHULZ, R., O'BRIEN, A. T., BOOKWALA, J., & FLEISSNER, K. (1995). Psychiatric and physical morbidity effects of dementia caregiving: Prevalence, correlates, and causes. *The Gerontologist, 35,* 771–791.

SEYLE, H. (1956). *The stress of life.* New York: McGraw-Hill.

SIEGEL, K., & KRAUSS, B. J. (1991). Living with HIV infection: Adaptive tasks of seropositive gay men. *Journal of Health and Social Behavior, 32,* 17–32.

SILVER, R., & WORTMAN, C. B. (1980). Coping with undesirable life events. In J. Barber & M. E. P. Seligman (Eds.), *Human helplessness* (pp. 279–375). New York: Academic Press.

STANTON, A. L., & DUNKEL-SCHETTER, C. (1991). Psychological adjustment to infertility: An overview of conceptual approaches. In A. L. Stanton & C. Dunkel-Schetter (Eds.), *Infertility: Perspectives from stress and coping research* (pp. 3–16). New York: Plenum.

STAPLES, S. L. (1996). Human response to environmental noise. *American Psychologist, 51,* 143–150.

STONE, A. A., NEALE, J. M., & SHIFFMAN, S. (1993). Daily assessment of stress and coping and their association with mood. *Annals of Behavioral Medicine, 15,* 8–16.

STONE, A. H., & SHIFFMAN, S. (1992). Reflections on the intensive measurement of stress, coping, and mood, with an emphasis on daily measures. *Psychology and Health, 7,* 115–129.

SULS, J., & MARTIN, R. E. (1993). Daily recording and ambulatory monitoring methodologies in behavioral medicine. *Annals of Behavioral Medicine, 15,* 3–7.

THAYER, R. E., NEWMAN, J. R., & MCCLAIN, T. M. (1994). Self-regulation of mood: Strategies for changing a bad mood, raising energy, and reducing tension. *Journal of Personality and Social Psychology, 67,* 910–925.

TURNER, R. J., & NOH, S. (1983). Class and psychological vulnerability among women: The significance of social support and personal control. *Journal of Health and Social Behavior, 24,* 2–15.

VINEY, L. L., & WESTBROOK, M. T. (1984). Coping with chronic illness: Strategy preferences, changes in preferences, and associated emotional reactions. *Journal of Chronic Disease, 37,* 489–502.

WEGNER, D. M., SCHNEIDER, D. J., CARTER, S. R., & WHITE, T. L. (1987). Paradoxical effects of thought suppression. *Journal of Personality and Social Psychology, 53,* 5–13.

WHEATON, B. (1990). Life transitions, role histories, and mental health. *American Sociological Review, 55,* 209–223.

WHEATON, B. (1994). Sampling the stress universe. In W. R. Avison & I. H. Gotlib (Eds.), *Stress and mental health* (pp. 77–114). New York: Plenum.

WHEELER, L., & REIS, H. T. (1991). Self-recording of everyday life events: Origins, types, and uses. *Journal of Personality, 59,* 339–354.

White, R. (1974). Strategies of adaptation: An attempt at systematic description. In G. Coelho, D. Hamburg, & J. Adams (Eds.), *Coping and adaptation* (pp. 47–68). New York: Basic Books.

ZARIT, S. H., & ZARIT, J. M. (1982). Families under stress: Interventions for caregivers of senile dementia patients. *Psychotherapy: Theory, Research, and Practice, 19,* 461–471.

ZAUTRA, A. J., BURLESON, M. H., SMITH, C. A., BLALOCK, S. J., WALLSTON, K. A., DEVELLIS, R. F., DEVELLIS, B. M., & SMITH, T. W. (1995). Arthritis and perceptions of quality of life: An examination of positive and negative affect in rheumatoid arthritis patients. *Health Psychology, 14,* 399–408.

II

Theory and Perspectives

2

The Nature of Chronic Stress

BLAIR WHEATON

PREFATORY NOTE

In 1984, the middle span of a bridge over a river on I-95 between New York and Boston collapsed near midnight, extinguishing the lights along the highway for miles leading up to a bridge. Without the usual light, cars hurtled off the last intact span into the black waters below, until the driver of a semi-trailer saw the gap, squealed to a stop, and purposely jackknifed his truck to block the way.

The sensational coverage that followed this event in the media centered on the possible cause of the collapse. The first questions asked had to do with precipitating events. Could it have been high wind that day? Could it have been an unusually high volume of traffic that day? Could it have been a boat that struck the foundation of the bridge and damaged it?

At the time, I was in the early stages of my developing interest in chronic stress. I had followed the important work of Len Pearlin in this area (Pearlin et al., 1981; Pearlin, 1983) and had incorporated the concept of chronic stress into some earlier work on stress-buffering (Wheaton, 1983) and on social class differences in mental disorder (Wheaton, 1980). I was struck by the kinds of questions posed about the cause of the collapse of the bridge: All searched for an event that could have precipitated the collapse. It seemed to me that this was misguided.

BLAIR WHEATON • Department of Sociology, University of Toronto, Toronto, Ontario, Canada M5T 1P9.

Coping with Chronic Stress, edited by Benjamin H. Gottlieb. Plenum Press, New York, 1997.

In fact, it has seemed to me a problem of stress research that we search for events as causes first. Observable, discrete events have an attractive quality as causes: They explain why the outcome happened when it did. It is more difficult to point to an insidious process and suggest that perhaps the wear-and-tear simply reached a threshold, a threshold of structural integrity.

This is in fact what happened to the bridge. There was no "life event" that triggered the collapse: The weather was normal, the traffic was normal, there had been no sudden trauma to the bridge. But long-term rusting, unmonitored by inspectors on their usual rounds because of the strategic location of a nearby coffee and doughnut shop, had finally reached the point where the current structure could survive no more. In Neil Young's immortal words, "Rust never sleeps."

The bridge had collapsed due to chronic stress. The scenario of the bridge collapse fit perfectly with a point I had wanted to make in writing about stress: It is not necessary to have a discrete or easily observable cause of an outcome that is itself discrete—such as the onset of an episode of depression. Even a small increment in the level of the long-term continuous pressure caused by chronic stress may be enough to result in a major shift in functioning. And the fact that such sources of stress are difficult to measure does not mean that they have a minor role to play in understanding the distress or disorders we regularly try to explain with event sources of stress. The problem is that the role of more chronic stressors may be central, but difficult to capture. On second thought, however, this is all the more reason for intensive and comprehensive study of the nature, course, and consequences of chronic stressors.

INTRODUCTION: OF STRESSORS, STRESS, AND STRESS OUTCOMES

The term "stress" has been used so widely in so many ways for so long that one could validly wonder whether yet another discussion of the meaning of this concept—after the thousands of articles, chapters, and books that have been written—could possibly be useful. And yet, in a research tradition in which the task of measurement has tended to define the concept, rather than vice versa, in which the questions asked have mined thoroughly a few veins while leaving others relatively untouched, and in which few have actually addressed *conceptual* or boundary issues, it seems almost necessary to return to the assumptions underlying the stress model and reconsider some basic questions.

Because stress as a concept touches on many disciplines, there is widespread uncertainty about the boundaries of the stress concept, about the point in the stress process where stress occurs, and about distinctions between stress and stress outcomes.

There are in fact two distinct areas of ambiguity surrounding the term stress. Concerning the stage of the stress process where stress occurs, there is either confusion, or unrealized disagreement, about whether the term stress should be reserved for a problem emanating from the social environment (as in *stressors*), defining a stimulus problem, or for a response state of the organism as manifested by biological definitions or as embodied by the term "psychological stress." This latter term has been used most often to refer to what is also called distress in much of the stress literature. Presumably, the reason that stress has been used in this way is that it reflects a tendency to define the stress as existing in the response of the organism. In the case of psychological stress, it may be assumed that a state of "feeling stressed," or feeling anxious, or feeling depressed amounts to *prima facie* evidence that stress has occurred. At the same time, it is likely that use of the term stress to refer at times to outcomes and at other times to the problem faced has added to a sense of confusion about what stress is and is not.

The second area of ambiguity in using the term stress has to do with the content of stressors themselves. A variety of terms have been used to refer to stress, including *role strains* (Pearlin, 1983), *life difficulties* (Brown & Harris, 1978), the somewhat problematic *daily hassles* (Kanner, Coyne, Schaefer, & Lazarus, 1981), and *traumas* (Norris, 1992). By using these terms, which avoid the word stress, we seem to be assuming the primacy of *stressful life change events* as the embodiment of what is implied by the term stress, although it is clear at the same time that these terms are intended to stand for *types* of stress.

In this chapter, I consider the nature of chronic stress as a distinct type of stress. But it is premature to consider a type of stress before providing a general definition of stress. This definition should give guidelines as to the problems posed by stressful events and situations. Given such a definition, it makes sense to then distinguish subtypes of stress, especially chronic stress as opposed to acute stress, as embodied by the tradition that defines stress in terms of discrete life events. Such a distinction is made possible by first defining a more inclusive stress domain than that which is implied by the life events tradition.

Defining Stress

Selye's classic work on stress (1956) is a useful reference point, since it influenced much of what is assumed about stress in the psychosocial model. Selye's stress model (1956) included four stages:

1. Stressors, in Selye's approach consisting of a wide variety of events and conditions that represent threat or insult to the organism.
2. Conditioning factors that alter the impact of the stressor on the organism, as in coping resources in the psychosocial model.
3. The general adaptation syndrome (G.A.S.), an intervening state of stress as indicated by a physiological state of the organism.
4. Behavioral responses, adaptive or maladaptive.

These distinctions still operate as a source of confusion in the literature (Goodyer, 1990; Kasl, 1984). I believe this confusion is conceptual and not just terminological and can be traced, unfortunately, and through no fault of his own, to Selye's work. For Selye, the heart of the matter of stress was the G.A.S. itself. This syndrome consisted of a three-stage response sequence to "noxious agents": the alarm reaction, the stage of resistance, and the stage of exhaustion (Selye, 1956). Selye's primary interest was in identifying and describing a biologically based and generalized response syndrome to threatening agents. To help with the metaphor, he adds that stress could be defined as the "state of wear and tear of the body" (1956, p. 55). Identifying stress as a physiological response state of the body and outlining the adrenal and other organ and hormonal changes involved, Selye then proceeds to define a stressor as "that which produces stress" (1956, p. 64). Nothing more is said about stressors by way of definition, but examples are used throughout that give some hints (see later in this chapter).

In psychosocial stress research, we typically do not observe physiological indications of stress directly, and yet we are interested in identifying features, states, and changes in the social environment that affect functioning. The problem we face as social scientists is that it is the *realm of stressors* that we must define and never have been able to define adequately. It is not "stress" in the sense of Selye's use of that term that is our problem. We have separated the parts of his model into stressors, resources, and outcomes, leaving out the black box of the G.A.S. But in effect, this most influential work in the history of stress research gives practically no guidance on what stressors are and are not, and it is this ambiguity that has plagued the history of psychosocial stress research. Perhaps more importantly, by extension the implication is that *one cannot use the biological stress model as a basis for derivation of any particular psychosocial stress model,* and yet that is precisely what we have done.

To provide a starting point for discussion, I define (social) stressors as *threats, demands, or structural constraints that, by the very fact of their occurrence or existence, call into question the operating integrity of the organism.*

There are a number of other features of stress not specified by this definition that nonetheless help delimit its meaning. For example, it should be clear that the kinds of environmental conditions or changes that operate as *potential* stressors must be capable of challenging the integrity of the organism if they occur in their more extreme form. This means that some things cannot qualify as stress by their nature because they do not occur in social reality at levels that could be considered challenging. While allowing for exceptions that prove the rule, there are many experiences in life that simply fail to meet minimal standards of serious threat or demand, even at their most extreme. Losing a tennis game to a long-term and valued partner is probably not an experience that will ever be stressful to any significant number of people. Such experiences dot the landscape of day-to-day life: They are defined by a combination of their regularity, their mundanity, and their inherently low potential for threat.

A stressor must also, by virtue of the threat it poses, represent a "problematic" that requires resolution and cannot be allowed to exist indefinitely without damage. The issue of need for resolution is more than a technicality. In fact, we need to understand still that we regularly blur distinctions between different stressors, and between stressors and allied concepts in the stress process, because we tend to overshoot the definition of what the stressor is. A divorce has a point of resolution. After that point, any stress that arises conditionally and separately, and does not follow automatically from the divorce process per se, is a separate stressor. We cannot call parental conflict after a divorce "part" of divorce as a stressor: It is not a necessary feature of divorce, it is not a ritual or defined part of the "event," and it often may reflect the continuation of a chronic stressor that predated the divorce.

Finally, I want to make explicit that a stressor must be *identity-relevant*. This means that the pressure exerted by the stressor in part derives its power from the fact that it has the potential to threaten or alter current identities. There are features of identities that are likely to be vulnerable to stress impacts. These include assumptions about personal self-worth and power, assumptions about personal control (Taylor & Brown, 1991), assumptions about roles or contributions a person has to offer, and needs to occupy mandated or valued roles or social statuses.

At first thought, this requirement may seem problematic, but a stressor need not be exclusively defined by consciousness of its existence. Awareness of the damage potential of a stressor is not a necessary condition of that stressor having negative consequences. In order to save the definition of a stressor from a requirement of perception, appraisal, or cognition, we must be able to specify stressors that are free of articulation as "problems" by the individuals they may affect, while including articulated problems as well. If perception were a required aspect of defining a stressor, we would restrict the stress domain to obvious, visible, and more discrete problems, and these are *not* the only kinds of problems, under our model, that have effects on functioning. The bridge, in effect, does not feel its rust. And the rust is not a static problem; it grows in scope and virulence, but imperceptibly, as slowly as the growth of a child whom one sees every day.

ELABORATING THE STRESS DOMAIN

When the word "stress" is used in psychosocial research, the image it invokes is a life event, a discrete, observable, and "objectively" reportable life change that requires some social and/or psychological adjustment on the part of the individual. If we look to Selye's examples for clues as to what stressors are, however, we find examples that are quite instructive. The noxious agents cited included toxic substances, noise, extreme heat or cold, injury, weight—even a colony of microbes (Selye, 1956). Although there are some agents here that qualify as "events," it is also clear that some may qualify as conditions or continuous states. This is generally reflected in biological research since that time—it has never been the case that biological stressors were restricted to the notion of an event (Hinkle, 1987).

An event is a specific concept in epistemology (Mestrovic, 1985). It implies by definition a change in the properties of something—but it requires change. Why our thinking about stress in the social sciences has been so closely tied to the notion of an event is not clear, beyond the operational convenience and efficiency of the life events inventory. I have argued elsewhere (Wheaton, 1994) that the life events inventory—a measure—unconsciously evolved into a functional equivalent of the concept of stress.

Our assumption of the necessity of an event has become so ingrained that we strain to find events in stressors that in no way qualify as such. It is well known that the original Holmes and Rahe (1967) list of "events" contained reference to a number of issues that could not easily be categorized as events. These items tended to start with references to "troubles with . . ." and were accorded, I think kindly, "ambiguous" status as events. The fact is that these are not events, but ongoing problems that contradict the idea of an event. Monroe and Roberts (1990) reflect this treatment of the event as the *sine qua non* of stress: "It may seem that life events are self-evident. Yet life is a continuous flow of experiences and transactions. Determining at what point ongoing experience becomes an event can be problematic" (1990, p. 211). This quote has ironic appeal, leading me to the conclusion that while the correct facts are cited, the need to transform a continuous reality into a discrete event leads to the wrong conclusion. Fundamentally, a stressor can exist as a "state," a continuous reality. It need not start as an event, but may evolve slowly. It need not be resolved with a particular act; instead, it may dissipate gradually. Such stressors are not sampled or even, in some cases, deemed allowable in an event approach.

Models of the Stress Concept—Reconsidered

Where does the modern stress concept come from? Dohrenwend and Dohrenwend (1974) trace their use of the term to the pioneering experiments of Cannon (1929) on the effects of pain, hunger, and emotions on bodily changes, as does Selye himself. In applying this model, Dohrenwend and Dohrenwend (1970) utilize a crucial distinction drawn from Koos (1946) between "troubles" and exigencies of daily life—the former referring to situations that block the usual patterns of daily activities and call for new ones, the latter referring to the patterns that persist over time. The notion of stress is restricted to issues that reflect change in the usual patterns of daily life. Dohrenwend and Dohrenwend frankly state: "We limit the term stressor to objective events" (1970, p. 115). In this approach, stress is linked to the requirement of change.

An alternative to the biological stress model is the stress model in engineering. My attention was drawn to the engineering stress model by an article in *Schizophrenia Bulletin* in 1987 called "The Stress Analogy," written by Warren Smith, a metallurgist. In the engineering model, stress is essentially an external force acting against a resisting body that may or may not operate within normative limits. Thus, one could say that stress also becomes a stressor when the level of force exceeds limits defining structural integrity. It appears at first glance that stressors and stress are not distinct phases in the engineering model—they both refer to the external force, pressure, or threat to the body. This immediately makes this model more amenable to translation into the psychosocial model, and it provides some direction in defining what stressors are. However, in the psychosocial model we need further help in defining what is stressful, due to the fact that there is variability in contextual factors that define whether a stressor is in fact stressful. For example, I have argued elsewhere that events such as divorce are only stressful when preceded by what was apparently a nonstressful marriage, even a good marriage (Wheaton, 1990). If one finds the marriage stressful, then divorce may not be a stressor at all, but a relief from stress. Thus, stressful stressors are a contextually defined subclass of stressors.

In fact, this additional link in defining what is stressful can be accommodated by the engineering model, as follows. Contextual factors may also enter into the definition of the current strength of the material. Thus, some materials can withstand less force without breaking when heated than at room temperature. This reflects a change in the relative force of the stressor defined by a reduction in the strength of the material by environmental conditions.

To be more precise about the definition of stress in the engineering model, it is the load exerted by a force divided by the capacity of the material to resist. This latter feature of the definition is actually a weakness of the engineering model, because it imagines coping capacity only as the denominator of stress loads. The psychosocial stress model offers a superior analogy in this area by allowing coping capacity to operate as a separate factor in the model, thus allowing us to *discover* how it combines with stress loads.

The engineering model, however, does offer a clarification of the relationship between the concepts of stress and strain—a terminological problem that in recent years has finally started to be clarified, thanks to a recent discussion in which the term chronic stressor, rather than chronic strain or role strain, is used explicitly (Pearlin, 1989). In the engineering model, of course, strain is the response state of the material, technically, the state of the elongation and compression of the material. Obviously, strain is the distress side of the model.

An important distinction in the engineering model refers to stress occurring below or above normative limits, technically, within or beyond the "elastic limit" of the material. The elastic limit is an important concept, since it refers to the strength of the material in resisting stress forces. Coping capacity, in effect, defines the current elastic limit, which the engineering model envisions is *not* static over time, but dynamic.

Figure 1 reproduces from Smith (1987) the curve showing the relationship between stress and strain in the engineering model. The level of stress is shown on the Y axis, the level of strain on the X axis (reversing our conventions in social science). As long as the stress applied does not exceed point A on the stress scale, the material will not exceed its elastic limit, and it will return to its original shape after the stress is removed. The model does allow for changes in the elastic limit of the material, however. When stress exceeds A, say to level B, the material is able to adjust by elongation or compression and, in the process, achieves a new, greater elastic limit. In other words, it is stronger.

This feature of the engineering model offers greater flexibility and,

THE NATURE OF CHRONIC STRESS

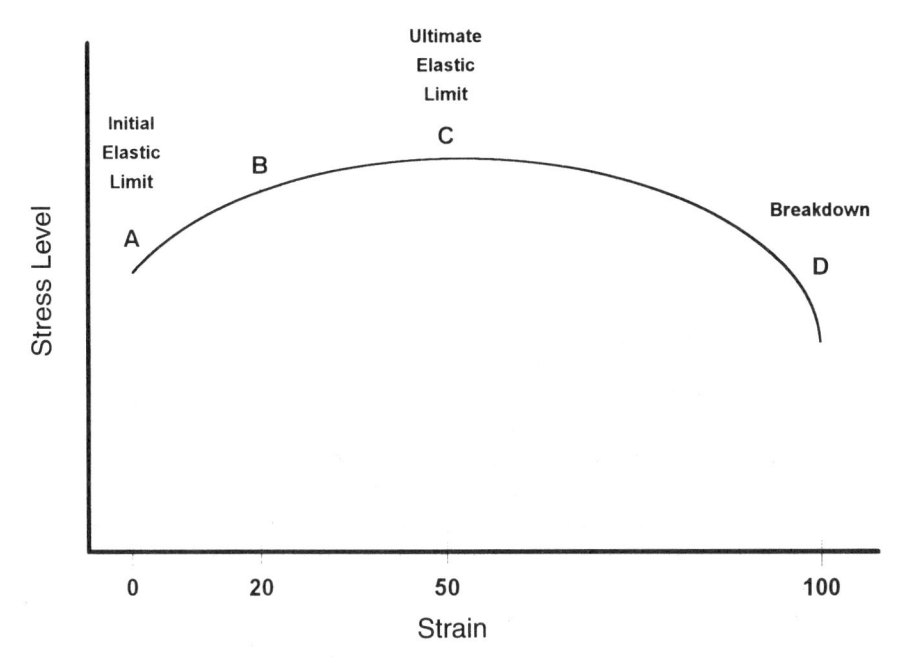

Figure 1. The stress versus strain curve in the engineering stress model (adapted from Smith, 1987).

I believe, applicability to psychosocial stress, compared to the biological stress model of Selye. The reason is that it allows for enhancement in coping capacity as a result of facing stressful situations, rather than just the minimization of damage to existing capacity. Even in the resistance phase of Selye's G.A.S., the best that is achieved is a return to prior levels of functioning.

The model also allows for deterioration of capacity to resist, since the material has a finite elastic limit. The implication is that at *some* point the individual's ability to respond with adjustments that enhance strength will be no longer possible. Point C in Figure 1 represents the ultimate elastic limit of the material—the point of maximum strength. If stress is applied beyond point C, the stress the material can resist actually decreases, heading toward point D, known in the engineering model as fracture or breakdown. The curve in Figure 1 can be considered a representative curve—materials and persons will differ in the amount of rise and fall of the curve and in the left-to-right distance for enhancements versus deteriorations in strength.

Rather than imagining stressors as a single class, the engineering model also allows for distinctions among types of stressors. The primary distinction is between *catastrophic* and *continuous* forces, a clear analogy to event versus chronic stressors. Why is this distinction useful in the engineering model? The issue is whether the process by which forces change materials is the same in the case of continuous versus catastrophic forces, and it is not. Thus, although the phenomenology of slow or insidious decay may make us feel less than satisfied in terms of explaining *how* something happened, the bridge collapse should instruct us that it is possible and plausible as a mode of explanation.

In addition, the types of adjustments possible on the part of the material are defined by whether the force is a trauma or a long-term force. Thus, we should expect that coping with a continuous stress is a very different phenomenon compared to coping with a discrete, sudden, and self-limiting force. For example, one can imagine that dealing with life event stress may involve a stronger role for resources that can be easily mobilized but only exist over short periods (e.g., unusually high levels of social support after a spouse dies), while chronic stress may demand more stable resources that are automatically rather than conditionally activated.

The engineering model is more than a metaphor. It is, in fact, a model, providing rationales for linkages in the human stress model, definitional guidelines, and conceptual distinctions. It is a reminder of features of human stress and coping that have been buried or left ambiguous or simply left out of the psychosocial model as it has evolved from the concept of biological stress. It reminds us that even inert materials have dynamic coping capacities—so, obviously, humans do, too. It reminds us that stress must be defined in conjunction with both contextual factors and coping capacities that define the current level of "force." It explicitly represents external forces as sometimes occurring within normative limits, thus representing a potential stressor in a prestressful state, and sometimes occurring beyond normative limits, thus representing the occurrence of stress. In either case, it places stress clearly in the realm of a stimulus issue, as opposed to an internalized process that is usually not measured in the social sciences. The stressor, in effect, is the stress applied. Finally, and most importantly for present purposes, it allows for—in fact, requires—heterogeneity in types of stressors, distinguishing principally between discrete and continuous forms of stress.

Events versus Chronic Stressors

Life events, as embodied in the literature, have the following characteristics: They are discrete, observable events standing for significant life changes and possessing a relatively clear onset and offset; between the onset and offset, they are made up of a relatively well-defined set of subevents describing the "normal" progress of the event. Some events, of course, have little internal structure, such as the death of a pet, but most others actually involve a process, often a partially ritualized process. Divorce, job loss, and the death of a spouse are classic examples. The defining issue in a life event is its discreteness, both in typical time course and in its onset and offset. Life events do not typically emerge slowly; rather, they begin with the announcement of the unfortunate news that begins the life change. As stressors, they typically have a clear offset, a point at which the stressor ends—for example, the court settlement of the divorce, or the last day of work, or the actual death of the spouse. The fact that events take time to come to fruition has been well documented by Avison and Turner (1988).

Taking events as a point of departure, then, we can define a very different form of stress that (1) does not necessarily start as an event, but develops slowly and insidiously as a continuing problematic condition in our social environments and roles and (2) typically has a longer time course than life events, from onset to resolution. Among a large set of alternative possibilities, we seem to have settled on the term *chronic stressors* to refer to this kind of stress.

The crux of the distinction between event stressors and more continuous stressors is the time course of the stressor, but there is more involved, including differences in the ways in which the stressor develops, exists, and ends. The term "chronic" has been applied less to designate a time course presumptuously than to designate the fact that this class of stressors will have a typical time course that is very unlike the notion of an event. Chronic stressors are continuous stressors in an approximate sense; standing for problems and issues that either are so regular in the enactment of daily roles and activities or are defined by the nature of daily role enactments or activities, and so behave as if they are continuous for the individual.

Chronic stressors are less self-limiting in nature than the typical life event. A life event, almost by definition, will end, while chronic stressors are typically open-ended, using up our resources in coping, but not promising resolution. Although chronic stress is most often associated with the problem of overload (i.e., excessive demand), it is more than that. Most generally, it arises from one of an array of problems: task or role demands, excessive complexity, uncertainty, conflict, restriction of choice, or underreward. In Pearlin's words these are "the enduring problems, conflicts, and threats that many people face in their daily lives" (Pearlin, 1989, p. 245).

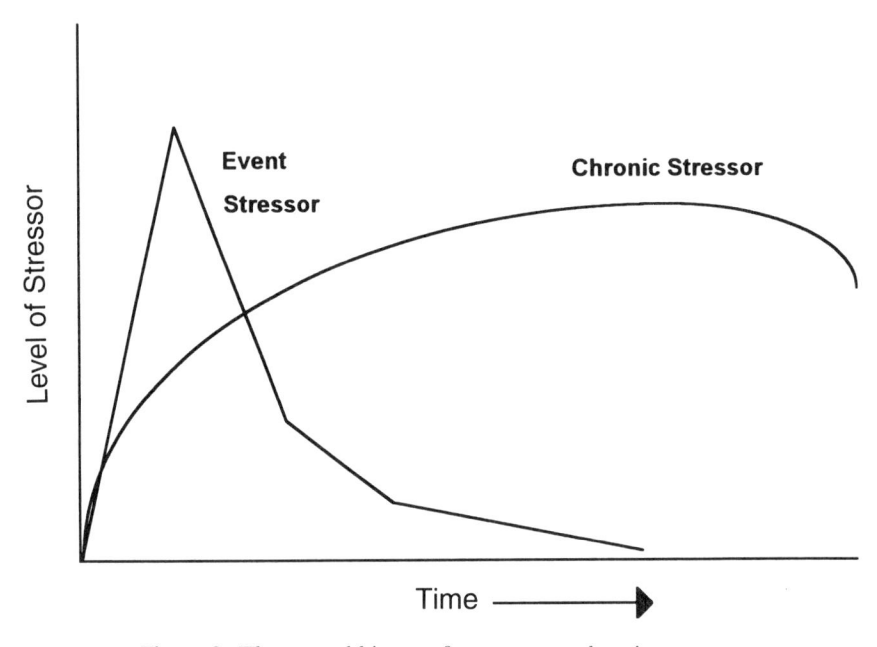

Figure 2. The natural history of event versus chronic stressors.

A typical chronic stressor is represented in Figure 2, along with a typical discrete event stressor. The onset of the chronic stressor is gradual, the course long-term and continuous (not a string of events), and the offset problematic and often unpredictable. If we were to envision the perfect opposite of this kind of stress (also in Figure 2), we would have a traumatic event that occurs suddenly and without warning, reflecting a clear and discretely defined onset. The actual length of the stressor would be short-term, followed by a definite resolution.

Why distinguish these forms of stress as two *types* of stress? Why not just measure the time course of stressors? The problem is one of defining a conceptual universe fully. If we begin with an event and just elaborate the time course, we still assume that "events" are the standard. And, of course, there are the important precedents in the work of Pearlin and colleagues (1978, 1981) and Brown and Harris (1978), who found it not only necessary but also conceptually useful to keep these types of stress separate. In the case of Pearlin's work, of course, this distinction helps to develop the whole notion of a stress process, where stressors are linked to each other. In the case of Brown and Harris, they point to the following example as evidence of the fact that events do not capture everything stressful:

THE NATURE OF CHRONIC STRESS

> A woman living for three years in two small damp rooms with her husband and two children would not have been picked up by our measures of events unless her situation has led to some kind of crisis in the year. . . . There clearly is no theoretical justification for dealing with such situations only when they give rise to a crisis. (p. 130)

There is, of course, the inevitable fact that some life events will be more chronic than others, and some chronic stressors will act more like discrete problems. This overlap in phenomenology is not at issue. Event stressors and chronic stressors represent two large and distinct classes of stressors, that is, the trajectories in Figure 2 represent modal patterns. We treat gender as a categorical variable, knowing that it stands for two categories with even more within-group variability than cross-group variability. This does not mean that gender does not operate in social terms as two distinct classes. The same can be said of event versus chronic stress: While they are classes of stress, they of course will exhibit overlapping distributions on many characteristics, such as time course, nature of onset, open-endedness, etc.

If we imagine a spliced curve in Figure 2, starting like the event but continuing like the chronic stressor, we would have the perfect borderline case. But in many cases this situation will actually be describing two stressors, not one. The distinction between event and chronic stressors allows us to distinguish the effects of *getting* divorced from *being* divorced. Keeping the stressors separate allows us to distinguish between the problems of identity loss and identity adjustment, on the one hand, and the problems of continual vigilance and pressure, on the other. Put another away, we are distinguishing between the loss of another and the abstract absence of another as two stressors.

Chronic Stress versus Role Strain. Even in recent discussions of chronic stress (Lepore, 1995), the impression is that chronic stress reduces to the concept of role stress. This is so because, fundamentally, chronic stresses are most visible in the literature as ongoing work or marital stressors, i.e., stresses within and defined by role conditions. This presumed equivalence is unfortunate. The conceptualization of chronic stress has in fact evolved over the years, so that chronic stress is now usually assumed to involve an array of problems beyond rolebound conditions. This is evident in Pearlin's (1989) discussion, in which the term "ambient stress" is used to refer to sources of chronic stress that cannot be attached to any one role situation; in fact, they span many role situations. These include issues such as generalized time pressure, fear of crime or personal assault, and spending too much time alone.

There are fundamental problems in assuming that chronic stress exists only in major social roles. The following scenario should make this clear. It is important to understand that stress in one role will be affected by the presence or absence of stress in other roles. That is, whether the stress of caring for an aging parent will be important or not may depend on the levels of demands in other roles, e.g., the parenting role. Even where one role is the focus, it will be necessary to consider other-role or nonrole levels of stress in order to understand how threatening stress in any one role is. If one wants to understand total stress burden, it will be necessary to aggregate sources of stress. In these cases, higher exposure to role stress accumulated across roles is confounded with social competence factors that determine the number of role occupancies. In other words, people who have a job, are married, have children, etc., tend to accumulate these roles and maintain them because of relative social competence. Thus, higher scores on role strain are typically related to being in more roles, which in turn suppresses the relationship between overall stress burden and stress outcomes. This problem follows from the equivalence of total chronic stress exposure with role stress only (Wheaton, 1991).

This is a point that can be elaborated upon to suggest that there are in fact four sources of chronic stress that must be considered, including but also beyond major roles (Pearlin, 1989; Wheaton, 1994):

1. Stressors due to role occupancy, as in the classic work on role strains.
2. Stressors due to role inoccupancy, such as the problems resulting from not having children when you want to, or not being in a relationship when you want to.
3. Role-defining stressors, i.e., stressors that do not result from role engagement but precipitate it, as in the appearance of a chronic illness or the entry into an intrinsically difficult social role situation, such as a single parent.
4. Ambient stressors that are not rolebound but instead are socially diffuse and general in origin, such as a recession, residential living space difficulties, time pressure, or social complexity.

In the instrument I have recently developed to measure chronic stress, all of these possibilities are represented (Wheaton, 1991). The items for this instrument are shown in the Appendix at the end of this chapter. Typical items include: "You're trying to take on too many things at once" (ambient), "You have a lot of conflict with your boss or coworkers" (role strain), "You don't get paid enough for what you do" (role strain), "Your relationship restricts your freedom" (role strain), "You find it is too difficult to find someone compatible with you" (strain due to role inoccupancy), and "You are often afraid you will be mugged, assaulted, or robbed" (ambient). The importance of sampling a range of sources is underscored by the finding that sources of stress for those *not* in major social roles (e.g., those who want to have children but cannot, those who want a relationship but feel that it is difficult to find someone) may be more virulent in impact than even the major role stresses usually studied (Wheaton, 1991, 1994).

FORMS OF CHRONIC STRESS

Chronic stress presents itself as an ongoing, open-ended problem located in the structure of the social environment. While there are many specific examples of chronic stress situations in the literature, most reflect one or more of a set of basic themes that recur as fundamental forms of chronic stress. Here I consider nine such forms: (1) threats, (2) demands, (3) structural constraints, (4) complexity, (5) uncertainty, (6) conflict, (7) restriction of choice, (8) underreward, and (9) resource deprivation.

Threats

Chronic stress is often defined by the continuing possibility or expectation of potential harm. This is the problem in such stressors as regular physical abuse by a spouse, life in a high crime area, and life in a war zone. In these cases, the episodes of actual danger are not the entire stressor. The chronic stressor at issue is the constant presence of the possibility of vulnerability to dangerous forces that cannot be controlled or avoided.

But these cases are only the most obvious examples in which continuing threat is the main issue. It is also the issue when a current identity is in question, for example, when a marriage is valued but also beset with continuing conflict or when a student begins to perform poorly after developing an expectation of success. The change in grades for the student may be gradual or sudden, but the threat to one's identity as a "good student" accumulates only with *persistent* evidence of performance problems.

Threat also exists as a form of pressure, for example, when the number of demands across roles begins to compromise the ability to perform in any role. Such is the case when the overload (or excessive demands; see the next section) becomes a threat to the normal operation of social roles that are essential to well-being.

In all of these cases, threat operates as a continuing reality that exists apart from the fruition of the threat and is a fundamental component of what is stressful about the situation. Between episodes of abuse, in a situation where performance in school may not change for the better, or when the inability to meet obligations in major roles is imminent, threat describes the operative problem.

Demands

The word "demands," and accompanying terms such as overload, are among the most commonly used in defining the nature of stress. There is simply too much to do, and the person feels pulled by multiple, independent, immediate, and uncontrollable demands that cannot be put aside. Among a set of chronic stress items elicited in open-ended questioning in the chronic stress study mentioned earlier (Wheaton, 1991), this sense of generalized overload came out in a number of ways: "Too much is expected of me by others," "I'm trying to take on too many things," or "I don't have enough time to myself." This is the generalized version of a sense of over-demand that does not pertain just to one role, but to the total of all role obligations. Other items also reflected overload within roles: "I have an unusual amount of work compared to others," or "I don't have enough time to talk to my spouse."

Although this is the most commonly cited source of stress—and in the popular notions of stress, the sense of being overwhelmed is presumably ubiquitous and cited by everyone as a "fact of life"—these items were never endorsed by over 40% of a random sample community survey in three cities (Wheaton, 1991). Thus, most people in fact believe that life is essentially under control. This makes the inclusion of reported overload—as a sense of undue expectation in others and/or level of demand beyond one's usual ability to meet obligations—essential in detecting the accumulation of excessive demand across situations.

Excessive demand is at the heart of many stressful situations, but often in conjunction with other important features of chronic stress. For example, being a caregiver may have elements of excessive demand, but these situations usually also include a sense of absence of alternatives and restricted choice.

Stress is usually defined to be bidirectional with respect to demand characteristics. That is, *it is possible for both overdemand and underdemand to be stress problems.* This feature would seem to beg the whole definitional issue, since we might legitimately wonder how something can be stressful when it stands for too little stimulation. First, it is important to see that some stress models explicitly incorporate a nonlinearity in the effects of demand. Gersten et al. (1974) used arousal theory to suggest the need for the specification of stressors beyond the notion of an "event." They noted that:

> [Some] arousal is necessary for the maintenance of efficient behavior; the well-documented inverse U-shaped function between arousal and behavior efficiency attests to this. . . . Accordingly, maladaptive behavior would occur either at levels of extremely low arousal or extremely high arousal. (1974, p. 167)

Second, underload, as it is often called, involves features of structural constraint. Boredom, by definition, is not chosen; it is a state of not having a choice when one wants to have a choice. Restriction of choice is a state defined by one's "social location," a place in a social structure. Third, there are forms of underdemand—a slow, boring, repetitive job, for example—that in fact represent high threat because of their lack of stimulation. Looked at this way, it should be clear that situations of low demand can under some conditions be stressful because they also represent high levels of structural constraint and/or threat.

Structural Constraints

I have included the notion of "structural constraints" in the definition of stress to make clear that there are problems posed strictly by the consequences of the structure of the social environment that leave the individual with reduced opportunities, choices, or alternatives. The idea of structural constraints is essential to understanding that stressors arise from and are embedded in locations in a social structure (Pearlin, 1989). Structural constraints come in many forms, from the influence of rules or regulations that impede dealing with a problem straightforwardly to the fact of severe and non-self-limiting social disadvantage resulting from inequality of opportunity or systemic discrimination. Restriction in access to means, as a form of structural strain (Merton, 1957), is a form of stress. In fact, this form of stress fits well with the notion of a continuous force acting on a material in the engineering model. It is the *disjunction* between shared goals and means to achieve goals that is the stressor.

Open-ended responses to questions about persistent problems sometimes reflect the issue of structural constraints. These include statements such as, "I am looking for a job but can't find one," "I want to achieve more at work but things get in the way," or "I am in the middle between two divorced parents." Other items reflect structural constraints by definition, such as, "I don't have enough money to buy the things I or my kids need."

The notion of structural constraints raises the problem of how to impute stress to social locations. Should we consider living in poverty, being a visible minority, or nonpromotion due to gender as *prima facie* evidence of the occurrence of stress? There is no easy answer to this question. Certainly, discrimination is experienced as stressful and it is often experienced pervasively. Asking about the experience of discrimination will often elicit this sense of disadvantage, and whether "real" or not, the perception of it operates as a stressor. Still, this may not be enough if restriction of opportunity is a reality, but the person is coping with it well and does not perceive a loss of opportunity. In this case, there may be a stressor that is not *also* stressful for a given person. This individual variability is a universal problem in stress measurement. It is important to try to measure and detect both appraised sources of disadvantage and direct indicators of disadvantage, such as low income, race, and physical disability.

Underreward

The notion of underreward is derived from Equity Theory (Walster, Berscheid, & Walster, 1976), a theory of social exchange that posits stable social exchange under conditions of equity, defined as an equal ratio of outputs to inputs for the two parties involved in a relationship. This feature of social relations has various incarnations in sociological theory (Blau, 1964; Homans, 1961). Equity Theory defines a specific condition for underreward that is quite general. In this formulation, importantly, it is outputs *relative to* inputs that matter, not absolute levels of outputs or rewards. The absolute problem of underreward is defined by the twin notions of restriction of choice and restriction of access to means. Relative underreward is also a structural constraint: The individual is faced with a problem of reduced returns on personal investments in another, and changing the situation is not entirely controllable. If we are to have a notion of stress that includes individuals in relationships in which the giving exceeds the receiving by large amounts, then underreward as defined by equity theory is a way of embedding this situation in a concept.

A basic prediction of Equity Theory is that inequity produces distress in both parties. This feature is reminiscent of the bidirectional assumption underlying the effects of demands, where either too much or too little is distressing. But the role of victim in the equity equation is probably more universally stressful than the role of harmdoer, for reasons offered by the theory: The harmdoer can rationalize harm by derogating the victim, without losing any outputs.

Many of the types of problems used to measure work or relationship stressors involve a form of inequity. These include not getting paid enough for a job, feeling you don't get what you deserve out of a relationship, feeling that you give more affection and understanding than you get in return, feeling that your spouse is not committed enough to your relationship, and having a spouse or child who does not contribute to household tasks. Inequity is probably a prevalent form of chronic stress, in that it expresses a structure for "feeling unappreciated." Often, such feelings have to do with presumption, the thoughtlessness of others, or simply "being taken for granted." Sometimes, the problem is outright volitional harmdoing. It is likely that the level of the stress in the latter form of inequity is much higher (Walster et al., 1976).

Complexity

Complexity can be a positive feature of social life, such as when it expresses the fine points of an enjoyed or understood activity or when it is the source of continued interest in work tasks (as in the substantive complexity of work). However, complexity can also represent a form of excessive demand, with its own unique characteristics. The complexity of demand is distinct from the level of demand in social roles. When demands are more contingent and yet also interdependent, the effects of the resulting complexity can amount to a form of chronic stress. People with complex jobs complain about the strain of facing constantly problematic issues without a standard or clear resolution.

Complexity of routines in social roles can also be a source of chronic stress. When a single parent has many contingent issues involved in each day—involving childcare, short-term changes in arrangements, and work demands that lead to staying late at work unpredictably—the whole fabric of daily life begins to be excessively complex. The amount of time devoted to logistics takes up a larger portion of each day. The complexity here has to do with three features:

1. The number of daily responsibilities and roles one is solely responsible for or has no choice about.
2. The level of uncertainty and contingency in how plans work out and the absence of stable solutions to logistics.
3. Scheduling problems that cannot be controlled.

These three problems amount to a phenomenology of complexity.

Complexity may be a source of stress that has been increasing in individual lives over the last half of the twentieth century. If contingencies increase in prevalence in daily life because in effect social institutions have not been responsive to social changes such as the prevalence of women in the labor force (e.g., sources of childcare, family-friendly work policies), then the average level of chronic stress experienced may be increasing historically as well. There are, of course, other sources of chronic stress besides complexity—such as threat—that may be adding to this possibility.

Complexity is also to some degree amenable to learning effects. Clearly, long-term residents of New York City notice the complexity of daily life less than the casual visitor. An important aspect of complexity is that it represents a set of daily issues that resist ritualization. Ritualization is a coping device that helps to defuse complexity; whether it works depends on the amount of exposure and accompanying reinforcements that offset the effects of complexity per se.

Uncertainty

A closely related problem is uncertainty. Complexity and uncertainty usually feed each other in the following sense: At a given level of complexity, uncertainty multiplies the effects of complexity, and at a given level of uncertainty, complexity multiplies the effects of uncertainty.

Uncertainty can also be a positive feature of daily life, but usually within well-known role situations or in clearly delimited amounts. Prolonged uncertainty about something that requires resolution, or for which resolution is desired, is itself stressful. This is a common situation in work roles where turnaround involves long periods of time or when the outcomes of tasks do not have a clear success–failure component.

The truth is that uncertainty is a feature of many social situations and social relations. However, it can become almost a defining feature of some situations. For example, if someone suspects that the company they are working for is on a downward trajectory, uncertainty about losing a job may be a constant issue and may pervade the atmosphere of work life. Often interpersonal relations are defined by varying levels of uncertainty over time. In premarital relationships, the interpretation of the other's commitment or seriousness may be a constant source of uncertainty and stress, if greater commitment is desirable. Mixed signals from another increase the constancy of a sense of uncertainty.

Often, uncertainty involves unwanted waiting for an outcome. Many processes in life involve a ritualized time period, but those caught in these processes want to have the result. This is true if one's fate is being decided in a tenure process in a university or if one is the defendant in a long trial. Where a judgment is to be made, the uncertainty of not knowing the outcome becomes the stressor. In these cases, one's future is being decided by others, and no action in one's own behalf can further alter the outcome.

When the time period for an outcome is not defined but is open-ended, the uncertainty can be worse. It has become increasingly common in Canada to analyze the "stress" of a possible separation of Quebec in terms of the stress of prolonged and open-ended uncertainty. The nature of this uncertainty is a desire for *some* resolution, *one way or the other*. When the desire for resolution begins to be greater than the desire for a specific result, it is clear that, at the system level, uncertainty itself is operating as a chronic stressor.

Conflict

It would be difficult to exclude conflict in a discussion of long-term sources of stress. Conflicts at work, in marriages, and in families become regular enactments, reflecting basic differences in viewpoints, values, principles, goals, or desires. Long-term conflicts tend to be those that are defined by the inability to agree on starting premises, or even on the common goal (Wheaton, 1974). Both the fear of bringing the conflict to the surface and the ritualized enactment of the conflict become sources of chronic stress. Our open-ended questioning about chronic stress in the stress measurement study revealed basic concerns about conflict at work and at home, and it was a prevalent source of concern.

As Simmel (1955) has made clear, it is not just overt conflict that is at issue. Often, the avoidance of overt conflict stands for the assumption of "silent conflict"; as Simmel eloquently argues, there are times when conflict stands for the strength of a group rather than its weakness. However, it is also true that group-strengthening conflicts are likely to be of a certain type, involving either (1) a high chance of resolution or (2) an assumption of common values or goals but disagreement about means or procedures (Wheaton, 1974).

Thus, in treating conflict as stress, we must be careful to (1) include cases of implicit conflict in which there is an assumed fundamental disagreement that cannot be resolved and (2) not count conflict that is in fact normative, unthreatening, and with a shared purpose that is clearly recognized by both parties.

Restriction of Choice

Restriction of choice can be considered to be a kind of structural constraint. Pearlin (1983) argued for the distinct importance of restriction of choice as manifest by the problem of role captivity—a situation in which exit from a role is desired but not really an option. When this occurs, this is likely to be a powerful source of stress, captured by the phrase "feeling trapped." This may be an important source of chronic stress in many lives, from the situation of caregivers, to the experience of a long-term debilitating chronic illness, to a marriage one cannot leave because of commitments to children, to the lack of alternative choices for jobs with no hope of promotion, to the absence of alternatives when your child is in a bad school. In all of these situations, it is the restriction of choice that is the source of stress, over and above the stress emanating from the situation itself.

Of course, restriction of choice need not occur within or because of roles. It may also occur directly as a function of ascriptive or achieved social status. Thus, reduced opportunities for education, training, or promotion may plague selected groups who are regularly discriminated against. This should be considered a kind of chronic stress that is structurally embedded and a function of social inequality in general.

Restriction of choice may also occur in situations that are not patterned by social inequality but may be defined by demographic or geographic limits on choice. Growing up in a small town may limit the choice of marital partners, or living in a mining town may define the choice of occupations. Whether these restrictions are in fact stressful depends on the larger goals of the individual—one cannot be defined without reference to the other.

At the same time, minor or ubiquitous restrictions cannot be considered a stress issue. It is true that some restriction of choice is involved in most social situations. The distinguishing features of problematic levels of restriction are:

1. When the restriction is fundamental in defining life chances.
2. When no alternatives are available in a clearly undesirable situation.
3. When restriction in choice is accompanied by other features of chronic stress, such as threat, complexity, or uncertainty of outcome.

Resource Deprivation

Whether resource deprivation should be considered a form of stress is a controversial issue. This is a closely related concept to the notion of restriction of choice. Insufficient means or resources to achieve desired goals qualifies as a restriction of choice or as a kind of structural constraint. However, what if the resource deprivation has to do with resources that are important in coping with stress, such as social support?

THE NATURE OF CHRONIC STRESS 65

Is a state of low social support also a kind of stress? In cases where the absence of a coping resource may also define a stressful state, a choice must be made. My preference it to leave certain forms of resource deprivation in the realm of coping resources and not stressors. This is in part because their presence—high social support, high mastery—indicates a specific resource in dealing with stress. More generally, however, there is a need to separate issues that stand for differences in coping, in any definition of the term, from differences in stress exposure, so that their respective roles can be estimated as part of empirical research into the stress process.

This does not mean that issues such as social isolation, as indicated by living alone when living with someone is preferred, cannot be studied separately from social support. A person living alone can still conceivably report high available support from family or from friends. This person could also be experiencing high levels of instrumental support from a work-based social network.

MEASURING CHRONIC STRESS

Although this chapter is not about measurement, a consideration of the issues that arise in measuring chronic stress is instructive. We learn about concepts further when we try to measure them. Often, in the process of operationalization, we realize some of the implicit boundaries we have set for our concept and the need for specification of these boundaries.

In preparation for the stress measurement study described earlier, I conducted a random sample pilot study in one of the three cities to elicit items for a chronic stress measure. As part of this survey, respondents were asked this open-ended question: "If you think about the main problems in your life right now, the problems that are there all the time or occur to you regularly and frequently, what would you say they are?" The answers that resulted from this question were first screened for their correspondence to chronic stress, and the resulting subset was used as the basis of the original 90-item measure used in the stress measurement survey. This background should make clear that these stressors are sampled from the experience of a general population, not by a priori assumption or by "expert" presumption. This procedure allows us to consider the resulting items as a *sample* of the universe of possible items we could use to measure chronic stress. Since it is difficult to imagine a set of items that collectively expresses the full universe of chronic stress, it is important that this is a random sample of items.

The original list of 90 items was reduced to 60 after multiple assessments of the validity of the items (Wheaton, 1991), resulting in the list of 60 items found in the Appendix to this chapter. Note that the wording of these items generally reflects the wording used by the original respondents wherever possible. The removed items are those that either failed to be related to any of the expected criteria for consequences of stress, including a wide range of physical and mental health problems, or were redundant with other items. Looking over this list gives an idea of the range of problems people describe when asked about chronic problems in their lives.

Three points should be made about these items, which speak to the concept of chronic stress. First, it is clear from the examples throughout this chapter, using the items in this list, that we can inductively learn from such a sampling of items what the content of stressors are. At the same time, it is also clear that theoretical discussions of chronic stress (e.g., Pearlin, 1983, 1989) have had empirical validity in terms of predicting the kinds of issues that arise under the rubric of chronic stress.

Second, it should be clear from this list that chronic stress cannot be reduced to or equated with role stress. Items such as #19 ("You are looking for a job and can't find the one you want"), #34 ("You wonder whether you will ever get married"), and #37 ("You wish you could have children but you cannot") measure possible stress resulting from *not* being in commonly valued social roles, such as worker, spouse, and parent. Despite the fact that the items are indeed heavily weighted toward role stress indices (e.g., items 9–18 for work stress and 21–32 for relationship stress), these "role inoccupancy" items have been shown to be among the most important sources of stress in this set of items (Wheaton, 1994). This means that role stress measures will likely miss the level of chronic stress in important segments of the population.

Finally, there is the issue of the subjectivity of some of these items. It is difficult to resolve whether objective features of the social environment or subjectively evaluated states of the social environment constitute the primary locus of chronic stress. Presumably, it would be helpful to have well-validated social conditions that could be measured without requiring subjective appraisal. However, there are a number of problems. Many of the social conditions that one might think generally qualify as stressors turn out to depend *essentially* on contextual specifiers. In effect, objective referents are usually insufficient to specify whether something is a stressor, and in the case of chronic stressors the problem of specifying a delimited set of objective referents is prohibitive.

Some of the items in the list come closer to specifying conditions with objective referents than others. This is as it should be, since there is natural variability in the degree to which chronic stressors *have* objective referents. Let us consider an item such as, "You have no control over the pace of work." This statement could be validated—to an extent—by using the *Dictionary of Occupational Titles* (DOT) to check the codings for job control attached to the person's occupation, as suggested by Kessler (1983). But even this kind of grounding of the item carries with it a number of interpretive problems. For example, we should expect, and I have observed, only modest correlations between personal assessments of control over the pace of work and DOT-rated control conditions (Wheaton, 1991). This is in part due to the fact that the criterion here is just a coding of the occupation, not the individual's particular job in that occupation. There is variability across jobs that is captured in the self-report.

More generally, the question is whether one *could* find a set of objective referents for this item that applied across occupations and could be asked of individuals, since indicators of the pace of work would depend on the nature of the occupation itself or are so abstract (e.g., available job mechanisms for changing the pace of work) that they invite unreliable reporting in any case.

This problem is even more obvious in the case of other items. For many situations we would want to include as chronic stressors, it is simply difficult to imagine what the objective referents could be. There is no DOT for marriage problems, such as, "My spouse doesn't understand me." In the pilot study to elicit items, a number of respondents mentioned living too far from or too close to their family as a long-term problem. In probing this statement, it became clear that the objective referent for these statements would have missed both cases. In the case of the complaint of living too far away, the respondent was a newlywed who lived only 20 blocks away from her parents; in the case of the complaint of living too close, the respondent lived in a city 90 miles from her parents.

Consider the item: "You are often afraid you will be mugged, assaulted, or robbed." The question is whether the actual stressor is the objectively measured crime rate or the *expected* crime rate. The issue for the individual, the factor that precipitates vigilance, is the understanding of the crime rate, not the actual aggregate reality. Following this reasoning, the actual crime rate may show little relation to mental health, and the misleading conclusion would be that chronic stressors are not really implicated in mental health problems.

Subjective assessment raises many measurement concerns, but, in the long run, it would be preferable to face these concerns than to not measure chronic stress at all simply because the job of doing so is complex. Ultimately, subjective measurement may be a better route to take than is sometimes assumed: It allows shorthand reference to a complex objective social reality and thus is an efficient approach. More importantly, it probably *does* reflect some reality that we would consider objectively stressful if we could ask enough questions. While such subjective reports cannot assumed to be veridical, the question is whether we should reach the opposite conclusion—that they are illusions constructed simply to justify the rest of our psychological experience.

It should be obvious that this is not the case. From the point of view of an "objective" social reality, these items could typically be described as looking through a somewhat distorted lens at stressful social situations that are actually there and can still be seen in main outline despite the distortion. Validity evidence for these items (Wheaton, 1991) shows that most of them have some grounding in more "objective" indicators of social situation. For example, an index of "generalized demand" constructed from these items is correlated with the number of social roles occupied; a financial strain index is related to life events reporting financial losses in the last year; going to social events alone is prevalent among the widowed, but not among the never married; and reporting a chronic illness is related to specific physical problem reports such as diabetes and asthma, but not to acute illnesses such as colds or flu.

In other words, these items reflect a negotiation of subjective and objective social realities. If one attempts to objectify chronic stress entirely, it is likely that much will be missed that is valid and essential to understanding its impacts. On the other hand, we should avoid the assumption that these are *only* subjective perceptions, as if such perceptions are entirely disengaged from objectively stressful features of the situation.

CONCLUSIONS

In the course of writing this chapter, a bridge collapsed in California due to flooding. The news reported that the force of the current of rushing flood water was too much for the bridge's structure. This was an event stressor. This was not a case of chronic stress on the bridge.

This chapter presents a model for defining *stressors*, as opposed to the *stress* of the biological model. I began by pointing out why the biological model does not particularly restrict the realm of stressors, but it doesn't specify it either. The engineering model explicitly distinguishes between catastrophic (event) and continuous (chronic) forces acting on materials. While a physical world, inert material metaphor for human stress seems farther afield than the biological version, it nicely complements the biological model emphasis on internal body processing of the stressor.

Unless the concept of chronic stress is explicitly derived and embedded in a general stress model, there will be little impetus to develop the notion of chronic stress as a coequal player in stress research. One reaction to the notion of a *separate* chronic stress concept is that it is simply unnecessary. But 30 years of research on life events since 1967 suggests otherwise. Some suggest that we just need to ask about stressors with a longer time course. But if we begin with events as the ideal, we will stretch events until they are not events at all and still not sample adequately stressors that take a longer and more gradual time course. The problem is that we simply will not ask the correct questions about what is stressful if events remain the sole ideal type. We will continue, as a consequence, to underestimate the impact of stress in understanding health outcomes.

This chapter develops a phenomenology of chronic stress involving a number of typical problems posed by chronic stress. This list is not exhaustive, but it does communicate the potential uniqueness of chronic stress as a stressor. If, as suggested earlier, chronic stress is essential to the stress process, then an understanding of coping and coping issues specific to chronic stress is just as essential. In effect, if we want to ask what is unique about coping with chronic stress, we must have a distinct concept of chronic stress.

APPENDIX: CLASSIFICATION OF THE CHRONIC STRESS ITEMS FROM THE STRESS MEASUREMENT SURVEY

General

1. You're trying to take on too many things at once.
2. There is too much pressure on you to be like other people.
3. Too much is expected of you by others.

Money and Financial Matters

4. You don't have enough money to buy the things you or your kids need.
5. You have a long-term debt or loan.
6. Your rent or mortgage is too much.
7. You don't have enough money to take vacations.
8. You don't have enough money to fix things.

Work

(Employed, 9–18)
9. You have a lot of conflict with your boss or coworkers.
10. You have an unusual amount of work these days.
11. Someone is always watching you at work.
12. You want to change jobs or career but don't feel you can.
13. You are often very tired at the end of work.
14. You want to achieve more at work but things get in the way.
15. You don't get paid enough for what you do.
16. Your work is boring and repetitive.
17. You have no control over the pace of work.
18. Your current job is a dead-end job.

(Nonemployed, 19)
19. You are looking for a job and can't the find the one you want.

(Nonemployed women, 20)
20. You feel like being a housewife is not appreciated.

Love and Marriage

(Married/in relationship, 21–32)
21. You have a lot of conflict with your spouse.
22. Divorced: You have a lot of conflict with your exspouse.
23. Your relationship restricts your freedom.
24. You have too little time to talk to your partner.
25. Your partner doesn't understand you.
26. Your partner expects too much of you.
27. You and your partner have different social needs.
28. You don't get what you deserve out of your relationship.
29. Your partner doesn't show enough affection.
30. Your partner is not committed enough to your relationship.
31. Your sexual needs are not fulfilled by this relationship.
32. Your partner is always threatening to leave or end the relationship.

(Nonmarried, 33–35).
33. There are too many changes in your relationships with others.
34. You wonder whether you will ever get married (again).
35. You find it is too difficult to find someone compatible with you.

(Everyone, 36).
36. You are alone too much.

Family and Children

(Nonparents, 37)
37. You wish you could have children but you cannot.

(Parents, 38–44)
38. One of your children seems very unhappy.
39. Your children don't help around the house.
40. One of your children spends too much time away from the house.
41. You feel your children don't listen to you.
42. One or more children do not do well enough at school.
43. You are a single parent and it seems like you have to do twice as much.
44. You think you are not a good parent.

Social Life and Recreation
45. You don't have enough time for a social life.
46. You have to go to social events alone and you don't want to.
47. Your friends are a bad influence.
48. You don't have time for your favorite leisure time activities.

Crime and Legal Matters
49. You are often afraid you will be mugged, assaulted, or robbed.

Residence
50. You want to live farther away from your family.
51. You would like to move but you cannot.
52. The place you live is too noisy.
53. The place you live is too polluted.
54. Your family lives too far away.

Religion
55. Your church/religion demands too much.

Health
56. Someone in your family or a close friend has a long-term illness or handicap.
57. You have a parent who is in bad health and may die soon.
58. Someone in your family has an alcohol or drug problem.
59. You have a handicap that makes you dependent on others.
60. A long-term illness prevents you from doing things you like to do.

ACKNOWLEDGMENTS Work on this chapter was supported in part by a Senior Research Fellowship from the Ontario Mental Health Foundation and by the W. T. Grant Foundation.

REFERENCES

Avison, W. R., & Turner, R. J. (1988). Stressful life events and depressive symptoms: Disaggregating the effects of acute stressors and chronic strains. *Journal of Health and Social Behavior, 29,* 253–264.
Blau, P. M. (1964). *Exchange and power in social life.* New York: Wiley.
Brown, G., & Harris, T. (1978). *The social origins of depression: A study of psychiatric disorder in women.* London: Tavistock.
Cannon, W. B. (1929). *Bodily changes in pain, hunger, fear, and rage.* New York: D. Appleton and Company.
Dohrenwend, B. S., & Dohrenwend, B. P. (1970). Class and race as status-related sources of stress. In S. Levine and N. Scotch (Eds.), *Social stress* (pp. 111–140). Chicago: Aldine.
Dohrenwend, B. S., and Dohrenwend, B. P. (1974). A brief historical introduction to research on stressful life events. In B. S. Dohrenwend and B. P. Dohrenwend (Eds.), *Stressful life events: Their nature and effects* (pp. 1–5). New York: Wiley.
Gersten, J. C., Langner, T. S., Eisenberg, J. G., & Orzeck, L. (1974). Child behavior and life events: Undesirable change or change per se? In B. S. Dohrenwend & B. P. Dohrenwend (Eds.), *Stressful life events: Their nature and effects* (pp. 159–170). New York: Wiley.
Goodyer, I. M. (1990). Family relationships, life events, and childhood psychopathology. *Journal of Child Psychology and Psychiatry, 31,* 161–192.
Hinkle, L. (1987). Stress and disease: The concept after 50 years. *Social Science and Medicine, 25,* 561–567.
Homans, G. C. (1961). *Social behavior: Its elementary forms.* New York: Harcourt, Brace, and World.
Kanner, A. D., Coyne, J. C., Schaefer, C., & Lazarus, R. S. (1981). Comparison of two modes of stress measurement: Daily hassles and uplifts versus major life events. *Journal of Behavioral Medicine, 4,* 1–39.
Kasl, S. V. (1984). Stress and health. *Annual Review of Public Health, 5,* 319–341.
Kessler, R. C. (1983). Methodological issues in the study of psychosocial stress: Measurement, design, and analysis. In H. B. Kaplan (Ed.), *Psychosocial stress: Recent developments in theory and research* (pp. 267–341). New York: Academic Press.
Koos, E. L. (1946). *Families in trouble.* New York: Kings Crowe.
Lepore, S. (1995). Measurement of chronic stressors. In S. Cohen, R. Kessler, & L. Underwood Gordon (Eds.), *Measuring stress: A guide for health and social scientists* (pp. 102–120). New York: Oxford University Press.
Merton, R. K. (1957). *Social theory and social structure.* New York: Free Press.
Mestrovic, S. G. (1985). A sociological conceptualization of trauma. *Social Science and Medicine, 21,* 835–848.
Monroe, S. M., & Roberts, J. E. (1990). Conceptualizing and measuring life stress: Problems, principles, procedures, and progress. *Stress Medicine, 6,* 209–216.
Norris, F. H. (1992). Epidemiology of trauma: Frequency and impact of different potentially traumatic events on different demographic groups. *Journal of Consulting and Clinical Psychology, 60,* 409–418.
Pearlin, L. I. (1983). Role strains and personal stress. In H. Kaplan (Ed.), *Psychosocial stress: Trends in theory and research* (pp. 3–33). New York: Academic Press.
Pearlin, L. I. (1989). The sociological study of stress. *Journal of Health and Social Behavior, 30,* 241–257.
Pearlin, L. I., Lieberman, M. A., Menaghan, E. G., & Mullan, J. T. (1981). The stress process. *Journal of Health and Social Behavior, 22,* 337–356.
Pearlin, L. I., & Schooler, C. (1978). The structure of coping. *Journal of Health and Social Behavior, 19,* 2–21.
Selye, H. (1956). *The stress of life.* New York: McGraw-Hill.
Simmel, G. (1955). *Conflict and the web of group affiliations.* New York: Free Press.
Smith, W. K. (1987). The stress analogy. *Schizophrenia Bulletin, 13,* 215–220.

Taylor, S. E., & Brown, J. D. (1991). Illusion and well-being: A social psychological perspective on mental health. *Psychological Bulletin, 103,* 193–210.

Walster, E., Berscheid, E., & Walster, G. W. (1976). New directions in equity research. In L. Berkowitz & E. Walster (Eds.), *Advances in experimental social psychology* (Vol. 9, pp. 1–42). New York: Academic Press.

Wheaton, B. (1974). Interpersonal conflict and cohesiveness in dyadic relationships. *Sociometry, 37,* 328–348.

Wheaton, B. (1980). The sociogenesis of psychological disorder: An attributional theory. *Journal of Health and Social Behavior, 21,* 100–123.

Wheaton, B. (1983). Stress, personal coping resources, and psychiatric symptoms: An investigation of interactive models. *Journal of Health and Social Behavior, 24,* 208–229.

Wheaton, B. (1990). Life transitions, role histories, and mental health. *American Sociological Review, 55,* 209–224.

Wheaton, B. (1991). *Chronic stress: Models and measurement.* Paper presented at the Society for Social Problems meetings in Cincinnati, Ohio, August 19–21, 1991.

Wheaton, B. (1994). Sampling the stress universe. In W. R. Avison & I. H. Gotlib, (Eds.), *Stress and mental health: Contemporary issues and prospects for the future* (pp. 77–113). New York: Plenum.

3

Theories of Coping with Chronic Stress
Illustrations from the Health Psychology and Aging Literatures

CAROLYN M. ALDWIN and JENNIFER BRUSTROM

Although theoretical models of stress processes have distinguished between chronic and acute stressors, the same cannot be said about models of coping, with some notable exceptions (Moos & Schaefer, 1984; Pearlin, 1989). One area of coping with chronic stress that has received increasing empirical examination is the ways in which patients and their caregivers and families cope with chronic illness. It is an open question, however, whether models of coping developed from an examination of acute stress are adequate for comprehending coping with chronic stress.

The purpose of this chapter is to provide a brief overview of general theories of coping and to review the few theoretical models of coping with chronic stress that do exist. Empirical studies of coping with chronic illness will also be reviewed to examine how coping changes over time. Common age-related changes in coping will be used as an instructive prototype for the examination of how individuals develop strategies for coping with chronic stress. Finally, we will present a deviation amplification model of the process of coping with chronic stress.

CAROLYN M. ALDWIN and JENNIFER BRUSTROM • Department of Human and Community Development, University of California, Davis, Davis, California 95616.

Coping with Chronic Stress, edited by Benjamin H. Gottlieb. Plenum Press, New York, 1997.

THEORETICAL MODELS OF COPING

Coping with Acute Stress

Currently in the literature there are three basic models of coping and adaptation: psychodynamic, coping styles, and coping processes (cf. Aldwin, 1994). The distinctions between these three areas are often blurred; indeed, all use similar terminology (e.g., denial, suppression), and there is often a substantial degree of overlap in the items in coping inventories. However, the three models differ in their assumptions concerning the source, development, and efficacy of adaptive strategies.

Psychodynamic Models. Psychodynamic approaches focus primarily on defense mechanisms, which are unconscious means of regulating negative affect, primarily anxiety. According to Freud (1966), defense mechanisms are ego processes for regulating anxiety generated by conflicts between the id and the superego that function primarily by distorting reality, whether through denial, projection, repression, or sublimation and, as such, are inherently pathological. Subsequent theorists expanded this list to include defenses such as intellectualization (see Tart, 1987, for a good description of defense mechanisms). Shapiro (1965) argued that the use of certain defense mechanisms can become habitual and result in what he termed neurotic styles.

More recent theorists, such as Vaillant (1977, 1993) and Haan (1977), developed what they called defensive hierarchies. In Vaillant's model, defense mechanisms are divided into four groups, depending upon the degree to which they distort reality: psychotic, immature, neurotic, and mature. Further, he argued that there are systematic developmental changes in defensive styles throughout adulthood. For example, neurotic mechanisms such as acting out or projection, which are common in early adulthood, decline with age, while more mature mechanisms such as suppression and sublimation increase. Thus, although Vaillant does not view defense mechanisms as inherently pathological, his model is still incomplete because its emphasis is on emotional regulation to the neglect of more problem-focused strategies used to change the problematic situation. Further, defense mechanisms are still viewed as largely unconscious, as are the developmental processes by which defense mechanisms are transformed (see Vaillant, 1993). Whereas Vaillant relied primarily on coding open-ended interviews to assess the use of defenses, there now are self-report inventories to assess defense mechanisms (Andrews, Singh, & Bond, 1993; Bond, Gardiner, & Siegel, 1983).

Haan (1977) developed a hierarchical model that divided coping into three modes: coping, defense, and fragmentation. Coping consists of conscious, flexible, and purposive attempts to regulate both the emotions and the environment, and defense mechanisms are unconscious, inflexible, and aimed primarily at the emotions; fragmentation processes, however, are rigid, automatic, and ritualistic and constitute a psychotic flight from reality. To paraphrase Haan, people cope when they can (usually when problems are not very stressful), defend when they must, and fragment under intolerable strain. Haan developed a coping inventory to test her scheme using the Gough California Psychological Inventory (CPI) and the Minnesota Multiphasic Personality Inventory (MMPI).

Coping Styles. The second major model, coping styles, assumes that people can be characterized by a consistent pattern of coping based on perceptual styles and/or personality characteristics. This pattern has been described generally in terms of a dichotomy, such as repression/sensitization, approach/avoidance, or blunting/monitoring, among many others (cf. Roth & Cohen, 1986). Basically, this model holds that people can be characterized by the manner in which they process information, either approaching or seeking information or avoiding or denying it. Approach/avoidance coping is generally measured via self-report inventories, which often have good internal reliability and stable factor structures (Amirkhan, 1990; Endler & Parker, 1990).

Although it is generally assumed that "approach is good, and avoidance is bad," Mullen and Suls (1982) showed that the effects of approach and avoidance coping vary as a function of the type of problem. For uncontrollable problems, avoidance coping may decrease negative affect. However, the effects of approach/avoidance may also vary over time. For example, for chronic health problems, avoidance coping may initially reduce negative affect, and approach coping may increase it. Over time, though, avoidance is associated with poorer adaptational outcomes than is approach coping.

Not all typologies of coping styles are organized in terms of simple dichotomies. Indeed, several researchers have attempted to describe various types of copers, generally based upon some characteristic way of dealing with a particular type of stressor. Reichard, Livson, and Peterson (1962), for example, described five different ways in which men coped with retirement, ranging from "rocking-chair men" who were content to sit passively to "armored men" who engaged in a hyperactive round of activities, primarily to ward off anxiety. There may also be characteristic ways of dealing with bereavement. Wortman and Silver's (1989) typology included acute grievers, chronic grievers, individuals who never appeared distressed, and those who experienced a delayed reaction. Millon (1982) identified eight different coping styles for dealing with illness, including minimization, denial, displacement, and taking a heroic stance.

In summary, both psychodynamic and coping styles approaches assume that stable characteristics of the person determine the coping behaviors that are employed. Hence, both of these approaches ignore the problem of environmental contingency, namely that situational characteristics may "pull" for different types of coping strategies.

Coping Processes. The coping process approach assumes that coping is flexible, planful, and responsive to both environmental demands and personal preferences (Lazarus & Folkman, 1984). Thus, researchers in this area study the cognition and behaviors of individuals in specific circumstances. Coping is assumed to derive from how people appraise the stressors they experience as to whether these entail threat, harm/loss, or challenge. Thus, appraisals and coping strategies are not necessarily stable characteristics of the person, but arise from a transaction between environmental demands and resources, on the one hand, and the individual's personal resources, such as coping skills and values, on the other.

The focus of coping efforts may be the environment (problem-focused coping) or the emotions (emotion-focused coping), but the overwhelming majority of people utilize both types of strategies (Folkman & Lazarus, 1980). The coping process is thought to unfold over time, in part as a function of changing environmental circumstances. However, people may also change their tactics based upon the successfulness of their initial coping efforts.

There is empirical support for this hypothesis that coping changes over time. For example, when Dunkel-Schetter and her colleagues examined the coping strategies of breast cancer patients over time, they found that most patients could not be characterized by a single coping style (Dunkel-Schetter, Feinstein, Taylor, & Falke, 1992). Swindle, Cronkite, and Moos (1989) assessed coping strategies over several time periods and found only modest correlations. Finally, Carver and Scheier (1994) had the same individuals fill out their COPE measure both in terms of their general styles of coping and for a specific problem and found that these two assessments were only modestly correlated. Together, these studies suggest that the way in which people cope does vary as a function of the situation and that coping is not necessarily a stable characteristic of the individual. However, the way in which people cope with their emotions may be more consistent than the way in which they cope with situational demands (Aldwin & Revenson, 1987; Folkman, Lazarus, Gruen, & DeLongis, 1986), and some forms of coping may be relatively automatic (Compas, Connor, Osourecki, & Welch, Chapter 4, this volume; Lazarus & Folkman, 1984). An interesting question is whether there are individual differences in the stability and flexibility of coping, but, as of this writing, there were no published studies examining this topic (but see Tennen & Affleck, 1996).

In process models, the efficacy of coping processes depends on various environmental contingencies. An important construct in the literature concerns the domain specificity of the efficacy of coping strategies. Mattlin, Wethington, and Kessler (1990), for example, found that emotion-focused coping was associated with poor outcomes in work situations, but with good outcomes among the bereaved. As Pearlin and Schooler (1978) noted, it is unlikely that we will find a single coping strategy that functions as a "magic bullet" by proving effective in all situations.

Since it has been found that problem and emotion-focused strategies are used conjointly in 90% of situations (Folkman & Lazarus, 1980), it may be less important to examine how particular strategies are related to outcomes than to study the overall pattern of their use. In other words, the relative proportion of emotion- and problem-focused coping may be more important for outcomes than the absolute level (cf. Vitaliano, De Wolfe, Maiuro, Russo, & Katon, 1985). For example, the use of relatively less emotion-focused coping compared to problem-focused coping may be more efficacious than the opposite pattern (Mattlin et al., 1990). Whereas a little emotion-focused coping may facilitate problem-solving efforts, exclusive reliance on this mode of coping may be harmful, at least in those situations that can be modified.

These two assumptions of variability in both the use and efficacy of coping strategies lead coping process researchers to assess coping in particular situations. As Aldwin (1994) pointed out, the types of strategies assessed by both coping style and process inventories are very similar. Often, the only difference lies in the instructions to the respondent. As mentioned earlier, coping style measures ask respondents to indicate how they usually cope with problems, while coping process measures ask for specific behaviors and cognitions used in managing a particular stressor. From a process point of view, measures of coping styles are not very accurate because individuals may provide idealized versions that may be contaminated by social desirability. By focusing on exactly what was done in a specific situation, coping process researchers hope to obtain more accurate assessment of the coping strategies used, regardless of whether they were helpful or harmful in managing the problem and reducing stress.

Critique

There are three primary critiques of the process approach to coping. The first lies in the method of assessment. Process approaches typically ask individuals to focus on a recent stressor, usually in the past week or month. Focusing on only one stressor leads to questions of representativeness and comparability across individuals. In any sample, problems may range from trivial spats with friends or coworkers to the death of a loved one; thus, environmental variance may overwhelm individual differences and confound coping strategies with the stressfulness of the problem, leading to spurious correlations between coping and outcomes. This problem can be mitigated somewhat by controlling for the stressfulness of the problem (e.g., Aldwin & Revenson, 1987) or by using proportional scoring (e.g., Vitaliano et al., 1987). Nonetheless, process approaches sacrifice generalizability for accuracy, specificity, and complexity.

Second, because process measures focus on variability and change, they may violate standard psychometric assumptions of cross-time reliability and factor invariance, leading some researchers to argue that simpler measures of coping styles are preferable (see Endler & Parker, 1990). For example, interpersonal strategies may or may not load on the same factor as problem-focused strategies, depending upon whether or not the types of problems studied involve other individuals. However, if one is interested in change and variability, adhering rigidly to statistics that assume invariance may be counterproductive (see Aldwin, 1994, for a more detailed discussion of this issue).

The third critique involves the emphasis on cognition in process models. Psychodynamicists often assume that cognitive psychologists overemphasize rationality and consciousness, and they argue that coping is not always conscious or logical. Thus, they may be uncomfortable with the terms coping "strategies" and "efforts," with their implication of planning. However, the focus on planfulness or effort does not mean that coping is necessarily rational or consistent. As Lazarus (1983) pointed out, a person with a terminal illness may oscillate between recognition and denial of his or her impending death, depending upon the supportiveness of others in the environment or his or her own fluctuating needs at any given moment. For example, a cancer patient may admit to a particularly supportive nurse that he or she may not have much longer to live but nonetheless continue planning for the next summer's vacation with a child or a spouse.

Process researchers often distinguish between emotional reactions and coping strategies. Emotional reactions that are not planful or effortful are not considered to be coping strategies per se. For example, involuntarily yelling "ouch" if a lab rat bites your thumb is not really a coping strategy; however, releasing a colorful and creative stream of invectives is considered to be emotion-focused coping because it requires some degree of effort. However, this distinction may be difficult to maintain in self-report inventories.

Application of Current Models to Chronic Stress

All three models—psychodynamic, coping styles, and coping processes—have some application to conditions of chronic stress. It is certainly plausible that chronic stress may activate defense mechanisms of various types. Chronic illness may trigger denial; a spinal cord injury patient, for example, may at first use denial to cope with the physician's prediction that he or she may never walk again. Many women may deny the significance of a lump in the breast and avoid seeing a physician until life-saving treatment is no longer possible. It is equally plausible that chronic use of defense mechanisms may engender chronic stress. Lifelong inability to have a successful marriage or career or chronic alcohol or drug abuse may stem from defense mechanisms that keep an individual from dealing with unresolved childhood trauma (cf. Werner & Smith, 1992).

Each of these models has its limitations. A major limitation of the psychodynamic model is that it tends to focus on emotions and thus cannot illuminate how individuals learn problem-focused strategies to manage chronic stressors. Even though Haan's (1977) model includes problem-focused efforts, her insistence that they are used primarily to deal with relatively minor stressors limits her theory's applicability to chronic stress, which often involves intense distress.

The coping styles model is also relevant to chronic stress. Much of the early work on coping with chronic illness, for example, focused on approach/avoidance dichotomies (for a review, see Aldwin, 1994). Further, there is little doubt that there are individual differences in how people cope with chronic stress. It is intuitively obvious that some people cope by gathering as much information as possible about the problem, whereas others may simply strive to avoid the problem. The drawback of this approach is that, by definition, coping styles are static properties of the person. Thus, they cannot capture the dynamics of how the coping process unfolds over time. These dynamics undoubtedly change as a function of the characteristics of the chronic stressor, such as its rapidity of onset and whether the problem stays in one domain or spills over into others. Nonetheless, it is extremely unlikely that the same coping processes characterize individuals at different stages of a chronic stressor.

Thus, the coping process model, with its emphasis on fluidity and flexibility, is the theoretical model most likely to apply to chronic stress. The demands of the chronic stressor necessitate a learning curve, in which different strategies are tried out and discarded until, hopefully, adaptive strategies can be found that allow for some level of orderly existence (cf. Gignac & Gottlieb, 1996). Further, this model does not use a priori criteria to designate which strategies are adaptive or maladaptive, but recognizes that different combinations of strategies may be efficacious for different people under different circumstances (cf. Aldwin, 1994; Lazarus & Folkman, 1984; Vitaliano et al., 1990).

It is also clear that coping does not exist in a vacuum, and how others in the social environment deal with the problem is highly relevant to the individual's coping outcomes (Coyne & Downey, 1991; DeLongis & O'Brien, 1990; O'Brien & DeLongis, Chapter 6, this volume). To a certain extent, the efficacy of approach or avoidance coping also depends upon its fit with the strategies used by others in the situation. For example, Miller and Mangan (1983) showed that congruence in approach/avoidance strategies in mother–child dyads was more adaptive than when there was discordance between the pair.

Although the coping process model may be more applicable to the management of chronic stress than psychodynamic or coping style models, the inventories currently in use may need some modification to capture the process of coping with chronic stress.

Models of Coping with Chronic Stress

As mentioned earlier, there are relatively few theoretical models for explaining how individuals cope with chronic stress. These models can be divided into two categories: sociological and behavioral medicine models.

Sociological Models. Pearlin and Schooler (1978) were the first to address coping with chronic stress. Rather than conceiving of stress in terms of either life events or hassles, Pearlin and Schooler coined the term "chronic role strain" to characterize the types of stressors they felt were most harmful—those involving difficulty in discharging the most basic social roles, such as marriage, parenting, work, and household management. For Pearlin and Schooler, coping strategies are role specific, that is, they are tailored to role demands. Thus, methods of disciplining children are specific to the parenting role, whereas strategies for dealing with supervisors are more relevant to the work role.

Importantly, Pearlin and Schooler conceived of coping as directed not only at the problem or the emotions, but also at changing the *meaning* of the stressful situation (see also Pearlin, Mullan, Semple, & Skaff, 1990). For example, individuals may cope with chronic role strain at work by decreasing their investment in their work identity and focusing more on their families. Indeed, meaning may play a more central role in coping with chronic stress, similar to the process of coping with trauma (cf. Epstein, 1991; Frankl, 1962). That is, both chronic stress and trauma have irresolvable or uncontrollable aspects, and thus meaning manipulation may play a crucial role in coming to terms with what cannot be changed. Ingestad's (1988) comparison of Norwegian and Botswanan parents who had disabled children provides a nice illustration of the importance of meaning in coping with a chronic stressor. The Norwegian parents were more likely to appraise the situation as extremely stressful, in part because they felt guilty and had "vague thoughts" that it was a punishment from God. In contrast, the Botswanan parents were less likely to feel guilty, as they were more likely to believe that the child's disability indicated God's trust in their ability as parents. Thus, coming to terms with the meaning of the chronic stressor may play a significant role in both the appraisal of stressfulness and how one copes with the problem.

In sociological schemes, coping may be less a function of personality than of shared meanings within a social context (Mechanic, 1978; Pearlin, 1989). Extending Coyne and Downey's (1991) observation that stress and coping largely take place within an interpersonal context, one could argue that nearly all chronic stress also takes place in an interpersonal context. Thus, the development of coping strategies as well as their efficacy cannot be fully understood without comprehension of the role of significant others in the shared management of chronic stress.

Behavioral Medicine Models. The second model of coping with chronic stress examines coping strategies in the context of coping with illness. Moos and Schaefer (1984) have developed a model of the major adaptive tasks that face individuals who are coping with illness. They divided the tasks into those that are specifically illness related and those that are necessary for the patient's well-being in general. The illness-related tasks include the following: coping with the physiological consequences of the illness, including symptoms, pain, and disability; coping with the treatment and hospital environment; and developing and maintaining good relations with healthcare workers. The more general tasks involve maintaining emotional equilibrium and a sense of self, including competence and mastery; maintaining good relations with family and friends; and preparing for future exigencies, such as disability or death. Even though Moos and Schaefer's seminal work has guided much of the literature on coping with chronic illness, most studies typically examine only one or two of these tasks. Further, we know of no coping instrument that encompasses the strategies that individuals use to accomplish all of these tasks.

Critique. There are three primary problems with the current models of coping with chronic stress. First, to our knowledge, there have been no studies that systematically attempt to differentiate how coping with chronic stress might differ from coping with acute stress. There have been qualitative studies that identify coping strategies specific to the situation, often a chronic illness, and the items on Pearlin and Schooler's (1978) inventory are specific to role strain. Clearer identification of strategies specific to general chronic stressors is needed.

Second, current models of coping with chronic stress do not address how people develop strategies for managing sustained stressors such as chronic illness or poverty. To what extent do people use simple trial and error, or do they seek models in how others cope? Are there characteristic temporal patterns in the development of coping strategies?

Finally, there is growing evidence that chronic stress occurs in an interpersonal context and that the appraisal and coping strategies used by others may have a significant impact on how the target individual copes. Thoits' (1986) theory of the role of social support in coping may provide a viable framework for examining this problem. She argued that a primary function of social support is to provide feedback to individuals on their appraisals of the seriousness of the problem, as well as the appropriateness of their emotional reactions. Further, members of the social support network often provide advice and/or serve as models for problem-focused efforts as well. Although Thoits' theory is promising, to our knowledge, it has not been empirically applied in studies of coping with chronic stress.

The next section reviews studies from both the health psychology and gerontological literatures in an attempt to synthesize what is known about coping with chronic stress.

PATTERNS OF COPING WITH CHRONIC ILLNESS

In general, studies of coping with chronic illness have focused either on the characterization of coping patterns or on the relationship between coping and particular outcomes. Each of these types of studies will be discussed for the purpose of characterizing the development of strategies for coping with chronic stress.

Predictors of Coping Patterns

A number of factors may influence the ways in which individuals cope with chronic stress. For the purposes of this discussion, we do not distinguish between studies investigating coping styles or coping processes because these approaches are often not differentiated clearly in the literature.

First, differences in coping may vary according to the type of chronic stressor encountered. For example, when the chronic stressor is breast cancer, patients tend to employ avoidance and positive reappraisal coping strategies (Dunkel-Schetter et al., 1992; Jarrett, Ramirez, Richards, & Weinman, 1992). Individuals coping with schizophrenia have reported focusing on aspects of the external environment in order to regulate their internal emotional state (Carr, 1988; Leete, 1989; Mates, 1992). A comparison of patients with either malignant melanoma or cardiovascular disease revealed that individuals with melanoma used significantly more repressive coping (Kneier & Temoshok, 1984).

Even in a single type of chronically stressful context, such as caring for a relative with dementia, individuals may employ different strategies depending on the specific stressful aspect of caregiving with which they are coping. In a study of family caregivers of relatives with Alzheimer's disease, Gottlieb and Gignac (1996) found that coping strategies were domain specific. Stressors related to the deprivations occasioned by the disease (e.g., loss of freedom, surrendering of retirement plans) were associated with the use of more positive reframing, acceptance, and support-seeking efforts. When they were coping with the symptoms of the disease, however, individuals employed more "making meaning" and verbal and behavioral management tactics.

Second, the manner in which an individual copes with a chronic stressor may also depend on his or her appraisal of the stressor. In a study comparing three groups of men—those coping with cancer, those coping with the long-term effects of myocardial infarction, and those coping with a nonthreatening chronic illness—Feifel and his colleagues (1987) found that individuals who considered their illness to be more serious used more confrontation, but individuals who did not expect to recover from their illnesses employed more acceptance/resignation. Believing that one's chronic condition was changeable or controllable was associated with the utilization of more active, problem-focused coping (Bombardier, D'Amico, & Jordan, 1990; Schussler, 1992). In contrast, perceiving one's illness as uncontrollable was associated with more emotion-focused coping (Schussler, 1992). Greenley (1986) found that families coping with schizophrenia were more likely to employ emotional expression (e.g., yelling at the patient) if they believed that the schizophrenic individual was able to control his or her symptoms.

Third, the individual's developmental stage may also be an important determinant of how he or she copes with a chronic stressor. For example, compared to 7- to 12-year-old sickle cell disease patients, adolescents coping with the same illness employed more negative thinking and passive adherence (Gil, Thompson, Keith, Tota-Faucette, Noll, & Kinney, 1993). Older adults used less information seeking, emotional expression, and self-blame to cope with a chronic illness than did middle-aged adults (Felton & Revenson, 1987). Compared to middle-aged adults, older adults used less active behavioral coping to deal with colon cancer (Keyes, Bisno, Richardson, & Marston, 1987).

Fourth, overall level of coping effort may be associated with the use of particular coping strategies. Breast cancer patients who reported high levels of coping effort coped with psychological distress by "crying and becoming desperate" and "taking tranquilizers or alcohol" (Hurny, Bernhard, Bacchi, van Wegberg, Tomamichel, Spek, et al., 1993). "Seeing a positive side of the problem" was associated with lower levels of coping effort.

Fifth, both coping effort and the types of strategies used may vary as a function of time and/or stage of the illness. In a 3-year longitudinal examination of breast cancer patients, Buddeberg and colleagues (1991) observed decreases in three types of coping strategies. Over time, patients employed less self-encouragement and distraction, depressive coping, and problem tackling. Another investigation also demonstrated that breast cancer patients employed fewer coping modes across time (Heim, Augustiny, Schaffner, & Valach, 1993). After 3 months, the group of respondents employed 12 coping modes with a high degree of frequency; after 5 years, only five coping modes were employed on a regular basis. Individuals were less likely to employ emotional release and attention and care strategies (e.g., seeking support) during the successive stages of their illness. However, particular coping strategies may become employed more frequently. Use of a "relativization" strategy (e.g., comparing oneself with others, downplaying one's fate) increased as the disease progressed (Heim et al., 1993). The participants in the

Bonn Longitudinal Study who were coping with a serious illness (e.g., heart attack, stroke) demonstrated an increase in active coping strategies over a 5-year period (Kruse & Lehr, 1989). Also, adolescents coping with sickle cell disease showed increases in passive adherence and decreases in the amount of negative thinking employed during a 9-month period (Gil et al., 1993).

Sixth, environmental factors such as cultural context also influence coping modes. An examination of American and Danish individuals with multiple sclerosis who were coping with disease-related depression revealed that Danes were more likely to cope by seeking medical care. The Americans, however, were more likely to use relaxation techniques such as meditation and yoga (McLaughlin & Zeeberg, 1993). When coping with disease-associated loneliness or alienation, the Americans were more likely to cope by talking with a spouse or confidante, whereas Danes were relatively unwilling to express negative emotions to others. In an investigation of Swiss breast cancer patients, Hurny and his colleagues (1993) found that, relative to their Italian-speaking counterparts, German-speaking patients were more likely to engage in downward comparisons, to consult a medical expert, or to use self-criticism when coping with disease-related distress. In contrast, the Italian-speaking patients employed more acceptance and coping by "keeping a stiff upper lip."

Life events are a second type of environmental influence that may affect coping modes. For example, number of life events experienced was positively associated with problem-solving and self-reflection strategies in myocardial infarction patients (Martin & Lee, 1992).

In summary, studies of the predictors of coping strategies suggest that there is no single determinant either of the types of strategies that are likely to be used or of their progression over time. Both contextual factors—such as the type of illness, the co-occurrence of other stressful life events, and culture—and person factors—such as temperament and appraisal—influence the types of coping strategies used. Nonetheless, there is some suggestion in the literature that the number of strategies that are used decreases over time. This pattern makes sense, if individuals are learning which strategies are efficacious and that they can indeed manage the illness (Gignac & Gottlieb, Chapter 9, this volume). However, if the illness becomes worse and/or leads to other stressful life events, more problem-focused coping or adherence strategies may be required.

Outcomes of Coping Efforts

Other investigations of coping with chronic stress have focused on the ways in which particular coping strategies relate to mental health outcomes. These studies suggest that specific strategies are associated with either positive or negative outcomes, that certain factors may modify the effects of coping strategies (e.g., context, perceptions of stressor), and that the amount of stressor-related distress may change over time.

Specific types of coping strategies have been linked consistently to either positive or negative outcomes. In general, the use of active, problem-focused coping strategies has been associated with positive outcomes among patients with chronic illnesses (e.g., Newman, Fitzpatrick, Lamb, & Shipley, 1990). For instance, seeking social support (Dunkel-Schetter et al., 1992) and seeking information (Felton & Revenson, 1984) were associated with less emotional distress. In contrast, employment of emotion-focused coping strategies has often been associated with poorer psychological outcomes (e.g., Bombardier et al., 1990). Using avoidance (Dunkel-Schetter et al., 1992; Feifel et al., 1987) and employing wish-fulfilling fantasy (Felton & Revenson, 1984) were associated with indicators of poor adjustment.

Studies involving caregivers also suggest that certain coping strategies are consistently associated with particular mental health outcomes. Active strategies, such as offering encouragement to the patient (Hinrichsen & Niederehe, 1994), relaxation, and seeking social support (Williamson & Schulz, 1993), were associated with less distress and better emotional adjustment among caregivers of persons with dementia. Utilization of active cognitive coping strategies such as "focusing on the positive" was associated with lower levels of distress and better mental health outcomes (Borden & Berlin, 1990; Hinrichsen & Niederehe, 1994). In contrast, emotion-focused strategies, such as wishful thinking (Borden & Berlin, 1990; Pruchno & Resch, 1989; Williamson & Schulz, 1993) and avoidance (Hinrichsen & Niederehe, 1994; Timko, Stovel, & Moos, 1992), were associated with poorer mental health outcomes among caregivers and family members of the chronically ill.

Contextual factors such as stressor type may predict the nature of the association between coping and indicators of adjustment. Certain coping strategies may be associated with poor outcomes for some illnesses but with positive adjustment for other illnesses. Although greater use of avoidance was associated with poor adjustment among breast cancer (Dunkel-Schetter et al., 1992) and heart patients (Feifel et al., 1987), use of this strategy predicted positive adjustment over a 6- to 12-month period in a group of alcoholics (Litman, Stapleton, Oppenheim, Peleg, & Jackson, 1984).

Timing is another contextual factor that may affect the outcomes of coping. Using denial may reduce negative emotional reactions in the early stages of some illnesses (e.g., myocardial infarction), but may have adverse consequences if it leads to the postponement of medical care (Hackett & Cassem, 1975) or interferes with problem-focused coping efforts (for a review, see Aldwin, 1994).

Studies of coping among family members and caregivers also suggest that contextual factors modify the association between coping strategy and mental health. In a study of the spouses of rheumatoid arthritis patients, Revenson and Majerovitz (1991) found an interaction between disease severity and network support in predicting depression: More severe illness accompanied by more network support was associated with less depression. An investigation of caregivers of persons with Alzheimer's disease revealed that the association between coping strategies and distress level varied across stressor domains (Williamson & Schulz, 1993). For example, increased use of relaxation was associated with less depression when caregivers were coping with a patient's memory-related deficit; however, use of this technique was unrelated to depression when individuals were coping with either communication problems or the decline of their loved one.

Perceptions of chronic stressors also may affect coping-related outcomes. In a 4-year study of adaptation of rheumatoid arthritis, Smith and Wallston (1992) found that helplessness appraisals led to passive coping, which in turn led to psychosocial impairment and maladaptation. A "holding back" appraisal (e.g., finding it necessary to use restraint) was associated with depression among persons with various chronic conditions (Bombardier et al., 1990). Perceived effectiveness of the coping strategy, but not the utilization of coping behaviors per se, was significantly related to continued abstinence over a 6- to 12-month period among recovering alcoholics (Litman et al., 1984). An investigation of men with HIV revealed that higher levels of perceived control were associated with better psychological adjustment (Thompson, Nanni, & Levine, 1994). Depression level was inversely correlated with the perceived ability to control disease-related outcomes, as well as with disease-related adjustment.

Longitudinal assessments suggest that sustained coping efforts may be accompanied by changes in distress level and that there are individual differences in the course of adjustment to chronic illness. An early study by Robinson and Thurnher (1979) found that caregiving was associated with increased anxiety, tension, and sense of confinement over the course of 5 years. However, Townsend and her colleagues (1989) found that, although 34% of the sample showed an increase in depressive symptoms over a 14-month period, 58% of the sample reported a decrease in depressive symptoms over time; this trend suggests that a majority of respondents were adapting to caregiving over time. Similarly,

Gilhooly (1984) found that a longer duration of caregiving was associated with higher morale and better mental health.

Cognitive appraisal processes may mediate these individual differences. In a longitudinal study of rheumatoid arthritis patients, cognitive distortion and perceived helplessness were associated with increased depression over the course of 4 years (Smith, Christensen, Peck, & Ward, 1994). Gender may also be an important mediator. A 6-year study of 8- to 13-year-old children coping with diabetes mellitus demonstrated that increased duration of illness was associated with increased depression and increased anxiety for girls but not for boys (Kovacs, Iyengar, Goldston, Stewart, Obrosky, & Marsh, 1990).

In summary, investigations relating coping to outcomes have shown that, although emotion-focused strategies are consistently associated with negative outcomes (e.g., depression), active, problem-focused strategies such as information-seeking usually predict positive outcomes. However, the association between coping and its consequences may be modified by contextual factors such as the duration or stage of an illness. Longitudinal assessments of coping among chronic illness patients and caregivers suggest that there are individual differences in the course of adaptation. Some individuals may improve over time (Gilhooly, 1984; Newman et al., 1990; Townsend et al., 1989), perhaps because they have revised their management skills (see discussion later in the chapter) and/or redefined the meaning of the situation.

Limitations of Studies

Studies examining coping with chronic illnesses are limited by several methodological factors. One limitation of these investigations is that the causal relationship between coping and adjustment is not clear. It is often assumed that coping strategies lead to mental health outcomes; however, individuals' mental health status may predict the frequency and type of coping strategies they employ (Coyne, Aldwin, & Lazarus, 1981; Folkman & Lazarus, 1986). Relative to their nondepressed counterparts, depressed persons used more coping strategies and were more likely to employ wishful thinking and to seek emotional support. In another study, individuals with more psychological symptomatology employed more maladaptive coping strategies (Aldwin & Revenson, 1987).

The disproportionate use of cross-sectional designs is another factor that limits the interpretability of the causal relationship between coping and its outcomes. Because chronic stressors are ongoing and require sustained coping, these processes cannot be characterized adequately with only one assessment. Thus, more longitudinal assessments are necessary to identify changes (and reasons for those changes) in coping. Surprisingly, we were unable to locate any longitudinal studies of coping with chronic illness that covaried changes in coping strategies with changes in outcome; however, this issue has been examined among individuals coping with other types of stressors (DeLongis, Folkman, & Lazarus, 1988; Stone, Neale, & Shiffman, 1993).

An additional limitation of these investigations is that stress, coping effort, and outcomes are confounded. Serious problems often lead to both heightened distress and more vigorous coping efforts (Aldwin, 1994). Confounding of stressors and outcomes is particularly problematic in assessing chronic coping situations because the effects of the stressor are ongoing (Pearlin, 1989). For example, it is not apparent whether observed decreases in coping over time (e.g., Buddeberg et al., 1991; Heim et al., 1993) are due to adaptation to the stressor, decreases in perceived stressfulness of the conditions, or a combination of the two.

Long-term examinations of coping may also be adversely affected by response biases occurring over time. Even though decreases in the number of coping strategies employed have been interpreted as a reflection of increased coping efficiency (Meeks, Carstensen, Tamsky, Wright, & Pellegrini, 1989), it is also possible that respondents tire of answering the same questions repeatedly, making these decreases an artifact of response bias.

A related concern is that coping scales designed to assess coping with acute stressors (e.g., the Ways of Coping scale), or modified versions of such scales, are often employed to assess coping with chronic problems. Because such instruments are designed to assess situation-specific coping, some of the items may not be relevant to coping with chronic illness (e.g., "Talked to the person responsible for the problem"). Furthermore, scales designed to assess acute stressors may not explore issues that are of wide concern to individuals coping with chronic problems, such as different ways of manipulating meaning. Because of the multiplicity of factors that contribute to chronically stressful conditions (cf. Charmaz, 1983), acute measures of situation-specific coping may not adequately characterize coping and related outcomes. As Turk and his colleagues (1980) argue, it is important to examine both the range of problems encountered during the course of coping with a chronic condition as well as the cumulative effects of coping with the stressor, which, we might add, can be negative or positive.

Qualitative studies such as Weitz' (1989) interviews with AIDS patients can yield insight into the process of coping with chronic stress. She documented coping strategies, such as learning to tolerate ambiguity by refusing to make concrete plans; learning to avoid sources of infection, including nonobvious ones such as bathroom mold; and manipulating the healthcare system to gain access to experimental medications, either by lying to researchers to qualify for a study, convincing the physicians to provide medications even if they were not eligible, or borrowing medications from friends who were eligible. The gerontology coping literature may also be a useful source of information about strategies specific to coping with chronic stress, given that 80% of the persons over the age of 65 have a chronic illness, and many cope quite successfully with increasing disabilities.

AGING AS A PARADIGM FOR COPING WITH CHRONIC STRESS

Research on aging and mental health presents an interesting conundrum for stress and coping researchers. On the one hand, old age is thought to be a time of great stress. An older person faces increasing disabilities: he or she may lose access to social roles, such as work and parenting, that may have been crucial to his or her identity; may experience bereavement of kith and kin; and may have severe financial constraints (especially in the case of widows and minority elderly). Although white males over the age of 65 have the highest suicide rates, in general, the mental health of the elderly is as good or better than that of younger adults. Older people routinely report high levels of life satisfaction and sometimes rate their problems as less stressful than do the young (for further discussion of this issue, see Aldwin, 1990, 1991). Older people thus may present a paradigmatic case of successful adaptation to chronic stress. Examining the coping strategies that they use may shed light on this process.

One of the most promising theoretical model of coping in late life is Baltes' (1987) model of selective optimization with compensation. As people age, they may lose certain capacities or abilities. However, people can and do learn to compensate for losses in abilities by developing alternative strategies and making greater use of the capacities that they do have. For example, the great pianist Vladimir Horowitz continued performing into his 80s by limiting his repertoire to more romantic composers such as Chopin. Although such pieces require great technical virtuosity, they may not demand as rapid a reaction time—a notorious loss with age—allowing Horowitz to focus on his strength, which was emotional interpretation. Unfortunately, there have been no published studies that have systematically investigated the extent to which and the ways in which the elderly utilize this strategy. However, its relevance to coping with chronic stressors is obvious and deserves greater investigation.

Second, older people may manipulate their environment to compensate for their physical limitations, thereby increasing their competence (cf. Lawton, 1989). As Johnson and Barer (1993) pointed out, older people may arrange heavy furniture in a pattern that allows them to grasp various pieces for balance as they move around their homes or to catch themselves if they fall. Alternatively, some elderly people may furnish their homes very sparsely to minimize housekeeping tasks. Certainly, people with chronic illnesses also engage in these strategies. Those in wheelchairs may install ramps or purchase cars with manual controls, and rheumatoid arthritis patients may replace buttons with velcro, for example.

Third, elderly people may develop routines that allow them to function despite disabilities. For example, many are acutely aware of a decrement in their driving skills and carefully plot routes that allow them to avoid challenges such as left-hand turns. In Johnson and Barer's (1993) study of coping among the old-old, individuals who could no longer drive took buses to remote supermarkets so that they would be assured of getting seats on the way back with their groceries. Elderly people with cognitive impairment may shop only at one, smaller supermarket in which the layout is familiar to them in order to avoid the confusion associated with large supermarkets. While routinization may result in limited choices, it affords elderly persons the structure to accomplish tasks that remain within their capabilities.

Fourth, changes in expectations may be crucial to positive adaptation to chronic stress. Researchers such as Brandtstädter and his colleagues (1993) have documented age-related decreases in the ideal self that allow older people to minimize the psychological distance between their actual and their ideal selves. We hypothesize that people with chronic impairments and their families also decrease their expectations. A good day may be one with only minimal pain, or a family with a child with developmental disabilities may rejoice when the child finally learns a simple task.

Fifth, manipulation of meaning may play a central role in coping with chronic stress. Downward comparisons (e.g., viewing one's own situation in a positive light, relative to others) may be especially important, as Taylor and Brown (1988) have demonstrated among patients with breast cancer. Among elderly people, such downward comparisons may explain why most older persons rate their health as better than average. As Johnson and Barer (1993) observed, most elderly individuals can point to an age peer whose health is worse than theirs. For example, one woman who could not get up unassisted thought that her health was better than others because she did not have "heart or breathing" problems.

Acceptance may also be a crucial element in the successful adaptation of the elderly. Older people expect some increase in aches and pains with age, and the loss of friends and family may become normative. For some, this acceptance may be strongly tinged with denial. As one woman in Johnson and Barer's (1993) study remarked, "What can I say, I've had by-pass surgery, I now have shingles, I'm isolated and lonely, I'm losing my strength and my confidence in myself. But glory to God, I'm feeling well" (p. 75).

Finally, elderly people may develop caregiving dyads in which each compensates for the other's incapacities. Dixon (1994), for example, has documented that individual memory impairment may be markedly improved when elderly people are allowed to work in pairs on memory tasks. We suspect that within elderly dyads, each person may compensate for the other's sensory impairments, although evidence for this remains anecdotal. Aldwin (1990) described the case of an 80-year-old couple, one of whom was nearly blind and the other nearly deaf. They rearranged the management of their household chores to accommodate each other's disabilities; the hearing-impaired man relied upon his wife to relay conversations to him, while she relied upon him to navigate the environment. Note that these arrangements may become so highly routinized that they may be barely conscious. On coping inventories, elderly respondents typically report less use of social support, but we suspect that elderly dyads may have routinized these types of social exchanges to the extent that they no longer consider them coping strategies per se.

In summary, the ways in which the elderly cope with their disabilities is clearly relevant to other chronically ill populations, and perhaps to people undergoing chronic stress in general. To the extent that coping strategies become routinized into generalized management skills, a disability may no longer be perceived as an everyday problem, but simply as part of the fabric of life. Thus, given sufficient psychological, social, and environmental resources, individuals may be able to adapt to chronic stress with a minimum of adaptive cost.

Clearly, there are individual differences in this process that depend upon both access to resources and the severity of the chronic stress. Pain and suffering are unavoidable and may have severe costs for both the individuals' and their families' well-being. However, it is also clear that some individuals are able to achieve positive outcomes, such as increased mastery and self-esteem, increased self-knowledge, a greater acceptance of self and others, adaptive changes in value systems, and closer ties to significant others (cf. Aldwin, 1994; Aldwin & Stokols, 1988; Beardslee, 1989; Elder & Clipp, 1989; Silver, Boon, & Stones, 1983). What is not clear is the process whereby this type of adaptation develops. The next section proposes a theoretical framework that may be useful in understanding how stress can have both positive and negative outcomes.

A DEVIATION AMPLIFICATION MODEL OF COPING WITH CHRONIC STRESS

As Aldwin (1994) recently pointed out, two major problems with coping theories is that they assume that (1) coping has primarily homeostatic functions that return the person to the original state and (2) coping is episodic in nature, meaning that it has a discrete beginning and end. It is clear that neither of these two assumptions applies to coping with chronic stress. It is unlikely that the situation will be resolved by the individual, although it may be managed. This is why Folkman and Lazarus (1980) carefully included the phrase "manage or resolve stress" in their definition of coping. However, a more dynamic model may be needed to describe the types of sustained coping efforts required of people experiencing chronic stress.

From reviews of the literature, it is clear that the development and outcomes of coping efforts are highly contextual and subject to the influence of a number of factors. This suggests that a systems theory model (von Bertalanffy, 1950) may be most applicable to this highly complex phenomenon. The initial formulation of systems theory focused on homeostatic processes, in which a system of multiple feedback loops allows an organism to maintain a steady state, for example, temperature or blood pressure regulation. However, a more dynamic model is needed for processes that are thought to change in systematic ways over time [cf. Ford and Lerner's (1992) discussion of developmental systems theory].

Maruyama (1963) described the processes by which a system either maintained homeostasis or promoted change. He proposed that there were two kinds of feedback loops: deviation countering and deviation amplification. Deviation countering loops function to prevent change, in the form of negative feedback loops such as those seen in regulation of body temperature. However, deviation amplification processes, or positive feedback loops, promote change by amplifying what might be initially small changes, similar to cascade effects seen in neurohormonal stress responses. Aldwin and Stokols (1988) suggested that this deviation amplification model can provide a framework for understanding how stress can result in change rather than homeostasis and, as such, may provide a promising theoretical framework for examining coping with chronic stress. Note, however, that this change may be positive, negative or, most likely, some combination of the two.

For example, Elder (1974) showed that the effect of economic deprivation on the lifecourse of people who were children during the Depression varied as a function of their social class. Working-class children exhibited a downward spiral, when compared to their nondeprived peers. They were less likely to finish school, had poorer career and marital histories, suffered more illness, and so on. Middle-class children, however, exhibited an upward spiral. Compared to their nondeprived peers, they attained higher levels of education, had better career and marital trajectories, enjoyed better relations with their children, and so on. Thus, the same type of stressor may result in different types of adaptive spirals.

At this point, one can only speculate on the factors that promote either deviation amplification or deviation countering processes. Aldwin and Stokols (1988) identified four characteristics of the stressor that might promote deviation amplification, including the timing, rapidity of onset, and scope of the change, as well as its meaning to the individual. A stressor that occurs suddenly, at an inopportune time (e.g., developmentally off-time), impacts on multiple domains, and is highly meaningful to the individual may be more likely to promote deviation amplification processes, while a stressor with a more gradual onset and limited scope may be more likely to promote deviation countering trends. For example, a severe myocardial infarction early in life that results in severe disability is likely to generate deviation amplification processes and require more sustained coping efforts than a mild case of coronary congestion late in life. Aldwin and Stokols (1988) also speculated that whether the long-term effect of this deviation process is positive or negative will depend upon personal resources, including coping efforts, social support, and chance.

It is widely acknowledged that people have an arsenal of coping resources to draw upon, although the process through which that arsenal develops is poorly understood. Rather than coping merely involving the expenditure of resources (Hobfoll, 1989), this perspective views stressful situations as the means through which individuals develop coping resources for future use, as Hobfoll and Lilly (1993) now suggest. Indeed, Pearlin, Lieberman, Menaghan, and Mullan (1981) have shown that problem-focused coping serves to reduce stress in future problems. Aldwin, Sutton, and Lachman (1996) conducted a series of studies in which they showed that the vast majority of people draw upon previous stressful experiences in coping with current problems and, indeed, felt that there were long-term positive outcomes of highly stressful events.

Thus, a corollary of deviation amplification theory is that stress can have positive effects, to the extent that individuals develop better resources to cope with future problems. For chronic stress, such a stance would argue that individuals can eventually adapt to persistent problems and even develop new strengths from managing such conditions.

At first glance, this would appear to contradict general assumptions in the stress literature concerning the long-term effects of stress. After all, the third stage of Selye's (1956) general adaptation syndrome is exhaustion and, eventually, death. The adverse effects of chronic work stress are well known (Hepburn, Loughlin, and Barling, Chapter 13, this volume; Karasek & Theorell, 1990). Yet the notion that chronic stress necessarily results in adverse outcomes has begun to be challenged in the literature. For example, Dienstbier (1989) suggested that stress can result in physiological toughening if the organism has sufficient respite periods. Townsend et al. (1989) have recently presented longitudinal data suggesting that caregivers can adapt to their situation and show improved psychological functioning in a few months. These data suggest that individuals can develop new coping strategies to manage even chronic stress successfully and may make extensive use of meaning management to adapt to persistent problems.

Indeed, adaptation level theory (Helson, 1964) suggests that people can become inured to even highly stressful situations. Salman Rushdie was recently interviewed on television by David Frost, who asked him how he could possibly cope with a *fatwa* (death sentence) hanging over his head. "Well," he said, "you get used to it." He had asked the same question of a friend of his who lived in Sarajevo, who said that one quickly learned to avoid and generally ignore the constant shelling, and that this was necessary if one were to survive.

Obviously, some people never learn to adapt and flee the problem, if they can, by physically leaving the situation, retreating into mental or physical illness, or developing social pathologies of some sort. However, we suspect that most people develop skills that allow them to routinely manage chronic stress, thereby minimizing its drain on resources. The process through which these skills develop, and the influences on their development, are poorly understood.

We hypothesize that coping with chronic stress requires the development of three types of resources. First, one must be able to turn coping strategies into management skills. With respect to chronic stressors, it is necessary to use anticipatory coping to minimize or prevent problems from occurring. For example, for asthmatics, it is more useful to carefully regulate medications, exercise, and exposure to environmental pathogens to decrease the probability of wheezing and bronchial spasms than to deal with them after they occur. Thus, through coping with problems, one can learn how to prevent certain types of flare-ups and develop routines that incorporate these preventive activities, similar to what Lazarus and Folkman (1984) called "automatic" coping processes. Over time, as one's management skills increase, a chronic illness may no longer be a daily stressor.

The second resource that needs to be developed is preplanned strategies for coping with the acute incidents that are likely to occur. This may range from back-up daycare arrangements for when a child or a regular caregiver is ill to storing oxygen tanks in the house in anticipation of a future myocardial infarction.

The third type of resource involves the regulation of the meaning of events within the context of chronic stress. This regulation may involve downplaying the occurrence or importance of negative aspects. Not becoming upset by uncontrollable events may be more efficacious than having to use emotion-focused coping after becoming upset. This may be aided by focusing more on the positive aspects. Some elders, for example, speak of the great joy that caring for an ill spouse gives them (cf. Gilmer, 1993). Small achievements may be proud accomplishments for the parents of a developmentally disabled child.

Through the development of these resources, management skills, anticipation of crises, and meaning manipulation, the requirement for acute types of coping strategies may decrease, which may be why the level of coping effort appears to decrease over time for some types of chronic illness. Further, it may explain why individuals appear to adapt to chronic stressors over time, although there is no doubt that individuals who cannot learn to minimize the stress may develop severe problems. However, as is the case for resilient children, it is likely that vulnerability and resilience are not absolute, or even necessarily stable, characteristics of the individual, but rather represent a patchwork of processes that are subject to change over time (Rutter, 1987).

FUTURE RESEARCH

More research is needed on the process by which people facing chronic stress learn new coping skills and on how coping skills become routinized into general management strategies. Understanding how chronically stressed individuals manipulate their environment to compensate for losses is also crucial, as is whether selective optimization is a viable coping strategy and how and when it occurs. Finally, more work is needed that examines the sources of individual differences in trajectories of chronic illnesses. In addition, the potential positive aspects of managing chronic stress need to be studied. Through successful management of chronic hardships, there is the possibility of increases in mastery and self-esteem. Further, it is possible that, through transformational coping, such stressors may become catalysts for positive change in the form of tangible gains. Specifically, we need to understand how individuals learn to manage chronic stress successfully and to identify the personal and environmental factors that aid them in the development of those strategies.

ACKNOWLEDGMENTS   Preparation of this chapter was supported by a FIRST Award (R29-07469) from the National Institute on Aging. We would like to thank the editor for his helpful suggestions on an earlier draft of this paper.

REFERENCES

ALDWIN, C. (1990). The Elders Life Stress Inventory (ELSI): Egocentric and nonegocentric stress. In M. A. P. Stephens, S. E. Hobfall, J. H. Crowther, & D. L. Tennenbaum (Eds.), *Stress and coping in late life families* (pp. 49–69). New York: Hemisphere.

ALDWIN, C. (1991). Does age affect the stress and coping process? Implications of age differences in perceived control. *Journal of Gerontology, 46,* 174–180.

ALDWIN, C. (1994). *Stress, coping, and development: An integrative perspective.* New York: Guilford.

ALDWIN, C. M., & REVENSON, T. A. (1987). Does coping help? A reexamination of the relation between coping and mental health. *Journal of Personality and Social Psychology, 53,* 337–348.

ALDWIN, C., & STOKOLS, D. (1988). The effects of environmental change on individuals and groups: Some neglected issues in stress research. *Journal of Environmental Psychology, 8,* 57–75.

ALDWIN, C., SUTTON, K., & LACHMAN, M. (1996). The development of coping resources in adulthood. *Journal of Personality, 64,* 91–113.

AMIRKHAN, J. H. (1990). A factor analytically derived measure of coping: The Coping Strategy Indicator. *Journal of Personality and Social Psychology, 59,* 1066–1074.

ANDREWS, G., SINGH, M., & BOND, M. (1993). The Defense Style Questionnaire. *Journal of Nervous and Mental Disease, 181,* 246–256.

BALTES, P. (1987). Theoretical propositions of life-span developmental psychology: On the dynamics between growth and decline. *Developmental Psychology, 24,* 611–626.

BEARDSLEE, W. R. (1989). The role of self-understanding in resilient individuals: The development of a perspective. *American Journal of Orthopsychiatry, 59,* 266–278.

BOMBARDIER, C. H., D'AMICO, C., & JORDAN, J. S. (1990). The relationship of appraisal and coping to chronic illness adjustment. *Behavior Research and Therapy, 28,* 297–304.

BOND, M., GARDINER, S. T., & SIEGEL, J. J. (1983). An empirical examination of defense mechanisms. *Archives of General Psychiatry, 40,* 333–338.

BORDEN, W., & BERLIN, S. (1990). Gender, coping, and psychological well-being in spouses of older adults with chronic dementia. *American Journal of Orthopsychiatry, 60,* 603–610.

BRANDTSTÄDTER, J., WENTURA, D., & GREVE, W. (1993). Adaptive resources of the aging self: Outlines of an emergent perspective. In M. E. Lachman (Ed.), *Planning and control processes across the life span* (pp. 323–250). Hillsdale, NJ: Lawrence Erlbaum.

BUDDEBERG, C., WOLF, C., SIEBER, M., RIEHL-EMDE, A., BERGANT, A., STEINER, R., LANDOLT-RITTER, C., & RICHTER, D. (1991). Coping strategies and cause of disease of breast cancer patients. *Psychotherapy and Psychosomatics, 55,* 151–157.

CARR, V. (1988). Patients' techniques for coping with schizophrenia: An exploratory study. *British Journal of Medical Psychology, 61,* 339–352.

CARVER, C. S., & SCHEIER, M. F. (1994). Situational coping and coping dispositions in a stressful transaction. *Journal of Personality and Social Psychology, 66,* 184–195.

CHARMAZ, K. (1983). Loss of self: A fundamental form of suffering in the chronically ill. *Sociology of Health and Illness, 5,* 168–194.

COYNE, J., ALDWIN, C., & LAZARUS, R. (1981). Depression and coping in stressful episodes. *Journal of Abnormal Psychology, 90,* 439–447.

COYNE, J., & DOWNEY, G. (1991). Social factors and psychopathology: Stress, social support, and coping processes. *Annual Review of Psychology, 42,* 401–426.

DELONGIS, A., FOLKMAN, S., & LAZARUS, R. S. (1988). The impact of daily stress on health and mood: Psychological and social resources as mediators. *Journal of Personality and Social Psychology, 54,* 486–495.

DELONGIS, A., & O'BRIEN, T. (1990). An interpersonal framework for stress and coping: An application to the families of Alzheimer's patients. In M. A. P. Stephens, J. H. Crowther, S. E. Hobfall, & D. L. Tennenbaum (Eds.), *Stress and coping in later life families* (pp. 221–239). New York: Hemisphere.

DIENSTBIER, R. A. (1989). Arousal and physiological toughness: Implications for mental and physical health. *Psychological Bulletin, 96,* 84–100.

DIXON, R. (1994, August). *Collaborative cognition in adulthood—contextualizing competence.* Address presented at the Annual Meetings of the American Psychological Association, Los Angeles, CA.

DUNKEL-SCHETTER, C., FEINSTEIN, L., TAYLOR, S. E., & FALKE, R. L. (1992). Patterns of coping with cancer. *Health Psychology, 11,* 79–87.

ELDER, G. (1974). *Children of the Great Depression.* Chicago: University of Chicago Press.

ELDER, G., & CLIPP, E. (1989). Combat experience and emotional health: Impairment and resilience in later life. *Journal of Personality, 57,* 311–341.

ENDLER, N., & PARKER, J. D. A. (1990). Multidimensional assessment of coping: A critical evaluation. *Journal of Personality and Social Psychology, 58,* 844–854.

EPSTEIN, S. (1991). The self-concept, the traumatic neurosis, and the structure of personality. In D. Ozer, J. H. Healy, & A. J. Stewart (Eds.), *Perspectives in personality* (Vol. 3, pp. 63–98). London: Kingsley.

FEIFEL, H., STRACK, S., & NAGY, V. (1987). Coping strategies and associated features of medically ill patients. *Psychosomatic Research, 49,* 616–625.

FELTON, B. J., & REVENSON, T. A. (1984). Coping with chronic illness: A study of illness controllability and the influence of coping strategies on psychological adjustment. *Journal of Consulting and Clinical Psychology, 52,* 343–353.

FELTON, B. J., & REVENSON, T. A. (1987). Age difference in coping with chronic illness. *Psychology and Aging, 2,* 164–170.

FOLKMAN, S., & LAZARUS, R. S. (1980). An analysis of coping in a middle-aged community sample. *Journal of Health & Social Behavior, 21,* 219–239.

FOLKMAN, S., & LAZARUS, R. S. (1986). Stress processes and depressive symptomatology. *Journal of Abnormal Psychology, 95,* 107–113.

FOLKMAN, S., LAZARUS, R. S., GRUEN, R. J., & DELONGIS, A. (1986). Appraisal, coping, health status, and psychological symptoms. *Journal of Personality and Social Psychology, 50,* 571–579.

FORD, D. H., & LERNER, R. M. (1992). *Developmental systems theory: An integrative approach.* Newbury Park, CA: Sage.

FRANKL, V. E. (1962). *Man's search for meaning: An introduction to logotherapy.* Boston: Beacon.

Freud, A. (1966). *The ego and the mechanisms of defense* (Rev. ed.). New York: International Universities Press.
Gil, K. M., Thompson, R. J., Keith, B. R., Tota-Faucette, M., Noll, S., & Kinney, T. R. (1993). Sickle cell disease pain in children and adolescents: Change in pain frequency and coping strategies over time. *Journal of Pediatric Psychiatry, 18,* 621–637.
Gilhooly, M. L. M. (1984). The impact of care-giving on caregivers: Factors associated with the psychological well-being of people supporting a dementing relative in the community. *British Journal of Medical Psychology, 57,* 35–44.
Gilmer, D. (1993). *"Young-old" and "old-old" patients post-discharge and spouse caregivers: A study of social support and developmental stage.* Unpublished doctoral thesis, University of California, Davis.
Gottlieb, B. H., & Gignac, M. A. M. (1996). Content and domain specificity of coping among family caregivers of persons with dementia. *Journal of Aging Studies, 10,* 137–155.
Greenley, J. R. (1986). Social control and expressed emotion. *Journal of Nervous and Mental Disease, 174,* 24–30.
Haan, N. (1977). *Coping and defending.* New York: Academic Press.
Hackett, T. P., & Cassem, N. H. (1975). Psychological management of the myocardial infarction patient. *Journal of Human Stress, 1,* 25–38.
Heim, E., Augustiny, K. F., Schaffner, L., & Valach, L. (1993). Coping with breast cancer over time and situation. *Journal of Psychosomatic Research, 37,* 523–542.
Helson, H. (1964). *Adaptation level theory: an experimental and systematic approach to behavior.* New York: Harper & Row.
Hinrichsen, G. A., & Niederehe, G. (1994). Dementia management strategies and adjustment of family members of older patients. *The Gerontologist, 34,* 95–102.
Hobfoll, S. (1989). Conservation of resources: A new attempt at conceptualizing stress. *American Psychologist, 44,* 513–524.
Hobfoll, S., & Lilly, R. (1993). Resource as a strategy for community psychology. *Journal of Community Psychology, 21,* 128–148.
Hurny, C., Bernhard, J., Bacchi, M., van Wegberg, B., Tomamichel, M., Spek, U., Coates, A., Castiglione, M., Goldhirsch, A., & Senn, H. (1993). The Perceived Adjustment to Chronic Illness Scale (PACIS): A global indicator of coping for operable breast cancer patients in clinical trials. *Support Care Cancer, 1,* 200–208.
Ingestad, B. (1988). Coping behavior of disabled persons and their families: Cross-cultural perspectives from Norway and Botswana. *Rehabilitation Research, 11,* 351–359.
Jarrett, S. R., Ramirez, A. J., Richards, M. A., & Weinman, J. (1992). Measuring coping in breast cancer. *Journal of Psychosomatic Research, 36,* 593–602.
Johnson, C. I., & Barer, B. M. (1993). Coping and a sense of control among the oldest old. *Journal of Aging Studies, 7,* 67–80.
Karasek, R., & Theorell, T. (1990). *Healthy work: Stress, productivity, and the reconstruction of working life.* New York: Basic Books.
Keyes, K., Bisno, B., Richardson, J., & Marston, A. (1987). Age differences in coping, behavioral dysfunction and depression following colostomy surgery. *The Gerontologist, 27,* 182–184.
Kneier, A., & Temoshok, L. (1984). Repressive coping reactions in patients with malignant melanoma as compared to cardiovascular disease patients. *Journal of Psychosomatic Research, 28,* 145–155.
Kovacs, M., Iyengar, S., Goldston, D., Stewart, J., Obrosky, D. S., & Marsh, J. (1990). Psychological functioning of children with insulin-dependent diabetes mellitus: A longitudinal study. *Journal of Pediatric Psychology, 15,* 619–632.
Kruse, A., & Lehr, U. (1989). Longitudinal analysis of the developmental process in chronically ill and healthy persons: Empirical findings from the Bonn longitudinal study of aging (BOLSA). *International Psychogeriatrics, 1,* 73–85.
Lawton, M. P. (1989). Behavior-relevant ecological factors. In K. W. Schaie & C. Schooler

(Eds.), *Social structure & aging: Psychological processes* (pp. 67–78). Hillsdale, NJ: Lawrence Erlbaum.

LAZARUS, R. S. (1983). The costs and benefits of denial. In S. Breznitz (Ed.), *The denial of stress* (pp. 1–30). New York: International Universities Press.

LAZARUS, R. S., & FOLKMAN, S. (1984). *Stress, appraisal, and coping.* New York: Springer.

LEETE, E. (1989). How I perceive and manage my illness. *Schizophrenia Bulletin, 15,* 197–200.

LITMAN, G. K., STAPLETON, J., OPPENHEIM, A. N., PELEG, M., & JACKSON, P. (1984). The relationship between coping behaviours, their effectiveness, and alcoholism relapse and survival. *British Journal of Addiction, 79,* 283–291.

MARTIN, P., & LEE, H. (1992). Indicators of active and passive coping in myocardial infarction victims. *Journal of Gerontology, 47,* P238–P241.

MARUYAMA, M. (1963). The second cybernetics: Deviation-amplifying mutual causal processes. *American Scientists, 51,* 164–179.

MATES, M. (1992). A clinical discussion of schizophrenia from the perspective of the schizophrenic. *Journal of Orthomolecular Medicine, 7,* 170–175.

MATTLIN, J., WETHINGTON, E., & KESSLER, R. C. (1990). Situational determinants of coping and coping effectiveness. *Journal of Health & Social Behavior, 31,* 103–122.

MCLAUGHLIN, J., & ZEEBERG, I. (1993). Self-care and multiple sclerosis: A view from two cultures. *Social Science and Medicine, 37,* 315–329.

MECHANIC, D. (1978). *Students under stress: A study in the social psychology of adaptation.* Madison, WI: The University of Wisconsin Press.

MEEKS, S., CARSTENSEN, L., TAMSKY, B., WRIGHT, T., & PELLEGRINI, D. (1989). Age differences in coping: Does less mean worse? *International Journal of Aging and Human Development, 28,* 127–140.

MILLER, S., & MANGAN, C. E. (1983). Interacting effects of information and coping style in adapting to gynecological stress: When should the doctor tell all? *Journal of Personality and Social Psychology, 45,* 223–236.

MILLON, T. (1982). On the nature of clinical health psychology. In T. Millon, C. Green, & R. Meagher (Eds.), *Handbook of clinical health psychology* (pp. 1–28). New York: Plenum.

MOOS, R. H., & SCHAEFER, J. A. (1984). The crisis of physical illness. In R. Moos (Ed.), *Coping with physical illness* (pp. 3–26). New York: Plenum.

MULLEN, B., & SULS, J. (1982). The effectiveness of attention and rejection as coping styles: A meta-analysis of temporal differences. *Journal of Psychosomatic Research, 26,* 43–49.

NEWMAN, S., FITZPATRICK, R., LAMB, R., & SHIPLEY, M. (1990). Patterns of coping in rheumatoid arthritis. *Psychology and Health, 4,* 187–200.

PEARLIN, L. I. (1989). The sociological study of stress. *Journal of Health and Social Behavior, 30,* 241–256.

PEARLIN, L. I., LIEBERMAN, M. A., MENAGHAN, E. G., & MULLAN, J. T. (1981). The stress process. *Journal of Health and Social Behavior, 22,* 337–356.

PEARLIN, L. I., MULLAN, J. T., SEMPLE, S. J., & SKAFF, M. (1990). Caregiving and the stress process. An overview of concepts and their measures. *The Gerontologist, 30,* 583–594.

PEARLIN, L., & SCHOOLER, C. (1978). The structure of coping. *Journal of Health and Social Behavior, 19,* 2–21.

PRUCHNO, R. A., & RESCH, N. L. (1989). Mental health of caregiving spouses: Coping as a mediator, moderator, or main effect? *Psychology and Aging, 4,* 454–463.

REICHARD, S., LIVSON, F., & PETERSON, P. G. (1962). *Aging and personality.* New York: Wiley.

REVENSON, T. A., & MAJEROVITZ, S. D. (1991). The effects of chronic illness on the spouse: Social resources as stress buffers. *Arthritis Care and Research, 4,* 63–72.

ROBINSON, B., & THURNHER, M. (1979). Taking care of aged parents: A family cycle transition. *The Gerontologist, 19,* 586–593.

ROTH, S., & COHEN, L. J. (1986). Approach, avoidance, and coping with stress. *American Psychologist, 41,* 813–819.

RUTTER, M. (1987). Psychosocial resilience and protective mechanisms. *American Journal of Orthopsychiatry, 57,* 316–331.

SCHUSSLER, G. (1992). Coping strategies and individual meanings of illness. *Social Science and Medicine, 34,* 427–432.
SELYE, H. (1956). *The stress of life.* New York: McGraw-Hill.
SHAPIRO, D. (1965). *Neurotic styles.* New York: Basic Books.
SILVER, R. L., BOON, C., & STONES, M. H. (1983). Searching for meaning in misfortune: Making sense of incest. *Journal of Social Issues, 39,* 81–102.
SMITH, T. W., CHRISTENSEN, A. J., PECK, J. R., & WARD, J. R. (1994). Cognitive distortion, helplessness, and depressed mood in rheumatoid arthritis: A four-year longitudinal analysis. *Health Psychology, 13,* 213–217.
SMITH, C. A., & WALLSTON, K. A. (1992). Adaptation in patients with chronic rheumatoid arthritis: Application of a general coping model. *Health Psychology, 11,* 151–162.
STONE, A. A., NEALE, J. N., & SHIFFMAN, S. (1993). Daily assessments of stress and coping and their association with mood. *Annals of Behavioral Medicine, 15,* 8–16.
SWINDLE, R. W., CRONKITE, R. C., & MOOS, R. (1989). Life stressors, social resources, coping, and the 4-year course of unipolar depression. *Journal of Abnormal Psychology, 98,* 468–477.
TART, C. (1987). *Waking up.* Cambridge, MA: Shambala Press.
TAYLOR, S., & BROWN, J. D. (1988). Illusion and well-being: A social psychological perspective on mental health. *Psychological Bulletin, 103,* 193–210.
TENNEN, H. & AFFLECK, G. (1996). Daily processes in coping with chronic pain: Methods and analytic strategies. In M. Zeidner and N. Endler (Eds.), *Handbook of coping: Theory, research applications* (pp. 151–180). New York: Wiley.
THOITS, P. (1986). Social support as coping assistance. *Journal of Consulting and Clinical Psychology, 54,* 416–423.
THOMPSON, S. C., NANNI, C., & LEVINE, A. (1994). Primary versus secondary and central versus consequence-related control in HIV-positive men. *Journal of Personality and Social Psychology, 67,* 540–547.
TIMKO, C., STOVEL, K., & MOOS, R. H. (1992). Functioning among mothers and fathers of children with juvenile rheumatic disease. *Journal of Pediatric Psychology, 17,* 705–724.
TOWNSEND, A., NOELKER, L., DEIMLING, G., & BASS, D. (1989). Longitudinal impact of interhousehold caregiving on adult children's mental health. *Psychology and Aging, 4,* 393–401.
TURK, D. C., SOBEL, H. J., FOLLICK, M. J., & YOUKILIS, H. D. (1980). A sequential criterion analysis for assessing coping with chronic illness. *Journal of Human Stress, 6,* 35–40.
VAILLANT, G. (1977). *Adaptation to life: How the best and the brightest came of age.* Boston: Little, Brown.
VAILLANT, G. (1993). *The wisdom of the ego.* Cambridge, MA: Harvard University Press.
VITALIANO, P., DE WOLFE, D. J., MAIURO, R. D., RUSSO, J., & KATON, W. (1990). Appraised changeability of a stressor as a modifier of the relationship between coping and depression: A test of the hypothesis of fit. *Journal of Personality and Social Psychology, 59,* 582–592.
VITALIANO, P. P., MAIURO, R. D., RUSSO, J., & BECKER, J. (1987). Raw versus relative scores in the assessment of coping strategies. *Journal of Behavioral Medicine, 10,* 1–18.
VON BERTALANAFFY, L. (1969). *General systems theory: Foundations, development, applications.* New York: Braziller.
WEITZ, R. (1989). Uncertainty and the lives of persons with AIDS. *Journal of Health and Social Behavior, 30,* 270–281.
WERNER, E. E., & SMITH, R. S. (1992). *Overcoming the odds.* Ithaca, NY: Cornell University Press.
WILLIAMSON, G., & SCHULZ, R. (1993). Coping with specific stressors in Alzheimer's disease caregiving. *The Gerontologist, 33,* 747–755.
WORTMAN, C. B., & SILVER, R. C. (1989). The myths of coping with loss. *Journal of Consulting & Clinical Psychology, 57,* 349–357.

4

Effortful and Involuntary Responses to Stress
Implications for Coping with Chronic Stress

BRUCE E. COMPAS, JENNIFER CONNOR,
DANA OSOWIECKI, and AMY WELCH

When Elaine received her diagnosis of breast cancer, she was faced with stress in virtually all aspects of her life. The diagnosis itself was unexpected and acutely stressful—her surgeon found and removed a 2 centimeter tumor and four positive lymph nodes. Yet the diagnosis was only the beginning of a long and frightening process. Her surgery was difficult and left her with the loss of her breast, feeling self-conscious and concerned about her appearance and her sexuality. In the ensuing months she faced several cycles of chemotherapy that left her fatigued, somewhat nauseous, and embarrassed about the loss of her hair. She felt unable to fulfill her responsibilities to her family or her job, because all of her daily routines at home and at work were disrupted. Her husband had withdrawn from her, apparently unwilling or unable to talk about her illness. She was worried about her oldest daughter, who was assuming far too many responsibilities for a 14-year-old girl by trying to care for Elaine, her siblings, and her father. And when she finally laid down at night, a time when she hoped to escape all of the stresses of her disease, Elaine was hounded by uncontrollable thoughts and images of

---

BRUCE E. COMPAS, JENNIFER CONNOR, DANA OSOWIECKI, and AMY WELCH • Department of Psychology, University of Vermont, Burlington, Vermont 05405-0134.

Coping with Chronic Stress, edited by Benjamin H. Gottlieb. Plenum Press, New York, 1997.

her cancer, the aversive treatment procedures, and fears about her own and her family's future.

Elaine's experiences exemplify an important aspect of the stress process. That is, virtually all enduring, clinically important effects of stress are the result of chronic rather than acute processes. The chronic processes that contribute to long-term difficulties in adjustment and well-being are represented in both *exogenous* (overt, environmental) processes and *endogenous* (covert, internal) processes. In Elaine's case, exogenous stress processes are reflected in the strain of disrupted roles at home and work, the repeated stress of chemotherapy, and ongoing difficulties in interpersonal relationships. Covert or endogenous processes are represented by the uncontrollable negative thoughts that she experiences at sleep onset and in other situations during her daily routines.

Central among the processes that buffer the long-term effects of stress are the cognitive and behavioral efforts made by an individual to master or manage ongoing stress—what researchers have come to refer to as *coping*. The massive and growing literature on coping with stress has told only half the story of patterns of response to stress, however. Theory and research on responses to stress has tended to focus on *effortful*, volitional responses to stress, thereby overlooking the importance of *involuntary*, nonvolitional responses. Failure to delineate the degree to which thoughts and behaviors are effortful versus involuntary has limited our understanding of the nature of responses to stress.

In this chapter we offer a conceptualization of effortful and involuntary reactions to stress, focusing on the implications for understanding adjustment to chronic stress. We argue that while the concept of coping is limited to effortful responses to stress, any conceptualization of coping will be incomplete without an understanding of the complex relationships between coping and involuntary or overlearned patterns of responding to stress. Involuntary processes frequently constrain the types of coping responses that an individual can generate and, in turn, effortful coping responses may unintentionally initiate involuntary processes that interfere with effective coping. Furthermore, we will distinguish between engagement (involvement with the stressor or one's mood) and disengagement (orienting away from the stressor or associated mood) responses that are both effortful and involuntary as a further step in delineating patterns of coping with chronic stress. Engagement and disengagement responses differ substantially in their efficacy in managing chronic stress. A critical distinction will be made between two types of effortful disengagement coping—avoidance and distraction. The former is typically associated with poor adjustment, whereas the latter most often has beneficial effects. Examples from research on psychological and physical health outcomes will be discussed; specifically, the association of effortful and involuntary stress responses will be examined in research on depression and cancer.

ACUTE AND CHRONIC STRESS

Conceptualizations of stress have been soundly criticized for a lack of clarity in definition and heterogeneity in measurement (e.g., Lazarus, 1991; Wheaton, Chapter 2, this volume). In no area have the criticisms been more pronounced than in the distinction between acute and chronic stress. On the surface, the distinction seems rather simple, one that is made on the basis of either the frequency or duration of a stressful event, circumstance, or condition. On closer consideration, however, the distinction begins to blur. For example, Baum, Cohen, and Hall (1993) point to three problems in distinguishing acute and chronic stress solely on the basis of the duration of the stressor: individuals may habituate to or adapt to a persistent stressor with repeated exposure, an acute stressor can lead to long-lasting appraisals of stress even after the event itself has ended, and distinctions based on the duration of acute and chronic stress are often arbitrary.

The distinction between acute and chronic stress is further blurred by the fact that these two types of stress are often related. Acute stressors exert their impact on well-being and adjustment partially through the ongoing minor, recurrent stressors that are the result of acute stress (e.g., Compas, Howell, Phares, Williams, & Ledoux, 1989; Wagner, Compas, & Howell, 1988; Wheaton, 1994). For example, parental divorce may affect children through the myriad of changes in ongoing daily routines, roles, and relationships. Acute stress can also affect adjustment through cognitive processes. The significance of cognitive mechanisms in chronic stress is found in research by Baum et al. (1993) on the enduring effects of the Three Mile Island (TMI) nuclear accident. Those residents of the TMI area who experienced high levels of intrusive thoughts and memories of the event had the most long-lasting emotional, physical, cognitive, and behavioral problems. Enduring intrusive thoughts and memories related to the accident served as a form of continued cognitive reexposure to the stressor for a subgroup of those who lived near TMI, creating chronic stress from a seemingly acute event.

Taken together, these findings suggest that there are two processes, one exogenous and the other endogenous, through which acute events contribute to chronic stress (see Figure 1). Exogenous processes are rep-

```
                    ┌──────────────────┐
                    │    Exogenous     │
                    │ Processes: Ongoing│
                    │   Minor Events   │
                    └──────────────────┘
              ↗                            ↘
┌──────────┐                              ┌──────────────┐
│  Acute   │                              │ Psychological│
│ Stressor │                              │  and Physical│
│          │                              │   Outcome    │
└──────────┘                              └──────────────┘
              ↘                            ↗
                    ┌──────────────────┐
                    │    Endogenous    │
                    │Processes: Involuntary│
                    │ Thoughts & Emotions│
                    └──────────────────┘
```

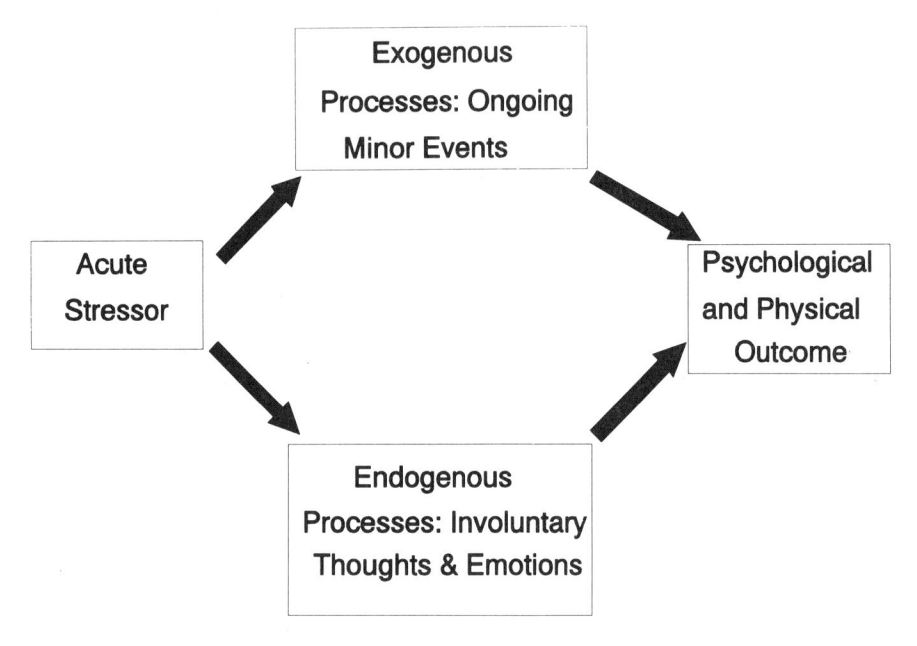

Figure 1. Exogenous and endogenous processes in chronic stress.

resented by the ongoing demands and threats that are produced in the environment. For example, the diagnosis of cancer represents an acute traumatic event for patients and their families and is associated with significant short-term psychological distress (e.g., Andersen, Andersen, & deProsse, 1989; Compas, Worsham, Epping-Jordan, Grant, Mireault, Howell, et al., 1994). As reflected in the case example presented here, however, the enduring effects of this event are played out through the disruptions that are created in the daily routines, family roles, and threats to goals and values of patients and their families (e.g., Grant & Compas, 1995). Endogenous processes are reflected in the persistent cognitive and affective reexperiencing of the stressor by patients and family members (e.g., Compas et al., 1994). Intrusive and uncontrollable thoughts and memories about the disease and reminders of it maintain appraisals of threat and emotional arousal (Baum et al., 1993). Involuntary negative thoughts are part of the response system that unwittingly prolong stress. Both of these processes are the direct consequence of the effects of acute stress on the individual and the environment.

The association of acute and chronic stress is imperfect, as not all acute events lead to chronic stress, nor do all individuals exposed to acute traumatic events experience chronic cognitive and affective sequelae of these events (see Wheaton, 1994, for a discussion of the continuum of stress processes). Further, not all chronic stressful conditions are the result of acute events (e.g., poverty, a congenital birth defect; see Compas, 1994). We will focus our attention on those chronic stressful conditions that are the result of acute stressors. These circumstances provide an opportunity to learn from the literatures on both acute and chronic stress and to identify consistent findings in these two typically separate lines of theory and research.

RESPONSES TO STRESS: EFFORTFUL AND INVOLUNTARY PROCESSES

Coping as an Effortful Process: Try and Try Again

The direction for much of current research on coping with stress was set by the landmark work of Lazarus and Folkman in the early 1980s (e.g., Folkman & Lazarus, 1980; Lazarus & Folkman, 1984). Among the important distinctions they made in defining the concept of coping was to distinguish coping as effortful responses to stress, as opposed to either innate, temperamentally based reactions or automatized, overlearned responses. Specifically, Lazarus and Folkman state, ". . . not all adaptive processes are coping. Coping is a subset of adaptational activities that involves effort and does not include everything we do in relating to the environment" (1984, p. 132). Effortful processes are hypothesized to become automatized through repeated practice—some responses to stress that initially require effortful control may become automatic as a result of overlearning and thus are no longer considered coping.

The distinction between effortful and automatic responses to stress was an essential step to move the field forward because it prevented researchers from relegating coping to the nonspecific status of encompassing all responses to stress. This also freed researchers to draw on self-reports of efforts to manage stressful experiences in naturally occurring contexts (e.g., Billings & Moos, 1981; Carver, Scheier, & Weintraub, 1989; Folkman & Lazarus, 1980; Stone & Neale, 1984). That is, researchers have assumed that individuals have reasonably good awareness of and can provide verbal reports on effortful cognitive and behavioral responses to stress. This was an essential step forward for research on chronic stress, as chronic stress can be studied only as it unfolds in the natural environment and self-reports of coping are one of the only methods of accessing information about coping in these circumstances.

Furthermore, the focus on effortful processes has led to the delineation of two broad intentions or goals of personal coping efforts—coping responses that are aimed at changing or resolving the source of stress (problem-focused coping) and coping efforts that are intended to manage or palliate one's emotional reaction to the stressor (emotion-focused coping). The distinction between problem- and emotion-focused coping has permeated much of the research on coping in the last 15 years (Lazarus, 1993).

The exclusive emphasis on effortful processes has not been without cost, however. The focus on effortful processes has led coping theorists and researchers to ignore the role of involuntary responses to stress with several consequences. First, research on involuntary responses to stress has developed independent of coping research. As a result, the conceptualization and measurement of coping have often lacked precision in distinguishing between these two broad categories of stress responses. Second, coping researchers have failed to recognize how involuntary processes may influence coping and how coping may trigger nonvolitional responses to stress. And third, possible interactions between effortful and involuntary processes in their effects on psychological and physical outcomes have been overlooked.

Involuntary Responses to Stress: Unwanted Effects of Unintended Reactions

A second realm of stress responses includes thoughts and behaviors that are involuntary or automatic. The significance of automatic or involuntary responses to stress is found in the literature on traumatic stress (e.g., Horowitz, 1982), on the relationship between stress and depression (Hartlage, Alloy, Vazquez, & Dykman, 1993) and stress and worry (Andrews & Borkovec, 1988), and in theories of mental control of automatic processes (Wegner, 1994). The seminal work on automatic cognitive processes dates to the late 1970s and the experimental work of Schneider and Shiffrin, who investigated the ways that cognitive processes can become automatic or involuntary (e.g., Schneider & Shiffrin, 1977; Shiffrin & Schneider, 1977). They conceptualized automatic processes as involving a sequence of cognitive nodes that are activated in response to internal or external cues. A cognitive or behavioral sequence can be activated automatically without the necessity of effortful (conscious) control or attention by the individual (Schneider & Shiffrin, 1977). Once an automatic attention process begins it is assumed that it is no longer under control of the person and will occur whenever its corresponding stimulus is presented (Shiffrin & Schneider, 1977).

Though much of the research on automatic cognitive processes has been conducted in laboratory contexts, it has important implications for the conceptualization of involuntary processes in adaptation to chronic stress. The basic premise of this research, that a cognitive response can be initiated and run to completion without effortful control by the individual, suggests that when a response has been overlearned it can preempt a conscious, effortful response (Shiffrin & Schneider, 1977). Exposure to chronic stress may represent a primary context in which overlearning can occur through repeated exposure to a stressor. For example, repeated involuntary negative thoughts about one's cancer may develop during prolonged treatment such as chemotherapy. These negative thoughts may disrupt the generation of coping responses to manage one's negative emotions and the stress of the disease. Furthermore, a key point of Shiffrin and Schneider's work is that these processes can generalize to other stimuli that are associated with the initial trigger for the involuntary response. Therefore, the processing of one piece of information may activate a larger category of information that could further impact on responses to stressful stimuli. For example, if a stimulus belongs in a category of distressing interactions with one's family, then a particular negative affective response related to family interactions may be initiated. The fact that automatic attention processes direct attention involuntarily to the target regardless of concurrent inputs or memory load has implications for understanding cognitive processes of individuals who are experiencing continued exposure to stressful conditions. Even if they are engaged in one task that requires direct attention (e.g., a task at work), they may still feel the effects of cognitions that are running their course automatically (e.g., negative thoughts about cancer).

Involuntary Stress Responses and Negative Affect. Research on involuntary negative cognitive processes has played a central role in research on stress and negative affect (e.g., anxiety, depression, anger). A prime example of automatic thought processes that are related to chronic stress can be found in the phenomenon of worry. As described by Borkovec and colleagues (e.g., Andrews & Borkovec, 1988; Stavosky & Borkovec, 1988), worry is a relatively uncontrollable chain of negative, affect-laden thoughts that, once initiated, is difficult to disrupt. Worry appears to be an intrusive, negative cognitive process to which some individuals ("worriers") are more susceptible than others ("nonworriers"). It resembles the automatic processes described by Shiffrin and Schneider in that it does not appear to be under the control of the worrier and does not require direct attention. The process of worrying has also been shown to lead to more negative intrusive thoughts and more negative daydreaming activity (Borkovec & Lyonfields, 1993). Thus, as Shiffrin and Schneider's work suggests, such automatic negative thought processes are also self-regenerating in that the associative network of negative thoughts and recollections is expanded each time the cycle is repeated. Worry becomes a habitual, overlearned, and seemingly uncontrollable cognitive response pattern.

Why are some individuals more susceptible than others to involuntary negative cognitive processes? One avenue of research that has a bearing on this question can be found in investigations of cognitive processes in depression. Hartlage et al. (1993) suggest that the relationship between involuntary and effortful responses plays a key role in depression and that this relationship is a central factor distinguishing individuals who are "depression-prone" from those who are not. In individuals who are prone to depression, exposure to stress leads to cognitive and affective arousal, which creates a narrowing of attentional focus toward stress-related, negative information and disrupts control of effortful processes. These individuals appear to lose the ability to attend to positive information and begin to automatically process the negative aspects of the stressful situation and recall related negative experiences. Furthermore, depression-prone individuals appear unable to disrupt such automatic negative thought patterns once they have begun or to reestablish effortful control of their cognitive processes, a step that is necessary in order to engage in coping. Like the worriers described by Stavosky and Borkovec (1988), depression-prone individuals appear trapped in an uncontrollable response pattern that prolongs and heightens their negative emotional tone.

Although non-depression-prone individuals are also confronted with stress and may initially experience some automatic negative thoughts, they appear to be able to escape the cycle of negative cognitions experienced by those who are depression-prone. A key factor in non-depression-prone individuals' responses to stress may be the ability to *reestablish effortful processing;* i.e., they are able to engage in effortful coping responses that disrupt the cognitions that lead to the development of depressed mood. For example, they engage in pleasant distracting thoughts or activities or positively reframe the negative situation. By generating an effortful response, they not only employ a coping strategy that may help to ameliorate the stressor, but they may also disrupt the automatic negative thought chain and the sequence of negative, self-focused attention.

Thus, depression-prone individuals, as compared with non-depression-prone individuals, appear particularly vulnerable to automatic negative thought processes that are triggered by stress. Each time these automatic negative thought processes are repeated, depression-prone individuals learn to attend to more negative, depression-relevant thoughts, thus enlarging and solidifying the network of related negative experiences. Such learning occurs quickly and is difficult to extinguish (Hartlage et al., 1993). Therefore, it may not take many repetitions before the narrowing of attentional focus toward negative thoughts moves out of conscious control and becomes automatic. Chronic stress, which entails frequent reexposure to negative events, may be a primary example of the conditions that contribute to this process.

Involuntary Processes and Effortful Coping: You Can't Always Think What You Want. If both effortful and involuntary responses are crucial to understanding adaptation to stress, then research on the reciprocal effects of these processes should provide essential information on adjustment. Recent research suggests that involuntary responses to stress may both constrain the resources individuals have available to cope and influence the coping responses they select. Additionally, some types of effortful coping may unintentionally set involuntary responses into motion.

Several converging lines of research indicate that effortful responses aimed at *avoidance and suppression of unwanted, involuntary thoughts* have the unintended effect of increasing the frequency and persistence of those thoughts (e.g., Wegner, 1994). For example, Wegner, Schneider, Carter, and White (1987) demonstrated the potential for "paradoxical effects" of attempted thought suppression. In this set of experiments, participants were asked to report their thoughts while they first tried either to think of the target "white bear" (expression) or to think of anything but the target (suppression), and then they participated in the opposite condition. Subjects participating first in the suppression condition reported more thoughts about the white bear during the expression period than did subjects with an initial expression period. This "rebound effect" suggests that initial attempts to suppress a thought may ultimately result in that thought becoming more salient, intrusive, and automatic. Thoughts used to distract one's attention from "white bear thoughts" are labeled "not white bear" and serve as primes for thoughts about white bears, leading to a rebound effect when subjects allow thoughts to roam freely. Subjects provided with a specific distractor (red Volkswagen) reported no rebound effect when placed in an expression condition, presumably because only the cue "red Volkswagen" was associated with "white bear" thoughts, whereas other readily available internal and external cues were free of such contamination.

If individuals cannot successfully suppress thoughts of a neutral target such as white bears, what happens when they attempt to suppress the more personally meaningful and emotion-laden thoughts associated with chronic stressors? Roemer and Borkovec (1994) used an experimental design similar to that of Wegner et al. (1987) but asked individuals to suppress either neutral, personalized anxious, or personalized depressing target thoughts. They found that, for all thought targets, initial suppression elicited an increase in anxious mood and tendency toward an increase in depressed mood. Roemer and Borkovec suggest that simply attempting to suppress a thought may lead to increased anxiety, whereas expressing that thought may lead to decreased anxiety. Attempts at suppression may initiate a cycle in which thought suppression leads to the formation of an association between that thought and negative emotion (arousal), the thought becomes intrusive because of its association with negative emotion, and the intrusiveness of the thought leads to enhanced attempts to suppress the thought. This position fits both with the common belief that it is helpful to talk about problems and with research indicating that the expression of negative thoughts, even in writing, can be beneficial (e.g., Pennebaker, Colder, & Sharp, 1990). Moreover, some forms of chronic stress are characterized by continued reexposure, leaving little opportunity for thought suppression. For example, caregivers of persons with dementia experience this type of constant exposure to stress with little opportunity to escape (Gottlieb & Gignac, in press).

Control of unwanted or unintended thoughts should be more difficult for individuals with preexisting depressed mood because effective thought suppression requires distraction via emotionally positive or neutral material (Wegner & Erber, 1992; Wegner, Erber, & Zanakos, 1993; Wenzlaff, Wegner, & Roper, 1988). Depressed individuals acknowledge that positive thoughts are the most efficacious distractors from negative thoughts. However, unlike subjects without depressed mood, subjects with depressed mood do not follow intrusive negative thoughts with positive thoughts (Wenzlaff et al., 1988). To some extent this appears to be due to the difficulty depressed subjects have generating positive distractors because they use fewer negative distractors when positive distractors are provided. This suggests that although depressed individuals seem to be aware of the best strategies for distraction, they are ultimately unable to implement them. Wegner et al. (1987) maintain that this apparent contradiction results from automatic mental processes; ineffective mental control strategies lower one's ability to suppress negative thoughts, leading to increased negative affect and a more pronounced inaccessibility of positive distractors. This lack of appropriate distractors leads to future ineffective attempts at mental control, further increasing depressed mood. Thus, an initially effortful attempt to suppress negative thoughts initiates an involuntary process that leads thoughts further from an individual's conscious control.

Engagement and Disengagement Responses to Stress

A second fundamental contrast in the coping literature has centered on those responses that involve engagement with or approach toward a stressor and the negative emotions associated with it, as opposed to those responses that are characterized by disengagement from the stressor and negative affect (e.g., Billings & Moos, 1981; Tobin, Holroyd, Reynolds, & Wigal, 1989). Engagement coping includes planful problem solving (e.g., making a plan of action and following it), cognitive restructuring (e.g., focusing on the positive aspects of the situation), and seeking social support (e.g., sharing one's feelings with others). These coping strategies all involve psychological contact with the source of the stressful interaction with the environment and/or the negative emotions that have resulted from the stressful encounter. Disengagement coping includes wishful thinking (e.g., just wishing that the problem had never happened), problem avoidance (e.g,. staying away from reminders of it), avoidance of negative emotions and thoughts (e.g., trying not to think about it), and social withdrawal (e.g., avoiding contact with others). Disengagement coping efforts involve either behavioral or psychological attempts to move away from the source of stress and/or negative emotions. Although the findings of research on the consequences of these two broad types of coping are not wholly consistent, the pervasive trend is that engagement coping is associated with lower affective distress and better physical health outcomes, whereas disengagement coping is associated with greater distress and poorer health (e.g., Carver, Pozo, Harris, Noriega, Scheier, Robinson, et al., 1993). The beneficial effects of engagement coping appear to be greatest in response to stressors that are either objectively controllable or are perceived as controllable by the individual (Compas, Malcarne, & Fondacaro, 1988; Forsythe & Compas, 1987; Osowiecki & Compas, 1996).

A related distinction has been made by Nolen-Hoeksema and her colleagues in their research on responses to depression (e.g., Nolen-Hoeksema, 1991; Nolen-Hoeksema & Morrow, 1991; Nolen-Hoeksema, Morrow, & Fredrickson, 1993; Nolen-Hoeksema, Parker, & Larsen, 1994). Nolen-Hoeksema has distinguished between response styles that she characterizes as *rumination* (thoughts and behaviors that focus attention on one's mood or depressive symptoms and the consequences of those symptoms; Nolen-Hoeksema et al., 1993) and *distraction* (thoughts and behaviors that take the individual's attention off depressive symptoms and shift it onto positive or neutral targets; Nolen-Hoeksema et al., 1993). Nolen-Hoeksema and colleagues have been specifically concerned with deleterious effects of attention focused on the self and one's negative mood as distinguished from rumination about a stressful event. In this way, rumination is similar to the process of self-focused attention, which has also been shown to be related to increased depressive mood and symptoms (Ingram, 1990). The distinction between rumination and distraction (or between self- and externally focused attention) closely parallels the engagement–disengagement dichotomy. Ruminative responses involve continued engagement with or focus on one's depressed mood and aspects of the self, whereas distraction involves deliberate disengagement or shifting of attention away from the self and negative mood.

In both laboratory analogue studies and correlational field studies, ruminative responses have been shown to increase and prolong depressed affect, whereas distraction is associated with decreased depressed mood (e.g., Nolen-Hoeksema & Morrow, 1991; Nolen-Hoeksema et al., 1993). Rumination maintains a focus on negative mood and negative aspects of the self, triggering other networks of associated memories and self-schema. Furthermore, self-focused rumination interferes with planful problem solving and other active forms of engagement coping. It is noteworthy, however, that Nolen-Hoeksema has not distinguished between rumination and distraction responses that differ in the degree to which they are effortful or involuntary. It is plausible, for example, that some ruminative responses are volitional (e.g., writing in a diary), whereas others are involuntary (e.g., intrusive thoughts prior to sleep onset). Whether effortful and involuntary rumination both lead to increased depressed mood has not been examined, although parallel research by Borkavec and colleagues suggests that the involuntary process of worrying is the most difficult to control and will lead to the greatest level of depressed and anxious mood (e.g., Stavosky & Borkavec, 1988).

Rumination, Avoidance, and Distraction

At first glance, it would appear that the findings from research on engagement–disengagement coping and research on rumination–distraction are at odds. That is, rumination appears to be a form of engagement coping (with negative emotions that may result from a stressor), yet it is associated with increased depressed mood. Distraction, which would appear to be a form of disengagement coping, is associated with decreased depressed mood. In contrast, engagement coping strategies generally have been found to reduce symptoms of distress in association with stress, and disengagement responses have been associated with increased distress. This suggests that more refined distinctions are needed among types of engagement and disengagement responses. For example, engagement with one's negative emotions and aspects of the self may be maladaptive, whereas engagement with external factors (e.g., characteristics of the environment that are experienced as stressful) may be relatively more adaptive. In contrast, disengagement that involves purely avoidance of an unwanted thought may be unsuccessful, whereas disengagement that includes a redirection of attention onto positive, distracting stimuli may have beneficial consequences.

The apparent contradiction in these findings centers on the distinctions between effortful and involuntary responses and between different intentions of engagement and disengagement responses. Effortful engagement responses that focus on controllable aspects of the stressor are generally effective in reducing negative affect, especially in situations that afford the opportunity for personal control. For example, problem solving and active coping aimed at changing a stressful situation are associated with lower symptoms of anxiety and depression in situations that are appraised as controllable (e.g., Compas et al., 1988; Forsythe & Compas, 1987; Osowiecki & Compas, 1995). In contrast, higher levels of emotional distress appear to be the result of engagement responses that focus on negative emotions and aspects of the self, especially when they are accompanied by efforts to disengage from the stressor or from the negative thoughts and emotions.

A Framework for Distinguishing Responses to Stress

An integrative framework for understanding responses to stress needs to reflect the three fundamental dimensions represented in the research described above. These dimensions contrast responses that (1) are effortful versus involuntary, (2) involve engagement versus disengagement, and (3) reflect problem-focused versus emotion-focused goals. The three dimensions and the resulting eight categories of responses are represented in a preliminary version of such a framework in Figure 2. This model builds on several previous efforts to develop multidimensional frameworks of coping responses (e.g., Carver et al., 1989; Endler & Parker, 1994; Folkman & Lazarus, 1980; Pearlin & Schooler, 1978; Rohde, Lewinsohn, Tilson, & Seeley, 1990; Tobin et al., 1989).

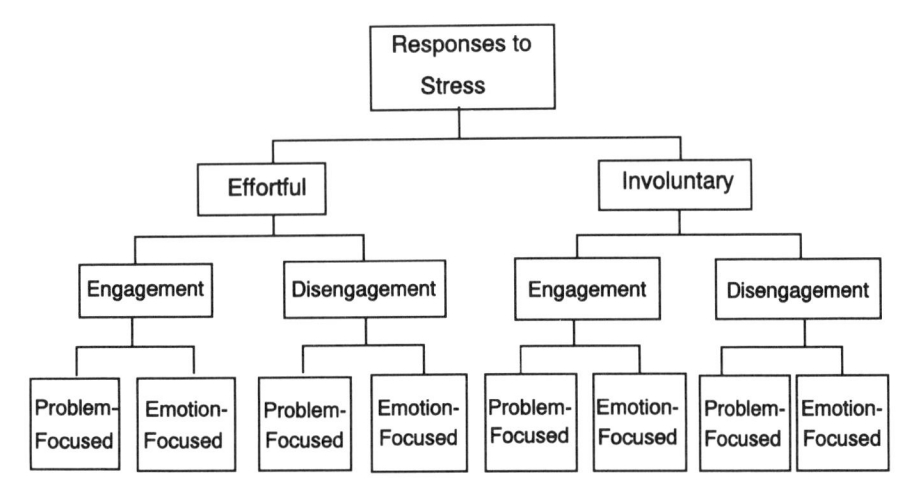

```
                    Responses to
                       Stress
          ┌───────────────┴───────────────┐
        Effortful                      Involuntary
    ┌──────┴──────┐                 ┌──────┴──────┐
Engagement   Disengagement       Engagement   Disengagement
  ┌─┴─┐        ┌─┴─┐              ┌─┴─┐        ┌─┴─┐
Problem- Emotion- Problem- Emotion- Problem- Emotion- Problem- Emotion-
Focused  Focused  Focused  Focused  Focused  Focused  Focused  Focused
```

Figure 2. Model of effortful and involuntary responses to stress.

However, none of these previous conceptualizations has included all three of the dimensions that we believe are essential to distinguishing among the various types of responses to stress.

First, responses to stress can be distinguished as effortful or involuntary. This is the most fundamental distinction among stress responses and distinguishes coping (effortful responses) from other reactions to stress that are nonvolitional. We recognize that attributions of volition may be based as much on the perceptions of the individual as on the actual causes or factors that control these responses (cf. Nisbett & Ross, 1980; Nisbett & Wilson, 1977). This concern notwithstanding, it remains important to distinguish those responses that are experienced as being under one's control from those that are experienced as involuntary because perceptions of the volitionality of responses may influence their efficacy in managing stress. Furthermore, responses to stress that are originally effortful and volitional may become involuntary through repeated practice (e.g., Lazarus & Folkman, 1984). Conversely, responses that are experienced as involuntary may be brought under personal control as well, through processes such as reattributing the causes of responses to controllable factors and subsequently increasing effortful control.

We have noted considerable confusion in the literature regarding the distinction between effortful and involuntary responses to stress. In some instances the distinction between the two categories of responses has been overlooked. For example, Tobin et al. (1989) and Nolen-Hoeksema (1991) include very few involuntary responses and do not differentiate between responses to stress that are effortful and those that are involuntary. Perhaps as a consequence, some items on the scales that these researchers have developed are ambiguous with regard to their volitionality. Others have mixed the concepts in ways that suggest that they are interchangeable. For example, Janoff-Bulman (1992) refers to "automatic efforts by survivors to come to terms with and integrate their traumatic experience" (p. 96). Although she goes on to distinguish denial (an unconscious, involuntary process of avoidance) from conscious efforts to avoid, she describes ways that individuals "choose" to engage in denial in spite of the involuntary nature of this response.

Finally, in some instances coping efforts have been labeled as entirely automatic responses. The fourth edition of the *Diagnostic and Statistical Manual of Mental Disorders* (DSM-IV) includes among its axes proposed for further study a category labeled "defensive functioning." The authors state, "Defense mechanisms (or coping styles) are automatic psychological processes that protect the individual against anxiety and from awareness of internal or external dangers or stressors" (American Psychiatric Association, 1994, p. 751). Thus, coping styles are labeled as automatic rather than effortful processes. Although some of these problems may involve simple semantic confusion surrounding the use of the terms effortful and involuntary, we believe that they also represent a fundamental misunderstanding of the distinction between these two broad categories of responses to stress. This failure to distinguish between effortful and involuntary responses leads to extremely different responses to stress being classified in a single category.

Second, stress responses involve either engagement or disengagement with the stressor, with negative mood, or with aspects of the self. Responses that involve approach or avoidance of the stressor or negative aspects of the self may be initiated either voluntarily or involuntarily. The engagement–disengagement dimension reflects the assumption that cognitive and behavioral responses to stress are *directed* either toward or away from a specific target. The target of one's engagement or disengagement may be a negative aspect of the person–environment relationship (the stressor or negative emotions), but it may also involve a positive focus, as in the case of distraction through pleasant thoughts or activities. Furthermore, avoidance in the form of respite from chronic stress may also involve engagement in pleasant activities (Repetti & Wood, Chapter 7, this volume). The direction of one's responses is not synonymous, however, with the function of the response, the subject of the third dimension of the framework we propose.

As the bottom row of Figure 2 reveals, the intentions or functions of the response can focus on the problem/stressor or address the emotions that arise in the stressful episode. This distinction involves the goals that the person is trying to accomplish or the function that is served by the response. Goal-directed responses are represented in the category of effortful responses, whereas involuntary responses are classified according to the function that is served by the response. The distinction between problem- and emotion-focused responses is widely represented in the literature on subtypes of coping (e.g., Lazarus, 1993). Problem-focused responses are those that alter some aspect of the stressful transaction between the person and the environment. Emotion-focused responses are palliative in nature, as they reduce or manage negative emotions in the context of the stressful episode.

We recognize that the problem- and emotion-focused dichotomy has become a bit worn after nearly 15 years of overuse. Furthermore, this simple dichotomy does not capture the variations in the goals or intentions of specific coping efforts. This problem can be appreciated when considering the rather distinct effects associated with distraction and avoidance, both of which are classified as emotion-focused coping. Many researchers have labeled these categories interchangeably or have conceptualized one as a subcategory of the other (e.g., Endler & Parker, 1994). The research reviewed earlier, however, indicates that they are distinct responses to stress, each of which is associated with unique outcomes. Within the traditional distinction between problem- and emotion-focused coping, both distraction and avoidance would be classified as effortful emotion-focused disengagement responses. There is a need to further differentiate these two responses, however. Avoidance is a purely disengagement form of responding (e.g., failing to comply with a chemotherapy regimen), whereas distraction includes an additional component of engagement through redirection of one's attention to positive thoughts, emotions, or activities—responses that direct attention or action toward a neutral or positive target that is separate from the stressor (e.g., reading a magazine while waiting in the physician's office). Based on this distinction, avoidance involves effortful disengagement from the problem or negative emotions by attempting to behaviorally avoid threatening situations or to suppress thoughts associated with the stressor. In contrast, distraction involves effortful engagement in positive activities or thoughts—the redeployment of attention or action onto an alternative target. The distinction between problem- and emotion-focused coping fails to capture these more subtle but important variations within these two broad categories.

The three dimensions can be found to varying degrees in other conceptualizations of coping and responses to stress. Failure to consider all three of these dimensions, however, has resulted in an incomplete understanding of the process of adjustment to stress. Most notably, the failure to consider effortful coping in light of involuntary responses has led to a fundamental misunderstanding of the basis for the efficacy of some coping strategies. For example, avoidance may frequently lead to poor outcomes or inefficacy in part because it does not result in successful resolution of the problem and in part because it increases the frequency and intensity of involuntary negative cognitions. Avoidance of some forms of chronic stress may be beneficial, however, if it provides relief from the stressful conditions and is accompanied by more positive cognitive or behavioral strategies (Gottlieb & Gignac, in press; Repetti & Wood, Chapter 7, this volume).

UNDERSTANDING RESPONSES TO CHRONIC STRESS

What is the role of effortful and involuntary response patterns in adjustment to chronic stress? Because it is characterized by repeated or continuous exposure to stressful conditions, chronic stress may make particular demands on effortful responding and may also trigger involuntary processes. The challenges presented by chronically stressful conditions warrant different coping responses than those presented by acute stressors. Because of their recurrent nature, and because these responses may be repeated with each reexposure to the condition of chronic stress, the effects on adjustment of effortful and involuntary responses to chronic stress may be greater. We offer the following hypothesis regarding the process of coping with chronic stress: *The most deleterious responses to chronic stress are characterized by high levels of involuntary engagement (intrusive or ruminative thoughts and/or unwanted exposure to stressful conditions) coupled with high levels of effortful disengagement (cognitive or behavioral avoidance).*

Involuntary Processes Contribute to Chronic Stress

A fundamental characteristic of chronic stress is repeated reexposure to stressful conditions. As described earlier, this reexposure can take place either through repeated contacts with stressful stimuli or contexts that are the source of stress or through cognitive reexposure through involuntary, unwanted thoughts about the stressor. Habituation to the stressful situation or intrusive thoughts is likely to occur only if there is an opportunity for new learning to take place. Negative emotional responses to stressful situations will continue even in contexts or situations other than the one in which the original habituation (extinction) took place (cf. Bouton, 1994). Furthermore, new learning may be seriously disrupted by coping efforts that are directed toward avoiding the stressful thoughts or situations.

Understanding the Cognitive Pathway from Acute to Chronic Stress. Intrusive thoughts and emotions, a particular pattern of involuntary responses to stress, contribute to the chronicity of a stressor or stressful episode. Intrusive thoughts and images of a stressor occur as an involuntary, conditioned response and represent repeated reexposure to the stressor. As a result, involuntary cognitive processes represent an internal mechanism through which a stressful event becomes a chronic stressor. This pattern is well represented in research by Baum and colleagues on the long-term adjustment of individuals exposed to the TMI nuclear accident (Baum, 1990; Baum et al., 1993). Those individuals who experienced high levels of intrusive thoughts about the event also showed the poorest long-term emotional adjustment. Kiecolt-Glaser and colleagues have also identified intrusive thoughts as an important marker of poor psychological adjustment of elderly individuals faced with the chronic stress of caregiving for a partner with Alzheimer's disease and subsequent bereavement over loss of the partner (e.g., Bodnar & Kiecolt-Glaser, 1994). Similarly, in our own research on psychological adjustment to cancer, intrusive thoughts about one's disease serve as a marker of poor adjustment, not only near the time of diagnosis but also continuing for months or more after the diagnosis (e.g., Compas et al., 1994).

Involuntary thoughts about a stressor may be triggered by both internal and external cues. Internal cues include thoughts, emotions, or physiological states that have come to be associated with the stressor itself. Similarly, external cues that trigger involuntary thoughts are conditioned stimuli that are associated with the stressor. Cancer patients may come to associate the stress of their disease with the internal physical states associated with the disease and its treatment, along with salient external cues that are associated with their cancer. Among breast cancer patients, for example, internal cues include pain or discomfort or physical changes associated with loss of a breast; external cues include conditioned reactions to specific treatment procedures, certain settings (e.g., the hospital), or certain temporal contexts, such as bedtime.

If chronic stressors are reexperienced, at least in part through involuntary cognitive processes, then effective coping with chronic stress will need to address these internal cues as well as ongoing threats in the environment. In the most extreme instances, chronic reexposure to the stressor occurs entirely through cognitive pathways. In these cases, coping efforts are entirely directed toward managing these intrusive thoughts and images. In most instances, however, chronic stress is likely to be the result of reexposure to stress in the environment, cognitive reexposure to unwanted thoughts, or both.

Affective and Physical Consequences of Avoidant Coping Efforts

Intrusive thoughts about a stressor are frequently accompanied by efforts to avoid these unwanted thoughts and images. Such avoidant efforts are typically unsuccessful, however, and contribute to increased frequency and intensity of the unwanted stimuli that are intended to be avoided. This pattern is suggested by the laboratory research by Wegner and colleagues (1987) described earlier and is found in studies of avoidance and intrusive thoughts reported by individuals exposed to significant stress. In our research on psychological adjustment to cancer we have found that avoidance and intrusive thoughts are moderately to strongly correlated. For example, we found in a sample of cancer patients that intrusive thoughts about the disease and efforts to avoid these thoughts were moderately correlated, $r = .51, p < .001$ (Epping-Jordan, Compas, & Howell, 1994). This indicates that intrusive thoughts about one's cancer are typically accompanied by efforts to avoid these unwanted cognitions. However, the simple correlation between intrusive thoughts and avoidance disguises possible combinations of these variables that may be important (Primo, Compas, Oppedisano, Epping-Jordan, & Krag, 1996). Those individuals who report high levels of both constructs are ineffectively avoiding the unwanted negative thoughts—their avoidance does not lead to decreased intrusive ideation. In contrast, individuals who report low intrusion and low avoidance are less threatened or are managing the threat in ways that do not contribute to intrusive thoughts. Smaller groups of individuals are represented by those who may successfully avoid the unwanted thoughts (high levels of avoidance and low intrusive thoughts) and those who are facing or accepting the negative thoughts (high levels of intrusive thoughts and low levels of avoidance). The outcomes of these latter two patterns of intrusion and avoidance have received little attention in research.

Intrusive thoughts and avoidance have been found to predict prolonged affective distress and poor health outcomes. For example, we have found that, after controlling for relevant aspects of initial disease severity and treatment, avoidance predicts poorer disease outcomes for cancer patients 1 year after their diagnosis (Epping-Jordan et al., 1994). Intrusive thoughts and levels of negative affect (symptoms of depression and anxiety) were not related to later disease status. In contrast, both intrusive thoughts and avoidance are related to prolonged affective distress, whereas avoidance is only related to distress cross-sectionally. In initial analyses of a prospective study of women with newly diagnosed breast cancer, participants were divided into those who experienced persistent and prolonged affective distress and those who remained low in distress in the months following their diagnosis. The persistently distressed group was distinguished at the time of their diagnosis by higher levels of intrusive thoughts, avoidance of these thoughts, and coping through employing emotional expression and wishful thinking (Compas, Oppedisano, Primo, Epping-Jordan, & Krag, 1995). Although avoidance was correlated with negative affect in cross-sectional analyses, the use of avoidance coping did not distinguish those who experienced chronic distress from those who did not.

Avoidant coping has also been found to be associated with poor outcomes in other types of chronic stress independent of intrusive ideation. For example, cognitive and behavioral avoidance in the context of marital distress is related to poorer outcomes for individuals in these relationships and to their spouses' adjustment as well. In a community sample of 153 couples coping with ongoing hassles and strains, Giunta and Compas (1993) found that psychological distress was associated with the use of avoidant coping for both husbands ($r = .50$) and wives ($r = .53$). Furthermore, husbands' psychological distress was related to their wives' use of avoidant coping ($r = .29$) whereas wives' distress was not related to husbands' avoidant coping. Cluster analysis was used to identify subgroups of couples as a function of their coping patterns. Those couples that were characterized by high levels of avoidance by both spouses also had the highest levels of psychological distress for both members. Carro, Gotlib, and Compas (1996) examined similar processes of coping during pregnancy and postpartum in a community sample of husbands and wives. Carro et al. found that husbands' and wives' use of avoidant coping was related to higher levels of their own depressive symptoms, both cross-sectionally during pregnancy and postpartum and prospectively over a period of 3–6 months. Husbands' and wives' use of avoidant coping was also related to higher depressive symptoms in their spouses, both cross-sectionally and prospectively. In the studies of both Giunta and Compas (1993) and Carro et al. (1996), spouses' use of avoidant coping was significantly correlated; that is, if husbands tended to use avoidant coping responses, their wives did as well, and vice versa. These findings suggest that the adverse effects of avoidance are not limited to personal adjustment—avoidance may be linked to interpersonal interactions within marital relationships and may have interpersonal consequences for the psychological adjustment of one's spouse (O'Brien & DeLongis, Chapter 6, this volume).

In some instances, avoidance and social withdrawal may offer the opportunity to engage in other forms of coping that may have beneficial consequences. For example, in a discussion of coping with chronic work-related stress, Repetti (1992) and Repetti and Wood (Chapter 7, this volume) suggests that social withdrawal may represent one type of avoidance that offers the opportunity for short-term adaptation to chronic stress. If individuals withdraw from others in order to engage in pleasant distraction or to take time to plan strategies to deal with the source of stress, then beneficial effects may ensue. If withdrawal is associated with increased rumination, however, negative outcomes would be expected. This highlights once again the need to distinguish between avoidance and distraction as distinct types of emotion-focused coping. As Repetti (1992) suggests, researchers need to pay greater attention to what individuals do in the course of withdrawal from a stressful situation.

Why might distraction be associated with better outcomes than avoidance? This is most likely a consequence of the redeployment of attention and/or behavior to positive thoughts or situations as a part of distraction, or seeking respite from chronic stress (Repetti and Wood, Chapter 7, this volume). Therefore, distraction involves at least a temporary escape from the negative emotions associated with a stressor as a result of engagement with a pleasant thought or activity. Avoidant responses do not include a shifting of attention onto a positive target and, as a consequence, may be especially susceptible to paradoxical effects of increasing involuntary negative thoughts (e.g., Wegner, 1994; Wenzlaff et al., 1988). The efficacy of distraction as opposed to avoidance in adjustment to chronic stress is not well understood, however. To the extent that distraction can provide relief from a process of negative rumination, it may increase the cognitive capacity of the individual to engage in problem solving and other forms of effortful engagement coping.

Involuntary Thoughts, Avoidance, and Effortful Engagement Coping

In addition to increasing affective distress, the pattern of intrusive thoughts and avoidance may further interfere with other coping efforts aimed at resolution of the stressor. To the extent that involuntary cognitive processes present a load that drains the capacity for effortful responding, repeated exposure to intrusive thoughts or chronic stress in the environment will diminish the individual's resources to engage in effortful problem-focused coping. Uleman (1989) has suggested a sequence in which chronic stress, as represented in repeated exposure to the stressor, results in the conditioned response of automatic cognitions, which in turn leads to disruption of effortful responses. Although exposure to the stressor should offer repeated opportunities to employ engagement coping responses, this process appears to be disrupted by the presence of involuntary cognitive responses.

Exposure to chronic stressors provides fertile ground for the development of such automatic or overlearned processes. Whether internally or externally produced, chronic stress would likely lead to a reduction in cognitive capacity as individuals attempt to respond to multiple or repeated or protracted/enduring negative events. Once cognitive capacity is reduced, automatic processes would be more likely to take place and effortful coping responses would become more difficult to initiate. Further, as negative cognitions are repeatedly experienced, which would be the case for chronic stress, practice effects would facilitate the learning process, thereby reinforcing the automaticity of the response pattern and expanding the network of negative cognitions. Individuals vulnerable to automatic processing would therefore be at risk for prolonged depressed mood, as well as for future depressive episodes.

Effortful engagement coping may be further disrupted by avoidance responses. Avoidant coping reduces contact with the source of stress and therefore reduces opportunities for use of engagement coping. Furthermore, avoidance may lead to increased affective distress, contributing to further interference with effortful engagement coping.

FUTURE DIRECTIONS

At least four important directions for future research on coping with chronic stress are suggested by the work described in this chapter. First, further attention should be given to the role of both involuntary and effortful processes in adjustment to chronic stress. Similar to the coping literature in general, studies of coping with chronic stress have emphasized effortful responses while overlooking the significance of involuntary processes. This will require refinement in the measures that are used to assess responses to stress. Many scales fail to distinguish between responses that are experienced by the individual as volitional as opposed to involuntary (e.g., Tobin et al., 1989). Furthermore, the validation of self-reports of effortful versus involuntary responses presents an additional challenge to researchers. The extent to which individuals can validly distinguish between effortful and involuntary cognitive and behavioral processes is open to question. This is further compounded by the fact that many involuntary cognitive processes occur out of the awareness of the individual (Uleman, 1989). It is incumbent on researchers to show that self-report measures can accurately reflect these important processes, especially because measurement of coping with chronic stress requires the use of retrospective recall methods (Coyne & Gottlieb, 1996; Ptacek, Smith, Espe, & Raffety, 1994).

Second, further research is needed to delineate specific subtypes of responses to stress, especially the distinction between distraction and avoidance as effortful emotion-focused disengagement. Within the framework that we have proposed, problem- and emotion-focused responses need to be further classified into more specific subtypes to account for these important differences in coping. For example, avoidance and distraction differ in their orientation toward negative or positive "targets." That is, avoidant responses involve disengagement from negative stimuli, whereas distraction involves a redirection of attention or behavior toward positive stimuli or activities. Further consideration of these distinctions among subtypes of coping are needed to account for the differences in the efficacy of these types of responses to stress.

Third, greater integration of the chronic and acute stress literatures is needed to identify the commonalities and differences. Research by Baum (1990) and others has highlighted the gray area between these two broad categories of stress. Acute and chronic stress are best distinguished along a variety of dimensions, rather than categorically (Wheaton, Chapter 2, this volume). Further, evidence suggests that chronic stress may be prolonged by internal, cognitive reactions of the individual as well as by repeated exposure to environmental stress. Given the uncertain distinctions between these two broad types of stress, researchers concerned with either acute or chronic stress would be well to draw on findings from both areas of research.

Finally, greater integration of field and laboratory research is needed. Beginning in the 1970s, stress researchers turned away from laboratory study due to concerns about the external validity of the types of stressful circumstances that can be represented in the laboratory (Lazarus & Folkman, 1984). The benefits of this shift from the laboratory to the field have been well documented in hundreds of studies of people coping with significant circumstances in their daily lives. However, the relative emphasis on field research has overlooked the unique contributions that laboratory research on stress and coping can offer. Research by Wegner and colleagues, Nolen-Hoeksema and associates, and others exemplifies the types of important questions about the coping process that can only be examined under controlled conditions.

Moreover, the strong database now available from coping research has set the stage for conducting careful intervention studies in which aspects of the coping process are manipulated and controlled in the natural environment. Intervention studies offer the best opportunity for experimental studies of coping in the natural environment. Further understanding of the process of coping with chronic stress is likely to depend on contributions from all of these areas—descriptive field studies, controlled laboratory studies, and intervention trials.

REFERENCES

AMERICAN PSYCHIATRIC ASSOCIATION. (1994). *Diagnostic and statistical manual of mental disorders (4th ed.)* Washington, DC: Author.

ANDERSEN, B. L., ANDERSEN, B., & DE PROSSE, C. (1989). Controlled prospective longitudinal study of women with cancer: II. Psychological outcomes. *Journal of Consulting and Clinical Psychology, 57,* 692–697.

ANDREWS, V. H., & BORKOVEC, T. D. (1988). The differential effects of inductions of worry, somatic anxiety, and depression on emotional experience. *Journal of Behavior Therapy and Experimental Psychiatry, 19,* 21–26.

BAUM, A. (1990). Stress, intrusive imagery, and chronic distress. *Health Psychology, 9,* 653–675.

BAUM, C., COHEN, L., & HALL, M. (1993). Control and intrusive memories as possible determinants of chronic stress. *Psychosomatic Medicine, 55,* 274–286.

BILLINGS, A. G., & MOOS, R. H. (1981). The role of coping responses and social resources in attenuating the impact of stressful life events. *Journal of Behavioral Medicine, 4,* 139–157.

BODNAR, J. C., & KIECOLT-GLASER, J. K. (1994). Caregiver depression after bereavement: Chronic stress isn't over when its over. *Psychology and Aging, 9,* 372–380.

BORKOVEC, T. D., & LYONFIELDS, J. D. (1993). Worry: Thought suppression and emotional processing. In H. W. Krobne (Ed.). *Attention and avoidance: Strategies in coping with adversities.* Gottingen, Germany: Hogrete and Huber.

BOUTON, M. B. (1994). Context, ambiguity, and classical conditioning. *Current Directions in Psychological Science, 3,* 49–53.

CARRO, M., GOTLIB, I., & COMPAS, B. E. (1996). *Postpartum depression: Coping, marital distress, and depressive symptoms in husbands and wives during pregnancy and postpartum.* Manuscript in preparation.

CARVER, C. S., POZO, C. P., HARRIS, S. D., NORIEGA, V., SCHEIER, M. F., ROBINSON, D. S., KETCHAM, A. S., MOFFAT, F. L., & CLARCK, K. C. (1993). How coping mediates the effect of optimism on distress: A study of women with early stage breast cancer. *Journal of Personality and Social Psychology, 65,* 375–390.

CARVER, C. S., SCHEIER, M. F., & WEINTRAUB, J. K. (1989). Assessing coping strategies: A theoretically based approach. *Journal of Personality and Social Psychology, 56,* 267–283.

COMPAS, B. E. (1994). Promoting successful coping during adolescence. In M. Rutter (Ed.), *Psychosocial disturbances in young people: Challenges for prevention.* Cambridge, England: Cambridge University Press.

COMPAS, B. E., HOWELL, D. C., PHARES, V., WILLIAMS, R. A., & LEDOUX, N. (1989). Parent and child stress and psychological symptoms: An integrative analysis. *Developmental Psychology, 25,* 550–559.

COMPAS, B. E., MALCARNE, V. L., BANEZ, G., & WORSHAM, N. L. (1993). Perceived control and coping with stress: A developmental perspective. *Journal of Social Issues, 47,* 23–34.

Compas, B. E., Malcarne, V. L., & Fondacaro, K. M. (1988). Coping with stressful events in older children and young adolescents. *Journal of Consulting and Clinical Psychology, 56*, 405–411.
Compas, B. E., Oppedisano, G., Primo, K., Epping-Jordan, J. E., & Krag, D. N. (1994). Predictors of individual differences in psychological adjustment to breast cancer. Manuscript submitted for publication.
Compas, B. E., Worsham, N. L., Epping-Jordan, J. E., Grant, K. E., Mireault, G., Howell, D. C., & Malcarne, V. L. (1994). When mom or dad has cancer: Markers of psychological distress in adult cancer patients, their spouses, and children. *Health Psychology, 13*, 507–515.
Coyne, J. C., & Gottlieb, B. H. (1996).
Endler, N. S., & Parker, J. D. A. (1994). Assessment of multidimensional coping: Task, emotion, and avoidance strategies. *Psychological Assessment, 6*, 50–60.
Epping-Jordan, J. E., Compas, B. E., & Howell, D. C. (1994). Predictors of cancer progression in young adult men and women: Avoidance, intrusive thoughts, and psychological symptoms. *Health Psychology, 13*, 539–547.
Folkman, S., & Lazarus, R. S. (1980). An analysis of coping in a middle-aged community sample. *Journal of Health and Social Behavior, 21*, 219–239.
Forsythe, C. J., & Compas, B. E. (1987). Interactions of coping and perceptions of control: Testing the goodness of fit hypothesis. *Cognitive Therapy and Research, 11*, 473–485.
Giunta, C. T., & Compas, B. E. (1993). Coping in marital dyads: Patterns and associations with psychological symptoms. *Journal of Marriage and the Family, 55*, 1011–1017.
Gottlieb, B. H., & Gignac, A. M. (in press). Content and domain specificity of coping among family caregivers of persons with dementia. *Journal of Aging Studies*.
Grant, K. E., & Compas, B. E. (1995). Stress and symptoms of anxiety/depression among adolescents: Searching for mechanisms of risk. *Journal of Consulting and Clinical Psychology, 63*, 1015–1021.
Hartlage, S., Alloy, L. B., Vazquez, C., & Dykman, B. (1993). Automatic and effortful processing in depression. *Psychological Bulletin, 113*, 247–278.
Horowitz, M. (1982). Stress response symptoms and their treatment. In L. Goldberger & S. Breznitz (Eds.), *Handbook of stress* (pp. 711–732). New York: Free Press.
Ingram, R. E. (1990). Self-focused attention in clinical disorders: Review and a conceptual model. *Psychological Bulletin, 107*, 156–176.
Janoff-Bulman, R. (1992). *Shattered assumptions: Towards a new psychology of trauma*. New York: Free Press.
Lazarus, R. S. (1991). *Emotion and adaptation*. New York: Oxford University Press.
Lazarus, R. S. (1993). Coping theory and research: Past, present, and future. *Psychosomatic Medicine, 55*, 232–247.
Lazarus, R. S., & Folkman, S. (1984). *Stress, appraisal, and coping*. New York: Springer.
Nisbett, R., & Ross, L. (1980). *Human inference: Strategies and shortcomings of social judgment*. Englewood Cliffs, NJ: Prentice Hall.
Nisbett, R. E., & Wilson, T. D. (1977). Telling more than we can know: Verbal reports on mental processes. *Psychological Review, 84*, 231–259.
Nolen-Hoeksema, S. (1991). Responses to depression and their effects on the duration of depressive episodes. *Journal of Abnormal Psychology, 100*, 569–582.
Nolen-Hoeksema, S., & Morrow, J. (1991). A prospective study of depression and post-traumatic stress symptoms after a natural disaster: The 1989 Loma Prieta Earthquake. *Journal of Personality and Social Psychology, 61*, 115–121.
Nolen-Hoeksema, S., Morrow, J., & Fredrickson, B. L. (1993). Response styles and the duration of episodes of depressed mood. *Journal of Abnormal Psychology, 102*, 20–28.
Nolen-Hoeksema, S., Parker, L. E., & Larson, J. (1994). Ruminative coping with depressed mood following loss. *Journal of Personality and Social Psychology, 67*, 92–104.
Osowiecki, D., & Compas, B. E. (1996). *Coping with cancer: Interactions of coping and control as predictors of psychological adjustment*. Manuscript submitted for publication.

Pearlin, L. I., & Schooler, C. (1978). The structure of coping. *Journal of Health and Social Behavior, 19,* 2–21.

Pennebaker, J. W., Colder, M., & Sharp, L. K. (1990). Accelerating the coping process. *Journal of Personality and Social Psychology, 58,* 528–537.

Ptacek, J. T., Smith, R. E., Espe, K., & Rafferty, B. (1994). Limited correspondence between daily coping reports and retrospective coping recall. *Psychological Assessment, 6,* 41–49.

Repetti, R. L. (1992). Social withdrawal as a short-term coping response to daily stressors. In H. S. Friedman (Ed.), *Hostility, coping and health* (pp. 151–165). Washington, DC: American Psychological Association.

Roemer, L., & Borkovec, T. D. (1994). Effects of suppressing thoughts about emotional material. *Journal of Abnormal Psychology, 103,* 467–474.

Rohde, P., Lewinsohn, P. M., Tilson, M., & Seeley, J. R. (1990). dimensionality of coping and its relation to depression. *Journal of Personality and Social Psychology, 58,* 499–511.

Scheier, M. F., Weintraub, J. K., & Carver, C. S. (1986). Coping with stress: Divergent strategies of optimists and pessimists. *Journal of Personality and Social Psychology, 51,* 1257–1264.

Schneider, W., & Shiffrin, R. M. (1977). Controlled and automatic human information processing: I. Detection, search, and attention. *Psychological Review, 84,* 1–66.

Shiffrin, R. M., & Schneider, W. (1977). Controlled and automatic human information processing: II. Perceptual learning, automatic attending, and a general theory. *Psychological Review, 84,* 127–190.

Stavosky, J. M., & Borkovec, T. D. (1988). The phenomenon of worry: Theory, research, treatment and its implications for women. *Women and Therapy, 6,* 77–95.

Stone, A. A., & Neale, J. M. (1984). New measure of daily coping: Development and preliminary results. *Journal of Personality and Social Psychology, 46,* 892–906.

Tobin, D. L., Holroyd, K. A., Reynolds, R. V., & Wigal, J. K. (1989). The hierarchical factor structure of the Coping Strategies Inventory. *Cognitive Therapy and Research, 13,* 343–361.

Primo, K., Compas, B. E., Oppedisano, G., Epping-Jordan, J. E., & Krag, D. N. (1996). *Intrusive thoughts and avoidance in breast cancer: Individual differences and association with psychological distress.* Manuscript submitted for publication.

Uleman, J. S. (1989). A framework for thinking intentionally about unintended thoughts. In J. S. Uleman & J. A. Bargh (Eds.), *Unintended thought* (pp. 425–447). New York: Guilford.

Wagner, B. M., Compas, B. E., & Howell, D. C. (1988). Daily and major life events: A test of an integrative model of psychosocial stress. *American Journal of Community Psychology, 16,* 189–205.

Wegner, D. M. (1994). Ironic processes of mental control. *Psychological Review, 101,* 34–52.

Wegner, D. M., & Erber, R. (1992). The hyperaccessibility of suppressed thoughts. *Journal of Personality and Social Psychology, 63,* 903–912.

Wegner, D. M., Erber, R., & Zanakos, S. (1992). Ironic processes in the mental control of mood and mood-related thought. *Journal of Personality and Social Psychology, 65,* 1093–1104.

Wegner, D. M., Schneider, D. J., Carter, S. R., & White, T. L. (1987). Paradoxical effects of thought suppression. *Journal of Personality and Social Psychology, 53,* 5–13.

Wenzlaff, R. M., Wegner, D. M., & Roper, D. W. (1988). Depression and mental control: The resurgence of unwanted negative thoughts. *Journal of Personality and Social Psychology, 55,* 882–892.

Wheaton, B. (1994). Sampling the stress universe. In W. R. Avison & I. H. Gotlib (Eds.), *Stress and mental health* (pp. 77–114). New York: Plenum.

III

The Social Context of Coping with Chronic Stress

5

Social–Environmental Influences on the Chronic Stress Process

STEPHEN J. LEPORE

OVERVIEW

The social environment can facilitate or hamper one's ability to cope with chronic stressors, but it can also be a direct source of chronic stress. This chapter examines three ways in which the social environment is implicated in chronic stress processes. First, it describes the variety of social sources of chronic stress. Second, it shows how the social environment can moderate, or alter, the impact of chronic stressors by mitigating or exacerbating people's responses to them. Finally, it illustrates how enduring and undesirable changes in the social environment, which often result from stressful life events, can mediate, or explain, the effects of major life events on health and well-being.

SOCIAL ORIGINS OF CHRONIC STRESS

The social environment can be a direct source of potent and continuing stressors (Eckenrode & Gore, 1981; Lepore, 1992; Pearlin, 1982;

STEPHEN J. LEPORE • Department of Psychology, Carnegie Mellon University, Pittsburgh, Pennsylvania 15213-3890.

Coping with Chronic Stress, edited by Benjamin H. Gottlieb. Plenum Press, New York, 1997.

Table 1. Sources of Chronic Social Stress

Source	Description
Loneliness	Stress associated with having few or no social relationships or lacking meaningful and fulfilling social relationships
Social stimulus overload	Stress associated with an excess of social stimulation, overload, frequent unwanted or undesirable social interactions, or high social density
Stressful life events	Stress associated with negative changes in the quality of social relationships because of normative life transitions (e.g., retirement, graduation) or irrevocable or traumatic life events (e.g., imprisonment, widowhood)
Social roles	Stress associated with conflicts, demands, disapointments, responsibilities, obligations, and expectations in social roles (e.g., gender roles, work roles, marital roles)
Stigma	Stress associated with having a culturally devalued trait or characteristic that others respond to in an undesirable or discriminatory manner
Migration	Stress associated with social isolation, changing social roles, unfamiliar social norms, and general social disorganization following migration from one culture to another

Shinn, Lehmann, & Wong, 1984). In a study by Bolger, DeLongis, Kessler, and Schilling (1989), emotional distress was more strongly correlated with social stressors (e.g., marital conflicts) than with nonsocial stressors (e.g., financial problems). Bolger et al. also found that people's emotional distress did not appear to habituate, or subside, in the face of enduring interpersonal stressors, such as marital conflicts. Indeed, the emotional impact of marital conflicts in their sample increased when episodes of conflict extended over several days. Ongoing social stressors are also related to biological outcomes that may be relevant to health. For instance, family members who have assumed the long-term responsibility of caring for a relative with Alzheimer's disease have poorer psychological and immunological functioning than matched controls who do not have such chronic social stress in their lives (Kiecolt-Glaser, Glaser, Dyer, Shuttleworth, Ogrocki, & Speicher, 1987).

Table 1 presents a list of six general social situations that can create chronic stress. These were derived from the literature on stress and coping and illustrate the diversity of chronic social stressors. Each of these potential sources of chronic social stress is briefly discussed in the following sections.

Loneliness

One source of social stress is a lack of social relationships. The importance of social bonds and social integration is reflected in the stress associated with social isolation, deprivation, separation, and loss. House, Landis, and Umberson (1989) reviewed numerous studies that have shown an inverse association between degree of social integration and mortality and, to a lesser extent, between social integration and morbidity. Recent studies have continued to reveal an inverse association between social integration and all-cause and coronary-related mortality and morbidity, even after controlling for potential confounding or competing explanatory factors such as age, socioeconomic status, race, blood pressure, smoking habits, body mass, physical disability, and cholesterol (e.g., Orth-Gomer, Rosengren, & Wilhelmsen, 1993; Hibbard & Pope, 1992; Seeman, Berkman, Kohout, Lacroix, Glynn, & Blazer, 1993; Sugisawa, Liang, & Liu, 1994). Thus, the finding that less integrated (more isolated) people are at increased risk for morbidity and mortality appears to be reliable.

Because many obvious factors, such as age and health habits, do not appear to explain the link between social integration and health outcomes, House and colleagues (1989) have identified a number of alternative explanations. Prominent among them is the notion that people who are socially isolated lack social support and are therefore more vulnerable to the adverse health effects of stressful life events. Another hypothesis, which has received relatively scant attention, is that a lack of social ties, or social isolation, may be a direct source of chronic stress or can exacerbate people's negative responses to other ongoing stressors. In a large-scale prospective Swedish study, isolated workers who experienced high levels of job strain due to heavy job demands had a higher age-adjusted risk ratio for coronary-related mortality than their counterparts working under less strained and more socially interdependent conditions (Johnson, Hall, & Theorell, 1989). Strained and isolated workers also had a higher probability of developing and dying of cardiovascular disease at a younger age.

Isolation may be a chronic stressor because it can lead to feelings of social deprivation and loneliness (Peplau & Perlman, 1982). Chronic loneliness might contribute to psychological disorders such as depression (Rook, 1984). Loneliness also has potential implications for physical health. In a large-scale study of the elderly living in Odense, Denmark, people who reported relatively high levels of loneliness at the start of the study were more likely to have died by the follow-up 14 years later than their counterparts who reported relatively little loneliness (Olsen, Olsen, Gunner-Svensson, & Waldstrom, 1991). Several studies have revealed poorer immune system functioning among students and psychiatric patients who were lonely compared with counterparts who were not lonely (see review by Kiecolt-Glaser & Glaser, 1991).

Social Stimulus Overload

In conditions of high social embeddedness, or high social density, people may experience unwanted and excessive levels of social interaction. Excessive social stimulation, in turn, can lead to stress because of sensory overload. Milgram (1970) applied the overload concept to explain why crowded urbanites often behave in a more apathetic, socially aloof, and less courteous manner than people in relatively uncrowded residential areas. Milgram has argued that the high population density and heterogeneity of city environments lead to excessive sensory inputs. Urbanites presumably have adapted to the overload by adopting strategies that minimize social inputs, including ignoring and filtering out low-priority social inputs, allocating less time to each social input, and establishing technologies (e.g., answering machines), services (e.g., doormen), and institutions that reduce the number of social demands to which they must respond (see also Krupat, 1985; Lipowski, 1975). As Milgram has noted, behavioral adaptations to overload may be responsible for the evolution of many undesirable social norms readily apparent in cities. These norms range from general incivilities, such as a lack of manners, politeness, and respect in day-to-day commerce with others, to the more disturbing problem of bystander apathy, which is a tendency of people to ignore the needs of others, even when that need is desperate and when lives may be at stake.

The costs of adapting to high levels of social density and concomitant stimulus overload are also evident at the level of individual households. People living in high-density households (i.e., households with a high ratio of persons per room) often experience excessive and unwanted social contact with housemates, exhibit heightened social withdrawal, feel diminished levels of social support, and have heightened psychological distress (for reviews see Baum & Paulus, 1987; Lepore, 1994). Crowded people may become socially withdrawn as a means of reducing unwanted social interactions (Evans, Lepore, & Schroeder, 1996). Evans and Lepore (1993) have found that in stressful laboratory situations, people from crowded homes are less likely than those from uncrowded homes to seek and respond to support from a peer or to offer support to a peer in need. These effects appear to be related to crowded residents' heightened social withdrawal during the laboratory interactions. Of course, as will be discussed later, social overload is not the only pathway linking crowding to stress reactions. But the overload concept appears to account for many of the social and psychological disturbances associated with chronic exposure to high-density social environments.

Stressful Life Events

Many stressful life events involve undesirable changes in the quality of social relationships (Eckenrode & Gore, 1981; Schulz & Tomkins, 1990; Shinn et al., 1984). Although stressful and traumatic life events are often transient or episodic, they can have a lasting impact on people's emotional or physical well-being by causing enduring changes in the configuration and quality of social relationships. Following the loss of a loved one, people may experience intense grief and a prolonged desire for reunion. Following a divorce, many social ties, in addition to the marital bond, become severed (Lin & Westcott, 1991). Being deprived of former social bonds is stressful in and of itself in the wake of divorce, but when there are dependent children involved, divorce also adds to chronic stress by increasing the role demands of the custodial parent (cf. Wheaton, 1991). Stressors that involve social exits and losses can transform social roles and simultaneously diminish the social resources that are available for responding to both familiar and novel demands in that role. For this reason, stressors that are fundamentally social in nature, such as bereavement, divorce, relocation, and interpersonal conflicts, may be particularly insidious: They represent deprivations and threats and arouse new demands, while simultaneously weakening and diminishing social coping resources.

Social Roles

A common approach to organizing social stressors is based on social role theory. Social roles comprise sets of interpersonal relationships, activities, expectations, and responsibilities that are easy to identify, tend to be stable over time, and affect many people in the general population (Lepore, 1995a). Because of the great investment people make in certain social roles, especially work and family roles, any difficulties or threats to functioning in these roles can be very stressful (Eckenrode & Gore, 1990; Pearlin, 1989). There are myriad social roles that people occupy and myriad ways in which occupancy of one or more social roles can engender chronic stress. A few of the many ways in which social roles can contribute to chronic stress are illustrated here (for more detailed discussions, see Pearlin, 1982, 1989; Pearlin, Lieberman, Menaghan, & Mullan, 1981).

Some social roles are essentially imposed on people by society. Such roles are difficult to avoid because members of a society generally value them to such a degree that they have developed institutions, laws, and norms of interacting that encourage people to act in a role-consistent manner. For example, a number of social institutions, including schools and churches, exert a strong influence on gender-role development. Gender-role expectations shape men's and women's behaviors and lives in powerful and sometimes stressful ways. As an illustration, consider the role of women in this culture as nurturers and caregivers for ill or dependent members of society. Women are socialized to respond to the needs and desires of their loved ones and tend to exhibit greater responsiveness to the needs of others than do men (Gilligan, 1982). Unfortunately, women's orientation toward caring is not without costs, as they appear to be more distressed than men by "network events," or stressors that affect significant others (Belle, 1982; Kessler, McLeod, & Wethington, 1985). Women's characteristically high involvement in and sensitivity to the daily hardships of their loved ones can be a source of chronic stress.

Other social roles are entered into voluntarily but, nevertheless, they can be sources of stress. In the context of self-selected roles, such as spouse, parent, or worker, social demands, conflicts, and disappointments abound and can contribute to ongoing stress. Certainly some stressful aspects of roles are not social in nature. For example, in the work world, role overload may result from excessive physical and cognitive demands. However, work-role overload also might result from excessive demands from insensitive coworkers and supervisors. People might feel stress in a work role if their social relationships in that role are demeaning, dissatisfying, or unsupportive (cf. Repetti, 1993). A review by Lepore (1995a) of the stress associated with two common and valued types of roles—work and marital—indicates that the most prevalent stressors in these roles can be characterized as social in nature: interpersonal conflicts, responsibility for other people, competing expectations and demands from others, verbal and physical abuse and neglect, unsupportive boss or coworkers, lack of emotional closeness and affection, problems in communication, difficulties with relatives or friends of a spouse, infidelity or sexual problems with spouse, and inequity in the division of labor in household or in work groups. As indicated previously, because roles are fairly stable and valued by people, role stressors or challenges to role functioning can be highly stressful and enduring.

Stigma

People who are stigmatized because of physical or mental conditions that are not culturally valued, such as AIDS, Alzheimer's disease, or retardation, may experience stress in several ways. First, contact with stigmatized people may be emotionally discomforting to nonstigmatized people (Langer, Fiske, Taylor, & Chanowitz, 1976), thereby evoking negative social responses and straining social interactions (Frable, Blackstone, & Scherbaum, 1990). Nonstigmatized people also tend to exert greater effort than stigmatized people in creating a positive social exchange, which may lead them to resent the stigmatized person because the relationship is imbalanced. The resentment may even result in discrimination against or rejection of the stigmatized person. Second, stigmatized people may engage in hypervigilance, which is a tendency to devote extra attention to various aspects of social interaction. Hypervigilance is a strategy for deciphering the attitudes of social partners toward the stigmatizing condition. This hypervigilance can be another source of chronic stress. For example, a person with a stigmatizing condition may pay particularly close attention to how near to them a business associate sits during a work meeting. Sitting very far away might be construed as a sign of fear, whereas sitting very close may be viewed as an attempt by the associate to prove that he or she is oblivious to the stigmatizing condition. In either situation, the ambiguity of the associate's attitudes and motives can be a source of stress. Finally, to reduce the stress associated with awkward social interactions and hypervigilance, stigmatized people may withdraw socially, which can also contribute to stress. In summary, stigmatized people may experience heightened chronic stress because of social strains, isolation, hypervigilance, and attributional ambiguity in interpersonal interactions.

Migration

In recent years, there has been an unprecedented number of large-scale, cross-cultural migrations involving millions of people around the globe (Rogler, 1994). Rapid sociocultural changes created by migration patterns can create chronic stress for both the receiving and sending societies. The infusion of a large concentration of foreigners into a host society can create stress for that society by exposing its members to unfamiliar customs and possibly increasing undesirable social interactions and competition for resources. The migrant faces the same stressors, but he or she may also have additional problems associated with being separated from loved ones, changing social status, forging new social relationships, and attempting to assimilate to new sociocultural norms.

In general, chronic social stress may arise from the extreme social disorganization that can result from migration. Animal studies suggest that social disorganization can have adverse health consequences, although the effects appear to be conditioned by dispositional characteristics of animals. For example, chronic social disorganization (changing social groupings in houses) appears to increase risk for atherosclerosis in male monkeys, but the effect is stronger in dominant males than subordinate ones (Kaplan, Manuck, Clarkson, Lusso, & Taub, 1982). Interestingly, among female monkeys, the stress associated with social reorganization appears to have greater atherogenic effects in submissive rather than dominant monkeys (Kaplan, Adams, Clarkson, & Koritnik, 1984).

The research with humans is more tentative and not as highly controlled as the animal work, but it too suggests that some people are more susceptible than others to the negative effects of the social disorganization that accompanies migration. In a series of studies on the health of migrant groups, Hinkle (1974) observed that major changes in social relationships, major deprivations and dislocations, and major changes in interpersonal relationships appear to be linked to physical illness only in people with the necessary biophysical factors (e.g., genetic predisposition) that would make them susceptible to illness. In a review of the literature, Creed (1987) has drawn a similar conclusion, but in relation to psychiatric outcomes: Predisposition to develop psychotic illness appears to be as important as the stress of migration in predicting psychoses. Thus, the social changes associated with migration may be a source of chronic stress, but such changes only trigger health problems among people who are already predisposed to such problems.

Summary

Exposure to social stressors is multiply determined by broad, sociocultural factors, as well as by characteristics of people, such as their gender identity, role occupancy, and stigmatizing traits. Many of the sociocultural and personal antecedents of social stress are difficult for people to alter, which might make social stressors especially pernicious and enduring. Although people's broad sociocultural and personal characteristics may predispose them to experience chronic social stress, other exogenous factors can influence whether or not chronic social stress has negative health consequences. The next section shifts from discussing how the social environment can be a direct source of chronic stress to considering how the quality of the social environment can influence responses to chronic stressors, whether they are social or not.

SOCIAL ENVIRONMENT AS A MODIFIER OF CHRONIC STRESS

Interpersonal processes, such as social support and social strains, are viewed as conditioning influences in moderator models of stress. That is, the impact of stressors on health outcomes is presumed to be moderated by, or dependent on, positive and negative transactions occurring in people's social relationships. In their simplest form, moderator models predict that positive, or supportive, social relationships will attenuate stress reactions and that negative, or strained, social relationships will exacerbate stress reactions. Although stress moderation is often used to describe situations in which an external factor, such as social support, can mitigate stress responses, it can also refer to situations in which external factors amplify stress reactions (see Evans & Lepore, in press).

An implicit assumption of moderator models is that stressors and conditioning social variables are independent factors. The notion here is that social contextual processes that moderate stress reactions are not affected by stressors; perhaps they are antecedent conditions preceding stress exposure and influencing people's reactions to stressors or are highly stable or immutable characteristics of social environments. The moderating effect is demonstrated by a significant interaction between social support and stress or between social strains and stress on some health outcome.

This section describes two moderating functions of the social environment in the context of chronic stressors. One function is the familiar stress-buffering effect of supportive social environments. The second is the stress-amplifying effect of strained social environments. This section also discusses some special issues to consider regarding the moderating function of the social environment when stressors are chronic.

Chronic Stress Buffer

In the past two decades, the major thrust of research on the role of social relationships in adaptation to stress has been to test the stress-buffering effects of social support (for detailed discussions, see Cohen & Wills, 1985; House, 1981; Veiel, 1992). The buffering model essentially maintains that social support mitigates the negative effects of stressors on physical and psychological health through a variety of mechanisms. For example, supporters might offer emotional support or comfort to people that help reduce the threat of stressors and thereby reduces the adverse physiological and psychological consequences of the stressors (see Lepore, 1995b; Lepore, Allen, & Evans, 1992). However, as Hobfoll and Vaux (1993) have noted, an abundance of research and analysis has yielded no consensus on the status of the buffering model, with reviewers concluding that the evidence is dubious, mixed, or adequate.

The mixed evidence and opinions regarding the buffering model suggest that there are many contingencies that determine when, whether, and how social support mitigates stress reactions. Some of these contingencies are articulated in the specificity or matching model of social support (Cohen & McKay, 1984). According to this model, social support resources and provisions must fit the needs of the person under stress in order to be effective stress buffers (also see Cutrona, 1990; Cutrona & Russell, 1990; Thoits, 1986). For instance, people may need to feel emotionally secure and bonded with loved ones after someone close to them has died. Of course, many life stressors, including bereavement, can pose multiple demands, thereby complicating the specificity model (Cutrona, 1990). In addition, different people facing the same stressor may be challenged in unique ways (Gottlieb, 1992). Therefore, knowing the stressor a person faces does not necessarily inform decisions about the type of support that should be marshalled (Rook & Dooley, 1985). Nevertheless, the specificity approach is useful for alerting researchers to the necessity of both identifying the nature of the demands posed by unique stressors and considering the types of support necessary to help people cope with these demands.

Another conditioning factor that could influence the stress-buffering potential of social support is the chronicity of the stressor. In one of the few studies to examine the buffering potential of social support in the context of a chronic stressor, the role of social support appeared to shift over time. Lepore, Evans, and Schneider (1991) found that after only 2 months of being exposed to the stress associated with crowding (living in a high-density household), college students who judged their housemates to be supportive were not adversely affected by the crowding stress. In contrast, crowded people who felt their housemates were not supportive exhibited increased levels of psychological distress relative to when they first moved into their apartment. These findings are consistent with the classic stress-buffering model. However, after 8 months of exposure to crowding, the buffering effect of social support disappeared. Moreover, a higher level of household crowding was associated with a lower level of perceived social support from housemates, which, in turn, was associated with heightened psychological distress. After statistically controlling for the effects of social support, the association between crowding and psychological distress at 8 months disappeared, suggesting that changes in social support in chronically crowded households accounted for the adverse effects of chronic crowding on psychological distress symptoms. As will be discussed later in this chapter, several other studies have shown that deterioration of social support can increase psychological distress, but to date no other studies have shown that the buffering effect of social support can disappear under chronic stress conditions.

There is some indirect evidence that social support can be beneficial to people coping with chronic stressors. For example, among spousal caregivers of urologic cancer patients, those with higher levels of social support exhibited greater immunocompetence (Baron, Cutrona, Hicklin, Russell, & Lubaroff, 1990). Similarly, among people facing the chronic stress associated with breast cancer, more emotional support from others has been shown to be positively correlated with psychological adjustment in the short term (Northouse, 1988) and in the long term (Funch & Mettlin, 1982). However, because all of these studies are correlational, it is unclear how much other factors that coincide with social support contributed to the better adjustment of the high-support groups. For instance, it is possible that people who are less disabled by their illness have more support and better mental health (see Bloom & Kessler, 1994).

To test the buffering potential of social support in chronic illness situations, or in other chronic stress situations, it is necessary to control for variations in contextual features of the stressor, such as controllability, intensity, and desirability. Stressors that on the surface are equivalent may be quite different from one another along these contextual dimensions. Contextual differences in stressors could account for differences in availability of support and adjustment outcomes, creating a spurious association between support and adjustment. For example, if a person experiences a stressor, such as cancer, that is more severe, less controllable, or has more undesirable side effects than a cancer in a comparison person, then that person might make more demands on his or her support network and may find that support deteriorates as a result of the excessive demands placed on the network. The person with the more disabling and demanding cancer affliction would presumably exhibit greater adjustment problems as well. One approach to examining these processes would be to consider the dynamic changes in interpersonal relationships among patients with distinct illness experiences (e.g., disabling versus nondisabling). One might observe that more severe and demanding chronic illnesses interfere with support processes over time and that both the illness and the adverse changes in social support have negative implications for adjustment. This type of mediating process is described in more detail later in this chapter (also see O'Brien & DeLongis, Chapter 6, this volume).

Finally, when considering the stress-buffering potential of social support in the context of chronic stressors, it is important to realize that many chronic stressors, almost by definition, are resistant to change or coping efforts. That is, many aspects of chronically stressful situations are probably beyond the control of individuals and their social networks. If chronic stressors tend to be uncontrollable, then they may always require a certain degree of palliative or emotion-focused types of support, rather than instrumental types of support (cf. Cutrona, 1990). If support providers attempt to give instrumental support or advice about how to "fix the unfixable," then support recipients could grow frustrated and resentful because they are not getting the kind of support they need or because the support providers are insensitive to the fact that the problem is not one that can be resolved easily. In addition, support providers might become frustrated or demoralized by their inability to remove or diminish chronic stressors.

Chronic Stress Amplification

Exposure to chronic stressors may be more detrimental to the physical and mental health of people whose social environments are characterized by negative, or strained, interpersonal relationships than it is to the health of people with positive, or nonstrained, social relationships. Social strains are social relational qualities, or behaviors of members of one's social network, that cause one to experience lingering, adverse psychological or physiological states (e.g., hostility, depression, arousal). Whether the negative psychological and physiological effects of social strains make people more reactive to chronic stressors or whether chronic stressors make people more reactive to social strains is an empirical question that is difficult to test. Nevertheless, there is some emerging evidence that social strains in combination with chronic stressors have multiplicative, or synergistic, adverse effects on people's well-being.

In one study, family caregivers of persons with Alzheimer's disease and a comparison group of noncaregivers were found to have equivalent degrees of perceived upset in their relations with others (Kiecolt-Glaser, Dyer, & Shuttleworth, 1988). More importantly, there was a significant group membership (caregiver versus noncaregiver) × upset (low versus high) interactive effect on depressive symptoms. More specifically, degree of upset in social relationships was positively associated with depressive symptoms among caregivers, but not among noncaregivers. These findings suggest that the chronic stress of caregiving exacerbates adverse psychological responses to social strains. Kiecolt-Glaser et al. (1988) argued that because caregivers may have smaller social networks and less time to devote to social relationships, any signs of strain in their relationships are particularly salient and influential.

Lepore, Silver, Wortman, and Wayment (1996) recently investigated the negative effects of unsupportive social relationships on mothers' adjustment following the loss of their child to Sudden Infant Death Syndrome (SIDS). Two frequent responses to a traumatic event are the tendencies to experience event-related intrusive thoughts and to talk about the event. Lepore et al. argued that intrusive thoughts are a marker of incomplete cognitive processing of traumatic events and talking with others is a method to facilitate cognitive processing and emotional recovery. They predicted that bereaved mothers who felt socially constrained in talking about their loss, because their social network responded in an unsupportive or negative manner to their attempts to talk about their loss, would be less likely to talk about the loss than mothers who felt relatively unconstrained. Lepore et al. also argued that the forced inhibition of talking about the loss would interfere with cognitive processing and, consequently, contribute to or prolong psychological distress in bereaved mothers.

Data for the bereavement study were collected from mothers at 3 weeks, 3 months, and 18 months after the death of their child. All analyses were prospective and controlled for initial level of psychological distress. Among mothers who felt socially constrained in talking about the death, having intrusive thoughts about the baby several weeks post-loss was associated with less talking about the baby's death 3 months (Figure 1, top) and 18 months later (Figure 1, bottom). Among mothers who felt relatively unconstrained, the associations were reversed (Figure 1, top and bottom). More importantly, there was a positive relation between intrusive thoughts several weeks post-loss and depressive symptoms 3 months (Figure 2, top) and 18 months (Figure 2, bottom) later among mothers who felt socially constrained. However, more intrusive thoughts several weeks after the loss were associated with decreased depressive symptoms 18 months post-loss among mothers with unconstrained social relationships (Figure 2, bottom). These findings suggest that social constraints can inhibit people's discussion of traumatic events when they are attempting to cognitively process or integrate them and can increase and prolong psychological distress.

In another study on the interaction between social strains and chronic stressors, Lepore, Evans, and Palsane (1991) found additional evidence of synergism. Specifically, they found that people experiencing frequent social hassles from their housemates were likely to have greater increases in psychological distress symptoms if they lived in a crowded household than if they lived in a relatively uncrowded household. This synergistic effect of hassles and crowding was found in an American college student sample and in a sample of male heads of household

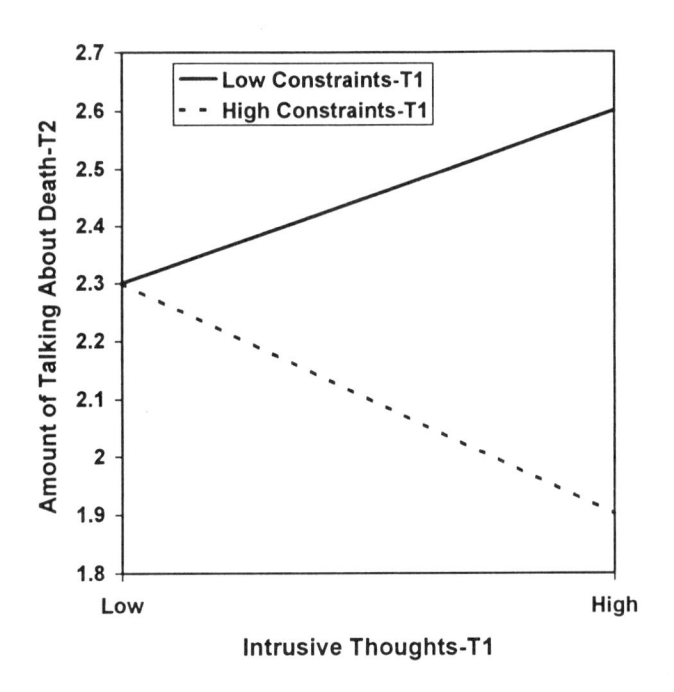

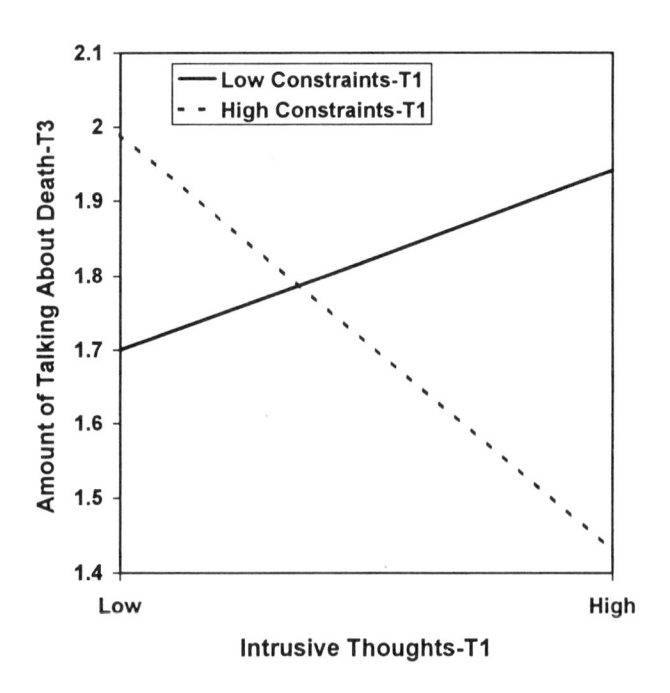

living in a city in India. The American data were longitudinal and adjusted for baseline levels of psychological distress symptoms. Subsequent analyses of this interaction indicated that crowded residents might have been more sensitive to social hassles because they had lower perceived control over their environment than did people facing social hassles in noncrowded households (Lepore, Evans, & Schneider, 1992). Perceptions of diminished control might have resulted from the limited behavioral coping options (e.g., ability to withdraw to another room) of people in crowded households compared to people in uncrowded households. Presumably, it would be more difficult to avoid or escape hassles in a crowded household than in an uncrowded one.

A variant of the "cost of coping" hypothesis offers one broad explanation of the interactive effects of social strains with other stressors. The cost of coping hypothesis maintains that there are adaptive costs associated with coping processes that are used to remove stressors or to ameliorate their negative biological, emotional, and psychological effects (Cohen, Evans, Stokols, & Krantz, 1986; Schonpflug, 1986). Recently, Lepore and Evans (1996) have extended the cost of coping hypothesis to multiple stressor situations. They argue that coping with one stressor can have negative adaptive consequences by interfering with a person's appraisals (i.e., evaluation of threat), capacity (i.e., resources), or motivation (i.e., incentive) to cope with a subsequent stressor. For instance, in the study by Kiecolt-Glaser et al. (1988), chronic caregiving stress seemed to have had negative implications for how people appraised upsetting social interactions, making the upsetting interactions more distressing than they would be otherwise. In the study by Lepore et al. (1992), crowding appears to have exacerbated the negative psychological effects of social hassles by constraining people's behavioral options for coping with the hassles. Finally, the deterioration of support that Lepore et al. (1991) observed in their study of the long-term effects of crowding is a "social cost" of coping that may be common following exposure to a wide range of chronic stressors.

←

Figure 1. Plot of the relation (slope) between intrusive thoughts about the dead infant at T1 and amount of talking about the death at T2 (top) and T3 (bottom) in mothers with high versus low levels of social constraints at T1. T1, T2, and T3 refer, respectively, to the period 3 weeks, 3 months, and 18 months after the child's death. The terms "high" and "low" refer, respectively, to +1 SD and −1 SD. All regression analyses were controlled for T1 psychological distress symptoms. Copyright (1996) by the American Psychological Association. Reprinted by permission from Lepore, Silver, Wortman, and Wayment (1996).

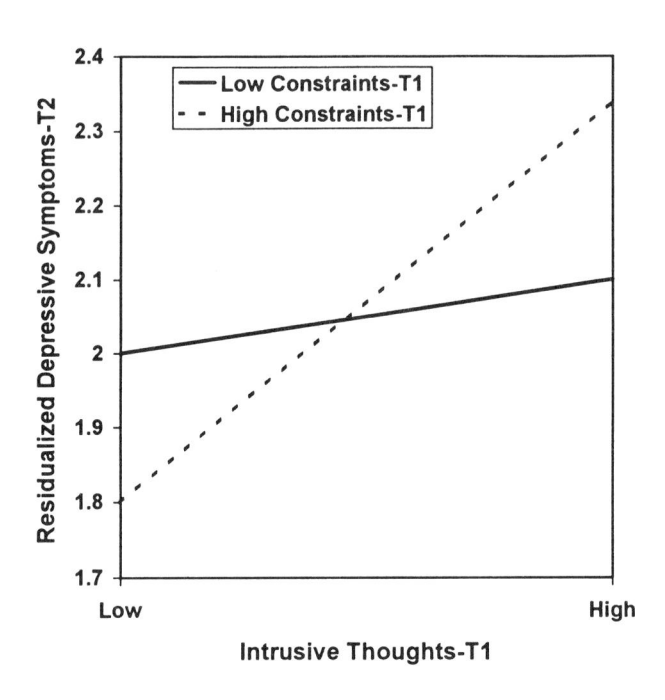

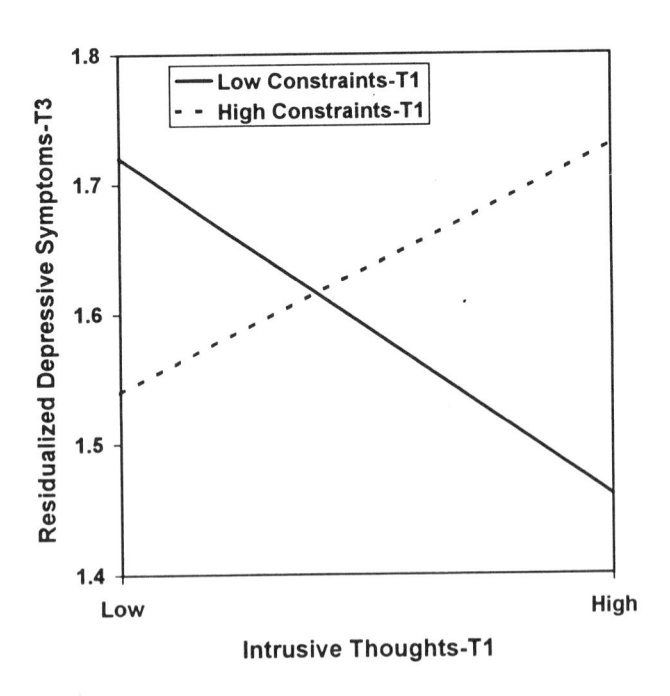

Summary

Theoretically, supportive social relationships can protect people from the negative effects of stressful life events. However, in the context of chronic stressors, people may experience difficulties in obtaining adequate social support. This may partially explain why social support research does not consistently produce evidence of stress-buffering. If investigators use cumulative stress measures, which tend to aggregate chronic and acute stressors, a buffering effect might be detected if the sample being studied is primarily exposed to acute stressors and might not be detected if the sample is primarily exposed to chronic stressors. In addition, because social needs of people can change over the course of a chronic stressor, buffering effects might be missed if the type of support measured is irrelevant to the stressed person at the time of measurement. Finally, emerging evidence indicates that people facing some chronic stressors, such as chronic crowding and disabling illnesses, might experience declines in the quality and amount of support they receive. An important direction for future research in this area is to examine the qualities of chronic stressors that can interfere with support processes and the types of support resources that are most durable and beneficial to people under chronic stress conditions. For instance, are there differences in the amount of time that people can maintain high-quality discretionary friendships versus family ties when they are facing a disabling illness or when they are forced to spend all of their time caring for an ill relative?

Strained social relationships can be a direct source of stress or a contributor to chronic stress processes by prolonging or intensifying negative reactions to other stressors. Coping with a chronic stressor can diminish a person's capacity to cope with social strains and vice versa. Thus, when social strains occur in the context of other chronic stressors, stress reactions can be amplified (i.e., can be greater than the unique effects of the independent stressors).

Figure 2. Plot of the relation (slope) between intrusive thoughts about the dead infant at T1 and increases in depressive symptoms at T2 (top) and T3 (bottom) in mothers with high versus low levels of social constraints at T1. T1, T2, and T3 refer, respectively, to the period 3 weeks, 3 months, and 18 months after the child's death. The terms "high" and "low" refer, respectively, to +1 SD and −1 SD. All regression analyses were controlled for T1 psychological distress symptoms. Copyright (1996) by the American Psychological Association. Reprinted by permission from Lepore, Silver, Wortman, and Wayment (1996).

SOCIAL ENVIRONMENT AS A MEDIATOR OF CHRONIC STRESS

Within a moderating framework, stressors and social relationship variables are assumed to be independent of one another. In fact, in some formulations of the stress-buffering model of social support, any correlation between stress and social support is undesirable and indicative of confounding between the stress and support constructs (Cohen & Wills, 1985; Thoits, 1982). From a statistical standpoint, independent and moderating factors should be orthogonal to get an unbiased estimate of their interactive effects (Evans & Lepore, in press). However, from a theoretical perspective, it is plausible and even likely that stressors influence interpersonal processes; hence, levels of stress could be correlated with indicators of relationship dynamics.

This section describes several studies that examine the influence of stress on social relational outcomes. These studies show that the impact of stressors on physical or psychological health is not so much determined by the quality of one's social relationships as it is by the changes in the quality of social relationships that can occur in the wake of some stressors.

Support Deterioration

According to the support deterioration model, some stressful events can erode social support resources, which, in turn, can have a negative influence on mental and physical health (Lepore et al., 1991; Kaniasty & Norris, 1993). Stressed people who lose social support may be in double jeopardy—they face the direct negative effects of the stressor and of having their support expectations violated. There are a number of plausible explanations of why social support might deteriorate in the face of various stressors.

One explanation is that observers sometimes react negatively to victims out of self-protective motives. For instance, Lerner and Miller (1978) have suggested that people wish to believe that the world is a just and fair place: If they behave appropriately and lead a "good" life, bad things will not happen to them. When observers see bad things happen to people they know, they are motivated to attribute the misfortune to the victims' bad behavior or negative traits. Lerner argues that by derogating victims, people are able to ward off negative feelings of personal vulnerability, because they can remain secure in the belief that the world is a fair and just place where people get what they deserve.

Another explanation is that stressed people might behave in ways that elicit negative social reactions. For example, it may be difficult for potential support providers to be around victims who engage in self-blame or expressions of negative affect (Coates, Wortman, & Abbey, 1979). Some victims might reject offers of support or have difficulty accessing support because of the way that they respond to stressors (i.e, being too withdrawn, inhibited, depressed, or helpless). In a study by Silver, Wortman, and Crofton (1990), it was observed that people who appear to be very well-adjusted or very poorly adjusted do not receive as much support as they need. Victims who appear well-adjusted and happy might not show the appropriate distress signals to others. It also may be discomforting to others when a victim appears to be unscathed by a traumatic experience, or supporters might perceive that the apparently nondistressed person does not need support. If a victim is extremely distressed, potential support providers can feel helpless or too highly distressed themselves when facing the victim, so they might avoid or withdraw from the person. Silver et al. (1990) also found, however, that people indicated that they would be willing to interact with, and would be comfortable with, victims who presented themselves as "balanced copers." Balanced copers are ones who admit their distress but also express optimism in coping with their problem.

The mechanisms of support deterioration can be quite complex. As noted earlier, the perceived and actual quality of social support can deteriorate because of supporters' reactions to victims or because of the dynamics between supporters and victims. There is also evidence that the structural elements of support networks (e.g., size, density, frequency of contact) can change under chronic stress. Access to support might be diminished by changes in the configuration of social networks in the context of chronic stressors, and changes in social networks might be an additional source of stress. For example, parents with a disabled child at home tend to be more socially isolated and to have less support than parents with a healthy child (Kazak & Wilcox, 1984). In addition, parents with a disabled child are more likely to have denser social networks (i.e., network members know one another to a greater degree) and to have more health care professionals in their networks (Kazak & Wilcox, 1984).

Social support also can diminish under chronic stress if the stressor has adverse effects on the support network. Some stressors have such a widespread impact that there is nobody available to support those who are most profoundly affected. Bereavement is a chronic stressor that has been characterized as a "social network crisis" (Vachon & Stylianos, 1988), in which the loss of a significant member of a social network can be distressing and debilitating to the entire group. Disasters, like floods, earthquakes, or war, also can affect entire communities. In a sample of elderly persons, Kaniasty and Norris (1993) found that following a severe flood, both the degree of personal loss and community-level destruction were associated with declines in social embeddedness, which, in turn, were associated with increases in psychological distress symptoms.

Interestingly, declines in social support do not inevitably contribute to increases in psychological distress. In the flood disaster study by Kaniasty and Norris (1993), degree of personal loss suffered during the flood was associated with a decrease in nonkin support, which was related to increases in psychological distress symptoms. Disaster stress also was related to decreases in support from kin, but these decreases did not appear to mediate the effects of disaster stress on psychological distress symptoms. These findings are interesting because they suggest that the mental health effects of support deterioration depend on other relationship qualities and expectations in relationships. Kaniasty and Norris argued that the negative psychological effects of decreases in nonkin support reveal the importance of companionate activities and the voluntary nature of the ties between the elderly subjects and nonkin.

Stress Transmission

Some stressful life events and situations can transmit their adverse effects to people indirectly by causing enduring and undesirable changes in their social environment. That is, stressful events can cause a ripple of chronic interpersonal stressors, thereby transmitting the stressor from one life domain to another. Norris and Uhl (1993) recently investigated how chronic stress in seven domains (e.g., marital, parental, filial, occupational, financial, ecological, physical) could mediate the effects of acute disaster stress (injury, life threat, property damage, and loss resulting from Hurricane Hugo) on psychological distress symptoms 1 year after the disaster. The chronic stressors they assessed primarily reflect difficulties and burdens in social roles. The investigators found that the level of acute stress experienced during Hurricane Hugo was positively associated with chronic stress, which, in turn, was positively associated with symptoms of psychological distress. More importantly, after statistically controlling for the effects of the chronic stress mediators, the association between the different acute disaster stressors and psychological distress outcomes generally disappeared. These latter findings suggest that the long-term, adverse psychological effects of the acute stressors caused by Hurricane Hugo were partly due to secondary, social-role stressors that arose in the wake of the disaster. Unfortunately, it is impossible to determine from Norris and Uhl's data which chronic stressors actually followed the hurricane and which ones preceded it, because the data are retrospective. However, the results are consistent with stress transmission.

Some life stressors can lead to chronic social stressors by transforming individuals' social roles. A wide range of normative life events, such as the birth of a child, retirement, marriage, and graduation from school, can alter or redefine one's social roles or cause one to assume a role that might be less satisfying or more demanding than a former role. For example, if a dual-career couple decides to have a child, they might have a lot of support from family and friends. However, if after the birth the mother is unable to return to her career because she is consumed by childcare demands, then the roles (i.e., behaviors, contributions, expectations) of the husband and wife may shift. These types of shifts may create tension in the couple, particularly if the husband or wife does not like the new role. When role transitions are not normative, such as widowhood at an early age, people may experience extraordinary levels of stress because they did not have time to prepare for the change or because they do not have peers who can empathize with their experience.

Summary

Research on victimization has shown that people's reactions to victims and victims' responses to stressors can undermine support processes. Chronic stressors can interfere with support processes by altering the configuration, or structural aspects, of social networks as well as the quality of support received from others. Over time, there may be changes in support providers' willingness or ability to give support, particularly if a stressed person does not show signs of recovery or if the stressor does not go away. Social networks might become "burned-out" when the support recipient is unreceptive to supportive efforts or when it seems futile to offer support because the stressful situation is insurmountable. The way that people adapt to chronic stressors also can undermine their social support. For example, withdrawal, inhibition of emotions, or hostility might preclude people from getting support or benefitting from it (cf. Evans & Lepore, 1993; Lepore, 1995b; Smith, 1992).

Sometimes support is not offered when needed because the stressful situation affects a wide range of people. During network crises, or large-scale disasters, people might not be able to help others because they are busy coping with their own problems or because the disaster destroys traditional social rituals and meeting places where support is exchanged. Declines in support appear to be associated with increases in psychological distress in some types of social relationships, but not in others. The mechanisms underlying this intriguing latter finding should be explored in future research.

Negative changes in the social environment, such as increases in social demands or social strains, are not uncommon following major life stressors. These negative changes can contribute to ongoing adjustment problems after the acute phase of the life stressor has passed. Indeed, the secondary effects of life events on social relationships may be more detrimental to people than the triggering event. When social roles and relationships change following non-normative life events (e.g., widowhood at an early age), they might be more distressing than normative life events. However, if normative life events (e.g., marriage) affect one's social role and relationships in unexpected ways, they too can be highly distressing.

CONCLUSION

This chapter has identified three general functions of the social environment in chronic stress processes: a direct source of chronic stress, a moderator of chronic stress, and a mediator of chronic stress. Here I will briefly summarize the main points of the chapter and note some implications for coping with chronic stress and for future research.

There are many roots of chronic social stressors. Some are deep in the bedrock of our collective cultural values and norms, far removed from any particular individual's control. Others are more proximal, emanating from diverse social relationships that are often voluntary, or at least nominally within a person's control. By investigating the social origins of chronic stress, it is possible to identify the groups of people in society who may be at greatest risk for exposure to chronic stressors. By examining the mechanisms through which people succumb to illness when exposed to various chronic social stressors, we might be able to develop social interventions to circumvent a number of health problems.

The social environment can indirectly affect human adjustment by moderating the effects of chronic stressors. Most research on the moderating influence of social relationships in the stress process has centered on the stress-buffering role of relationships on acute stress reactions. Relatively few studies have examined the stress-buffering potential of social support for people facing chronic stressors. There is some evidence that informal social support is beneficial to people facing chronic stressors, such as chronic illness or caregiving stress, but the evidence is subject to many alternative explanations. More carefully controlled, prospective longitudinal studies need to be conducted on the buffering potential of social support for people at various stages of exposure to chronic stressors. It is especially important that future investigations control for other nonequivalencies between high and low support populations that might explain differences in adjustment. In particular, it is important to control for variations in the stressor, such as its intensity, degree of long-term threat, and undesirability, since these contingencies may influence both the quality of people's social support and their adjustment. At least one study (Lepore et al., 1991) has shown that the buffering effect of social support may be short-lived. If this finding applies to a wider range of chronic stressors, such as caregiving and chronic illness, it may be necessary for people coping with such stressors to turn to alternative sources of support that are less prone to decay over time or take steps to provide extra support to the informal system to prevent it from becoming exhausted.

The social environment can also amplify reactions to a stressor. When social strains coincide with other chronic stressors, negative reactions to either the chronic stressor or to the social strains appear to be exaggerated. This stress amplification process was described in terms of the costs of coping: People coping with a chronic stressor may be less motivated or capable of coping with another irritant, or they may be more sensitized to the irritant (Lepore & Evans, 1996; Lepore & Miles, 1996). If social stressors intensify reactions to other chronic stressors, some subgroups of people in our society could be particularly vulnerable. For instance, chronic stressors, such as ongoing marital conflicts, could have a more adverse effect on people who live in very high-density social environments (e.g., crowded urban housing projects) or extremely isolated regions (e.g., rural farmers) than on those who are in moderate-density social environments (e.g., suburbs). Investigators who aggregate stressors, with the underlying assumption that multiple stressors have an additive effect on health outcomes, could miss a great deal of explainable individual variation in stress responses. Hence, rather than aggregating in this way, investigators could examine the independent and interactive effects of stressors among people who are exposed to different combinations of stressors (e.g., people with different levels of work- and marital-role stress).

Stressors can also lead to a cascade of changes in interpersonal relationships, ranging from declines in the quantity and quality of social support to increases in social conflicts and strains. Some stressors can be quick, point-in-time events, but can contribute to chronic stress because they create long-term, undesirable changes in people's social roles or relationships. More work of the sort described by O'Brien and DeLongis (Chapter 6, this volume) is needed to understand the interactional processes between victims of life stressors and their potential support providers that erode support processes and provoke social strains. It is clear that chronic stressors can effect dramatic changes in the conduct and character of social relationships over time.

Simple moderator models, which presume that the social environment is unaffected by stressors, may not capture the true nature of the social environment and its role in the chronic stress process. An underlying theme throughout this chapter is that chronic stressors can alter the social environment. To capture the dynamic quality of the social environment and interpersonal relationships in the context of chronic stress, it will be necessary to develop theoretical models that can account for changes in social relationships, research designs or methods of measurement that can assess changes in social relationships, and statistical models that are sensitive to change. Recent work that has examined changes in social relationships under conditions ranging from chronic crowding (Lepore et al., 1991) to ongoing parenting stress (Quittner, Gluekauf, & Jackson, 1990) to long-term disaster stress (Kaniasty & Norris, 1993) provides a starting point. Increasingly sophisticated methods of conducting and analyzing repeated measures data using diaries, electronic devices, and other means have greatly improved our potential to study the dynamic interplay between stressors and social processes (cf. Eckenrode & Bolger, 1995). Nevertheless, we are still far from understanding the general principles that determine changes in the quality of social relationships in the chronic stress process and from discerning those changes that are detrimental to health and well-being. These latter two topics should be a central focus in future research designed to explain how the social environment is implicated in chronic stress processes.

ACKNOWLEDGMENTS Preparation of this chapter was partially supported by a grant from the American Cancer Society (IRG-58-33) and National Institute of Mental Health (MH1-54217). I am grateful to Martha Alibali and Ben Gottlieb for their comments on an earlier draft of this chapter.

REFERENCES

BARON, R. S., CUTRONA, C. E., HICKLIN, D., RUSSELL, D. W., & LUBAROFF, D. M. (1990). Social support and immune function among spouses of cancer patients. *Journal of Personality and Social Psychology, 59,* 344–352.

BAUM, A., & PAULUS, P. B. (1987). Crowding. In D. Stokols & I. Altman (Eds.), *Handbook of environmental psychology* (pp. 533–570). New York: Wiley.

BELLE, D. (1982). The stress of caring: Women as providers of social support. In L. Goldberger & S. Breznitz (Eds.), *Handbook of stress: Theoretical and clinical aspects* (pp. 496–505). New York: Free Press.

BLOOM, J. R., & KESSLER, L. (1994). Emotional support following cancer: A test of the stigma and social activity hypothesis. *Journal of Health and Social Behavior, 35,* 118–133.

BOLGER, N., DELONGIS, A., KESSLER, R. C., & SCHILLING, E. A. (1989). Effects of daily stress on negative mood. *Journal of Personality and Social Psychology, 57,* 808–818.

COATES, D., WORTMAN, C. B., & ABBEY, A. (1979). Reactions to Victims. In I. H. Frieze, D. Bar-tal, & J. S. Carroll (Eds.), *New Approaches to social problems* (pp. 21–52). San Francisco, CA: Jossey-Bass.
COHEN, S., EVANS, G. W., STOKOLS, D., & KRANTZ, D. S. (1986). *Behavior, health, and environmental stress.* New York: Plenum.
COHEN, S., & MCKAY, G. (1984). Social support, stress, and the buffering hypothesis: A theoretical analysis. In A. Braum, S. E. Taylor, & J. E. Singer (Eds.), *Handbook of psychology and health* (pp. 253–267). Hillsdale, NJ: Lawrence Erlbaum.
COHEN, S., & WILLS, T. A. (1985). Stress, social support, and the buffering hypothesis. *Psychological Bulletin, 98,* 310–357.
CREED, F. (1987). Immigrant stress. *Stress Medicine, 3,* 185–192.
CUTRONA, C. E. (1990). Stress and social support: In search of optimal matching. *Journal of Social and Clinical Psychology, 9,* 3–14.
CUTRONA, C. E., & RUSSELL, D. (1990). Type of social support and specific stress: Toward a theory of optimal matching. In B. R. Sarason, I. G. Sarason, & G. R. Pierce (Eds.), *Social support: An interactional view* (pp. 319–366). New York: Wiley.
ECKENRODE, J., & BOLGER, N. (1995). Daily and within-day event measurement. In S. Cohen, R. Kessler, & L. Gordon (Eds.), *Measuring stress: A guide for health and social scientists* (pp. 80–101). New York: Oxford University Press.
ECKENRODE, J., & GORE, S. (1990). Stress and coping at the boundary of work and family. In J. Eckenrode & S. Gore (Eds.), *Stress between work and family* (pp. 1–16). New York: Plenum.
ECKENRODE, J., & GORE, S. (1981). Stressful events and social supports: The significance of context. In B. H. Gottlieb (Eds.), *Social networks and social support* (pp. 43–68). Beverly Hills, CA: Sage.
EVANS, G. W., & LEPORE, S. J. (1993). Household crowding and social support: A quasiexperimental analysis. *Journal of Personality and Social Psychology, 65,* 308–316.
EVANS, G. W., & LEPORE, S. J. (in press). Moderating and mediating processes in environment-behavior research. In G. T. Moore & R. W. Marans (Eds.), *Advances in environment, behavior, and design* (Vol. 4). New York: Plenum.
EVANS, G. W., LEPORE, S. J., & SCHROEDER, A. (1996). The role of interior design elements in human responses to crowding. *Journal of Personality and Social Psychology, 70,* 41–46.
FRABLE, D. E., BLACKSTONE, T., & SCHERBAUM, C. (1990). Marginal and mindful: Deviants in social interactions. *Journal of Personality and Social Psychology, 59,* 140–149.
FUNCH, D. P., & METTLIN, C. (1982). The role of support in relation to recovery from breast surgery. *Social Science and Medicine, 16*(1), 91–98.
GILLIGAN, C. P. (1982). *In a different voice: Psychological theory and women's development.* Cambridge, MA: Harvard University Press.
GOTTLIEB, B. H. (1992). Quandaries in translating support concepts to intervention. In H. O. F. Veiel & U. Baumann (Eds.), *The meaning and measurement of social support* (pp. 293–309). New York: Hemisphere.
HIBBARD, J. R., & POPE, C. R. (1992). Women's employment, social support, and mortality. *Women and Health, 18,* 119–133.
HINKLE, L. E. (1974). The effect of exposure to culture change, social change, and changes in interpersonal relationships on health. In B. S. Dohrenwend & B. P. Dohrenwend (Eds.), *Stressful life events: Their nature and effects* (pp. 9–44). New York: Wiley.
HOBFOLL, S. E., & VAUX, A. (1993). Social support: Social resources and social context. In L. Goldberger and S. Breznitz (Eds.), *Handbook of stress: Theoretical and clinical aspects* (pp. 685–705). New York: Free Press.
HOUSE, J. S. (1981). *Work stress and social support.* Reading, MA: Addison-Wesley.
HOUSE, J. S., LANDIS, K. R., & UMBERSON, D. (1989). Social relationships and health. *Science, 241,* 540–544.
JOHNSON, J. V., HALL, E. M., & THEORELL, T. (1989). Combined effects of job strain and social isolation on cardiovascular disease morbidity and mortality in a random sample of the Swedish male working population. *Scandinavian Journal of Work, 15,* 271–279.

KANIASTY, K., & NORRIS, F. H. (1993). A test of the social support deterioration model in the context of natural disaster. *Journal of Personality and Social Psychology, 64,* 395–408.

KAPLAN, J. R., ADAMS, M. R., CLARKSON, T. B., & KORITNIK, D. R. (1984). Psychosocial influences on female "protection" among cynomolgus macaques. *Atherosclerosis, 53,* 283–295.

KAPLAN, J. R., MANUCK, S. B., CLARKSON, T. B., LUSSO, F. M., & TAUB, D. M. (1982). Social status, environment, and atherosclerosis in cynomolgus monkeys. *Arteriosclerosis, 2,* 359–368.

KAZAK, A. E., & WILCOX, B. L. (1984). The structure and function of social support networks in families with handicapped children. *American Journal of Community Psychology, 12,* 645–661.

KESSLER, R. C., MCLEOD, J. D., & WETHINGTON, E. (1985). The costs of caring: A perspective on the relationships between sex and psychological distress. In I. G. Sarason, & B. R. Sarason (Eds.), *Social support: Theory, research and applications* (pp. 491–506). The Hague, the Netherlands: Martinus Nijhoff.

KIECOLT-GLASER, J. K., DYER, C. S., & SHUTTLEWORTH, E. C. (1988). Upsetting social interactions and distress among Alzheimer's disease family caregivers: A replication and extension. *American Journal of Community Psychology, 16,* 825–837.

KIECOLT-GLASER, J. K., & GLASER, R. (1991). Stress and immune function in humans. In R. Ader, D. L. Felten, & N. Cohen (Eds.), *Psychoneuroimmunology* (2nd edition) (pp. 849–867). New York: Academic Press.

KIECOLT-GLASER, J. K., GLASER, R., DYER, C., SHUTTLEWORTH, E., OGROCKI, P., & SPEICHER, C. E. (1987). Chronic stress and immunity in family caregivers of Alzheimer's disease victims. *Psychosomatic Medicine, 49,* 523–535.

KRUPAT, E. (1985). *People in cities.* New York: Cambridge.

LANGER, E., FISKE, S., TAYLOR, S., & CHANOWITZ, B. (1976). Stigma, staring, and discomfort: A novel-stimulus hypothesis. *Journal of Experimental Psychology, 12,* 451–463.

LEPORE, S. J. (1992). Social conflict, social support, and psychological distress: Evidence of cross-domain buffering. *Journal of Personality and Social Psychology, 63,* 857–867.

LEPORE, S. J. (1994). Crowding: Effects on health and behavior. In V. S. Ramachandran (Ed.), *Encyclopedia of human behavior* (Vol. 2, pp. 43–51). San Diego, CA: Academic Press.

LEPORE, S. J. (1995a). Measurement of chronic stressors. In S. Cohen, R. Kessler, & L. Gordon (Eds.), *Measuring stress: A guide for health and social scientists* (pp. 102–120). New York: Oxford University Press.

LEPORE, S. J. (1995b). Cynicism, social support, and cardiovascular reactivity. *Health Psychology, 14,* 210–216.

LEPORE, S. J., ALLEN, K. A. M., & EVANS, G. W. (1992). Social support lowers cardiovascular reactivity to an acute stressor. *Psychosomatic Medicine, 55,* 518–524.

LEPORE, S. J., & EVANS, G. W. (1996). Coping with multiple stressors in the environment. In M. Zeidner & N. Endler (Eds.), *Handbook of coping: Theory, research, and applications* (pp. 350–377). New York: Wiley.

LEPORE, S. J., EVANS, G. W., & PALSANE, M. N. (1991). Social hassles and psychological health in the context of chronic crowding. *Journal of Health and Social Behavior, 32,* 357–367.

LEPORE, S. J., EVANS, G. W., & SCHNEIDER, M. L. (1991). Dynamic role of social support in the link between chronic stress and psychological distress. *Journal of Personality and Social Psychology, 61,* 899–909.

LEPORE, S. J., EVANS, G. W., & SCHNEIDER, M. L. (1992). Role of control and social support in explaining the stress of hassles and crowding. *Environment and Behavior, 24,* 795–811.

LEPORE, S. J., & MILES, H. J. (1996, March). *Chronic stressors increase cardiovascular reactivity to acute stressors.* Paper presented at the Fourth International Congress of Behavioral Medicine, Washington, DC.

LEPORE, S. J., SILVER, R. C., WORTMAN, C. B., & WAYMENT, H. A. (1996). Social constraints, intrusive thoughts, and depressive symptoms among bereaved mothers. *Journal of Personality and Social Psychology, 70,* 271–282.

LERNER, M. J., & MILLER, D. T. (1978). Just world research and the attribution process: Looking back and ahead. *Psychological Bulletin, 85,* 1030–1051.

LIN, N., & WESTCOTT, J. (1991). Marital engagement/disengagement, social networks, and mental health. In J. Eckenrode (Ed.), *The social context of coping* (pp. 213–238). New York: Plenum.

LIPOWSKI, Z. J. (1975). Sensory and information inputs overload: Behavioral effects. *Comprehensive Psychiatry, 16,* 199–221.

MILGRAM, S. (1970). The experience of living in cities. *Science, 167,* 1461–1468.

NORRIS, F. H., & UHL, G. A. (1993). Chronic stress as a mediator of acute stress: The case of Hurricane Hugo. *Journal of Applied and Social Psychology, 23,* 1263–1284.

NORTHOUSE, L. L. (1988). Social support in patients' and husbands' adjustment to breast cancer. *Nursing Research, 37*(2), 91–95.

OLSEN, R. B., OLSEN, J., GUNNER-SVENSSON, F., & WALDSTRON, B. (1991). Social networks and longevity. A 14 year follow-up study among elderly in Denmark. *Social Science and Medicine, 33,* 1189–1195.

ORTH-GOMER, K., ROSENGREN, A., & WILHELMSON, L. (1993). Lack of social support and incidence of coronary heart disease in middle-aged Swedish men. *Psychosomatic Medicine, 55,* 37–43.

PEARLIN, L. I. (1982). The social contexts of stress. In L. Goldberger & S. Breznitz (Eds.), *Handbook of stress: Theoretical and clinical aspects* (pp. 367–379). New York: Free Press.

PEARLIN, L. I. (1989). The sociological study of stress. *Journal of Health and Social Behavior, 30,* 241–256.

PEARLIN, L. I., LIEBERMAN, M., MENAGHAN, E., & MULLAN, J. (1981). The stress process. *Journal of Health and Social Behavior, 22,* 337–356.

PEPLAU, L. A., & PERLMAN, D. (Eds.) (1982). *Loneliness: A sourcebook of current theory, research and therapy.* New York: Wiley–Interscience.

QUITTNER, A. L., GLUEKAUF, R. L., & JACKSON, D. N. (1990). Chronic parenting stress: Moderating versus mediating effects of social support. *Journal of Personality and Social Psychology, 59*(6), 1266–1278.

REPETTI, R. L. (1993). The effects of workload and the social environment at work on health. In L. Goldberger & S. Breznitz (Eds.), *Handbook of stress: Theoretical and clinical aspects* (2nd ed.) (pp. 368–385). New York: Free Press.

ROGLER, L. H. (1994). International migrations: A framework for directing research. *American Psychologist, 49,* 701–708.

ROOK, K. (1984). Interventions for loneliness: A review and analysis. In L. A. Peplau & S. E. Goldston (Eds.), *Preventing the harmful consequences of severe and persistent loneliness* (DHHS Publication No. 84-1312, pp. 47–80). Washington, DC: US Government Printing Office.

ROOK, K. S., & DOOLEY, D. (1985). Applying social support research: Theoretical problems and future directions. *Journal of Social Issues, 41,* 5–28.

SCHONPFLUG, W. (1986). Behavior economics as an approach to stress theory. In M. H. Appley & R. Trumbull (Eds.), *Dynamics of stress: Physiological, psychological, and social perspectives* (pp. 81–98). New York: Plenum.

SCHULZ, R., & TOMPKINS, C. (1990). Life events and changes in social relationships: Examples, mechanisms, and measurement. *Journal of Social and Clinical Psychology, 9,* 69–77.

SEEMAN, T. E., BERKMAN, L. F., KOHOUT, F., LACROIX, A., GLYNN, R., & BLAZER, D. (1993). Intercommunity variations in the association between social ties and mortality in the elderly. A comparative analysis of three communities. *Annals of Epidemiology, 3,* 325–335.

SHINN, M., LEHMANN, S., & WONG, N. W. (1984). Social interaction and social support. *Journal of Social Issues, 40,* 55–76.

SILVER, R. L., WORTMAN, C. B., & CROFTON, C. (1990). The role of coping in support provision: The self-presentational dilemma of victims in life crises. In B. R. Sarason, I. G. Sarason, & G. R. Pierce (Eds.), *Social support: An interactional view* (pp. 397–426). New York: Wiley.

SMITH, T. W. (1992). Hostility and health: Current status of a psychosomatic hypothesis. *Health Psychology, 11,* 139–150.

Sugisawa, H., Liang, J., & Liu, X. (1994). Social networks, social support, and mortality among older people in Japan. *Journal of Gerontology, 49*, 3–13.

Thoits, P. A. (1982). Social support as coping assistance. *Journal of Clinical and Consulting Psychology, 54*, 416–423.

Thoits, P. A. (1986). Conceptual, methodological, and theoretical problems in studying social support as a buffer against life stress. *Journal of Health and Social Behavior, 23*, 145–159.

Vachon, M. L. S., & Stylianos, S. K. (1988). The role of social support in bereavement. *Journal of Social Issues, 44*(3), 175–190.

Veiel, H. O. F. (1992). Some cautionary notes on the buffer effect. In H. O. F. Veiel and U. Bauman (Eds.), *The meaning and measurement of social support*. New York: Hemisphere.

Wheaton, B. (August, 1991). *Chronic stressors: Models and measurement*. Paper presented at the Society for Social Problems Meeting, Cincinnati, Ohio.

6

Coping with Chronic Stress
An Interpersonal Perspective

TESS BYRD O'BRIEN and ANITA DeLONGIS

Whether chronic stress stems from persistent relationship difficulties, shared adversities, or personal problems, the hardships associated with it rarely stop at one person's doorstep. Most often, chronic stress exerts widespread effects on the lives of entire families and other close intimates (Flor, Turk, & Scholz, 1987; Gottlieb, 1987; Stephens, Crowther, Hobfoll, & Tennenbaum, 1990). For many months or even years at a time, all those affected must find ways to cope. The consequences of one person's coping generally reverberate far beyond the confines of the individual (Pearlin, 1991). The coping of one family member may facilitate, constrict, or interfere with the coping efforts of loved ones. In turn, the expectations, emotional reactions, and coping actions of loved ones may influence the individual's appraisals and attempts to cope. Family members labor not only with their own distress but also with the distress of their loved ones. Finding ways to maintain personal well-being while simultaneously trying to address the needs of loved ones is one of the supreme challenges that people face when coping with chronic stress (Coyne & Smith, 1991; DeLongis & O'Brien, 1990).

If our models of chronic stress consider only individual coping and well-being, we may fail to develop an understanding of how the interper-

---

TESS BYRD O'BRIEN and ANITA DeLONGIS • Department of Psychology, University of British Columbia, Vancouver, British Columbia V6T 1Z4.

Coping with Chronic Stress, edited by Benjamin H. Gottlieb. Plenum Press, New York, 1997.

sonal context affects individual appraisals, coping, and coping outcomes (Pearlin, 1991). When the individual's perceptions and coping processes are considered in a social vacuum, we may unwittingly create an illusion that people generally adapt to chronic stress in an autonomous, solitary fashion, and we may be more likely to view adaptational problems as primarily a function of personality, faulty perceptions, or a lack of personal initiative. More importantly, an individualistic focus may obscure our understanding of interpersonal processes, such as negotiation, collaboration, accommodation, and affective sharing, which may be central to managing chronic stress in interpersonal contexts.

In this chapter, we offer a conceptualization of coping that spotlights interpersonal processes involved in managing chronic stress. We examine dyadic patterns of coping and their significance for personal and relationship well-being, assess the interpersonal consequences of particular forms of coping, explore the interplay between coping and support processes, and specify interpersonal functions and dimensions of coping. We focus on an interpersonal function of coping that has garnered increasing attention in the literature: relationship-focused coping (e.g., Coyne & Smith, 1991; DeLongis & O'Brien, 1990; Kramer, 1993a; Lepore, Chapter 5, this volume; Lyons, Sullivan, & Ritvo, 1995; O'Brien & DeLongis, 1996; Revenson, 1994). Relationship-focused coping consists of coping efforts geared toward managing and maintaining relationships during stressful periods. We will emphasize empathic coping as one mode of relationship-focused coping that may be of special significance to families who face the challenges of chronic stress. The studies reviewed in this chapter illustrate the importance of interpersonal processes in determining numerous aspects of adjustment to chronic stress, including the selection and efficacy of coping strategies, the persistence of coping efforts, and the impact of stress on physical and psychological well-being.

THE INTERPERSONAL CONTEXT OF COPING

To illustrate the interpersonal nature of stress and coping processes within families under chronic stress, we review literature that spans a variety of chronic stressors that couples or families face, including having a family member with a chronic illness or disability, the death of a child, stepfamily strains, and chronic relationship difficulties.

Sources of Strain in Chronic Stress Contexts

A growing body of work suggests that interpersonal stressors have a particularly deleterious effect on well-being (e.g., Baumeister & Leary,

1995; Bolger, DeLongis, Kessler, & Schilling, 1989; Kiecolt-Glaser, Dyer, & Shuttleworth, 1988; Pagel, Erdly, & Becker, 1987; Schuster, Kessler, & Aseltine, 1990). Bolger et al. (1989) found that interpersonal stressors, such as marital conflict or tension with friends or coworkers, were important predictors of personal distress, accounting for more than 80% of the explained variance in mood. Further testifying to the impact of interpersonal stressors, increasing evidence indicates that upsetting interactions with family and social network members play a significant role in the etiology and maintenance of depression and other emotional difficulties among those coping with chronic stress (Beach, Sandeen, & O'Leary, 1990; Fince & Zautra, 1992; Fiore, Coppel, Becker, & Cox, 1986; Kiecolt-Glaser et al., 1988; Rook, 1990). Moreover, changes in levels of distressing social interactions over time predict changes in levels of depression (Pagel et al., 1987).

Although some chronic stress situations may be directly attributable to poor quality relationships, increased family or social network conflict is often the result of chronic stress (Rook, 1990; Sheehan & Nuttall, 1988; Zautra & Manne, 1992). This heightened conflict may ensue from the increased day-to-day strains involved in managing chronic stress. In turn, the resultant interpersonal tension may diminish each family member's ability to adapt within a chronic stress context.

Many chronic stressors affect several members of a family or social network simultaneously. In such cases, family members may be less able to provide support to one another (Coyne, Wortman, & Lehman, 1988; DeLongis & O'Brien, 1990; Gottlieb & Wagner, 1991). Consequently, individuals may be compelled to seek other sources of support. Such support-seeking may, in and of itself, be an additional source of strain. Formal sources of support may not be readily available, accessible, or appealing to the individual (Zarit & Pearlin, 1993). Building new relationships or finding others outside of one's support network to provide support may not be easy.

In conceptualizing the stress and coping processes of couples and families in chronic stress contexts, we consider the metaconstructs of agency and communion to have particular heuristic value (e.g., Bakan, 1966; Helgeson, 1993, 1994; Wiggins & Trapnell, 1996). The metaconstruct of agency encompasses strivings for independence, mastery, power, competency, achievement, instrumentality, and task completion. The metaconstruct of communion encompasses strivings for intimacy, love, emotional relatedness, connectedness, friendship, communality, solidarity, belongingness, and relationship maintenance. Recently, these metaconstructs have been used to develop typologies to classify a diverse set of constructs (see Wiggins & Trapnell, 1996, for a review). For example, Moskowitz (1993) has classified situations according to whether they involve work (agentic) versus family and friends (communal).

We have recently used an agentic-communal typology to classify stressors (O'Brien & DeLongis, 1996). We found that whether the stressful situation described by our study participants was primarily agentic versus communal in nature tended to account for a much larger proportion of the variance in coping responses than did dimensions of personality (i.e., neuroticism, extraversion, openness to experience, agreeableness, and conscientiousness). The agentic versus communal nature of the situation accounted for between 2 and 48% of the variance in coping responses, depending upon the type of coping predicted in the model. In addition, there were significant person X situation interactions predicting coping responses, further suggesting the utility of these constructs for stress research.

Many sources of chronic stress threaten both agentic and communal aspects of life. For example, those who care for a family member with Alzheimer's disease may face a beleaguering number of agentic demands, such as the instrumental tasks of providing around-the-clock supervision and physical care for their loved one, increased financial strains due to loss of wages or increased medical costs, and the instrumental tasks involved in maintaining their households and caring for dependent children (DeLongis & O'Brien, 1990). They also may face increased interpersonal or communal demands, such as dealing with the emotional distress of family members, increased family conflicts, trying to mobilize social support, and maintaining their relationships with each other amidst the strain of providing constant care for their ill family member. Caregivers also face the loss of the supportive aspects of their prior relationship with the ill family member as the person's cognitive and physical capabilities diminish.

Dyadic Patterns of Coping and Their Significance for Well-Being

There are several ways that coping in chronic stress contexts may increase interpersonal conflict or tension. Conflict may ensue when one person's coping hinders the coping efforts of another person. Increased tension may also occur when one person's coping negatively affects another person's well-being. Mismatches in coping approaches among family members may also heighten interpersonal tensions. For example, it is not uncommon for couples to present in marital therapy with chronic relationship problems that appear to be maintained by the couple's differences in coping with the problem. One spouse (most often the husband) tends to rely on avoidance strategies (e.g., distancing, withdrawal, escape–avoidance) to deal with marital conflict, while the other spouse (most often the wife) tends to rely on approach strategies (e.g., attempts to seek intimacy, confrontation, "pursuing"). Christensen and Shenk (1991) found this mismatching pattern of dyadic coping with marital conflict to be more common among couples who are maritally distressed or divorcing than among nondistressed couples. More generally, although facing a chronic stressor together as a couple or as a family may be a source of solace, it may also become an additional source of strain when coping efforts among couples or families are incompatible. When others are involved in the stressful context, definitions of coping efficacy must be construed more broadly than in terms of individual well-being. Marital satisfaction, family functioning, and the well-being of the individual's spouse, children, and other network members must all be considered.

Although there have been relatively few dyadic coping studies reported in the literature, the results of a handful of studies have advanced our understanding of interpersonal processes in coping. One finding that has emerged from such studies is that strategies that are beneficial to the individual's well-being are not necessarily beneficial to the individual's spouse, and vice versa. Particularly when loved ones are affected by the individual's coping efforts, the efficacy of an individual's coping cannot be determined outside of his or her social context. Stern and Pascale (1979), for example, found that myocardial infarction (MI) patients who denied the seriousness of their illnesses were less anxious, less depressed, and more likely to carry out their usual role responsibilities than were those who did not engage in denial. However, their wives were more prone to depression than were the wives of nondeniers.

Studies such as these raise important issues. What criteria do we use to determine coping effectiveness? Can we really say that a particular strategy that improves the well-being of the individual is effective if it is associated with deleterious consequences for the individual's loved ones? Further complicating the picture are the studies that we will discuss next, which indicate that an individual may cope in a manner that has a positive impact on the spouse but a negative impact on one's self. In addition to providing a more complex picture of coping efficacy, studies of dyadic coping also render a richer understanding of interpersonal factors that may lead people to cope in ways that diminish their own well-being, the well-being of loved ones, or the well-being of their relationships.

Gottlieb and Wagner's (1991) study of the parents of children who have a serious chronic illness (i.e., cystic fibrosis or juvenile diabetes) illustrates that coping responses may be constrained by the reactions of other family members. They found that husbands actively attempted to alter their wives' coping when it clashed with their own coping. Husbands who relied on autonomous emotional self-control coping strategies (e.g., stoic acceptance, keeping feelings to oneself, denial, or distraction) verbally pressured their wives to inhibit interpersonally oriented coping efforts that involved emotional expression and seeking emotional intimacy. Over time, to smooth their relationships, wives adopted a more stoic stance in the presence of their husbands. They hid their emotional distress from their husbands and even shielded their husbands from bad news about their child's health status. However, as their public and private efforts to manage their emotions became more discrepant, wives reported greater psychological distress as well as a growing sense of emotional isolation and resentment. In acquiescing to their husband's demands to avoid emotional expression, wives may have maintained their marriages, but they forfeited their husbands as a source of emotional intimacy. When the coping between spouses is marked by a lack of emotional intimacy and emotional acceptance, the quality of the marriage may be sorely diminished (Coyne & DeLongis, 1986). Previous research indicates that when a spouse is unavailable to offer support as a confidant, support from other sources does not adequately fill the void (Brown & Harris, 1978; Coyne & DeLongis, 1986).

Coyne and Smith (1991) and Smith and Coyne (1988) also found that patterns of spousal coping that thwart emotional intimacy may have deleterious consequences, at least for women. These researchers have examined the use of coping strategies that are geared toward protecting and buffering another person from stress. Protective buffering strategies included hiding worries and concerns from one's spouse and attempting to avoid conflict by yielding to one's spouse. These investigators found that the use of such strategies by wives of MI patients was associated with enhanced self-efficacy for the husbands. The opposite effect was found for their wives, however. The impact of both their own and their husbands' protective buffering was to increase the wives' distress. These findings suggest that those who gear their coping efforts toward protecting the well-being of a loved one may not always benefit themselves. Although there may be personal costs involved in trying to protect the well-being of others, individuals may choose to shoulder these costs if their relationships are threatened or if their loved ones' well-being is at stake.

The constructs of unmitigated agency and unmitigated communion (Helgeson, 1994) are relevant to understanding the coping dynamics among spouses that were reported in the preceding studies. Helgeson

(1994) reviews evidence suggesting that negative consequences occur when a person's agentic orientation to life is not balanced by an adaptive communal orientation, and vice versa. More specifically, the construct of unmitigated agency refers to an extreme agentic orientation that promotes an intense focus upon the self to the exclusion of communion with others. Unmitigated communion refers to an extreme communal orientation that promotes both an intensive focus upon others and the maintaining of relationships to the exclusion of personal agency and self-protection. Helgeson suggests that unmitigated agency is associated with an egoistic power motivation that leads to a relentless promotion of one's self-interests and to acts of aggression and hostility. In contrast, unmitigated communion is associated with a power motivation to exert control over one's relationships and others' lives and to keep others dependent on the individual. Having an extreme communal orientation is thought to lead to acts of overprotection and emotional overinvolvement. Helgeson posits that people with a more extreme or unmitigated communal orientation would be likely to provide support for others, but not to seek support from others in times of need. We speculate that people who take an unmitigated communal approach to coping with the distress of others would tend to engage in support attempts that ultimately fail to help the intended recipient. This may occur because these support providers may have an excessive investment in others following their advice.

Helgeson suggests that a less extreme communal orientation is associated with an intimacy motivation and a "surrender of manipulative control." In the dyadic coping studies previously discussed, the shielding of emotions and hiding of concerns may reflect a more extreme or unmitigated communal approach to coping because these attempts to protect the spouse and the marriage thwart emotional intimacy. It should be noted that the wives in Gottlieb and Wagner's study indicated a clear preference for coping with their negative emotions by seeking emotional intimacy with their husbands. However, the husbands' responses to the wives' emotional expression discouraged the wives from persisting in their attempts to gain emotional support and understanding from their husbands. The husbands' persistence in coping via self-control, taken together with their relentless attempts to redirect their wives' coping to suit their own stoic coping preferences, may reflect an unmitigated agentic approach to coping. Individual differences in the extent to which each partner engages in agentic and communal patterns of coping may be an important cause of coping clashes among spouses.

One recent study has examined the impact of agentic and communal orientations on the psychological adjustment of men recovering from their first coronary event (Helgeson, 1993). This study found that nonextreme levels of agency were associated with better adjustment among patients, and nonextreme levels of communion were associated with better partner adjustment among both patients and their spouses. The couples who tended to be most distressed consisted of a husband who had an unmitigated agentic orientation and a wife who had an unmitigated communal orientation. Clearly, one avenue for future research that might be usefully explored is the adaptational significance of coping patterns that are characterized by unmitigated attempts to promote one's self-interests or to control relationships and other people's lives. More research is also needed to distinguish patterns of coping that have an adaptive agentic and communal orientation from patterns of coping that may reflect more extreme or maladaptive orientations.

Findings from our studies of dyadic coping (DeLongis, Bolger, & Kessler, 1987) are consistent with the findings of Helgeson (1993). Our results suggest that the coping strategy employed by any one member of a family system has a tendency to reverberate through the system—not only in terms of its impact on others' coping but also in terms of its impact on others' well-being. In our studies of community-residing married couples, we have examined two patterns of dyadic coping: symmetrical coping and complementary coping (Bateson, 1972). Symmetrical coping occurs when one spouse's coping spurs the other spouse to engage in the same type of coping (e.g., positive reappraisal elicits positive reappraisal). Complementary coping occurs when one spouse's coping spurs the other spouse to engage in a different, counteractive form of coping (e.g., confrontation elicits withdrawal).

The results of these studies (Daylen, 1993; DeLongis, Bolger, & Kessler, 1987) indicate that, in coping with marital tension, the use of a given coping strategy by one spouse tends to evoke the same strategy from the other spouse. For example, compromise begets compromise, and confrontation often begets confrontation. Further, these data suggest that the effect of dyadic coping on the individual's well-being is synergistic. For example, when husbands engaged in confrontation, they tended to experience an increase in distress. Wives' use of confrontation was also associated with increases in husbands' distress, even after controlling for the husbands' own use of confrontation and prior levels of distress. When both spouses used confrontation simultaneously, the increase in their distress was multiplicative. Alternatively, when both spouses engaged in compromise strategies, it generally had a positive effect on both of their moods. However, if one spouse attempted to compromise and the other engaged in confrontation or withdrawal, the effect of using compromise (on the mood of the person who engaged in compromise) tended to be negative. Thus, some coping strategies may be effective only when the spouse or partner uses the same or a similarly constructive form of coping. Consequently, the effectiveness of any given coping strategy may be determined, in part, by the coping responses of others in the chronic stress context. In the next section, we will discuss further ways that coping may be influenced by close relationships.

The Role of Close Relationships in Coping and Well-Being

In a study of parents coping with the loss of an infant (DeLongis, Silver, & Wortman, 1986), the responses of close friends and family members to the parents' efforts to cope with their grief by expressing their emotions predicted several aspects of the parents' coping. When close others' responses lacked empathy and reflected efforts to minimize the parents' loss, bereaved parents exhibited both a reduced desire to cope via emotional expression and a decline in coping effort over time. Further, nonempathic responses from others during the first month after the infant's death were associated with higher levels of depression 18 months later, even after controlling for prior levels of depression. Examples of nonempathic responses included telling parents that they were lucky that it happened now instead of later when the child was older, saying that the parents could always have other children, or suggesting that the infant's death was "God's will." In contrast, empathic responses from others that invited emotional sharing were associated with declines in the level of depression. These findings suggest that the efficacy of coping efforts may be heavily determined by the nature of others' responses. When such coping efforts are blocked or disrupted by the actions of others, individual distress may rise and adjustment may become a slower, more arduous process.

Even when individuals do not rely on coping strategies that require a loved one's participation, the strategies that people choose may be influenced by the degree of support that they receive from others in the stressful context. For example, among women with rheumatoid arthritis (RA), Manne and Zautra (1989) found that spousal criticism and support were differentially related to the women's coping. In their study, spousal criticism was assessed in interviews with the husband and operationalized as the number of complaints that the husband made about the negative impact that his wife's illness had on his life. Women with critical spouses were more likely to cope with their disease via wishful thinking. In turn, higher levels of wishful thinking were associated with higher psychological distress and lower well-being in the women. Conversely, women who reported more supportive behaviors from their husbands were more likely to cope with their disease via information-seeking and cognitive restructuring, which in turn were associated with lower distress and higher well-being. These findings suggest that spouses who have a negative orientation to the stressful situation may inadvertently foster their partner's use of more solitary, maladaptive forms of coping. In contrast, spousal support may increase a person's sense of agency and spur more proactive ways of managing the chronic stress.

Findings from our study of chronic stress among stepfamilies also illustrate the impact of others' responses on coping (O'Brien, DeLongis, & Campbell, 1997). We examined dyadic patterns of stress, coping, and support via structured interviews and structured daily diaries. Common sources of stress reported by the 150 stepfamilies in our study included conflicts between spouses about how to discipline and raise children and stepchildren, competing demands between meeting the needs of one's own children and the needs of stepchildren, child visitation issues, conflicts between biological children and stepchildren, and conflicts between stepparents and stepchildren. In examining the interrelations between coping and spousal support, we found that in stressful family situations where wives were disappointed with their husband's response to the situations, the wives coped by using more wishful thinking and confrontation. In turn, the use of these coping strategies was associated with increases in marital tension, family tension, and psychological distress, even after controlling for prior levels of these variables. Further, we (Morris, O'Brien, DeLongis, & Campbell, 1995) found that stepparents who reported low levels of support from family and friends were more inclined to engage in ruminative coping. The use of ruminative coping was associated with higher levels of depression at the follow-up interview 2 years later. These findings suggest that when support is lacking from significant others, individuals may be less able to cope effectively and more likely to engage in maladaptive or counterproductive modes of coping that have negative repercussions for their own well-being and for their marital and family relationships.

Not only do others' responses appear to influence the coping of the individual, but recent evidence also indicates that even anticipating a negative response from others can deter individuals from using particular coping strategies. For example, Pearlin and McCall (1990) found that when individuals anticipated criticism or other negative responses from family members, they were less likely to cope with their difficulties by seeking support from those family members. No doubt the anticipation of a negative response from others is based on experience with them in past stressful situations. It is not surprising that the prior quality of various family relationships has emerged as a significant predictor of coping and well-being within chronic stress contexts (Burman & Margolin, 1992; Kramer, 1993b). The prior relationship history and experience with loved ones in past stressful situations may enable individuals to discern the expectations of others and to anticipate others' emotional responses and coping tendencies. This accrued knowledge may influence appraisals of the current situation and coping, in that individuals may try to forecast on the basis of past experience what coping strategies may or may not work in the current situation with this family member or close tie (DeLongis & O'Brien, 1990). When the past behaviors of family members or other close ties create negative expectations, a vicious cycle of interpersonal tension, maladaptive coping, and heightened distress may ensue and prevent the resolution of the stressful situation.

Taken together, these studies underscore the significance of family and other close relationships in determining both the manner in which people cope and the effects that these coping strategies have on well-being. Given the deleterious impact of negative interpersonal interactions on emotional well-being and the significance of social relationships for health (Burman & Margolin, 1992; House, Umberson, & Landis, 1988), an examination of both relationship-disrupting modes of coping and relationship-sustaining modes of coping is needed. Modes of coping that damage relationships with others or negatively affect others may lead to not only diminished support and cooperation from those involved in the present stressful episode, but also to a long-term reduction of available support and cooperation in future stressful encounters (DeLongis & O'Brien, 1990; Lane & Hobfoll, 1992). Over time, the breakdown of supportive coping alliances among family members may perpetuate a chronic state of interpersonal tension and dissatisfaction, evoke coercive or maladaptive attempts to regain interpersonal support (Beach et al., 1990; Coyne et al., 1988), and diminish the ability of others to positively influence the individual's appraisal and coping processes (DeLongis & O'Brien, 1990).

The Role of Coping in Disrupting Relationships and Diminishing Support

Lane and Hobfoll (1992) examined stress and support processes among people with chronic obstructive pulmonary disease. They found that when their respondents managed their emotions by displaying irritability or venting anger to significant others, the significant others experienced heightened anger themselves and over time offered less support to the respondents. These findings indicate that forms of coping that alienate or distress others may alter the quality of relationships and lead others to withdraw support, leaving the individual more isolated in facing the tides of chronic adversity.

Additional research suggests that when individuals cope by engaging in angry, combative attempts to alter the situation, their own well-being and the well-being of their relationships are diminished. The use of confrontive coping has been repeatedly linked with negative psychological outcomes for the individual engaging in confrontation (Daylen, 1993; Folkman & Lazarus, 1988; Folkman, Lazarus, Dunkel-Schetter, DeLongis, & Gruen, 1986). We have found that the use of confrontation is also associated with negative interpersonal consequences. In our study of stepfamilies, the use of confrontive coping predicted higher levels of family and marital tension (Maris, 1993; O'Brien et al., 1997). Further, the use of confrontive coping by wives predicted higher levels of depression and disappointment with their husbands' responses to them (O'Brien et al., 1997). Not surprisingly, when both spouses engaged in confrontive coping, the increase in both marital tension and personal distress (O'Brien et al., 1997) was significantly greater than if only one of them had used it.

Individuals who use confrontive coping and other coping strategies involving the expression of anger may be able to coerce others into acquiescing to their position or into doing what is needed to solve the immediate problem. Nonetheless, the gains of using confrontational strategies may be outweighed by the injurious interpersonal consequences. At times, the use of confrontive coping may be spurred by a sense of commitment to improving the relationship by forcefully making other people aware of dissatisfaction and complaints. However, an excessive use of this strategy may antagonize others and cause them to respond in a way that perpetuates a coercive pattern of communication. Confrontive coping may also propel others to distance themselves from their relationship partners in an effort to avoid the unpleasantness of such exchanges (Beach et al., 1990). Consequently, with its potential to harm the relationship and to diminish the support and cooperation provided by those involved, a pronounced reliance upon confrontive coping strategies, particularly in family contexts, may contribute to both short-term and long-term problems of adaptation.

Collectively, these findings suggest that when individuals cope in ways that threaten their closeness with others, they may diminish their social resources for managing chronic stress. Clearly, the role of social relationships in determining well-being points to the importance of fostering ways of coping that sustain, rather than damage, those relationships. In the next section, we discuss how the ways that people regulate their family relationships and other important social relationships may play a pivotal role in managing chronic stress.

RELATIONSHIP-FOCUSED COPING: SUSTAINING SOCIAL RELATIONSHIPS DURING PERIODS OF CHRONIC STRESS

There is a general consensus in the coping literature that coping serves at least two basic functions (Endler & Parker, 1990; Folkman, Lazarus, Dunkel-Schetter et al., 1986; Folkman, Lazarus, Gruen, & DeLongis, 1986; Lazarus & Folkman, 1984): (1) a problem-focused function that denotes active attempts to alter and resolve the stressful situation and (2) an emotion-focused function that encompasses efforts to regulate one's emotions. In addition, the conceptualization of coping has been recently expanded to include coping efforts that serve an interpersonal regulation function. We and others have termed this function relationship-focused coping (Coyne & Smith, 1991; DeLongis & O'Brien, 1990). Relationship-focused coping refers to modes of coping that are aimed at managing, regulating, or preserving relationships during stressful periods (DeLongis & O'Brien, 1990; O'Brien & DeLongis, 1996). Such coping involves efforts to manage and sustain social relationships during stressful periods. Particularly when chronic stressors affect couples and families, successful coping may involve not only solving problems and managing emotions but also maintaining and protecting social relationships.

Our research has examined several forms of coping that are involved in maintaining relationships. In initial attempts to construct measures of relationship-focused coping, we specified three facets: intrapsychic empathic processes, conveying empathic understanding and support to others, and compromise. Relationship-focused items were drawn from the empathy literature, the social support literature, and the close relationships literature. Factor analyses from two separate populations, namely undergraduates and stepfamilies, have provided initial support for relationship-focused coping as a distinct function of coping. Relationship-focused coping items loaded separately from emotion-focused and problem-focused items in both samples (O'Brien, 1992; O'Brien et al., 1997). Further, relationship-focused, emotion-focused, and problem-focused forms of coping were differentially associated with individual difference and situational variables, as well as with indices of psychological distress and well-being.

Because the intercorrelations between intrapsychic empathic strategies and empathic communication strategies were high and the pattern of results with these two facets were very similar, we combined these two subscales into one scale, which we termed *empathic responding* (O'Brien & DeLongis, 1996). We chose to keep compromise as a separate subscale because the pattern of results with this facet differed from the other two facets. Having discussed findings regarding compromise in a previous section, we turn to a discussion of empathic coping in the next section.

Empathic Coping

The need for belongingness and the desire to form and maintain strong affective bonds with others is a fundamental human motivation that shapes cognition and emotion (Baumeister & Leary, 1995). Those who are deprived of social relationships characterized by mutual concern and emotional connectedness are prone to develop a host of psychological difficulties (e.g., Brown & Harris, 1978; Coyne & DeLongis, 1986). As Bowlby (1977) pointed out, "The psychology and psychopathology of emotion is found to be in large part the psychology and psychopathology of affectional bonds" (p. 203). Maintaining a sense of emotional relatedness may be one of the critical factors that determines the ability of people who face chronic stress to persist in their coping efforts and to maintain well-being (DeLongis & O'Brien, 1990; Lyons et al., 1995; Sarason, Pierce, & Sarason, 1990). Failure to do so may result in depression (Beach et al., 1990; Brown & Harris, 1978; Hammen, 1992), passivity (Kuiper & Olinger, 1989), anxiety (Baumeister & Leary, 1995), and guilt (Coyne, 1989; Coyne et al., 1988). One of the major determinants of people's ability to maintain satisfying relationships with family members and other close ties during periods of prolonged stress may be the extent to which they adopt an empathic orientation to managing sources of strain that are interpersonal in nature.

Although rarely considered in models of stress and coping, empathy has long been considered a quintessential mediator of prosocial behavior, the glue that cements affective bonds, and a central catalyst that propels caring, supportive actions between people (Burleson, 1990; Clark, 1991; Eisenberg & Miller, 1987; Eisenberg & Strayer, 1987; Hansson & Carpenter, 1990; Thoits, 1986). Though few coping measures tap empathy as a mode of coping, the notion that people use empathy as a means of managing stressors within the social context is not a new one. For example, Haan (1977) identified empathy as a mode of coping that involves attempts to formulate an understanding of another person's feelings and thoughts. Current conceptualizations of empathy have emphasized not only *cognitive* role-taking processes but also *affective* processes that involve subjectively sharing or experiencing the other person's affective state, as well as *behavioral* processes that involve attempts to sensitively communicate one's perceptions of another person's feelings and thoughts (Goldstein & Michaels, 1985; Strayer, 1987). Based on previous research regarding empathic processes (for reviews, see Clark, 1991; Hoffman, 1984; Strayer, 1987), empathic coping can be seen as involving the following dimensions: (1) efforts to engage in perspective taking or to take the role of another person by attempting to view the world as that person sees it, (2) efforts to vicariously experience the other person's feelings and concerns and to evoke one's own affective and cognitive associations with that experience, (3) efforts to interpret the feelings and thoughts underlying the other person's verbal and nonverbal communication, (4) subsequent efforts to sensitively respond to the other person out of a state of concern, and (5) efforts to express caring and understanding in an accepting, nonjudgmental, emotionally validating manner. Expressions of empathy may be verbal or nonverbal. Nonverbal expressions of empathy include mirroring the other person's facial expressions, showing compassion and affection through facial expressions and physical touch, and caring gestures, such as sharing another person's tasks, respecting the other person's wishes, and showing tolerance for the other person's current manifestations of stress.

The Situational Specificity of Empathic Coping. There are undoubtedly individual differences in tendencies and abilities to engage in empathic processes (Davis & Oathout, 1992; Eisenberg, Fabes, Murphy, Karbon, Maszk, Smith, et al., 1994). We (O'Brien & DeLongis, 1996) examined the role of the Big Five personality traits (neuroticism, extraversion, openness to experience, agreeableness, and conscientiousness) in predicting empathic coping and found that, taken as a whole, components of the five-factor model of personality (see McCrae, 1992, for a review) accounted for only 2% of the variance in empathic coping. In contrast, we found that the social context of the stressor accounted for 48% of the variance in the use of empathic coping to manage stress, with personality by social context interactions accounting for an additional 4% of the variance. Our findings suggesting that social context plays a large role in influencing the use of empathic coping are consistent with previous research. Several features of the social context have been identified as influencing the occurrence of empathic processes, such as another person's overt behavioral cues of distress (Buck, 1989; Goldstein & Michaels, 1985; Strayer, 1987), concern for the welfare of another person in the situation (Batson, Turk, Shaw, & Klein, 1995; Dovidio, Allen, & Schroeder, 1990), and the presence of a friend or loved one in the situation

(Burleson, 1985; Cramer, 1985, 1987). Taken together with the findings of our study, these findings suggest that it may be more useful for coping researchers to consider empathy a process that is elicited by social interactions than to view it as a stable characteristic of the person (Buck, 1989; Burleson, 1990; Hoffman, 1984; Lazarus, 1991).

Empathic Coping in Chronic Stress Contexts. Particularly in times of chronic interpersonal stress, such as during periods of family or marital tension or conflict, the need for empathy may be great. One family member may do and say things that hurt, frustrate, disappoint, or anger other family members. The use of empathy may enable family members to understand the feelings and thoughts that may underlie the other person's actions. Particularly when people do not share their loved one's point of view, empathy may allow them to recognize that their loved one's actions and feelings make sense in light of that other person's vantage point or position (Beach et al., 1990; Gottman, 1993). Gaining a better understanding of the underlying causes of another person's actions via empathy may allow individuals to alter their own cognitive appraisals of the situation, their emotional reactions to the other person, and their behavioral responses toward the other person.

Individuals may also engage in empathic coping to try to determine how their own actions may be affecting the well-being of others and contributing to the interpersonal discord in the relationship or the family. By imagining themselves in the other person's shoes, individuals may be more able to see how their own actions could be a source of distress for the other person. Understanding why one's own behaviors may have a negative impact on others may allow people to generate alternative ways of behaving and responding that are less disconcerting and more favorable to others.

The communication of empathy to others may be necessary to resolve or reduce conflict and interpersonal tension. Listening and allowing others to disclose their feelings, acknowledging and accepting others' feelings, communicating in a way that validates others' feelings, and expressing concern and affection for others are all empathic coping responses that may be attempted to reduce interpersonal tension and to repair damaged relationships (Beach et al., 1990; DeLongis & O'Brien, 1990; Gottman, 1993). Those who respond empathically to their loved ones during times of conflict or tension may also help their loved ones to more fully express and process their feelings, which may help loved ones to diminish their negative affect as well as foster greater emotional intimacy and connectedness in the relationship. Therefore, empathic coping may be a communally oriented mode of coping that helps family members achieve and maintain emotionally satisfying relationships with each other (cf. Long & Andrews, 1990).

Findings from our study of stress and coping among stepfamilies illustrate some of the potential outcomes of using empathy to manage interpersonal tensions or conflicts. We (O'Brien et al., 1997) found that wives' use of empathic coping in managing difficulties with spouses, children, and stepchildren was associated with decreases in marital tension, family tension, and negative mood, even after controlling for prior levels of these dependent variables. Wives who employed higher levels of empathic coping reported higher levels of both marital satisfaction and spousal support than did those who used less empathic coping. Among both husbands and wives, those who employed higher levels of empathic coping in managing marital and parenting stressors reported less disappointment with their spouse's response to them than did those who engaged in less empathic coping.

These findings suggest that the use of empathic coping may help to ameliorate the negative emotions that are associated with interpersonal conflict as well as to increase relationship satisfaction. When others perceive that they are understood and accepted, they may be inclined to be more emotionally attuned to the individual and to freely offer support in return. Clearly, more research is warranted to determine the possible reciprocal relations between the use of empathic coping and the receipt of social support.

In addition to employing empathic coping to manage interpersonal conflicts that occur in chronic stress contexts, individuals may also engage in empathic coping to manage the stress associated with living with family members who are emotionally distressed. Living with an emotionally distressed person may be a source of enormous strain in and of itself (Coyne et al., 1987), above and beyond the event or circumstance that precipitated the family's stress. There are a number of ways that the distress of other family members may affect the individual. It may be upsetting for the individual to see a loved one experience the pain and struggle that may accompany chronic stress. The emotional contagion of a loved one's distress may also heighten levels of personal distress in the individual as well as increase the individual's sense of vulnerability (Silver, Wortman, & Crofton, 1990). Another important reason why living with distressed family members may be a source of strain for the individual is that when family members are stressed themselves, they may act differently toward the individual than they do in times of relative calm (Pearlin & McCall, 1990). For example, distressed family members may become more detached, more needy, or more irritable toward each other. In ways such as these, the qualitative nature of the interactions that persons have with their family members may change during times of stress, and such changes may have significant implications for the well-being of the relationship.

There is some evidence to suggest that the ways that individuals respond to the distress of others influences both personal well-being and the well-being of the other person. Studies suggest that individuals who cope with the distress of others by responding empathically experience less upset than do those who use less sensitive interpersonal strategies (Burleson, 1985, 1990; Notarius & Herrick, 1988), such as denying the feelings and perspective of the other person, condemning or challenging the legitimacy of the other person's feelings, and advising the other person what to do or how to feel (Burleson, 1985). Further, those who use less sensitive strategies when responding to a distressed person are more likely to be anxious and depressed following social interactions than are those who respond empathically. Those who respond empathically are perceived more positively by others than those who respond in a less sensitive manner (Burleson & Samter, 1985).

Empathic strategies are generally more efficacious in alleviating the other person's distress (Burleson, 1990; Lehman, Ellard, & Wortman, 1986). When others receive empathic responses, their sense of emotional relatedness may be heightened, and they may derive a great deal of comfort from knowing that they are not facing their adversities alone (Burleson, 1990; Lehman et al., 1986). Empathic responses may, therefore, be a potent form of coping assistance that ameliorates the recipient's levels of distress (Thoits, 1986).

The chronic stress context of caregiving for a family member with Alzheimer's disease (AD) offers an illustration of how empathic coping may be used to manage the stress of dealing with distressed family members (DeLongis & O'Brien, 1990). AD is a progressive, degenerative disease that produces severe cognitive, physical, and emotional deficits that markedly increase the patient's dependency on others. Extreme forgetfulness, confusion, disorientation, irascibility, agitation, and abrupt mood swings are all characteristic symptoms of AD that are disturbing to both the patient and the caregiver (Brody, 1988; Tune, Lucas-Blaustein, & Rovner, 1988). Caregivers who cope with these disturbing behaviors by constantly trying to remind their afflicted family member of things that they have forgotten may only increase their afflicted family members' confusion, distress, and irascibility (Safford, 1986). If, on the other hand, caregivers attempt to deal with these symptoms by trying to identify the emotion underlying the patient's statements or actions, they may be able to offer validating understanding that could quell the emotional turmoil in the afflicted family member. Caregivers who can enter the ill family member's inner world through empathic processes may be more inclined to accept and validate the family member's emotions than to struggle to reinstate lost capabilities that have no hope of regeneration. Caregivers may find it more effective to reassure the patient (Safford, 1986) and to allow the patient to express his or her feelings of frustration and confusion (Tune et al., 1988).

An elderly retired physician from one of our focus groups serves as an example of empathic coping (DeLongis & O'Brien, 1990). After a period of regularly bathing his AD-afflicted wife, he found that his wife started to adamantly object to being bathed by him. She had reached the point where she no longer knew him, sometimes thinking he was her uncle, her neighbor, or her son. No longer recognizing him as her husband, she could not permit him to bathe her. Understanding why she now saw him as an inappropriate helper, he engaged the help of a female homemaking service provider. The wife happily agreed to her help. There are a wide variety of strategies that the husband could have applied to cope with this situation, but they may not have been as successful. If the husband had adopted an exclusively emotion-focused orientation that ignored both the problem (the wife's need for a bath) and the relationship with his wife, he may have relied on palliative coping efforts, such as drinking or turning to other activities to escape the situation. Alternatively, if the husband had taken a purely problem-focused approach, he may have persisted in trying to bathe his wife, despite the distress that she expressed. However, by adopting a relationship-focused approach that allowed him to develop an understanding of the source of his wife's distress, he was able to implement an appropriate and effective problem-focused strategy, which minimized damage to the social relationship.

In a study of wives caring for husbands with AD, Kramer (1993a) found that adaptation to chronic stress may be critically determined by the ways that people manage their relationships with others. Wives who engaged in higher levels of empathic coping strategies experienced higher levels of satisfaction with their caregiver roles than did those who used less empathic coping. Caregivers who engaged in strategies such as confrontation, withdrawal, and blaming others were significantly more depressed, less satisfied with their social involvement, and reported fewer social resources than those who did not use these maladaptive strategies. Also, caregivers who engaged in these relationship-disrupting strategies were more likely to engage in more maladaptive emotion-focused coping efforts (i.e., wishful thinking, self-blame, escape–avoidance), which were associated with depression. In contrast, those who engaged in empathic relationship-focused coping were more likely to engage in planful problem-solving strategies, which were related to greater caregiver satisfaction.

These findings suggest that ways in which individuals manage their relationships may be an important determinant of the use of problem- and emotion-focused forms of coping. When the coping strategies that individuals use alienate others, individuals may find themselves more alone in their struggle and more distressed as a result, creating a greater need to engage in emotion-focused coping. With the increased understanding of others that might result from the use of empathic coping, individuals may be better able to engage in constructive problem-focused coping. The notion that problem-solving may be enhanced by empathic processes is consistent with standard clinical interventions. Generally, psychotherapists attempt to establish rapport with their patients and a sense of empathic understanding before proceeding to more active phases of problem solution or management (for reviews, see Beach et al., 1990; Safran & Segal, 1990). Therapists also attempt to help their clients respond empathically in their daily lives as a fundamental way of shifting attributions and creating new ways of perceiving and behaving that may reduce negative interactions and facilitate more adaptive personal relationships. Couple and family therapy interventions often begin by helping clients develop empathic listening skills as a means of increasing levels of marital or family cohesion, perceived support, intimacy, emotional acceptance, and effective problem-solving communication (e.g., Beach et al., 1990; Carter & McGoldrick, 1988; Cordova & Jacobson, 1993).

Those who rely on purely problem-focused or agentic orientations in their attempts to cope with the distress of a loved one may be acting out of sympathetic intentions to alleviate their loved one's distress. However, when their loved one primarily desires emotional support, attempts to engage their loved one in problem-solving processes may be unwelcome or unappreciated (Gottlieb & Wagner, 1991; Lehman et al., 1986; Pearlin & McCall, 1990). Without the understanding that may be gleaned from engaging in empathic coping processes, individuals may attempt to cope with their loved one's distress in ways that do not reflect an adequate appreciation of the other person's feelings or concerns, causing their loved one to feel more distressed and emotionally isolated (see Coyne et al., 1988). If empathic efforts are taken to understand the feelings and thoughts of a loved one, subsequent problem-solving attempts to find a solution that is beneficial to decrease the loved one's distress may lead to better outcomes (Beach et al., 1990). The use of empathic coping may enable the person to discern the types of emotion-focused and problem-focused coping strategies that would be most effective and appropriate for dealing with others involved in the stressful situation. The use of such strategies also may enable the coper to minimize the use of coping strategies that could damage relationships with others (DeLongis & O'Brien, 1990).

Barriers to the Use of Empathic Coping. For those experiencing chronic stress, there are several factors that may deter or impede the use of empathic coping. They include energy depletion, high levels of personal distress brought on or exacerbated by the chronic stressor, a lack of information, and a lack of understanding and support from others in the chronic stress context. Despite the potential benefits of employing empathic coping, it takes a great deal of coping effort both to accurately perceive the psychological world of another person and to convey empathy to another person (Burleson, 1990). Because chronic stress may severely tax the coper's energy and generate distress for him or her, it may be difficult at times for individuals to maintain empathic coping efforts. High levels of personal distress, anxiety, or alarm inhibit empathy. Batson, Fultz, and Schoenrade (1987) found that when faced with a distressed person, those subjects who were highly aroused were more likely to choose to escape from the situation rather than to help the distressed person, at least under conditions in which escape from the distressed person was relatively easy. Further, Lehman et al. (1986) found that although individuals know in the abstract that empathic responses would benefit those facing serious life crises, when they actually come face-to-face with a distressed person, they are often unable to cope with the person by responding with empathy. Instead they respond in a cheery or distress-minimizing manner that leaves the recipient feeling emotionally invalidated and misunderstood. Lehman et al. interpreted these findings as signifying that interactions with distressed others caused individuals to experience high levels of personal anxiety, which in turn elicited a greater use of emotion-focused strategies. They posited that individuals who shift their coping efforts toward managing their own levels of personal distress are less able to respond empathically to their distressed loved ones.

In a study examining the role of personality in coping (O'Brien & DeLongis, 1996), we found that those high in neuroticism, a personality dimension that is characterized as having a tendency toward high levels of emotional distress, were less likely to use empathic coping when close others were involved in a stressful situation than were those lower in neuroticism. Those high in neuroticism were also less likely to engage in planful problem solving and more likely to use escape–avoidance coping strategies than were those lower in neuroticism. These findings suggest that those higher in neuroticism may be more likely to cope with their elevated levels of personal distress in maladaptive ways.

This picture of the ways that those higher in neuroticism cope is consistent with the findings of other studies. For example, Buss, Gomes, Higgins, and Lauterbach (1987) found that those with high levels of neuroticism were more likely to use the "silent treatment," coercion, debasement, or pouting and sulking in interactions with their spouses. Similarly, McCrae and Costa (1986) found that those with high levels of neuroticism more often coped using withdrawal, assessing blame, and via a "hostile reaction." Taken together, these findings suggest that individuals with high levels of neuroticism may find it particularly difficult to cope with the distress of those they care about most, especially when it is compounded by their own already high levels of distress. Given the effort needed to manage their own emotions, those with high levels of neuroticism may find themselves less able to take the perspective of others and to empathically respond to others who are distressed. Consistent with this, recent research suggests that among those who have difficulty regulating their own emotions, the process of vicariously experiencing the distress of another person may lead to "empathic over-arousal" (Eisenberg et al., 1994), which may impair the individual's ability to engage in perspective-taking.

There are also several situational and relationship factors that may hamper empathic coping efforts. First, in close relationships, which typically have a long history of interactions, another person's actions may be construed as symbolic of a larger issue or problem in the relationship, and this may impede the coper's ability to be empathic in the current interaction. Second, when loved ones hide or shield their emotions or are uncommunicative regarding their needs, it may be more difficult to make accurate empathic formulations. Further, without feedback on the accuracy of their empathic perceptions, individuals may fail to realize how their perceptions of others are inaccurate or distorted (Buck, 1989; Colvin, 1993), leading to less effective coping.

Third, the use of empathic coping may prove less efficacious if only one member of a family employs it. If one person is constantly providing empathic responses to others but is not receiving empathic responses from others, over the long haul that person may experience burnout and a diminished capacity to be empathic. A fourth factor that may inhibit the communication of empathy is a fear that such communications will increase a loved one's distress. Although expressions of empathy may indeed elicit crying and other types of emotional ventilation in the other person, such emotional expression may have a therapeutic effect (Pennebaker, 1989). However, those who are extremely protective of their loved ones may not always recognize the therapeutic value of encouraging emotional expression and showing acceptance of their loved one's emotional expression.

Costs of Engaging in Empathic Coping. Although initial studies suggest that empathic coping may be an adaptive way to manage stress that is interpersonal in nature, other research suggests that there are costs associated with caring and providing support to others (Kessler, McLeod, & Wethington, 1985). However, little research has attempted to differentiate the types of caring behaviors that are ultimately most costly to the caring person. More research is needed to determine the nature of the personal costs that may be involved in the use of empathic coping and to determine whether or not these costs are offset by positive, long-term adaptational outcomes. For those who are uncomfortable with the display of emotions or unable to withstand others' expressions of distress, the use of empathic coping may serve to increase personal levels of distress. Nonetheless, these increases in personal distress may be outweighed by the potential benefits to the individual's sense of emotional relatedness and connectedness with others. We speculate that if empathic coping increases the emotional intimacy of close ties, it will lead to more adaptive outcomes in terms of personal well-being and relationship satisfaction. However, if others are unwilling to become emotionally intimate with the individual, the use of empathic coping may not lead to positive adaptational outcomes.

Other Forms of Relationship-Focused Coping

Coyne and Smith (1991) have identified two forms of relationship-focused coping: active engagement (e.g., discussing the situation with involved others, asking others about their feelings, and constructive attempts at interpersonal problem solving) and protective buffering (e.g., attempts to hide worries and concerns from involved others and to avoid conflict by yielding to the other person). As noted previously, the use of protective buffering strategies by wives of MI patients was associated with higher levels of self-efficacy for husbands but with higher levels of personal distress for wives. Among wives reporting low marital satisfaction, the husband's use of protective buffering also contributed to the wife's level of personal distress. No significant relations between the use of active engagement strategies and outcome variables emerged.

There are additional forms of relationship-focused coping or interpersonal regulation that could be usefully explored. First, because interpersonal tensions and conflicts are such a common source of stress in families, modes of interpersonal negotiation, conflict resolution, and interpersonal accommodation should receive increased scrutiny (Canary & Cupach, 1988; Gottman, 1993; Rusbult, Verette, Whitney, Slovik, & Lipkus, 1991). Second, although empathic coping is one way that individuals cope with the distress of others, we know from the social support literature that there are many other ways that individuals attempt to cope with the distress of others by engaging in support behaviors (Midlarsky, 1991), some of which, although well-intentioned, can lead to negative adaptational outcomes for both the individual and the recipient (e.g., offering advice, "cheering-up" strategies) (Barbee, 1990; Lehman et al., 1986). Thus, many of the support behaviors and social responses identified by the social support literature could also be construed as coping efforts to manage the stress that accompanies living with or interacting with distressed others. Adopting a more interpersonal perspective on the stress process may eventually result in a greater integration of coping and social support constructs (cf. Thoits, 1986).

Third, since there is evidence that in close relationships individuals may try to redirect one another's coping attempts (Gottlieb & Wagner, 1991), greater exploration of the coping strategies that individuals use to influence one another's thoughts and actions is also warranted. Buss (1992) has developed a typology of interpersonal manipulation tactics that could be applied to identifying coping strategies that are geared toward influencing others. In particular, the use of criticism in attempts to alter others' behaviors should be explored more thoroughly in light of the literature documenting the negative effects of living in critical and coercive family environments (Coyne, 1989). Fourth, greater consideration could be given to the ways that specified modes of problem- and emotion-focused coping serve interpersonal regulation functions. For example, the short-term use of withdrawal could not only help to ameliorate personal distress but could also serve as a means for individuals to create a space in their relationships so that they do not say or do things that could damage their relationships, essentially allowing a cooling-off period before re-engaging with others (see Repetti and Wood, Chapter 7, this volume). These are only a few of the many possible ways that individuals attempt to regulate their relationships and the actions of others in the face of chronic stress.

CONCLUSION

In developing more comprehensive models of stress adaptation, it is important to depict not only the ways that individuals attempt to achieve mastery over their adversities but also the ways they attempt to establish and maintain closeness and communion with others (Helgeson, 1993; Riger, 1993). Because interpersonal relationships and social transactions within chronic stress contexts have been shown to profoundly influence adaptation, research efforts aimed at delineating processes of interpersonal regulation and other interpersonal dimensions of stress and coping could greatly expand the explanatory power of stress and coping models.

Without a doubt, the development of standard measures of interpersonal modes of coping is urgently needed to advance the field's progress. To advance our knowledge of chronic stress processes, greater use of process-oriented methodologies (Lazarus & DeLongis, 1983), such as the structured daily diary methodology and other intensive time-sampling methods (for reviews, see DeLongis, Hemphill, & Lehman, 1992; Tennen, Suls, & Affleck, 1991) is also needed. Such methodologies may allow us to delineate more adequately the dynamic processes of stress and coping within and between family members. The measurement of multiple family members' stress and coping processes is decidedly more costly and labor-intensive. It also presents a host of statistical challenges in dealing with the interdependence between family members' reports (Bryk & Raudenbush, 1992). However, our efforts may be immensely rewarded by our increased ability to depict faithfully the complexities of family adaptation in chronic stress contexts.

ACKNOWLEDGMENTS The preparation of this chapter has been supported by grants to A. DeLongis from the Social Sciences and Humanities Research Council of Canada (SSHRC; 410-94-1718 and 410-91-1596) and a fellowship to T. Byrd O'Brien from SSHRC and the British Columbia Health Care Research Foundation. We thank Ben Gottlieb, Darrin Lehman, Steve Lepore, Ron Pound, and Jerry Wiggins for their suggestions regarding the manuscript and Marie Habke and Jodi Morris for their assistance with data analysis.

REFERENCES

BAKAN, D. (1966). *The duality of human existence.* Chicago: Rand McNally.
BARBEE, A. (1990). Interactive coping: The cheering-up process in close relationships. In S. Duck (Ed.), *Personal relationships and social support* (pp. 46–65). London: Sage.
BATESON, G. (1972). *Steps to an ecology of mind.* New York: Ballantine.
BATSON, C. D., FULTZ, J., & SCHOENRADE, J. (1987). Adults' emotional reactions to the distress of others. In N. Eisenberg & J. Strayer (Eds.), *Empathy and its development* (pp. 163–184). New York: Cambridge University Press.
BATSON, C. D., TURK, C. L., SHAW, L. L., & KLEIN, P. R. (1995). Information function of

empathic emotion: Learning that we value the other's welfare. *Journal of Personality and Social Psychology, 68,* 300–312.
BAUMEISTER, R. F., & LEARY, M. R. (1995). The need to belong: Desire for interpersonal attachments as a fundamental human motivation. *Psychological Bulletin, 117,* 497–529.
BEACH, S. R. H., SANDEEN, E. E., & O'LEARY, K. D. (1990). *Depression in marriage: A model for etiology and treatment.* New York: Guilford.
BOLGER, N., DELONGIS, A., KESSLER, R. C., & SCHILLING, E. A. (1989). Effects of daily stress on negative mood. *Journal of Personality and Social Psychology, 57,* 808–818.
BOWLBY, J. (1977). The making and breaking of affectional bonds. I. Aetiology and psychopathology in light of attachment theory. *British Journal of Psychiatry, 130,* 201–210.
BRODY, E. M. (1988). The long haul: A family odyssey. In L. F. Jarvik & C. H. Winograd (Eds.), *Treatments for the Alzheimer's patient: The long haul* (pp. 107–122). New York: Springer.
BROWN, G. W., & HARRIS, T. (1978). *The social origins of depression.* New York: Raven.
BRYK, A. S., & RAUDENBUSH, S. W. (1992). *Hierarchical linear models: Applications and data analysis methods.* Newbury Park, CA: Sage.
BUCK, R. (1989). Emotional communication in personal relationships: A developmental-interactionist view. *Review of Personality and Social Psychology, 10,* 144–163.
BURLESON, B. R. (1985). The production of comforting messages: Social-cognitive foundations. *Journal of Language and Social Psychology, 4,* 253–273.
BURLESON, B. R. (1990). Comforting as social support: Relational consequences of supportive behaviors. In S. Duck (Ed.), *Personal relationships and support* (pp. 66–82). Newbury Park, CA: Sage.
BURLESON, B. R., & SAMTER, W. (1985). Consistencies in theoretical and naive evaluations of comforting messages. *Communication Monographs, 52,* 103–123.
BURMAN, B., & MARGOLIN, G. (1992). Analysis of the association between marital relationships and health problems: An interactional perspective. *Psychological Bulletin, 112,* 39–63.
BUSS, D. M. (1992). Manipulation in close relationships: Five personality factors in interactional context. *Journal of Personality, 60,* 477–500.
BUSS, D. M., GOMES, M., HIGGINS, D. S., & LAUTERBACH, K. (1987). Tactics of manipulation. *Journal of Personality and Social Psychology, 52,* 1219–1229.
CANARY, D. J., & CUPACH, W. R. (1988). Relational and episodic characteristics associated with conflict tactics. *Journal of Social and Personal Relationships, 5,* 305–325.
CARTER, B., & McGOLDRICK, M. (1988). *The changing family life cycle: A framework for family therapy.* New York: Gardner.
CHRISTENSEN, A., & SHENK, J. L. (1991). Communication, conflict, and psychological distance in nondistressed, clinic, and divorcing couples. *Journal of Consulting and Clinical Psychology, 59,* 458–463.
CLARK, M. S. (Ed.). (1991). *Review of Personality and Social Psychology: Prosocial behavior, 12.*
COLVIN, C. R. (1993). "Judgable" people: Personality, behavior, and competing explanations. *Journal of Personality and Social Psychology, 64,* 861–873.
CORDOVA, J. V., & JACOBSON, N. S. (1993). Couple distress. In D. H. Barlow (Ed.), *Clinical handbook of psychological disorders* (pp. 481–512). New York: Guilford.
COYNE, J. C. (1989). Thinking postcognitively about depression. In A. Freeman, K. M. Simon, L. E. Beutler, & H. Arkowitz (Eds.), *Comprehensive handbook of cognitive therapy* (pp. 227–244). New York: Plenum.
COYNE, J. C., & DELONGIS, A. (1986). Going beyond social support: The role of social relationships in adaptation. *Journal of Consulting and Clinical Psychology, 54,* 454–460.
COYNE, J. C., KESSLER, R. C., TAL, M., TURNBULL, J., WORTMAN, C. B., & GREDEN, J. F. (1987). Living with a depressed person. *Journal of Consulting and Clinical Psychology, 55,* 347–352.
COYNE, J. C., & SMITH, D. A. F. (1991). Couples coping with a myocardial infarction: A contextual perspective on wives' distress. *Journal of Personality and Social Psychology, 61,* 404–412.
COYNE, J. C., WORTMAN, C. B., & LEHMAN, D. R. (1988). The other side of support: Emo-

tional overinvolvement and miscarried helping. In B. H. Gottlieb (Ed.), *Marshaling social support* (pp. 305–330). Newbury Park, CA: Sage.

CRAMER, D. (1985). Psychological adjustment and the facilitative nature of close relationships. *British Journal of Medical Psychology, 58,* 165–168.

CRAMER, D. (1987). Self-esteem, advice giving, and the facilitative nature of close relationships. *Person-Centered Review, 2,* 99–110.

DAVIS, M. H., & OATHOUT, H. A. (1992). The effect of dispositional empathy on romantic relationship behaviors: Heterosexual anxiety as a moderating influence. *Personality and Social Psychological Bulletin, 18,* 76–83.

DAYLEN, J. L. (1993). *Gender differences in spouses' coping with marital tension.* Unpublished doctoral dissertation, University of British Columbia, Vancouver, British Columbia, Canada.

DELONGIS, A., BOLGER, N., & KESSLER, R. C. (1987, August). *Coping with marital conflict.* Paper presented at the annual meeting of the American Psychological Association, New York, NY.

DELONGIS, A., HEMPHILL, K. J., & LEHMAN, D. R. (1992). A structured diary methodology for the study of daily events. In F. B. Bryant, J. Edwards, L. Heath, E. J. Posavac, R. S. Tinsdale, & E. Henderson (Eds.), *Methodological issues in applied social psychology* (pp. 81–109). New York: Plenum.

DELONGIS, A., & O'BRIEN, T. (1990). An interpersonal framework for stress and coping: An application to the families of Alzheimer's patients. In M. A. P. Stephens, J. H. Crowther, S. E. Hobfoll, & D. L. Tennenbaum (Eds.), *Stress and coping in later life families* (pp. 221–239). Washington, DC: Hemisphere.

DELONGIS, A., SILVER, R. C., & WORTMAN, C. B. (1986, August). *The interpersonal implications of personal coping strategies among parents who have lost a child.* Paper presented at the annual meeting of the American Psychological Association, Washington, DC.

DOVIDIO, J. F., ALLEN, J. L., & SCHROEDER, D. A. (1990). Specificity of empathy-induced helping: Evidence for altruistic motivation. *Journal of Personality and Social Psychology, 59,* 249–260.

EISENBERG, N., FABES, R. A., MURPHY, B., KARBON, M., MASZK, P., SMITH, M., O'BOYLE, C., & SUH, K. (1994). The relations of emotionality and regulation to dispositional and situational empathy-related responding. *Journal of Personality and Social Psychology, 66,* 776–797.

EISENBERG, N., & MILLER, P. A. (1987). The relation of empathy to prosocial and related behaviors. *Psychological Bulletin, 101,* 91–119.

EISENBERG, N., & STRAYER, J. (1987). *Empathy and its development.* New York: Cambridge University Press.

ENDLER, N. S., & PARKER, J. D. A. (1990). Multidimensional assessment of coping: A critical evaluation. *Journal of Personality and Social Psychology, 58,* 844–854.

FINCH, J. F., & ZAUTRA, A. J. (1992). Testing latent longitudinal models of social ties and depression among the elderly: A comparison of distribution-free and maximum likelihood estimates with nonnormal data. *Psychology and Aging, 7,* 107–118.

FIORE, J., COPPEL, D. B., BECKER, J., & COX, G. B. (1986). Social support as a multifaceted concept: Examination of important dimensions for adjustment. *American Journal of Community Psychology, 14,* 93–111.

FLOR, H., TURK, D. C., & SCHOLZ, O. B. (1987). Impact of chronic pain in the spouse. *Journal of Psychosomatic Research, 31,* 63–71.

FOLKMAN, S., & LAZARUS, R. S. (1988). Coping as a mediator of emotion. *Journal of Personality and Social Psychology, 54,* 466–475.

FOLKMAN, S., LAZARUS, R. S., DUNKEL-SCHETTER, C., DELONGIS, A., & GRUEN, R. J. (1986). Dynamics of a stressful encounter: Cognitive appraisal, coping, and encounter outcomes. *Journal of Personality and Social Psychology, 50,* 992–1003.

FOLKMAN, S., LAZARUS, R. S., GRUEN, R. J., & DELONGIS, A. (1986). Appraisal, coping, health status, and psychological symptoms. Journal of Personality and Social Psychology, 50, 571–579.

GOLDSTEIN, A. P., & MICHAELS, G. Y. (1985). *Empathy development, training, and consequences.* Hillsdale, NJ: Lawrence Erlbaum.

GOTTLIEB, B. H. (1987). Marshalling social support for medical patients and their families. *Canadian Psychology, 28,* 201–217.
GOTTLIEB, B. H., & WAGNER, F. (1991). Stress and support processes in close relationships. In J. Eckenrode (Ed.), *The social context of coping* (pp. 165–188). New York: Plenum.
GOTTMAN, J. M. (1993). The roles of conflict engagement, escalation, and avoidance in marital interaction: A longitudinal view of five types of couples. *Journal of Consulting and Clinical Psychology, 61,* 6–15.
HAAN, N. (1977). *Coping and defending.* New York: Academic Press.
HAMMEN, C. (1992). Cognitive, life stress, and interpersonal approaches to a developmental psychopathology model of depression. *Development and Psychopathology, 4,* 189–206.
HANSSON, R. O., & CARPENTER, B. N. (1990). Relational competence and adjustment in older adults: Implications for the demands of aging. In M. A. P. Stephens, J. H. Crowther, S. E. Hobfoll, & D. L. Tennenbaum (Eds.), *Stress and coping in later life families* (pp. 131–151). Washington, DC: Hemisphere.
HELGESON, V. F. (1993). Implications of agency and communion for patient and spouse adjustment to a first coronary event. *Journal of Personality and Social Psychology, 64,* 807–816.
HELGESON, V. F. (1994). Relation of agency and communion to well-being: Evidence and potential explanations. *Psychological Bulletin, 116,* 412–428.
HOFFMAN, M. L. (1984). Interaction of affect and cognition in empathy. In C. E. Izard, J. Kagan, & R. B. Zajonc (Eds.), *Emotions, cognition, and behavior* (pp. 103–131). New York: Cambridge.
HOUSE, J. S., UMBERSON, D., & LANDIS, K. (1988). Structures and processes of social support. *Annual Review of Sociology, 14,* 293–318.
KESSLER, R. C., MCLEOD, J. D., & WETHINGTON, E. (1985). The costs of caring: A perspective on the relationship between sex and psychological distress. In I. G. Sarason & B. R. Sarason (Eds.), *Social support: Theory, research, and applications* (pp. 491–506). Dordrecht, the Netherlands: Martinus Nijhoff.
KIECOLT-GLASER, J. K., DYER, C. S., & SHUTTLEWORTH, E. C. (1988). Upsetting interactions and distress among Alzheimer's disease family caregivers: A replication and extension. *American Journal of Community Psychology, 16,* 825–837.
KRAMER, B. J. (1993a). Expanding the conceptualization of caregiver coping: The importance of relationship-focused coping strategies. *Family Relations, 42,* 383–391.
KRAMER, B. J. (1993b). Marital history and the prior relationship as predictors of positive and negative outcomes among wife caregivers. *Family Relations, 42,* 367–375.
KUIPER, N. A., & OLINGER, L. J. (1989). Stress and cognitive vulnerability for depression: A self-worth contingency model. In R. W. J. Neufeld (Ed.), *Advances in the investigation of psychological stress* (pp. 115–142). New York: Wiley.
LANE, C., & HOBFOLL, S. E. (1992). How loss affects anger and alienates potential supporters. *Journal of Consulting and Clinical Psychology, 60,* 935–942.
LAZARUS, R. S. (1991). Progress on a cognitive-motivational-relational theory of emotion. *American Psychologist, 46,* 819–834.
LAZARUS, R. S., & DELONGIS, A. (1983). Psychological stress and coping in aging. *American Psychologist, 38,* 245–254.
LAZARUS, R. S., & FOLKMAN, S. (1984). *Stress, appraisal, and coping.* New York: Springer.
LEHMAN, D. R., ELLARD, J. H., & WORTMAN, C. B. (1986). Social support for the bereaved: Recipients' and providers' perspectives on what is helpful. *Journal of Consulting and Clinical Psychology, 54,* 438–446.
LEHMAN, D. R., & HEMPHILL, K. J. (1990). Recipients' perceptions of support attempts and attributions for support attempts that fail. *Journal of Social and Personal Relationships, 7,* 563–574.
LONG, E. C. J., & ANDREWS, D. W. (1990). Perspective taking as a predictor of marital adjustment. *Journal of Personality and Social Psychology, 59,* 126–131.
LYONS, R. F., SULLIVAN, M. J., & RITVO, T. G. (with COYNE, J. C.) (1995). *Relationships in chronic illness and disability.* Thousand Oaks, CA: Sage.
MANNE, S. L., & ZAUTRA, A. J. (1989). Spousal criticism and support: Their association with

coping and psychological adjustment among women with rheumatoid arthritis. *Journal of Personality and Social Psychology, 56,* 608–617.
MARIS, C. L. (1993). *Dyadic coping, marital tension, and overall marital adjustment in step-family couples.* Unpublished master's thesis, University of British Columbia, Vancouver, British Columbia, Canada.
MCCRAE, R. R. (Ed.). (1992). The five-factor model: Issues and applications [Special issue]. *Journal of Personality, 60*(2).
MCCRAE, R. R., & COSTA, P. T. (1986). Personality, coping, and coping effectiveness in an adult sample. *Journal of Personality, 54,* 384–405.
MIDLARSKY, E. (1991). Helping as coping. *Review of Personality and Social Psychology, 12,* 238–264.
MORRIS, J., O'BRIEN, T., DELONGIS, A., & CAMPBELL, J. D. (1995, August). *Social support and coping among spouses in stepfamilies.* Poster presented at the annual meeting of the American Psychological Association, New York, NY.
MOSKOWITZ, D. S. (1993). Cross-situational generality and the interpersonal circumplex. *Journal of Personality and Social Psychology, 66,* 921–933.
NOTARIUS, C. I., & HERRICK, L. R. (1988). Listener response strategies to a distress other. *Journal of Social and Personal Relationships, 5,* 97–108.
O'BRIEN, T. B. (1992). *The role of personality and situation factors in three modes of coping: Emotion-focused, problem-focused, and relationship-focused.* Unpublished master's thesis, University of British Columbia, Vancouver, British Columbia, Canada.
O'BRIEN, T. B., & DELONGIS, A. (1996). The interactional context of problem-, emotion-, and relationship-focused coping: The role of the Big Five personality factors. *Journal of Personality, 64,* 775–813.
O'BRIEN, T. B., DELONGIS, A., & CAMPBELL, J. D. (1997). Stress and coping processes in stepfamilies: The significance of relationship-focused coping and other interpersonal processes as determinants of stepfamily well-being. Manuscript in preparation.
PAGEL, M. D., ERDLY, W. W., & BECKER, J. (1987). Social networks: We get by with (and in spite of) a little help from our friends. *Journal of Personality and Social Psychology, 53,* 793–804.
PEARLIN, L. I. (1991). The study of coping: An overview of problems and directions. In J. Eckenrode (Ed.), *The social context of coping* (pp. 261–276). New York: Plenum.
PEARLIN, L. I., & MCCALL, M. E. (1990). Occupation stress and marital support: A description of microprocesses. In J. Eckenrode & S. Gore (Eds.), *Stress between work and family* (pp. 39–60). New York: Plenum.
PEARLIN, L. I., TURNER, H., & SEMPLE, S. (1989). Coping and the mediation of caregiver stress. In E. Light & B. Liebowitz (Eds.), *Alzheimer's disease treatment and family stress: Directions for research* (NIMH Publication no. 89–1569, pp. 198–217). Washington, DC: U.S. Government Printing Office.
PENNEBAKER, J. W. (1989). Confession, inhibition, and disease. In L. Berkowitz (Ed.), *Advances in Experimental Social Psychology* (Vol. 22, pp. 211–244). Orlando, FL: Academic Press.
REVENSON, T. A. (1994). Social support and marital coping with chronic illness. *Annals of Behavioral Medicine, 16,* 122–130.
RIGER, S. (1993). What's wrong with empowerment. *American Journal of Community Psychology, 21,* 279–292.
ROOK, K. S. (1990). Parallels in the study of social support and social strain. *Journal of Social and Clinical Psychology, 9,* 118–132.
RUSBULT, C. E., VERETTE, J., WHITNEY, G. A., SLOVIK, L. F., & LIPKUS, I. (1991). Accommodation processes in close relationships: Theory and preliminary empirical evidence. *Journal of Personality and Social Psychology, 60,* 53–78.
SAFFORD, F. (1986). *Caring for the mentally impaired elderly: A family guide.* New York: Henry Hall.
SAFRAN, J. D., & SEGAL, Z. V. (1990). *Interpersonal process in cognitive therapy.* New York: Basic Books.
SARASON, I. G., PIERCE, G. R., & SARASON, B. R. (1990). Social support and interactional processes: A triadic hypothesis. *Journal of Social and Personal Relationships, 7,* 495–506.

SCHUSTER, T. L., KESSLER, R. C., & ASELTINE, R. H. (1990). Supportive interactions, negative interactions, and depressed mood. *American Journal of Community Psychology, 18,* 423–438.
SHEEHAN, N. W., & NUTTALL, P. (1988). Conflict, emotion, and personal strain among family caregivers. *Family Relations, 37,* 92–98.
SHINN, M., LEHMAN, S., & WONG, N. W. (1984). Social interaction and social support. *Journal of Social Issues, 40,* 55–76.
SILVER, R. C., WORTMAN, C. B., & CROFTON, C. (1990). The role of coping in support provision: The self-presentational dilemma of victims of life crises. In I. G. Sarason, B. R. Sarason, & G. Pierce (Eds.), *Social support: An interactional perspective* (pp. 397–426). New York: Wiley.
SMITH, D. A. F., & COYNE, J. C. (1988, August). *Coping with myocardial infarction: Determinants of patient self-efficacy.* Symposium presentation at the 96th Annual Convention of the American Psychological Association, Atlanta, GA.
STEPHENS, M. A. P., CROWTHER, J. H., HOBFOLL, S. E., & TENNENBAUM, D. L. (Eds.). (1990). *Stress and coping in later life families.* Washington, DC: Hemisphere.
STERN, M. J., & PASCALE, L. (1979). Psychosocial adaptation to post-myocardial infarction: The spouse's dilemma. *Journal of Psychosomatic Research, 23,* 83–87.
STRAYER, J. (1987). Affective and cognitive perspective on empathy. In N. Eisenberg & J. Strayer (Eds.), *Empathy and its development* (pp. 218–244). New York: Cambridge University Press.
TENNEN, H., SULS, J., & AFFLECK, G. (1991). Personality and daily experience [Special issue]. *Journal of Personality, 59*(3).
THOITS, P. A. (1986). Social support as coping assistance. *Journal of Consulting and Clinical Psychology, 54,* 416–423.
TUNE, L. E., LUCAS-BLAUSTEIN, M., & ROVNER, B. W. (1988). Psychosocial interventions. In L. F. Jarvik & C. H. Winograd (Eds.), *Treatments for the Alzheimer patient: The long haul* (pp. 123–136). New York: Springer.
WIGGINS, J. S., & TRAPNELL, P. D. (1996). A dyadic-interactional perspective on the five-factor model. In J. S. Wiggins (Ed.), *The five-factor model of personality: Theoretical perspectives* (pp. 88–162). New York: Guilford.
ZARIT, S. H., & PEARLIN, L. I. (1993). Family caregiving: Integrating informal and formal systems for care. In S. H. Zarit, L. I. Pearlin, & K. W. Shaie (Eds.), *Caregiving systems: Formal and informal helpers* (pp. 303–316). Hillsdale, NJ: Lawrence Erlbaum.
ZAUTRA, A. J., & MANNE, S. L. (1992). Coping with rheumatoid arthritis: A review of a decade of research. *Annals of Behavioral Medicine, 14,* 31–39.

7

Families Accommodating to Chronic Stress
Unintended and Unnoticed Processes

RENA L. REPETTI and JENIFER WOOD

The results of prolonged exposure to stressors can be observed in an individual's emotions, cognitions, behaviors, and social life. Somehow, difficult life circumstances permeate and influence all aspects of psychological functioning. Finding a way to capture that phenomenon—the process by which persistent demands or strains gradually infiltrate and change an individual's life—is a special challenge facing researchers. We approach that challenge by noting that when even small amounts of variance are explained in particular situations, the underlying processes can account for important long-term outcomes if the situations recur and the effects cumulate (Abelson, 1985). Chronic stress, by definition, recurs, and the effects certainly cumulate. One way to study this process of cumulation, then, is by examining acute responses to short-term increases in common daily stressors.

This chapter focuses on the small, often subtle, changes in social behavior and interpersonal relations that are instigated by common chronic stressors. In particular, we present evidence suggesting that job stressors, like work overload or conflict with coworkers and supervisors, influence behavior at home and patterns of family interaction. In addition to our emphasis on the interpersonal effects of daily stressors, we

---

RENA L. REPETTI and JENIFER WOOD • Department of Psychology, University of California, Los Angeles, Los Angeles, California 90095-1563.

Coping with Chronic Stress, edited by Benjamin H. Gottlieb. Plenum Press, New York, 1997.

also focus on nondeliberate responses to stress and their often unnoticed impact on social relations. The coping literature relies almost exclusively on individuals' own assessments of their coping responses. Current inventories of coping strategies therefore seem biased toward intentional or effortful responses to stressors. It seems reasonable to expect that people make major, conscious efforts to cope with salient changes in life routines, such as those that result from the loss of a job or the death of a spouse. However, we maintain that many chronic stressors, including those that represent long-term repercussions of major life events, are difficult to notice and to recognize as circumstances that require special coping efforts. We therefore believe that many responses to chronic stress are unintentional and remain largely unacknowledged by the people who use them.

COPING AS AN INTERPERSONAL PROCESS

The Unintentional Involvement of Others in Coping

Researchers are becoming more interested in interpersonal aspects of coping (Coyne & Smith, 1991; Eckenrode, 1991). In our work in this area, we begin by distinguishing the intentional involvement of others in the coping process from the casual or involuntary roles that others often play. Most analyses of coping as an interpersonal process focus on the assistance that one person actively and intentionally provides to another. Although there are other unintentional or indirect ways in which social support transactions take place in daily life, these support mechanisms generally are not studied by psychologists (Gottlieb, 1985). In psychological research, social support is almost always conceived as *conscious* or *intentional* efforts to seek, provide, or exchange emotional or instrumental assistance. Thus, the provision of social support might include loaning a friend money, offering advice or guidance, or holding a loved one's hand while listening to his or her problems. Even though such efforts may not always succeed in actually helping the person in need, the behavior of the support provider is assumed to be motivated by a desire or an intention to be helpful. It makes sense to define social support as a subjective appraisal if one presumes that a conscious motivation to provide, or to seek, help underlies most or all supportive social transactions. Afterall, who is in a better position to know of the desire to help, or of the wish for assistance, than the individuals involved in the interaction? It is therefore not surprising that measures of social support are typically based on self-reports of the providers or recipients of support.

We are primarily interested in the roles that individuals may inadvertently play in the coping behavior of others. There are at least two mechanisms through which others can become an integral part of one's responses to a stressor. First, we consider how the behavior of a partner in a social interaction may influence coping. Second, we discuss how chronic stressors may induce changes in the social behavior of stressed individuals. The resulting altered patterns of social interaction may become a part of the coping response.

Nondeliberate Social Influence. The first mechanism linking coping with social context is direct social influence. As in any social interaction, a coping behavior that is social in nature is partly shaped by the responses of the partner in the interaction. This is illustrated by the observation that one is more likely to persist in seeking advice from a friend if the friend demonstrates that she is willing and able to give good advice. However, reciprocal influences in social interactions may not always be easily recognized by the parties involved. For example, in an observational study, the expression of dysphoric affect by depressed mothers effectively suppressed aggressive behavior by children and fathers (Hops, Biglan, Sherman, Arthur, Friedman, & Osteen, 1987). Consider also research with chronic pain patients suggesting that solicitous spouses may inadvertently reinforce certain pain behaviors, like complaining, moaning, or grimacing (Flor & Turk, 1985). It seems likely that the children and spouses in these studies were not consciously aware of the ways in which their behavior may have helped to maintain the expression of dysphoric affect and pain. In a similar way, family members and friends may encourage or discourage the use of certain coping strategies without actively attempting to do so and without recognizing the extent to which they have shaped another's coping response.

Imagine the different ways that one might respond to a phone call from a friend who is distressed because her husband just stormed out of the house following a boisterous argument. Having heard about the strains in this marriage many times, the friend who received this call may not wish to listen to the details of yet another incident of discord and may therefore suggest that they meet to see a movie together. Hence, without specifically intending to do so and without necessarily realizing it, the friend might encourage the use of distraction as a coping strategy. Alternatively, because the phone call reminds the friend of her own failed marriage, she might suggest that the two of them meet at the local pub where the friend hopes that alcohol will help her to forget her own marital sorrows and regrets. In this instance, without any deliberate effort, the friend would encourage the use of a different avoidance coping strategy.

In both cases, the friend's suggestion that they meet for a social outing might be intended, and received, as an act of social support. However, there is more than a supportive transaction going on here. As pointed out before, the distressed friend's mode of coping could be shaped by the nature of the social event itself. It seems likely that social influence processes that encourage the use of problem-focused or action-centered forms of coping, which attempt to directly manage or change the stressful situation (Lazarus, 1991), would tend to result from a conscious intention on the part of the social partner. An illustration in this case might be the supportive friend suggesting the name of a good marital therapist in the community. However, as shown earlier, the encouragement of emotion-focused or cognitive coping strategies, such as distraction, could involve nondeliberate or unintended social influence processes.

The expectation of another's likely response to a particular coping behavior can also influence whether or not a stressed individual uses that coping behavior. Expectations might be based on past experience or knowledge of the other person's resources or personality. Consider a situation in which all members of a social network are exposed to the same stressful event, such as a natural disaster. Under these circumstances, an affected individual might feel reluctant to ask for help because potential support providers, who are attempting to cope with the same adversity, might not have the necessary resources or might expect to be repaid in the near future. The perceived plight of others may thus reduce or prohibit the use of support-seeking as a coping response. This might be especially true of individuals who believe that they were less harmed by the event than were others in the community. Disaster researchers have identified a "rule of relative needs," which dictates that the extent to which social support is mobilized by an individual is partly determined by the degree to which he or she was affected by the commonly experienced disaster (Kaniasty & Norris, 1995). Thus, unknowingly and without engaging in any particular behavior, members of a social network may shape the coping responses of another. It is the stressed individual's appraisal of the current state of his support resources that influences his choice of coping strategies.

Stress-Induced Change in Social Behavior. A second mechanism through which coping may involve others is through changes in social behavior that are associated with increases in stress. For example, mothers who have experienced more stressful life events have been found to be less sensitive and responsive to their young children (Crnic, Greenberg, Robinson, & Ragozin, 1984; Weinraub & Wolf, 1983). Other researchers have observed a similar response to stress on a day-to-day basis, such that mothers appear more irritable on days when they experience more minor stressful events (Dumas, 1986; Patterson, 1983; Snyder, 1991). A similar change in parenting behavior is also found among fathers. In a study of male air traffic controllers (ATCs), Repetti (1994) found that on days when the ATCs reported more distressing encounters with coworkers and supervisors at work, their behavior at home in the evening changed. One rather striking change was that they expressed more negative affect, such as anger, with their children. They also reported using more disciplinary tactics, such as yelling and punishing, on high social stress days. The term "spillover" is often used to refer to the expression of emotion in one setting that was generated in response to events that occurred in a different setting. The spillover responses observed in the ATCs illustrate how social behavior at home may change in response to an increase in stressors at work. In addition, by becoming drawn into an aversive parent–child interaction, the children in this study (unintentionally) became a part of their fathers' responses to job stress.

In addition to having direct effects on social behavior, such as those seen in spillover responses, stress may also have an indirect impact on social behavior. Repetti (1989, 1992, 1994, 1996) has suggested that some strategies for coping involve interpersonal relations. This may be true even when the stressed individual is not using social relationships as part of a deliberate effort to cope, as would be the case with strategies like seeking social support. For example, without necessarily intending to do so, parents of a chronically ill child may attempt to cope with their own emotional pain, and even feelings of guilt, by showing preferential treatment to the child with the chronic illness, such as by spending more time with that child in pleasurable activities. Research suggests that parents do spend more play time and positive time with a chronically ill child and that they perceive their time spent with a healthy sibling as significantly more negative than time spent with the ill child (Quittner & Opipari, 1994).

Another example of what may be a nonintended effect of coping on interaction with family members was observed in the study of ATCs. Repetti (1989, 1994) found that husbands and fathers were more withdrawn from social interaction at home following high workload shifts at the airport, compared to their level of family involvement after shifts with lower workloads. During after-work hours on high-load days, they described themselves as more distracted, less involved, and less responsive with their wives and children. A social withdrawal response to job stress does not appear to reflect a direct mood-spillover process. Instead, it may be part of a more complex reaction to job stress, perhaps a coping strategy. Among adults, social withdrawal may facilitate a short-term recovery process. By helping to return mood, arousal, and energy back to baseline levels, social withdrawal may alleviate some of the negative aftereffects of certain types of stressful encounters (Repetti, 1992). However, social withdrawal may be more of an automatic response than a voluntary or conscious effort to reduce stress. In addition, because it represents a subtle qualitative change in behavior that takes place following exposure to a stressor, rather than a direct proactive response to the stressor, it may not be recognized by the stressed individual as a coping strategy.

Children may also adjust their social behavior following an increase in daily stressors. In particular, evidence suggests that children's aggressive behavior may increase when they are under stress. For example, after witnessing a live simulation of an angry conflict between two adults, 4- and 5-year-old children were observed acting more aggressively toward a playmate (Cummings, 1987). Margolin, John, and Burman (1993) reported that on days when preadolescent children experienced more problems at school, they and their parents characterized their interactions as more angry and involving the use of parental discipline. In a study of 4th through 6th graders, Repetti (1996) also found that preadolescent children's behavior with parents changed on days when they had experienced more social and academic failures at school, such as feeling rejected by classmates or receiving a poor grade on a test. On those evenings, the children were more demanding and difficult at home. Interestingly, other researchers have found that preadolescents only rarely mention venting negative emotions or "taking it out on others" when asked in open-ended questions to describe how they cope with the types of stressors that were assessed in the Margolin et al. (1993) and Repetti (1996) studies (Band & Weisz, 1988). And, when asked to rate their use of specific types of coping strategies on a checklist, they tend to indicate that they only sometimes engage in aggressive responses in these situations (Causey & Dubow, 1992).

Although the child may not recognize it as coping, might an increase in aggressive behavior reflect attempts to cope, perhaps attempts that have gone awry? For example, it seems possible that a child's efforts to secure parental comfort and reassurance following a difficult day at school can unintentionally escalate into demanding and aversive behaviors, such as whining, nagging, or uncontrollable behavior (Repetti, 1996). Depending on the child's age, she may simply lack the language or social skills that are needed to request emotional support. It would be especially difficult for the child to effectively communicate her needs if she were feeling distressed or if she failed to recognize that her current state of distress and wish for comforting reflected lingering effects of negative events that occurred earlier at school. Instead, the child might resort to immature or indirect bids for attention, such as clinging, whining, or nagging, and become frustrated if the parent failed to recognize and respond to her need for comfort and reassurance. In addition, parents might respond to the child's negative behavior with expressions of intolerance or anger and the use of discipline. This would presumably cause the child to feel even more frustrated and distressed. The situation could also be aggravated by lingering negative affect that was initially generated at school.

It seems that any connection in a child's mind to earlier stressful events and efforts to cope with them would be lost if, as described here, the child's efforts to secure emotional support go awry and escalate into aversive parent–child interactions. Unfortunately, parents also would not be in a strong position to help the child understand how her current state of mind might be tied to events that took place earlier at school. They would more likely notice and respond to the child's aversive behavior, rather than its underlying cause. To summarize, whether through aversive behavior or social withdrawal, both children and adults may involve others in their coping without necessarily recognizing the link between their own social behavior and their efforts to manage distress associated with previous stressful encounters.

Though not typically incorporated into stress and coping research, family systems theory may help to explain the findings described here. According to this perspective, any pressure exerted on one part of a system will necessarily have repercussions throughout the system. Thus, stress experienced by one member of a family has an impact on other members through changed patterns of social interactions within the family (Thomson & Vaux, 1986). One finding from the air traffic controller (ATC) study illustrates the complex ways in which an individual's attempts to cope can become part of a family's dynamics. Over all days studied, there was a general association between increased workload at the airport and the ATCs' withdrawal from marital interaction. However, when the spouses' behavior was examined, Repetti (1989) found that the association between work overload and social withdrawal was moderated by the level of emotional support that wives provided on each evening. The ATCs responded to increased workload with withdrawal only on evenings in which wives were described as being highly supportive. Perhaps the wives expressed their support by taking over some of their husbands' usual housework and childcare tasks or by reducing other demands on their husbands' time and energy. It seems possible for a spouse to provide a high level of support simply by facilitating a period of social withdrawal at home after a difficult day.

The next section presents an empirical analysis of the dynamic relationship between daily stressors and patterns of social interaction described here. We investigated both of the proposed mechanisms through which social partners may become involved in an individual's response to stress. Daily mother–child interactions were observed both to examine stress-induced changes in the mothers' behavior and to explore the influence of their social partners, in this case their preschool children. In particular, we were interested in finding out whether there was a feedback loop, a child's reaction to maternal coping behaviors influencing the mother's subsequent short-term coping.

The Daycare Study

Mother–child dyads were videotaped at a worksite childcare center during daily 10-minute play sessions that took place immediately after the mother's day at work. Based on the findings from the ATC study, we expected that mothers who had experienced high workload days (characterized by more demands than usual, a subjective sense of being overwhelmed, etc.) or an increase in negative social interactions with coworkers or supervisors would appear to observers to be more behaviorally and emotionally withdrawn during interactions with their children after work. Due to the demands of our procedure and the everyday caregiving responsibilities of this sample of predominantly single mothers, we knew that these mothers would not be able to withdraw entirely from interaction with their children. We therefore anticipated that any attempts to withdraw would be manifested in subtle ways. For example, a mother experiencing stress might be less likely to focus her attention on the child or the child's activities or she might not speak as much as usual. Alternatively, a mother might seem to "go through the motions" without expressing as much affection and warmth as she does on other days.

We were also interested in the effects that diminished maternal behavioral and emotional involvement might have on the children. How might the preschoolers in our sample respond to changes in their mothers' social behavior after stressful days at work? More importantly, how might children's responses subsequently shape their mothers' efforts to manage their own distress? We expected that signs of diminished maternal attention and emotional involvement would be distressing to children. Preschooler distress could be manifested through a change in mood or through the child's own emotional withdrawal. The child might appear less happy and affectionate or not as comfortable or at ease during the interaction.

We also expected that the children might alter their own behavior in an attempt to elicit greater parental involvement and responsiveness.

Thus, without realizing it, the children could prevent their mothers from persisting in efforts to cope through social withdrawal. There are many different ways that a child might try to engage a behaviorally and emotionally withdrawn mother. One strategy would be to increase positive attempts to elicit maternal attention. For example, a preschooler could smile, express pride in an accomplishment ("Look at what I made!"), or ask her mother a question ("Can you help me with this?"). Some children might simply reduce their level of aversive behavior by, for example, behaving in a more cooperative manner or engaging in fewer behaviors that tend to trigger maternal disapproval. Other children might try the opposite approach, increasing their level of disruptive behavior simply to get a response (albeit a negative one) from their mothers.

Thirteen mother–child dyads were videotaped and provided daily self-ratings for 5 consecutive days (Monday through Friday). These thirteen dyads were part of a larger sample of 30 dyads recruited through four worksite childcare centers. However, only one of the four centers agreed to the daily videotaping procedure. The child participants were preschoolers (3–6 years old) enrolled full time in the childcare program. The typical mother recruited through the center where videotaping occurred was an ethnic minority single parent employed in a low-income government job. At the end of each day at work, but before being reunited with their children, mothers completed subjective measures of two daily job stressors: workload and negative interactions with coworkers and supervisors. Mother–child dyads were then videotaped while they played during a 10-minute reunion period before leaving the childcare center. Mothers also completed daily ratings of parent–child interaction each evening after the child had gone to bed.

Our research group developed a reliable minute-by-minute coding system with eight indicators of mothers' behavioral and emotional involvement with the child and ten ratings of child behavior. The measures of maternal behavioral and emotional involvement were intended to assess withdrawal in response to increased job stress. As described below, our analyses indicated that five of the eight involvement variables represented a "withdrawal response" to increased job stress.

Each minute of interaction was scored on all 18 variables. A list of the mother and child coding variables is presented in Table 1. Four different coders rated each minute of parent–child interaction. Two coders independently rated mother behavior and two rated child behavior during each reunion episode. Two types of codes were used. First, parent and child behavior in each minute of the play session were coded for instances of discrete behaviors, such as verbal or nonverbal expressions

Table 1. One-Minute Codes for Videotaped Mother and Child Behavior

Mothers' behavior
  Behavioral involvement
    Amount of speaking[a]
    Degree to which attention focused on child[a]
    Degree to which actively engaged in activity
    Instances of teaching or explaining
  Emotional involvement
    Verbal or physical expressions of affection[a]
    Degree to which parent appeared caring[a]
    Degree to which parent appeared loving[a]
    Communications of approval
Children's behavior
  Aversiveness
    Instances of aversive behavior (e.g., whining, crying)
    Degree to which child appeared uncooperative
  Behavioral attempts to engage parent
    Expressions of success or pride
    Attempts to amuse the parent
    Demonstration of interest in the activity
    Asking questions
  Emotional withdrawal or dysphoria
    Verbal or physical expressions of affection
    Extent to which child appeared happy/sad
    Extent to which child appeared at ease/anxious
    Laughing or verbal indication of enjoyment

[a]A withdrawal response to increased job stress (Repetti & Wood, 1997).

of affection (0 = no instances of the behavior, 1 = one instance of the behavior, and 2 = more than one instance of the behavior during the 1-minute segment). Second, parent and child behavior were also rated on a number of descriptive dimensions, such as loving/warm–cold/distant, using 5-point Likert scales. Inter-rater agreement on the discrete behavioral codes ranged from 68% complete agreement (degree to which the mother was actively engaged in the interaction during a 1-minute interval) to 94% complete agreement (child's verbal or physical expressions of affection). Inter-rater agreement for the descriptive ratings, within 1 point on a 5-point Likert scale, ranged from 95% (loving/warm–cold/distant) to 98% (cooperative–uncooperative). The two observers' ratings of mother or child behavior during each 1-minute segment of videotape were averaged.

In order to assess reactivity to the videotaping procedure, we tested for patterns of change in parent–child interaction over the 5 days. In particular, we wanted to see whether the mothers appeared more attentive and involved early in the week, when the videotaping was a more novel and salient change in their daily routine. Our analyses showed no pattern of change in the mothers' behavior over the 5 days.

Independent observers rated mothers as significantly more withdrawn on days when the mothers reported higher workloads and on days when they reported greater social stress at work (Repetti & Wood, 1997). After these more stressful days at work, mothers spoke less and paid less attention to the children and their activities during the reunion episodes. They also appeared less caring and loving. Moreover, they displayed fewer instances of physical or verbal affection, such as calling the child by a pet name. The degree to which mothers appeared actively engaged in the interaction, expressed approval of their children's activities, and attempted to teach or demonstrate activities were not significantly related to mothers' reports of increased job stress. Thus, five of the eight indicators of mothers' daily behavioral and emotional involvement were related to increased job stress. In the following analyses, we use them as our five indicators of the "withdrawal response" to job stress.

In their daily ratings of parent–child interaction, the mothers also described their own behavior at home as more withdrawn and less involved on evenings following more difficult days at work (Repetti & Wood, 1997). There were significant associations between relatively minor fluctuations in daily job stress that occur within a normal work week and subtle but observable changes in maternal behavior. Thus, one of the main findings from the study of ATCs was replicated in our sample of employed mothers. Social withdrawal appears to be a common response to two types of job stressors: overload and negative social interactions with coworkers and supervisors.

Child Responses to Maternal Withdrawal. In order to understand coping as an interpersonal process, we believe it is necessary to study the behavior of both parties in social interactions that follow stressful episodes. We therefore also examined preschoolers' behavior during the daily reunion episodes in the daycare study. We were interested in two general issues. First, because social withdrawal appears to be a common response to short-term increases in job stress, we wanted to know whether and how the preschoolers in our study responded to the five indicators of the maternal withdrawal response to job stress that we observed. Second, just as mothers' attempts to manage distress through withdrawal may elicit changes in child behavior, changes in child behavior may reciprocally shape mothers' coping efforts. Our analyses of child behavior in the videotapes centered on these two key points.

We used weighted least squares (WLS) multiple regression analyses to examine the link between a mother's withdrawal behaviors and her child's behavior on the same day. For each mother and child coding variable, a daily mean score was computed for each dyad by averaging over their 10 minutes of observational data. The 5 days of videotape data from each of the 13 mother–child dyads were then pooled and treated as 65 independent observations. We have described our WLS regression model in greater detail elsewhere (Repetti, 1994; Repetti & Wood, 1997). The general approach, which is described by West and Hepworth (1991) as least squares with dummy variables, is often considered the method of choice for analyzing daily report data. Using this analytic strategy, various steps are taken in order to treat each day of data as an independent observation. For example, dummy variables (one for each dyad) are included in order to control all between-subjects variance.

The regression model allows us to examine within dyad changes in patterns of interaction from one day to the next. That is, we examine how a child's behavior changes on a given day, compared to her 5-day average or baseline level of behavior. We relate these day-to-day fluctuations in the child's behavior to day-to-day fluctuations in her mother's behavior (i.e., changes compared to the mother's 5-day average or baseline level of behavior). Thus, the dummy variables first control for each dyad's tendency to behave in a particular way during that week's reunion episodes; only then do we examine the link between mother and child behavior on each day.

Separate regression equations were computed predicting each of the ten child outcome variables from each of the five maternal withdrawal predictor variables (for a total of 5 × 10 or 50 separate equations). More than one third (20 out of 50) of these bivariate regression analyses produced significant results, which are summarized in Table 2. The results reveal an association between daily fluctuations in maternal social withdrawal and three aspects of children's behavior: (1) child aversive behaviors, (2) child attempts to engage the parent, and (3) child emotional state.

First, when their mothers were more withdrawn, children did not show increases in aversive child behaviors. Rather, they showed decreases. Children appeared to respond in this way to signs of both behavioral and emotional withdrawal. For example, children were less likely to whine, demand, and argue (i.e., less likely to engage in aversive behav-

Table 2. Significant Results from Multiple Regression Analyses Predicting Daily Child Behavior from Mother's Daily Behavioral and Emotional Withdrawal

Child outcome variable	Maternal withdrawal predictor variable	WLS B[a]
Child aversive behaviors		
Aversive behavior	Less affection	−.42[e]
Aversive behavior	Less speaking	−.21[c]
Uncooperativeness	Less speaking	−.23[d]
Child attempts to engage parent		
Success/pride	Less speaking	.26[d]
Success/pride	Less attention	.21[b]
Success/pride	Less affection	.33[d]
Success/pride	Less caring	.17[b]
Success/pride	Less loving	.15[b]
Attempt to amuse	Less attention	.20[d]
Interested/engaged	Less speaking	.35[d]
Interested/engaged	Less attention	.23[c]
Interested/engaged	Less affection	.58[e]
Asking a question	Less affection	.28[c]
Child emotional withdrawal or dysphoria		
Anxious	Less caring	.13[b]
Anxious	Less loving	.16[c]
Happy	Less caring	−.21[c]
Happy	Less loving	−.23[c]
Affection	Less speaking	−.16[e]
Affection	Less attention	−.09[b]
Affection	Less affection	−.17[c]

Note: These are the 20 significant results from 50 separate regression analyses testing the bivariate association between 5 measures of maternal withdrawal and 10 measures of child behavior. The analyses were based on pooled data from 13 mother-child dyads resulting in a total of 65 videotaped reunion episodes.
[a]Beta from weighted least squares regression analysis; [b]$p \leq .05$; [c]$p \leq .01$; [d]$p \leq .001$; [e]$p \leq .0001$.

iors) on days when their mothers were less affectionate. Decreases in maternal speech were met not only with decreases in child aversive behaviors, but also with less uncooperativeness. In sum, as their mothers behaved in a more withdrawn manner than was typical for that dyad, preschoolers displayed less aversive behavior and less uncooperativeness. It seems possible that the children were reacting to maternal withdrawal by attempting to be on their "best behavior" and control, or at least limit, their difficult behaviors.

Second, children seemed to increase their attempts to engage the parent in positive ways on days when their mothers were less involved. For example, in response to every indicator of maternal withdrawal, children increased the frequency with which they expressed success, competence, or pride. This included statements like, "I know how" or "I can do it" or "Look what I did!" Statements like these typically preceded or followed the child's demonstration of something to the mother (e.g. modeling something out of clay). Thus, just when their mothers appeared disengaged, both emotionally and behaviorally, children seemed to attempt to direct them back into the play activity.

In a similar manner, on days when mothers seemed less attentive, children increased their attempts to amuse the parent by trying to make the parent laugh, by "playing cute," or by engaging in some other behavior clearly designed to evoke a positive reaction from the parent. The children also appeared more engaged or interested in the play going on during the reunion episode on days when their mothers seemed less involved (i.e., when mothers spoke less, paid less attention, and displayed less affection). They also asked more questions when their mothers expressed less affection than usual. We believe these findings indicate that preschoolers will use different means of enticing their mothers back into an interaction when they detect that mothers are less involved than usual.

Third, despite decreases in aversive behavior and increases in positive behaviors on days when their mothers were less involved, the preschoolers' affect was rated as more dysphoric on those days. On days when mothers appeared, to the pair of observers who rated mothers, to be a bit less caring and loving, the independent pair of observers who rated the children saw them as more anxious and less happy. It is important to point out that both the children and the mothers were generally extremely happy to see one another and there were many kisses and hugs during the reunion episodes. The term dysphoria is used here only in comparison to the child's typical behavior and mood on other days. It may be more accurate to describe the children as less euphoric on days when their mothers appeared less caring and loving.

Children were also less affectionate on days when their mothers were less behaviorally and emotionally involved. For example, a child was less likely to initiate affectionate or playful touching, such as hugging or climbing onto her mother's lap, on days when her mother spoke less or appeared less attentive or less affectionate herself. Decreases in child affection may reflect the child's own emotional withdrawal from the mother during the interaction. That is, child withdrawal may be part of a defensive response to a mother who seems less available and involved than usual.

To summarize, the videotaped reunion episodes suggest that children display a multifaceted pattern of behavior when parents appear less behaviorally and emotionally involved after difficult days at work. First, the child's attempts to please and to engage the parent may represent a proactive response to parental withdrawal, one that is aimed at preventing or inhibiting the parent's continued withdrawal. Second, children may nonetheless feel rejected and hurt at these times and may attempt to manage their distress by decreasing their emotional involvement in the interaction.

Bidirectional Associations between Maternal and Child Behavior. The results presented here tell us that there is a same-day association between changes in certain mother and child behaviors. In additional exploratory analyses we attempted to discern the order in which the behavioral changes occurred. For example, did children react with dysphoria to maternal withdrawal, or was withdrawal a maternal response to a child who seemed more anxious than usual? We were particularly interested in whether the child behaviors that we observed served to shape subsequent maternal behavior. For example, when children seem more anxious than usual, do mothers alter their own behavior in a manner that might interfere with their own coping efforts but would serve to reassure the child? That is, are mothers' efforts to cope through behavioral and emotional withdrawal inhibited by signs of child distress? Although it seems highly unlikely that preschoolers would try to appear more anxious as part of a conscious plan to elicit greater reassurance from their mothers, they may automatically and naturally respond to diminished maternal involvement in ways that serve to increase it. This line of reasoning is consistent with Bell's (1977) observation that children may effectively influence and control their parents' behavior without a conscious or willful intention to do so.

We explored the direction of effects between maternal and child behavior by conducting cross-lagged panel correlation analyses. The analyses were performed for the 20 pairs of maternal withdrawal and child behavior variables represented by the significant multiple regression results in Table 2. We compared (1) the correlation between mothers' behavior in the first 5 minutes of the reunion episode and children's behavior in the second 5 minutes to (2) the correlation between children's behavior in the first 5 minutes of the reunion episode and mothers' behavior in the second 5 minutes. The division of the play session into two 5-minute segments was essentially arbitrary but seemed to be a reasonable way to begin to determine whether children were actually responding to changes in maternal behavior earlier in the play session and whether certain child behaviors were eliciting maternal responses.

Maternal influences on child behavior would be indicated by a pat-

Table 3. Significant Results of Cross-Lagged Panel Correlation Analyses Suggesting Maternal Influences on Child Behavior

First 5 minutes	Second 5 minutes	r
Parent: speaking	Child: interest	$-.25^a$
Child: interest	Parent: speaking	$-.11$
Parent: affection	Child: success	$-.30^b$
Child: success	Parent: affection	$-.17$
Parent: speaking	Child: aversive	$.37^c$
Child: aversive	Parent: speaking	$.18$
Parent: caring	Child: happy	$.36^b$
Child: happy	Parent: caring	$.17$
Parent: loving	Child: happy	$.29^b$
Child: happy	Parent: loving	$.16$

$^a p \leq .05$; $^b p \leq .01$; $^c p \leq .001$.

tern of correlations such that the correlation between mothers' behavior in the first 5 minutes of the play session and children's behavior in the second half was significant, whereas the comparison correlation (between children's behavior in the first 5 minutes of the session and mothers' behavior in the second half) was not significant. The opposite pattern (i.e., only the correlation between child behavior in the first half of the play session and maternal behavior in the second half is significant) might suggest that child behaviors are effectively shaping later maternal responses. Out of the 20 pairs of correlations that were tested, nine fit one of the two patterns. The five correlation pairs that fit the first pattern (suggesting maternal influences on child behavior) are presented in Table 3, and the four correlation pairs that fit the second pattern (suggesting child influences on maternal behavior) are presented in Table 4.

As can be seen in Table 3, only 5 minutes after being reunited with their mothers, children seemed to respond to early signs of maternal withdrawal with positive attempts to re-engage the parent and with dysphoria. In these variable pairs, positive attempts to engage the parent in the second 5 minutes of the episode were significantly associated with earlier indicators of maternal withdrawal, and not vice versa. That is, when mothers were observed speaking less or displaying less affection toward the child early in the reunion period, the children appeared

Table 4. Significant Results of Cross-Lagged Panel Correlation Analyses Suggesting Child Influences on Maternal Behavior

First 5 minutes	Second 5 minutes	r
Child: aversive	Parent: affection	.43[c]
Parent: affection	Child: aversive	.18
Child: interest	Parent: affection	−.32[b]
Parent: affection	Child: interest	.06
Child: success	Parent: speaking	−.24[a]
Parent: speaking	Child: success	−.21
Child: affection	Parent: speaking	.27[a]
Parent: speaking	Child: affection	.14

[a]$p \leq .05$; [b]$p \leq .01$; [c]$p \leq .001$.

more interested in the activity or increased their demonstrations of success or competence in the second half of the play session. One sign of maternal withdrawal early in the reunion, less speaking, was also linked to decreased child aversiveness in the second half of the session. Child dysphoria in the second half of the play session (ratings of less child happiness) was associated with maternal emotional withdrawal during the first half of the reunion (ratings of mothers as less caring and loving), whereas the reverse was not true. In sum, the results presented in Table 3 suggest that mothers' efforts to manage their distress after stressful days at work through withdrawal may affect the subsequent social behavior of their children. Children show some evidence of dysphoria (or less euphoria) while behaving in a less aversive manner and engaging in more positive behaviors, perhaps in an attempt to engage the parent in the interaction.

As shown in Table 4, child behaviors during the first half of the play session were also associated with maternal responses in the second half of the session. In general, the mothers of children who appeared to be distressed or in need of help during the first half of the session displayed increased affection and spoke more to their children later in the session, possibly in an attempt to comfort or engage the children. Aversive child behavior during the first 5 minutes of the reunion was associated with increases in mothers' expressions of physical and verbal affection later in the play session. Children also appeared to elicit more maternal involvement (in the form of more maternal affection or speech) during the second half of the play session when they appeared less interested or expressed less pride during the first few minutes of the reunion. The observed increases in maternal speech and affection support Bell's (1977) contention that when children seem unable to apply themselves to a task or appear to lack competence, their parents respond with more prompting and directing, as well as more protective behavior. Thus, the mothers in this study may have been sensitive to very subtle signs of their child's distress or need for assistance and altered their behavior in ways that could help their children manage the situation. Most important, the mothers adjusted their behavior in ways that necessarily interfered with what appeared to be the most common coping response to an increase in daily job stress, namely social withdrawal.

One set of correlations in Table 4, which did not fit this general pattern of findings, suggests a different strategy that also increased mothers' involvement. More child initiations of affection during the first 5 minutes of the reunion were linked to more maternal speech during the second 5 minutes. Thus, there were also positive ways for children to engage their mothers without having to resort to behaving in a difficult or withdrawn manner.

Although these results are provocative and warrant further investigation, we regard them as only a first step toward understanding how chronic job stress is associated with changes in parental and child behavior. Unfortunately, limitations imposed by the sample size and the brief duration of the observational period in this study precluded the use of other methods for testing bidirectional influences, such as sequential analysis. Nonetheless, the results of the videotape analyses suggest that mothers respond to daily experiences of job stress with social withdrawal and that children react to this behavior in ways that may redirect their mothers' coping response. The present study illustrates how coping with one source of chronic stress is an interpersonal process. Although the involvement of other family members may not be deliberate, it appears that children are affected by, and help to shape, parents' responses to at least one type of chronic stressor.

LONG-TERM IMPLICATIONS OF COPING AS AN INTERPERSONAL PROCESS

What Can Short-Term Responses to Stress Tell Us about Coping with Chronic Stress?

Up to this point, our discussion has focused on immediate responses to short-term increases in common daily stressors. However, the goal of this research is not simply to monitor short-term changes in a family's normal pattern of interaction. We hope to extrapolate from small daily adjustments in behavior to incremental changes in family dynamics. That is, immediate responses to short-term increases in common daily stressors may provide a window for studying a family's long-term adjustment to chronic stress. For example, research cited earlier suggested that a problem with peers in the classroom may influence a child's subsequent interactions with parents at home. According to Repetti (1995), the changes in the child's behavior may have reflected a coping response gone awry. Research on this type of short-term association could help uncover new information about the role that parents play in children's coping with a chronic pattern of rejection by peers.

Our approach to coping with chronic stress situations acknowledges that coping responses unfold over time. First, it recognizes that reactions to a stressor can persist after the stressful incident or event has occurred. Just as children may continue to respond to a minor peer rejection hours after it has occurred, there is evidence of more extreme forms of persistent stress responding in the aftermath of a major disaster, such as the nuclear accident at Three Mile Island (Baum, 1992; Baum, Cohen, & Hall, 1993). Second, our approach takes seriously the observation that different types of coping come into play during different stages of a chronic stressor (Lazarus, 1993; Stone & Kennedy-Moore, 1992). For example, Aspinwall and Taylor (in press) have noted that proactive coping, which takes place in advance of a stressful event, can lessen or avert the full impact of stress that the individual will encounter, ultimately minimizing the individual's burden of chronic stress. Consider the case of a worker who receives a negative evaluation from a new supervisor at work. This situation may have several of the characteristics that Aspinwall and Taylor (in press) believe offer opportunities for proactive coping: It may reflect a slow-rising problem, with warning signals and possibly severe outcomes, that is potentially controllable.

Proactive responses may represent only the first stage in a long-term process of coping with a chronic problem at work. We would expect to observe different coping behaviors over time. Consider the social withdrawal findings from the worksite daycare study presented in the preceding section. What might be the long-term repercussions of a repeated pattern of parent withdrawal in the face of chronically high levels of job stressors? Would a parent attempt to pull back a little more at home each time he or she felt an added amount of pressure at work or when interpersonal relations with coworkers worsened? It seems reasonable to expect a gradual drift of baseline or typical behavioral patterns toward less emotional and instrumental involvement in the family. For example, over time, a father might reduce the average amount of time that he spends talking to his wife and children each day, or he might participate in fewer household chores or childcare tasks, like helping the children with their homework.

But there are limits to a continual process of parental withdrawal. First, the realities of family life demand a minimum amount of parent involvement; some social interaction must take place among family members. The absolute minimum tolerable level of participation in daily family life probably differs depending on the sex of the parent and on certain structural characteristics of the family, such as the number and ages of children and how many adults are present in the home. An individual's values and expectations for her own and her spouse's involvement in family life will also determine the point at which no further withdrawal can be tolerated.

Second, there will be protests and resistance to withdrawal long before a parent reaches an absolute, rock-bottom level of behavioral and emotional involvement in family life. Even the preschoolers in the work-site daycare study appeared to try different strategies to engage a mother who was less involved than usual. Those attempts to correct parent behavior were observed only 5 minutes into their reunion at the end of the day. Imagine the pressure for greater participation in the instrumental tasks and emotional life of the family after repeated hours, days, weeks, and months of withdrawal. Those demands could take on countless forms, ranging from seduction (e.g., a smiling preschooler's request to "look at what I did") to direct verbal requests (e.g., "please help me with my class project") to whining and nagging to anger and confrontation. Whether the pressure for increased involvement is subtle or direct, engaging or punishing, there is an effort to thwart the stressed parent's attempts at withdrawal, and he or she must respond in some way. Some parents may have the physical and emotional resources to respond like the mothers in our daycare study did. They reacted to subtle signs of distress in the preschoolers with affection and greater involvement. Other parents may react with irritability and frustration.

Clearly, the impact that chronic job stress has on the family is the result of a complex, dynamic process. It is determined not simply by the stressed parent's coping behaviors, but also by the responses of other family members to that way of coping. In some instances, family members may interfere with a stressed parent's coping responses, and at other times they may facilitate the same coping response. For example, Bolger, DeLongis, Kessler, and Wethington (1989) found, in a community sample, that husbands' overloads at work were associated with their wives' reports of increased workload at home. These women may have supported their husbands' recovery on hectic days by relieving them of some of their usual household responsibilities. This would be consistent with our interpretation of the finding that ATC husbands' withdrawal responses to increased workload occurred only on evenings when their wives were supportive (Repetti, 1989).

Chronic job stress probably does not have a simple, unimpeded monotonic relationship with parental involvement. For example, what would be the long-term implications of being part of a team at work in which there are conflictual interpersonal relationships among the members of the group? In the study of ATCs, fathers who were part of work teams with unsupportive or conflictual social climates were not simply less involved with their children. Compared to ATCs who were part of teams with supportive and congenial social climates, they described a more negative emotional tone in the father–child relationship (Repetti, 1994). Confidence in this finding was increased by the fact that it was based on other team members' descriptions of the group's social climate, rather than on the father's own perception of social conditions at work. The ATCs who were assigned to teams that had unfriendly and tense social atmospheres (as described by coworkers) reported more anger, hostility, and tension, as well as less closeness and warmth, during interactions with a school-age child. It is possible that, for these fathers, weeks or months of membership on a team with a hostile or unsupportive social climate lead to repeated daily attempts at withdrawal that gradually escalated into more aversive patterns of interaction with their children. That is, a more aversive parent–child relationship may have been the cumulative product of repeated instances of parental withdrawal that evoked an escalating pattern of aversive parent–child interactions. For example, a child's bids for attention may have become increasingly demanding and aversive, and the father may have responded with more and more impatience and hostility. Christensen and Pasch (1993) have similarly noted that one of the ways stressors may grind away at marital harmony and cause conflicts between husbands and wives is by decreasing the spouses' ability to empathize and provide support.

Family Accommodation to Chronic Stress

We use the term "accommodation" to refer to the long-term implications of the type of short-term coping strategies that are discussed in this chapter. Accommodation is the state of equilibrium within a family that results from the members' continual efforts to meet *immediate* physical and psychological needs. For example, the ATC findings discussed earlier might suggest that a father's tense and distant relationship with his child could reflect an accommodation to an unpleasant social climate at work. According to our perspective, this form of accommodation could have evolved from the father's daily efforts to cope with feelings of anxiety and anger that remained after workdays that were filled with unpleasant interactions with coworkers and supervisors. That is, the father's daily efforts to recover emotionally and physically from work, over time, created this unfortunate equilibrium in the parent–child relationship.

Accommodation is most likely to occur under chronically stressful circumstances in which there are *persistent, multiple, uncontrollable demands*. We believe that many chronic stressors that involve multiple, uncontrollable demands become "invisible" over time. As a result, a process of accommodation (as we have defined it) is usually difficult to recognize and, therefore, difficult to study. The persistence of the stressors, or their chronicity, may obscure them over time. Individuals who are accustomed to living with the stress of a difficult job, an unhappy marriage, a chronically ill child, or the fear of violence in the community may not recognize or appreciate that these situations continually siphon their energy and resources. Moreover, when other members of their social network share the same or similar chronic stressors, the individual may be even less likely to notice them (see Lepore, Chapter 5, this volume). A high daily tax on physical and emotional well-being becomes part of the normal background of life, and there is no one to point out the constant hardship that this entails.

Multiple, uncontrollable stressors require constant coping in the short term to meet basic immediate physical and/or psychological needs, such as the need to rest, recover, feel safe, and feel esteemed. Under these circumstances, one would expect to observe more emotion-focused coping and less planful, problem-oriented coping. In order to formulate an effective plan of action, one must reflect on the demands in the situation and develop goals. This may be impossible to do in the kind of chronic stress situation we are describing because the individual's time and energy are focused on coping with immediate needs. Aspinwall and Taylor (in press) have pointed out that in "busy" environments, which are characterized by many distractors and a high cognitive load, the quality of information processing suffers and, therefore, proactive coping is less likely to take place. They similarly argue that heavy chronic burdens, which are associated with environments that are oppressive, interfering, and hard to manage, favor reactive coping skills rather than proactive ones. Aspinwall and Taylor's analysis is consistent with the observation that chronic stress can exacerbate the negative effects of other family vulnerability factors. For example, a recent study found that under conditions of high daily stress, greater differences between spouses (i.e., differences in demographic factors, personality, and attitudes) were linked to a dysfunctional style of child rearing in which the parents undermined each other. Among families exposed to relatively few daily hassles, however, there was no association between the extent of spousal differences and the degree to which parents supported each other during interactions with their children (Belsky, Crnic, & Gable, 1995).

In addition, to the extent that a stressful situation is uncontrollable, it would not permit what Lazarus (1991) has called problem-focused or action-centered forms of coping. These are attempts to change the stressful situation. Lazarus contrasts these with emotion-focused or cognitive coping strategies that mostly involve thinking rather than acting. These responses change the meaning or the appraisal of the stressor, for example, by avoiding thoughts of it or denying that anything is wrong. In chronic stress situations, individuals may strive to ignore or minimize the difficult and demanding aspects of their daily lives as their only way of coping. This would further obscure the chronically stressful circumstance, whatever it may be, a demanding and unsupportive boss, role overload, a depressed wife, or a high level of violence in the community.

Implications for Coping Assessment

Self-Report Assessment Strategies. We have argued that some chronic stressors, over time, become invisible to those who are exposed to them. We have also suggested that an individual's social partners can play unintended and unnoticed roles in coping. If we are correct, then many of the responses used to cope with chronic stressors, particularly emotion-focused coping responses, must surely go unrecognized. However, most coping theorists conceive of coping as purposeful or effortful attempts to manage a stressor (Compas, 1987; and Compas, Connor, Osourecki, & Welch, Chapter 4, this volume). Because this type of definition implies a *conscious intent* on the part of the coper, we believe it excludes a significant portion of the coping that actually takes place in daily life. In accordance with the dominant conceptualization of coping, traditional methods of assessing coping ask individuals to describe how they typically cope with a variety of stressful experiences or how they have attempted to cope with a recent specific event. Others have delineated many of the problems that researchers encounter when they use self-report instruments, particularly checklists, to assess coping (Stone & Kennedy-Moore, 1992; Coyne & Gottlieb, in press). We focus our comments here on one general limitation associated with this approach to measurement: Most people cannot possibly describe all the different responses that comprise their gradual accommodation to conditions of chronic stress. In particular, we expect that the nondeliberate coping responses discussed in this chapter would *not* be included in most subjects' responses to coping questionnaires and interviews.

An individual's description of coping responses, even in the short-term, involves a three-step process:

1. A keen awareness and accurate recall of recent behavior, affect, and cognition
2. The detection of a recent change in behavior, affect, and cognition (from some baseline or typical pattern)
3. An inference that the change in behavior, affect, and cognition was in response to a specific stressful event or condition

Consider two typical emotion-focused or cognitive coping response options on coping questionnaires: "I avoided thinking about the problem" and "I watched TV." For each of these items, the individual would be required to accurately recall how much she thought about the problem or watched TV over the past day or week, to compare that amount with an estimate of her "usual" level of cognitive or television-viewing activity, and to infer that any change was in direct response to stress caused by the problem under consideration. Unless the response was part of a conscious and deliberate effort to cope with the stressor, it would appear impossible for most people to recognize the connection between the change in their behavior or thoughts and the stressor under investigation. The process is even more complex when applied to chronic stress. Here, any self-report strategy to assess coping requires that subjects use some type of complex calculus at the second and third steps in the process in order to compute long-term changes in their behavior, affect, and cognition and to link those changes to chronic or worsening conditions in the environment.

Besides random error due to the complexity of the task, systematic biases may influence self-reports of coping. For example, subjects may be more likely to recall coping responses that, in retrospect, they believe produced a desired outcome (Stone & Kennedy-Moore, 1992). Biases that have been identified in self-reports of social support may also apply to the measurement of coping. For example, Lakey and Cassady (1990) maintain that differences between perceptions of support and the actual enactment of support are due to individual differences in cognitive style and beliefs that cause biases in attentional and judgment processes, as well as in the recall of interpersonal transactions.

Because most of the coping efforts discussed in the literature are based on self-report data, they represent only those behaviors that are relatively easy to recognize and are linked (in the subject's mind) to the stressful situation. Thus, the reliance on self-report assessment devices has restricted the range of coping responses that are studied by psychologists. Many coping responses are not intentional and, we believe, cannot be thoroughly understood with self-report instruments alone. We would therefore encourage researchers to supplement self-report assessment strategies with other methodologies.

One alternative approach, illustrated in some of the research presented here, places the responsibility for making inferences about coping on the investigator, rather than on the subject. This approach to coping assessment involves three steps. The first two steps are designed into the data collection stage of a study. Short-term changes in specific contextual stressors, such as increases in workload or interpersonal conflicts, are assessed. This can be done by examining day-to-day changes in both subjective appraisals and objective indicators in the environment. The second step is an assessment of short-term changes in the subject's behavior, affect, and cognition. This can be done by examining change in both subjective reports and independent ratings of the subject. The third step, which takes place at the data analysis stage, links the short-term changes in environmental stressors to the corresponding short-term changes in the subject's mood, behavior, or cognition.

This approach requires prior definitions of the specific stressors and, more important, identification of the specific short-term responses to study. It also requires some notion of the time course of the coping response. Over what time frame can one expect to observe a change in the environment, and over what time frame do we expect to observe the subject's response to that environmental change? Is this a coping process that takes place over minutes, hours, days, or weeks? Clearly, the direct application of this approach would become increasingly complex as the time frame for observing a coping response increased beyond days or weeks. The logic behind this strategy is that the study of acute responses to common daily stressors will provide clues to the process of cumulation by which chronic stressors gradually infiltrate and change an individual's life.

Adaptive versus Maladaptive Coping. Our analysis of coping with chronic job stressors has another implication for the assessment of coping with chronic stress. It supports the notion that distinctions between adaptive and maladaptive coping are too simplistic (Lazarus, 1993). At the very least, the adaptiveness of a coping response depends on three characteristics of the outcome under consideration. The first is the aspect of adaptation that is assessed. Is the outcome an individual's physical health, is it psychological well-being, or is it the quality of social relationships? The second is the time frame for gauging the outcome. For example, if the outcome is psychological well-being, is adaptation measured as a change in mood minutes after a stressful event occurred or as depressed affect months later? The third characteristic is the person (or persons) whose adjustment is assessed. The unit of analysis might be the individual who directly experienced the stressor, another family member, or a dyadic relationship.

These issues can be illustrated by social withdrawal as a coping response. A period of social withdrawal may facilitate recovery from the immediate physical and emotional residues of a stressful encounter (Repetti, 1992). If, in the short run, social withdrawal does accelerate mood repair and recovery from physical arousal, it may also, in the long run, help reduce the health risks associated with chronic overloads at work. One would be tempted to categorize social withdrawal as an adaptive coping response. Yet, as suggested here, daily repetitions of this response in the face of chronic stress may erode the individual's most important and most sustaining relationships. Thus, the same coping response that is highly adaptive with regard to short-term and long-term health outcomes may be disasterous for the individual's important social relations. When one adopts an interpersonal approach to coping and considers the perspectives of other family members, the inadequacy of a single dimension to describe the adaptiveness of a coping response becomes obvious. Even considering only short-term outcomes, it might fall into the adaptive category for the adult who is using it. However, the same coping behavior might be categorized as maladaptive for other family members.

Accommodation to Poverty and Community Violence

In this final section, we attempt to extend some of the concepts and processes discussed in this chapter to two other types of chronically stressful situations—poverty and community violence. Low-income families, like the mothers and preschoolers in our daycare study, are likely to be exposed to multiple, persistent, uncontrollable demands and to live in environments characterized by what Aspinwall and Taylor (1995) call "chronic burden." Investigators who study the effects of poverty and community violence on families have described responses to stress that are strikingly similar to those we have described as reflecting a process of accommodation.

Poverty and community violence are among the chronic stressors that may require constant coping in the short term—coping that is likely to be unintentional and less planful or action-oriented. Researchers in this area have pointed out that chronic economic strain may "grind away and deplete emotional reserves" (McLoyd & Wilson, 1991, p. 105), possibly resulting in a diminished ability to reflect upon and develop a problem-focused plan of action. Belle (1984) suggests that continuous exposure to negative life events, such as those experienced by low-income families, does not allow time for "recuperation." Families facing chronic poverty must react immediately and regularly to constant demands, and, for this reason, their coping may be, at times, less planful. For example, Wahler (1990) has pointed out that it is a great challenge for a poor mother facing multiple daily stressors to put other pressing problems aside in order to focus on formulating an effective problem-solving strategy for dealing with a difficult child.

A similar phenomenon has been observed with regard to chronic community violence. After interviewing mothers of young children in a public housing development, Dubrow and Garbarino (1989) concluded that these mothers developed ways to cope with this dangerous environment that were largely unintentional. That is, although these mothers devised coping strategies, such as staying physically close to their children, they generally did not see them as part of a planned effort to keep their children safe. The researchers contrast this with coping strategies observed among mothers living in a nearby community characterized by relatively low levels of violence. Unlike their chronically stressed counterparts, these mothers had made careful observations of their surroundings and had developed plans to cope with sources of danger that, in many cases, were explicitly communicated to children. The reappraisal of stressors that Lazarus (1991) contends is the essence of emotion-focused coping has also been observed in these populations. For example, Richters and Martinez (1993) report that parents tend to underestimate their children's exposure to community violence. These parents may be trying to deny or minimize the danger that their children face in an attempt to reappraise a stressful situation.

Consistent with our observations of parent behavior after high-stress days at work, a number of researchers have found a relationship between chronic economic strain and parental behavior that is indicative of social withdrawal. For example, Lempers, Clark-Lempers, and Simons (1989) conclude that economic hardship is directly related to parents' diminished emotional involvement. Parents experiencing greater economic hardship report that they are less nurturing during parent–child interactions; for example, they compliment their children less often and display less affection toward them. The association between poverty and parental nurturance appears to be mediated by parents' psychological distress (McLoyd & Wilson, 1991). Flanagan (1990) observed that, over time, parents appeared to adjust to economic deprivation by adopting a "laissez-faire" attitude toward adolescent behavior, which may also suggest less behavioral and emotional involvement.

Finally, when considering families' responses to chronic poverty and community violence, a distinction between adaptive and maladaptive coping may be too simplistic. For example, Martinez and Richters (1993) suggest that, although short-term reactions to chronic community violence (such as hypervigilance) may be adaptive in a dangerous environment, these reactions may have negative consequences for healthy social, emotional, and cognitive development. As pointed out earlier, a determination of the adaptiveness (or maladaptiveness) of a coping response may depend on the aspect of adaptation being assessed. Hypervigilance may help keep some children safe while traveling to and from school each day, but it may become dysfunctional once the child is in the classroom and is no longer in physical danger. There, a constant perception of threat to one's safety may interfere with performance on tasks that require focused attention and concentration (Cicchetti & Lynch, 1993; Garbarino, Kostelny, & Dubrow, 1991). Hypervigilance may also lead to the development of a personality style that appears overly suspicious and mistrustful to others, such as teachers who do not live in the same community.

SUMMARY

Three themes have been repeated throughout this chapter. First, research on immediate responses to stressors may open a window into the process of cumulation that underlies the long-term effects of chronic stress. Second, changes in social behavior and interpersonal relations are important stress outcomes that are worthy of study not only in their own right, but also because of the role that they play in individual coping. Third, many responses to chronic stress may be unintentional and go unnoticed by the people involved. All three themes were illustrated by research findings suggesting that social withdrawal is a common response to increased job stress. However, we believe the framework presented here also may apply to other types of chronic stress situations.

ACKNOWLEDGMENTS   The authors would like to thank Ben Gottlieb for his helpful comments on an earlier draft of the chapter and the students who assisted in the collection and coding of data. We are also grateful to the parents and children who participated in the study. Preparation of this manuscript was supported by a FIRST award (R29-48593) from the National Institute of Mental Health awarded to Rena Repetti.

REFERENCES

ABELSON, R. P. (1985). A variance explanation paradox: When a little is a lot. *Psychological Bulletin, 97,* 129–133.
ASPINWALL, L. G., & TAYLOR, S. E. (in press). A stitch in time: Self-regulation and proactive coping. *Psychological Bulletin.*
BANK, E. B., & WEISZ, J. R. (1988). How to feel better when it feels bad: Children's perspectives on coping with everyday stress. *Developmental Psychology, 24,* 247–253.
BAUM, A. (1992). Chronic stress and health. *Psychological Science Agenda, 5,* 10–12.
BAUM, A., COHEN, L., & HALL, M. (1993). Control and intrusive memories as possible determinants of chronic stress. *Psychosomatic Medicine, 55,* 274–286.
BELL, R. Q. (1977). Socialization findings reexamined. In R. Q. Bell & L. V. Harper (Eds.), *Child effects on adults* (pp. 53–84). Hillsdale, NJ: Lawrence Erlbaum.
BELLE, D. (1984). Inequality and mental health: Low-income and minority women. In L. Walker (Ed.), *Women and mental health policy* (pp. 135–150). Beverly Hills, CA: Sage.
BELSKY, J., CRNIC, K., & GABLE, S. (1995). The determinants of coparenting in families with toddler boys: Spousal differences and daily hassles. *Child Development, 66,* 629–642.
BOLGER, N., DELONGIS, A., KESSLER, R. C., & WETHINGTON, E. (1989). The contagion of stress across multiple roles. *Journal of Marriage and the Family, 51,* 175–183.
CAUSEY, D. L., & DUBOW, E. F. (1992). Development of a self-report coping measure for elementary school children. *Journal of Clinical Child Psychology, 21,* 47–59.
CHRISTENSON, A., & PASCH, L. (1993). The sequence of marital conflict: An analysis of seven phases of marital conflict in distressed and nondistressed couples. *Clinical Psychology Review, 13,* 3–14.
CICCHETTI, D., & LYNCH, M. (1993). Toward an ecological/transactional mode of community violence and child maltreatment: Consequences for children's development. *Psychiatry, 56,* 96–118.
COMPAS, B. E. (1987). Coping with stress during childhood and adolescence. *Psychological Bulletin, 101,* 393–403.
COYNE, J. C., & GOTTLIEB, B. H. (1996). The mismeasure of coping by checklist. *Journal of Personality, 64,* 173–202.
COYNE, J. C., & SMITH, D. A. F. (1991). Couples coping with a myocardial infarction: A contextual perspective on wives' distress. *Journal of Personality and Social Psychology, 61,* 404–412.
CRNIC, K. A., GREENBERG, M. T., ROBINSON, R. M., & RAGOZIN, A. S. (1984). Maternal stress and social support: Effects on the mother–infant relationship from birth to eighteen months. *American Journal of Orthopsychiatry, 54,* 224–235.
CUMMINGS, E. M. (1987). Coping with background anger in early childhood. *Child Development, 58,* 976–984.
DUBROW, N. F., & GARBARINO, J. (1989). Living in the war zone: Mothers and young children in a public housing development. *Child Welfare, 58,* 3–20.
DUMAS, J. E. (1986). Indirect influence of maternal social contacts on mother–child interactions: A setting event analysis. *Journal of Abnormal Child Psychology, 14,* 205–216.
ECKENRODE, J. (Ed.). (1991). *The social context of coping.* New York: Plenum.
FLANAGAN, C. A. (1990). Change in family work status: Effects on parent–adolescent decision making. *Child Development, 61,* 163–177.
FLOR, H., & TURK, D. C. (1985). Chronic illness in an adult family member: Pain as a prototype. In D. C. Turk & R. D. Kerns (Eds.), *Health, illness, and families: A life span perspective* (pp. 255–278). New York: Wiley.
GARBARINO, J., KOSTELNY, K., & DUBROW, N. (1991). What children can tell us about living in danger. *American Psychologist, 46,* 376–383.
GOTTLIEB, B. H. (1985). Social support and the study of personal relationships. *Journal of Social and Personal Relationships, 2,* 351–375.
HOPS, H., BIGLAN, A., SHERMAN, L., ARTHUR, J., FRIEDMAN, L., & OSTEEN, V. (1987). Home

observations of family interactions of depressed women. *Journal of Consulting and Clinical Psychology, 55,* 341–346.

KANIASTY, K., & NORRIS, F. H. (1995). Mobilization and deterioration of social support following natural disasters. *Current Directions in Psychological Science, 4,* 94–98.

LAKEY, B., & CASSADY, P. B. (1990). Cognitive processes in perceived social support. *Journal of Personality and Social Psychology, 2,* 337–343.

LAZARUS, R. S. (1991). *Emotion and adaptation.* New York: Oxford University Press.

LAZARUS, R. S. (1993). Coping theory and research: Past, present, and future. *Psychosomatic Medicine, 55,* 234–247.

LEMPERS, J. D., CLARK-LEMPERS, D., & SIMONS, R. L. (1989). Economic hardship, parenting, distress, and adolescence. *Child Development, 60,* 25–39.

MARGOLIN, G., JOHN, R., & BURMAN, B. (1993, March). *Family factors and children's maladjustment: Daily variability.* Paper presented at the 60th Anniversary Meeting of the Society for Research in Child Development. New Orleans, LA.

MARTINEZ, P., & RICHTERS, J. E. (1993). The NIMH Community Violence Project: II. Children's distress symptoms associated with violence exposure. *Psychiatry, 56,* 22–35.

McLOYD, V. C., & WILSON, L. (1991). The strain of living poor: Parenting, social support, and child mental health. In A. C. Huston (Ed.), *Children in poverty: Child development and public policy* (pp. 105–135). Cambridge, England: Cambridge University Press.

PATTERSON, G. R. (1983). Stress: A change agent in the family. In N. Garmenzy & M. Rutter (Eds.), *Stress, coping, and development in children* (pp. 235–264). New York: McGraw-Hill.

QUITTNER, A. L., & OPIPARI, L. C. (1994). Differential treatment of siblings: Interview and diary analyses comparing two family contexts. *Child Development, 65,* 800–814.

REPETTI, R. L. (1989). Effects of daily workload on subsequent behavior during marital interaction: The roles of social withdrawal and spouse support. *Journal of Personality and Social Psychology, 57,* 651–659.

REPETTI, R. L. (1992). Social withdrawal as a short-term coping response to daily stressors. In H. Friedman (Ed.), *Hostility, coping, and health* (pp. 151–165). Washington, DC: American Psychological Association.

REPETTI, R. L. (1994). Short-term and long-term processes linking job stressors to father–child interaction. *Social Development, 3,* 1–15.

REPETTI, R. L. (1996). The effects of perceived daily social and academic failure experiences on school-age children's subsequent interactions with parents. *Child Development, 67,* 1467–1482.

REPETTI, R. L., & WOOD, J. (1997). The effects of daily stress at work on mothers' interactions with preschoolers. *Journal of Family Psychology, 11,* 90–108.

RICHTERS, J. E., & MARTINEZ, P. (1993). The NIMH Community Violence Project: I. Children as victims of and witnesses to violence. *Psychiatry, 56,* 7–21.

SNYDER, J. (1991). Discipline as a mediator of the impact of maternal stress and mood on child conduct problems. *Development and Psychopathology, 3,* 263–276.

STONE, A. A., & KENNEDY-MOORE, E. (1992). Commentary to part three: Assessing situational coping: Conceptual and methodological considerations. In H. S. Friedman (Ed.), *Hostility, coping, & health* (pp. 203–214). Washington, DC: American Psychological Association.

THOMSON, B., & VAUX, A. (1986). The importation, transmission, and moderation of stress in the family system. *American Journal of Community Psychology, 14,* 39–57.

WAHLER, R. G. (1990). Some perceptual functions of social networks in coercive mother–child interactions. *Journal of Social and Clinical Psychology, 9,* 43–53.

WEINRAUB, M., & WOLF, B. M. (1983). Effects of stress and social supports on mother–child interactions in single- and two-parent families. *Child Development, 54,* 1297–1311.

WEST, S. G., & HEPWORTH, J. T. (1991). Statistical issues in the study of temporal data: Daily experiences. *Journal of Personality, 59,* 609–662.

8

Reciprocity in the Expression of Emotional Support among Later-Life Couples Coping with Stroke

MARY ANN PARRIS STEPHENS and SARAH L. CLARK

STROKE AS A CHRONIC STRESSOR FOR MARRIED COUPLES

One of the consequences of increased life expectancy is the growing likelihood that older adults will experience chronic illnesses or disabling conditions that can dramatically impact the quality of their own and their family members' lives. Most older adults in the United States have at least one chronic health condition, and many have multiple chronic conditions (American Association of Retired Persons [AARP] & Administration on Aging [AoA], 1993). Nearly 30% of adults over the age of 65 and almost 60% of those over the age of 85 are limited in their activities of daily living due to health problems (AARP & AoA, 1993). In this chapter we focus on older adults who have experienced a recent stroke, particularly on how they and their caregiving spouses cope with its emotional aftermath.

The third-leading cause of both death and disability among older adults is cerebrovascular accident, or stroke (Kerson & Kerson, 1985).

MARY ANN PARRIS STEPHENS and SARAH L. CLARK • Department of Psychology, Kent State University, Kent, Ohio 44242-0001.

Coping with Chronic Stress, edited by Benjamin H. Gottlieb. Plenum Press, New York, 1997.

Estimates of the annual incidence of stroke in the United States range from 600,000 to 750,000, and the incidence increases with age (Schulz, Tompkins, & Rau, 1988). Among stroke survivors, functional improvements usually peak between 2 and 3 months following the stroke, and any additional improvements occur very gradually, such that recovery usually continues over many years (McCaffrey & Fisher, 1987). Despite the long-term recovery process, most stroke survivors continue to live with complex behavioral limitations and with marked changes in personality and affect (Binder, Howieson, & Coull, 1987; Kerson & Kerson, 1985). Hence, stroke and its aftermath typically occasion chronic stress that requires patients to undergo considerable psychosocial adaptation.

Because of the limitations imposed by a stroke, patients often must rely on others for assistance with many basic activities and for emotional support (Kerson & Kerson, 1985; Thompson, Sobolew-Shubin, Graham, & Janigian, 1989). Research indicates that older adults who are disabled or chronically ill turn first to their spouses in times of need (Chappell, 1991). In comparison to friends and family, spouses have been found to give the most coping assistance to patients during periods of illness, which may be due to the proximity, accessibility, interdependence, and intimacy they share (Burke, Weir, & Harrison, 1976; Primono, Yates, & Woods, 1990).

In addition to changing patients' lives, illness can also alter their spouses' lives in profound ways. Many spouses must assume caregiving responsibilities for the ill partner (such as assisting with personal care and other daily activities), perform new or additional household tasks, and provide more emotional support to the patient than usual (Flor, Turk, & Scholz, 1987; Revenson & Majerovitz, 1990). Caregivers to stroke patients also report problems such as having no time for themselves, alterations in the marital and other family relationships, and a decline in physical and mental health (Schulz et al., 1988). Living with an ill person often creates unique emotional distress, and as a result, many spouses experience depression, anxiety, and marital dissatisfaction (Flor et al., 1987). Thus, stroke and its aftermath can engender chronic stress for spouses as well as for patients. Like patients, spouses also need a long time to adjust to changes that illness brings to their lives.

EMOTIONAL SUPPORT IN THE CONTEXT OF CHRONIC ILLNESS

Because of the considerable changes that result from a stroke, both patients and their spouses must contend with a plethora of emotional demands. During the recovery period, spouses have to cope with both their own and their partner's emotional reactions. Each partner is faced with at least three potentially conflicting challenges to adjustment: managing his or her own distress, attending to various instrumental tasks, and grappling with the other partner's presence and emotional needs (Coyne & Fiske, 1992).

Research on close relationships has begun to emphasize how strongly interdependent partners in an intimate relationship are. It is well understood that partners share each other's stresses and satisfactions and that the difficulties faced by one partner can have profound implications for the well-being of the other (Anderson & McCulloch, 1993; Coyne & Fiske, 1992; Rook, Dooley, & Catalano, 1991). In marriage, because partners share many life experiences, they are often attempting to cope with the same or related stressful events at the same time. The irony is that when stressors affect both partners, the partners feel a greater need to rely on one another for emotional support while simultaneously feeling less able to help one another (DeLongis & O'Brien, 1990). To complicate the situation further, for many couples who are coping with the consequences of a stroke, the functional limitations of the ill spouse restrict the social involvements of both partners. The result is that the two partners often become more socially isolated and more dependent on one another for support.

Given the importance of marital relationships in maintaining good health and well-being (Burman & Margolin, 1992), emotional support between partners may be critical to married couples' adjustment to the chronic stress imposed by an illness or disabling condition. The expression of emotional support, however, may be associated with a number of difficulties, including the possibility that the support required to maintain and regulate a marital relationship may be different from and even oppose the efforts that are needed to manage one's own emotions or address the instrumental changes brought about by illness. Both partners face dilemmas such as how to contribute to their spouse's well-being while taking care of themselves, and thus have to balance their own and their spouse's emotional needs (Coyne & Fiske, 1992; Gottlieb & Wagner, 1991).

Despite the limited personal resources available to each partner during the stroke recovery period, when one of them is emotionally distressed, the other is likely to try to help out. Partners' responses to the emotional needs of their spouses may vary considerably across individuals and situations, and some responses appear to be more crucial to the relationship than others. The ability to respond empathically to one's spouse—to take the spouse's perspective—has been identified as important for maintaining marital relationships (Hansson & Carpenter, 1994). Empathy allows partners to understand and feel each other's upset and to respond in a way that communicates this understanding (Davis & Oathout, 1987). When marital partners are able to share emotions, they are more likely to respond to one another's distress in warm and caring ways. Furthermore, when spouses receive empathic responses, they interpret them as helpful and are more satisfied with the relationship (Davis & Oathout, 1987). The social support literature has shown that distressed people invariably regard expressions of affection and appreciation as helpful (Clark & Stephens, 1996; Dakof & Taylor, 1990: Lehman, Ellard, & Wortman, 1986; Lehman & Hemphill, 1990).

In contrast, the inability to experience another's feelings or to take his or her perspective may predispose one partner to respond insensitively to the other (Davis & Oathout, 1987). Marital research indicates that insensitive communications, such as one partner's criticism of and disrespect for the other, are perceived as unhelpful and occur more often in troubled marriages (Davis & Oathout, 1987; Long & Andrews, 1990). In addition, research on social support has consistently found that such communications from relational partners are deemed unhelpful by individuals facing a variety of life stressors (Clark & Stephens, 1996; Dakof & Taylor, 1990; Lehman et al., 1986; Lehman & Hemphill, 1990).

Older adults' perceptions of the helpfulness of social interactions with network members can have serious consequences for their emotional well-being. One of the most consistent findings in research on social support in later life is that the social interactions of older adults, including those who have experienced a stroke, are characterized by more supportive than problematic exchanges. The supportive interactions that have been examined include communications of understanding and caring, whereas the more problematic interactions involve insensitive communications, such as hostile criticism and unwanted advice. Although they occur less often, when problematic interactions do occur, they are usually more strongly related to psychological distress than are more supportive exchanges (Norris, Stephens, & Kinney, 1990; Pagel, Erdly, & Becker, 1987; Rook, 1984; Rook, 1990; Stephens, Kinney, Norris, & Ritchie, 1987). In addition, these problematic exchanges typically involve individuals with whom the older adult shares a close relationship. For stroke patients, the vast majority of problematic interactions involve their primary caregivers, most of whom are their spouses (Norris et al., 1990).

Although all marriages inevitably involve "give-and-take" in the communication of support between partners, considerable variability exists in the degree to which support is reciprocated. Some partners provide more emotional support than they receive, and others receive more than they provide. Equity theorists have argued that an imbalance between the support that one receives from a partner and the support that one gives to that partner may result in emotional distress for both partners (Walster, Walster, & Berscheid, 1978). Underbenefitted partners (those who give more support than they receive) are likely to experience feelings of unfairness and resentment in the relationship, whereas overbenefitted partners (those who receive more support than they give) are likely to experience guilt concerning this inequity (Walster et al., 1978).

Research on close relationships in later life has provided some evidence to support the propositions of equity theory. The extent to which an older adult receives as much support (including emotional support) from network members as he or she provides has been shown to be related to better psychological well-being and less emotional distress (Ingersoll-Dayton & Antonucci, 1988; Rook, 1987). Those older adults who are either overbenefitted or underbenefitted in their social networks tend to experience greater distress than those whose networks are characterized by reciprocity (Rook, 1987). In addition, reciprocated support in older married couples is related to greater marital satisfaction and well-being for both husbands and wives (Acitelli & Antonucci, 1994).

Taken together, the research on marriage and social support suggests that the character of the communications between stroke patients and their caregiving spouses may be vital to each partner's psychological adjustment. Communications that convey empathy have the potential to offset the stroke's emotional impact, whereas those that convey insensitivity have the potential to exacerbate it. Furthermore, equity theorists would argue that the reciprocity between partners in these communications may also be a critical factor in each partner's adjustment.

A DYADIC STUDY OF COUPLES COPING WITH STROKE

We conducted a study of later-life married couples who were attempting to adjust to the changes that a stroke had brought to their lives. We were most keenly interested in two issues: (1) how one partner responded to his or her spouse when the spouse was feeling emotionally distressed and (2) how couples' styles of responding to one another were related to each partner's psychological well-being. Because both partners were undergoing a period of recovery and adjustment as a result of the stroke, we were interested not only in how the caregiving spouse communicated to the ill spouse when the latter was feeling upset, but also in the communications that occurred in the other direction as well. We were operating under the assumption that, like patients, caregivers have special needs for emotional support during this time, and, like caregivers, patients could be sources of significant support for their spouses.

Our study focused on communications that occurred between partners when one of them was upset about the stroke and its impact on their lives. Through these communications, one partner may have been attempting to help the other partner cope more effectively with his or her negative emotions, appraise the situation differently, or express less emotional distress. Because efforts by one partner to be supportive to another frequently miscarry and are perceived as being unsupportive (e.g., Lehman et al., 1986), we focused on the kinds of interpersonal communications that previous research has identified as unhelpful and unsupportive, as well as those that have been shown to be helpful and supportive.

Based on previous research, we expected that both patients and caregivers would report engaging in supportive communications more often than unsupportive ones. We also predicted that patients would report engaging in supportive communications less often and in unsupportive communications more often than caregivers. This prediction was based on assumptions about the roles that each partner occupied. On the one hand, people who occupy the sick role are often exempted from the responsibilities of normal living (Parsons, 1964), and as such, that may feel little need to offer support to their spouses and may feel justified in being insensitive to them. On the other hand, according to the norm of social responsibility (Berkowitz, 1972), people are expected to help those who are dependent on them. This expectation, coupled with the fact that the caregiving role by definition is a supportive one, may lead caregivers to feel an especially great need to offer support to their ill spouses and to refrain from insensitivities.

Our study also examined the effects of reciprocity in partners' ways of communicating with one another. We predicted that the more equitable partners were in their responses to each others' emotional distress, the less distress each partner would experience. More specifically, we predicted that married partners whose supportive communications were more reciprocal (i.e., where partners provided as much support as they received) would experience less distress than those partners whose supportive communications were more imbalanced (i.e., where one partner provided more support than the other).

A similar prediction was made regarding reciprocity in unsupportive communications. We reasoned that, although unsupportive communications have the potential to be hurtful, when partners engage in insensitive communications to a similar degree, such communications may seem less inappropriate and may become less salient to each partner. Therefore, it was predicted that the negative impact of unsupportive communications on distress would be lessened for marital partners who reciprocated such communications.

We also predicted that partners' level of distress would be unrelated to the type of imbalance that existed in the couple's communications. According to equity theory, both partners in nonreciprocal relationships experience discomfort with the imbalance. Therefore, we expected that there would be no differences in distress between the group that was imbalanced due to patients' communications being more supportive (or unsupportive) and the group that was imbalanced due to caregivers' communication being more supportive (or unsupportive).

Sample Characteristics

Our sample comprised 57 couples in which one partner had been discharged from inpatient stroke rehabilitation within the previous 2 years. Patients were identified through medical records at two rehabilitation hospitals. To be eligible, patients had to be at least 55 years of age and currently residing in the community with their spouses, and their spouses had to have served as primary caregiver since the stroke occurred. Personal interviews were conducted with couples in their homes. Patients and their spouses were interviewed separately on the same day, both to facilitate openness in responding and to avoid the couple's discussing the interview before both had participated.

Most patients in our sample were men (82.5%), and thus most caregivers were women (82.5%). The average age of patients was about 68 years, and caregivers' average age was about 66 years. Couples had been married for an average of 37 years. Both patients and caregivers had completed an average of 12 years of education. Approximately 90% of couples were Caucasian, 7% were interracial (Caucasian and African-American), and the remaining 3% of couples were African-American. Studies of the incidence of stroke indicate that men and African-Americans are more likely than women and Caucasians to have a stroke (Kerson & Kerson, 1985). Thus, our sample adequately represented the stroke population in terms of gender but under represented African-Americans.

Many of the patients required assistance with basic activities of daily living. Three fourths reported requiring assistance with at least one daily activity, half required assistance with both bathing and dressing, and one third required assistance moving around the house. Caregivers reported providing extensive assistance to patients. Three fourths of the caregivers reported that they assisted patients with at least one basic activity. Over three fifths assisted patients with bathing and dressing, and two fifths assisted with mobility inside the house.

Measures of Interpersonal Communication and Distress

In constructing our measures of supportive and unsupportive communications, we examined the literature on those verbal and nonverbal communications from others that people under stress find helpful and unhelpful (Dakof & Taylor, 1990; Dunkel-Schetter, Blasband, Feinstein, & Herbert, 1992; Lehman et al., 1986). Helpful communications most often include expressions of love, concern, and empathy for the distressed person, whereas unhelpful communications most often include criticism, unwanted advice, minimization of the effort required to cope, and insistence that feelings improve. Helpful communications typically involve assurance and affirmation of the other person's worth; unhelpful communications generally involve judgmental evaluations about actions and feelings.

On the basis of these studies, we developed eight items to reflect supportive communications and eight items to reflect unsupportive communications. These items are shown in Tables 1 and 2. Each spouse

Table 1. Percent of Patients and Caregivers Endorsing Supportive Communication Items ($N = 57$)

Item	Patient	Caregiver
How often . . .		
Do you try to show concern and interest in how your spouse is feeling?	98.2	100.0
Are you just there for him or her?	98.2	100.0
Do you tell your spouse that you appreciate what he or she has done to cope with the stroke?	94.7	86.0
Do you tell your spouse that you really care about him or her?	93.0	100.0
Do you try to point out your spouse's strengths or good qualities?	91.3	96.5
Do you tell your spouse that you love him or her?	91.2	93.0
Do you let your spouse know that you are trying to understand his or her feelings?	91.3	93.0
Do you listen to your spouse talk about his or her feelings?	75.4	94.7

Table 2. Percent of Patients and Caregivers Endorsing Unsupportive Communication Items ($N = 57$)

Item	Patient	Caregiver
How often . . .		
Do you try to convince your spouse that the changes in his or her life could have been much worse?	89.5	42.1
Do you tell your spouse that there is a reason for everything, even the stroke?	87.8	56.1
Do you give your spouse advice on how to cope better?	87.8	75.4
Do you try to change the conversation to a happier topic?	79.0	61.5
Do you encourage your spouse to forget about the upset and to get on with his or her life?	72.0	43.9
Do you tell your spouse that you know exactly what he or she is going through?	70.2	73.7
Do you encourage your spouse to overcome the situation and to take charge of his or her own life?	70.2	43.9
Do you try to act cheerful even if you don't feel that way?	61.4	47.4

was asked about the things he or she typically said or did whenever the partner was feeling down or upset about the changes that had occurred since the stroke. Specifically, they were told, "Since the stroke, your spouse may have felt upset at times. I'll be asking you about the things you have said or done when your spouse seems to be feeling down or upset about the changes that have occurred in (his or her) life because of the stroke."

In the interview, the items reflecting supportive and unsupportive communications were alternated to reduce acquiescence bias in responding. For each supportive communication item, respondents were asked to indicate how often they had used this form of communication using a four-point scale ranging from 1 (rarely or none of the time) to 4 (most or all of the time). These ratings were summed to yield a single score that could range from 8 to 32. A similar procedure was used to score unsupportive communications. The alpha coefficient for patients' supportive communications was .79; for their unsupportive communications, it was .72. The alpha coefficient for caregivers' supportive communications was .72; for their unsupportive communications, it was .69.

Because we asked partners how they responded to their spouses' upset concerning the stroke, we were interested in how these communications related to their spouses' emotional distress concerning the stroke, rather than to distress in general. Stroke negative affect was assessed using a nine-item scale designed for this study. Three domains of negative affect were assessed: anxiety (e.g., fear about the effects of the stroke), anger (e.g., resentment about the stroke and its effects on daily life), and sadness (e.g., disappointment that the future may not be as good as had been hoped because of the stroke).

Each item was rated on the four-point scale described previously. These items were summed; total scale scores could range from 9 to 36. The mean score for patients' stroke negative affect was 22.2 (SD = 7.3; range = 10–36), and the mean score for caregivers was 20.7 (SD = 6.8; range = 10–35). The ranges indicate that every patient and caregiver in this sample reported experiencing at least some distress related to the stroke. The alpha coefficient for both patients and caregivers on this measure was .87.

Supportive and Unsupportive Communications

To describe the kinds of communications used by patients and caregivers, we used two approaches. First, we examined supportive and unsupportive communications within each group, and second, we examined these same forms of communication across the two groups. The correlation between patients' reports of their supportive and unsupportive communications was −.50 ($p < .01$), and the correlation between caregivers' reports of their supportive and unsupportive communications was −.37 ($p < .01$). Because the sample size was small, we allowed effects that were significant at the .10 level to be interpreted as evidence for our hypotheses. As we predicted, both patients and caregivers expressed supportive communications significantly more often than unsupportive communications ($t = 3.43$; $p \leq .001$ and $t = 12.15$; $p < .001$, respectively). The mean for patients' supportive communications was 26.4 (SD = 4.9, range = 12–32), and the mean for their unsupportive communications was 22.4 (SD = 5.5; range = 9–32). The mean for caregivers' supportive communications was 28.8 (SD = 3.5; range = 18–32), and the mean for their unsupportive communications was 17.1 (SD = 5.2; range = 8–28).

Table 1 shows the percentages of patients and caregivers who indicated that they engaged in each supportive communication at least some of the time when their spouse was experiencing upset because of the stroke. Most striking is that each form of supportive communication was endorsed by at least three quarters of patients and caregivers and that most of these communications were endorsed by over 90% of both groups. Virtually all patients reported both demonstrations of concern and interest in the distressed spouse and "just being there" for the spouse. All caregivers reported using these same two forms of communication as well as telling their spouse that they cared about them. In line with our predictions, caregivers used supportive communications significantly more often ($m = 28.8$) than did patients ($m = 26.4$; $t = -3.43$; $p < .001$).

The percentages of patients and caregivers expressing unsupportive communications are presented in Table 2. Unsupportive communications used by at least 85% of patients including stating that everything in life has a reason, telling their spouses that things could be worse, and giving advice to their spouses on how to cope better. About three fourths of caregivers reported that they also gave advice to their spouses on how to cope better and that they told their spouses that they knew exactly how the spouses felt. Four of the eight forms of unsupportive communications were reported by less than half the caregivers. In contrast, every form of unsupportive communication was reported by at least 60% of patients. As we predicted, patients engaged in unsupportive communications significantly more often ($m = 22.4$) than did caregivers ($m = 17.1$; $t = 5.58$; $p < .001$).

Because not all of our patients were men (and conversely, not all of our caregivers were women) we attempted to determine the extent to which supportive and unsupportive communications may have been due to gender rather than role. We used two strategies to examine potential gender effects in supportive and unsupportive communications. Our first strategy was to compare the supportive and unsupportive communications of the men and women in our sample, regardless of their patient or caregiver status (e.g., female patients and caregivers were combined into one group and male patients and caregivers were combined into another group). Significant differences were found for both supportive and unsupportive communications. Women expressed supportive communications significantly more often ($m = 28.5$) than did men ($m = 26.8$; $t = -1.98$; $p \leq .05$), and they expressed unsupportive communications significantly less often ($m = 17.7$) than did men ($m = 21.8$; $t = 3.95$; $p < .001$). Because of the high degree of overlap between gender and role (over four fifths of patients were men and over four fifths of caregivers were women), it is not surprising that the means for analyses based on gender are almost identical to those based on role status.

Our second strategy was to examine the effects of gender within groups by comparing the supportive and unsupportive communications of male and female patients and those of male and female caregivers. No significant differences were found in any of these comparisons. These null findings may have been due to the lower statistical power of these analyses compared to the former ones. However, an inspection of means suggests that the differences in supportive and unsupportive communications may be due more to role than to gender. For example, whereas the differences between men and women on unsupportive communications in the previous analyses were quite large (4.1 scale points), the differences between men and women on unsupportive communications in these latter analyses were quite small (averaging 1.3 scale points across these analyses—the means for male and female patients' unsupportive communications were 22.6 and 21.5; the means for male and female caregivers' unsupportive communications were 18.2 and 16.8).

Comparing Partners on Psychological Distress and Communications

Our next set of analyses was concerned with the extent to which marital partners were similar to one another regarding their states of distress about the stroke, as well as their use of supportive and unsupportive communications. The correlation coefficient between patients and caregivers for stroke negative affect revealed a significant relationship ($r = .26$; $p \leq .05$). These findings are consistent with previous research suggesting that each partner's well-being influences and is influenced by his or her spouse's well-being (e.g., Acitelli & Antonucci, 1994; Coyne & Smith, 1991).

The relationship between partners' supportive communications was similar to that for negative affect. The correlation coefficient representing this relationship was .27 ($p < .05$). In contrast, the relationship between partners' unsupportive communications was not significant ($r = .10$).

Further analyses examined the correspondence between one partner's supportive and unsupportive communications and the other partner's stroke negative affect. Neither of the correlation coefficients between either type of patients' communications and caregivers' distress were significant. Similarly, there were no significant findings for relationships between caregivers' communications and patients' distress.

Reciprocity in Communications

We used two strategies to test our hypothesis that less distress would be found among those couples whose supportive (or unsupportive) communications were more reciprocal. The first strategy examined reciprocity without taking into consideration whether patients were more supportive (or unsupportive) than their spouses or whether caregivers were more supportive (or unsupportive) than their spouses. In contrast, the second strategy emphasized these differences in partners' supportive (or unsupportive) communications.

Using the first strategy to test our hypothesis, we computed difference scores between patients and caregivers in the amount of supportive and unsupportive communications they reported. Each caregiver's supportive communication score was subtracted from his or her spouse's score on that same scale. We performed the same computations for unsupportive communications. Because these analyses were concerned only with the degree of reciprocity in communications, we used the absolute values of the difference scores. These scores ranged from 0 (greatest reciprocity) to 20 (least reciprocity) for both supportive and unsupportive communications.

We computed Pearson product-moment correlation coefficients to assess the association between these difference scores and each partner's negative affect. Positive associations would provide evidence that the more reciprocal partners were in their ways of communicating with one another (reciprocity scores closer to 0), the less distress each partner would experience. The correlation between reciprocity in couples' supportive communications and caregivers' distress was .22 ($p \leq .10$), and the coefficient for patients' distress was not significant. In analyses examining the associations between reciprocity in unsupportive communications and each partner's distress, the coefficient for caregivers was .23 ($p < .10$), and the coefficient for patients approached significance ($r = .20; p = .14$).

Our second strategy for testing the hypothesis focused on three groups: (1) patients expressing more supportive (or unsupportive) communications, (2) partners expressing supportive (or unsupportive) communications in similar amounts, and (3) caregivers expressing more supportive (or unsupportive) communications. We again computed difference scores, and unlike the first analytic strategy (where absolute values were used), in this strategy we retained the signs of these difference scores. The difference scores for supportive communications ranged from 9 to −20. For unsupportive communications, the difference scores ranged from 20 to −13.

Using these difference scores on the supportive measure, couples were classified into three groups. Partners were considered to be more reciprocal in their communications if their difference score was 0 or near 0. Because the number of couples whose difference score was equal to 0 was too small to permit confident statistical analysis ($n = 6$), we considered couples whose difference score was between +2 and −2 to be characterized as more reciprocal in supportive communications. Couples whose difference score was either above or below these values were considered to be less reciprocal in supportive communications. Group 1 (patients reporting more supportive communications) had 11 couples; Group 2 (partners reporting similar amounts of supportive communications) had 19 couples; and Group 3 (caregivers reporting more supportive communications) had 27 couples.

A similar procedure was used to classify couples according to differences in unsupportive communications. Here Group 1 (patients reporting more unsupportive communications) had 36 couples; Group 2 (patients and caregivers reporting similar amounts of unsupportive communications) had 9 couples; and Group 3 (caregivers reporting more unsupportive communications) had 12 couples. Classifying couples on the basis of supportive and unsupportive communications yielded different groups of individuals; for example, only 32% of couples classified into Group 2 based on supportive communications were also classified into Group 2 based on unsupportive communications.

One-way analyses of variance (ANOVA) were conducted to examine differences in stroke negative affect among couples classified according to differences in supportive communications and differences in unsupportive communications. Before conducting these analyses, we examined groups for differences on 19 patient and caregiver demographic and health variables (e.g., age, income, functional limitations). Because no significant differences were found among these groups for any of these variables, no covariates were used.

Student Newman Keuls post hoc analyses were used to compare cell means in those analyses that attained statistical significance. For our hypotheses to be fully supported, the distress levels of individuals in Group 2 (where supportive/unsupportive communications occurred in similar amounts) would have to be significantly lower than those for individuals in both Groups 1 and 3 (where supportive and unsupportive communications occurred in different amounts). In addition, no significant differences would exist in levels of distress between individuals in Group 1 (where patients were more supportive/unsupportive) and Group 3 (where caregivers were more supportive/unsupportive).

The top half of Table 3 reports the results of analyses for groups that were classified by supportive communications. Only the ANOVA for caregivers' stroke negative affect was significant ($p < .10$). Post hoc analyses revealed that only the means for Groups 1 and 2 differed significantly. As predicted, caregivers in Group 2 experienced less distress than those in Group 1, but contrary to our prediction, they did not experience significantly less distress than caregivers in Group 3. Also as predicted, no significant differences were found between Groups 1 and 3 for caregivers' stroke negative affect.

The bottom half of Table 3 presents the analyses for groups that

Table 3. Analyses of Variance in Stroke Negative Affect for Groups Classified on Supportive and Unsupportive Communications

	Supportive group means (SD)[a]				
	Group 1 (n = 11)	Group 2 (n = 19)	Group 3 (n = 27)	F(2,54)	Post hoc[b]
Patients	22.9 (7.0)	20.7 (7.5)	22.9 (7.4)	0.6	—
Caregivers	23.9 (5.6)	18.2 (7.1)	21.2 (6.5)	2.7[d]	1 and 2[e]
	Unsupportive group means (SD)[c]				
	Group 1 (n = 36)	Group 2 (n = 9)	Group 3 (n = 12)	F(2,54)	Post hoc[b]
Patients	22.9 (7.4)	15.3 (6.5)	25.2 (4.6)	6.1[f]	1 and 2,[e] 2 and 3[e]
Caregivers	21.7 (6.6)	15.6 (6.1)	21.7 (6.5)	3.3[e]	1 and 2,[e] 2 and 3[e]

[a]Group 1, patients more supportive; Group 2, patients and caregivers about equally supportive; Group 3, caregivers more supportive.
[b]Groups that are significantly different using the Student Newman Keuls analysis.
[c]Group 1, patients more unsupportive; Group 2, patients and caregivers about equally unsupportive; Group 3, caregivers more unsupportive.
[d]$p \leq .10$; [e]$p \leq .05$; [f]$p \leq .01$.

were classified on unsupportive communications. The ANOVAs for both patients' and caregivers' stroke negative affect reached significance ($p < .01$ and $p < .05$, respectively). The post hoc analyses for patients' stroke negative affect were significant and in the direction we had predicted. Compared to patients in Groups 1 and 3, patients in Group 2 experienced significantly less negative affect, and patients in Groups 1 and 3 did not differ from one another. Post hoc analyses also revealed significant differences between groups for caregivers' stroke negative affect. Again consistent with our predictions, caregivers in Group 2 experienced significantly less stroke-related distress than caregivers in the two other groups, and caregivers in Groups 1 and 3 did not differ from one another.

SOME OBSERVATIONS ON COUPLES COPING WITH STROKE

Our study clearly demonstrates that marital partners who are experiencing a period of significant adjustment communicate with each other in a variety of ways during episodes of emotional distress. It also points out that, whereas many of the communications they use may not be considered to be helpful, other communications may be considered to be quite helpful. In our study, both patients and caregivers frequently used forms of communication that prior research has found to be insensitive and unsupportive, such as minimizing the distressed partners' emotional pain and avoiding upsetting topics. However, they more often used communications that have been shown to be emotionally supportive, such as expressing love and attempting to understand. These findings—taken from the perspective of the support provider—are remarkably similar to findings from previous research taken from the perspective of the support recipient (Pagel et al., 1987; Rook, 1984; Rook, 1990; Stephens et al., 1987). This convergence enhances the confidence that can be placed in the constructs that represent supportive and unsupportive responses of significant others to people in need.

Our findings also suggest that individuals experiencing a chronic illness are not only recipients of emotional support from their spouses, but they are also active support providers who attend to their spouses' emotional needs. In line with our predictions, however, when compared to caregivers, patients were less often supportive and were more often unsupportive in responding to their partners' distress. We based these predictions on assumptions about the expectations and obligations that patients may have had as occupants of the sick role, such as believing that they did not have to work at maintaining the relationship because they were sick, as well as the expectations and obligations of caregivers in their role as support providers, such as believing that it was up to them to work extra hard to maintain the relationship during the patients' recovery period. It is also quite possible that patients may not have been able to respond with greater support because their health condition limited the amount of resources and energy they could devote to the relationship with their spouses. Furthermore, patients' frequent use of unsupportive communications, such as criticism and disrespect, may have been indirect expressions of resentment about their disability and the limitations it imposed on their lives. Whatever the explanation, it appears that these differences in responding may have been due more to communicators' roles as patients or caregivers than to their gender.

We found some evidence to suggest that equity in partners' communications is related to how well patients and their spouses emotionally adjust to the occurrence of a chronic illness and its aftermath. The strongest evidence to support our hypothesis that couples whose communications are characterized by reciprocity would experience less stroke-related distress was found in the analyses of unsupportive communications. Analyses of supportive communications also provided limited evidence for this hypothesis, but only for caregivers' distress. Furthermore, consistent with the predictions of equity theory, we found no differences in levels of distress for individuals in relationships where communications were imbalanced, either because the patient was more supportive (or unsupportive) or because the caregiver was more supportive (or unsupportive).

Regarding unsupportive communications, we found evidence to support our hypothesis for both patients and caregivers. As we had predicted, the least amount of distress was found among partners in couples in which unsupportive communications were mutually reciprocated, whereas the greatest distress was experienced by partners in couples in which there were unequal amounts of these communications. These findings held regardless of the source of the inequity, that is, whether patients' communications were more unsupportive than spouses' or vice versa.

It has been argued that the powerful effects of unsupportive or problematic interactions on psychological well-being may be due to their salience to the recipient, the suspicious attributions they engender, or the threats to personal safety they imply (Rook, 1990). However, we found no evidence that one partner's use of unsupportive communications was directly related to the other partner's distress. It was only when couples' styles of responding to one another were considered simultaneously that the negative effects of such communications were evidenced. In couples where one partner is more unsupportive than the other, the recipient may perceive these communications as prominent, maliciously motivated, or threatening, and the unsupportive partner may experience guilt and remorse about his or her insensitivity. As a result, distress appears to be the outcome. In contrast, when partners are insensitive with one another to the same degree, the salience, suspiciousness, and threat that often accompany such expressions may be lessened because they represent a normal way of interacting, and their generally benign motivations may be understood by both partners.

These findings raise an intriguing issue concerning the applicability of equity theory under extreme conditions of interpersonal insensitivity, namely, whether the principles of reciprocity hold when interactions between marital partners are intensely negative and hostile. That is, it might be questioned whether there is an upper limit or point beyond which the ameliorative effects of reciprocity in unsupportive communications are reduced. We have some, albeit limited, data to examine this possibility.

Our findings revealed that couples in the more reciprocal group varied greatly in their use of unsupportive communications, with some exchanging high levels of unsupportive communications and others exchanging low levels. These findings would suggest that the expression of intensely negative communications may not impose serious limitations on the propositions of equity theory. However, it is not certain how well our findings would generalize (or how well equity propositions would apply) to couples who are even more insensitive to one another than those couples who comprised our more reciprocal group. Evidence from other research has shown that distressed couples (including those with violent husbands) reciprocate negative behaviors, such as arguments and criticism, to a greater degree than nondistressed couples, suggesting that there indeed may be some upper limit on the principles of equity theory as they pertain to negative interpersonal interactions (Cordova, Jacobson, Gottman, Rushe, & Cox, 1993). However, the couples in our sample had been married for many years, and it may be that long-standing patterns of interactions that are characterized by high doses of mutual insensitivity have different effects on emotional distress than patterns of insensitivity with a shorter history.

In line with our prediction, caregivers whose spouses reciprocated supportive communications to a greater degree experienced less distress than caregivers whose spouses' communications were more supportive than their own. Contrary to our prediction, however, caregivers in the more reciprocal relationships did not experience less distress than caregivers whose spouses' communications were less supportive than their own. Perhaps caregivers in the latter group were not highly distressed because the imbalance in supportive communications may have seemed justifiable in the context of their spouse's chronic illness. The sense of unfairness or resentment that might ordinarily result from being under-benefitted may have been offset by the differential expectations caregivers had of supportiveness from their ill partners and from themselves as support providers.

The modest findings for reciprocity in supportive communications may have been due in part to ceiling effects in the measurement of supportive exchanges. Supportive communication scores were highly skewed in the direction of greater support. Thus, it is possible that our measures of supportive communications were not able to register the true variability that existed in such communications.

One reason for the skewed distribution of the supportive communication scores may be because individuals frequently overestimate the amount of support they provide to others (Ingersoll-Dayton & Antonucci, 1988). The demand characteristics of the social support items and the data collection procedures we used may have also caused the skewed distribution. Because the support items reflect obvious and important social values and expectations concerning intimate relationships, respondents' reports may have been colored by the need to present a positive image to the interviewer. Subsequent research on support from the perspective of the support provider may wish to employ less potentially reactive methods of data collection, such as daily diaries.

CONCLUDING COMMENTS

Although our study documented some of the empathic and insensitive ways partners typically responded to one another during episodes of emotional upset, it did not examine more subtle aspects of these communications. Factors such as the communicator's motivations and intentions, as well as the receiver's interpretations, may be critical to understanding the impact of a communication on the receiver. Especially when both spouses are undergoing the same chronically stressful situation, both often have emotional needs that deserve attention, and helping one's self can sometimes conflict with, or preclude, helping the partner. Thus, in some situations, the motivation of the communicator may be more to deal with his or her own needs and emotional states than with those of the partner (Batson, 1991).

Even when the communicator is altruistically motivated to deal with the emotional needs of the partner, his or her intended support may miscarry in at least two ways. On the one hand, the communicator might use a form of communication that has generally been shown to be helpful, although the recipient does not perceive it as such. For example, a husband, listening patiently to his wife who is emotionally aroused, may think that he is being supportive by "being there" for her, while the wife, perceiving that her husband is doing nothing overtly to help, interprets his silence as being unsupportive. On the other hand, the communicator's positive intent may be mismatched with a less than helpful way of expressing support. For example, a wife may attempt to be empathic with her husband by assuring him that things really could be worse, and he may interpret her communication as being insensitive. As a result, his negative emotional state may not be alleviated as she had hoped. Although such nuances of interpersonal communication were not the focus of the current study, they may be important for a more complete understanding of marital communications in the context of a chronic stressor.

Our findings challenge some traditional assumptions about what constitutes a healthy relationship and what the goals of psychological interventions with couples should be. Traditionally, a major goal of couples' therapy has been to minimize the unsupportive communications between partners and maximize the supportive ones. However, our findings suggest that negative communications are not necessarily deleterious to well-being, unless they are one-sided or imbalanced in a relationship. Furthermore, there is mounting evidence to suggest that, although negative communications between marital partners may be disruptive to the relationship in the short term, they do not appear to be related to any long-term effects (Smith, Vivian, & O'Leary, 1991).

Our findings have other implications for clinical practice with couples who are attempting to adjust to the chronic stress of an illness. Even though patients may be seriously ill and physically disabled, they often can remain emotionally involved with their spouses. As such, one goal of interventions with these couples may be to create a climate in which patients' emotional support of their spouses is encouraged. A climate of mutual exchange could be beneficial for both patients and caregivers. By staying active in the relationship, patients may gain a stronger sense of self-worth, which is especially important when such feelings have been undermined by the illness. In contrast, by having a spouse who is emotionally accessible, caregivers may be better psychologically prepared to withstand the chronic stress of their caregiving roles.

ACKNOWLEDGMENTS   This research was supported in part by a Biomedical Research Support grant from the National Institutes of Health. The authors wish to thank Edwin Shaw Hospital in Akron, Ohio, and Hillside Hospital in Warren, Ohio, for their cooperation in soliciting respondents for this study.

REFERENCES

ACITELLI, L. K., & ANTONUCCI, T. C. (1994). Gender differences in the link between marital support and satisfaction in older couples. *Journal of Personality and Social Psychology, 67,* 688–698.
AMERICAN ASSOCIATION OF RETIRED PERSONS (AARP), PROGRAM RESOURCES DEPARTMENT, & ADMINISTRATION OF AGING (AoA), U.S. DEPARTMENT OF HEALTH AND HUMAN SERVICES. (1993). *A profile of older Americans: 1993* [Report No. PF3049 (1293) - D996]. Washington, DC: Author.
ANDERSON, T. B., & MCCULLOCH, B. J. (1993). Conjugal support: Factor structure for older husbands and wives. *Journal of Gerontology: Social Sciences, 3,* S133–142.
BATSON, C. D. (1991). *The altruism question: Toward a social–psychological answer.* Hillsdale, NJ: Lawrence Erlbaum.
BERKOWITZ, L. (1972). Social norms, feelings, and other factors affecting helping and altruism. In L. Berkowitz (Ed.), *Advances in experimental social psychology* (Vol. 6, pp. 63–108). New York: Academic Press.
BINDER, L. M., HOWIESON, D., & COULL, B. M. (1987). Stroke: Causes, consequences, and treatment. In B. Caplan (Ed.), *Rehabilitation psychology desk reference.* Rockville, MD: Aspen.

BURKE, R. J., WEIR, T., & HARRISON, D. (1976). Disclosure of problems and tensions experienced by marital partners. *Psychological Reports, 38*, 531–542.

BURMAN, B., & MARGOLIN, G. (1992). Analysis of the association between marital relationships and health problems: An interactional perspective. *Psychological Bulletin, 112*, 39–63.

CHAPPELL, N. L. (1991). Living arrangements and sources of caregiving. *Journal of Gerontology: Social Sciences, 46*, S1–8.

CLARK, S. L., & STEPHENS, M. A. P. (1996). Stroke patients' well-being as a function of caregiving spouses' helpful and unhelpful actions. *Personal Relationships, 3*, 171–184.

CORDOVA, J. V., JACOBSON, N. S., GOTTMAN, J. M., RUSHE, R., & COX, G. (1993). Negative reciprocity and communication in couples with a violent husband. *Journal of Abnormal Psychology, 102*, 559–564.

COYNE, J. C., & FISKE, V. (1992). Couples coping with chronic and catastrophic illness. In T. J. Akamatsu, M. A. P. Stephens, S. E. Hobfoll, & J. H. Crowther (Eds.), *Family health psychology* (pp. 129–149). Washington, DC: Hemisphere.

COYNE, J. C., & SMITH, D. A. K. (1991). Couples coping with a myocardial infarction: A contextual perspective on wives' distress. *Journal of Personality and Social Psychology, 61*, 404–412.

DAKOF, G. A., & TAYLOR, S. E. (1990). Victims' perceptions of social support: What is helpful from whom? *Journal of Personality and Social Psychology, 58*, 80–89.

DAVIS, M. H., & OATHOUT, H. A. (1987). Maintenance of satisfaction in romantic relationships: Empathy and relational competence. *Journal of Personality and Social Psychology, 53*, 397–410.

DELONGIS, A., & O'BRIEN, T. (1990). An interpersonal framework for stress and coping: An application to the families of Alzheimer's patients. In T. J. Akamatsu, M. A. P. Stephens, S. E. Hobfoll, & J. H. Crowther (Eds.), *Family health psychology* (pp. 221–239). Washington, DC: Hemisphere.

DUNKEL-SCHETTER, C., BLASBAND, D. E., FEINSTEIN, L. G., & HERBERT, T. B. (1992). Elements of supportive interactions: When are attempts to help effective? In S. Spacapan & S. Oskamp (Eds.), *Helping and being helped: Naturalistic studies* (pp. 83–114). Newbury Park, CA: Sage.

FLOR, H., TURK, D. C., & SCHOLZ, O. B. (1987). Impact of chronic pain on the spouse: Marital, emotional and physical consequences. *Journal of Psychosomatic Research, 31*, 63–71.

GOTTLIEB, B. H., & WAGNER, F. (1991). Stress and support processes in close relationships. In J. Eckenrode (Ed.), *The social context of coping* (pp. 165–188). New York: Plenum.

HANSSON, R. O., & CARPENTER, B. N. (1994). *Relationships in old age: Coping with the challenge of transition*. New York: Guilford.

INGERSOLL-DAYTON, B., & ANTONUCCI, T. C. (1988). Reciprocal and nonreciprocal social support: Contrasting sides of intimate relationships. *Journal of Gerontology: Social Sciences, 43*, S65–73.

KERSON, T. S., & KERSON, L. A. (1985). *Understanding chronic illness: The medical and psychological dimensions of nine diseases*. New York: Free Press.

LEHMAN, D. R., ELLARD, J. H., & WORTMAN, C. B. (1986). Social support for the bereaved: Recipients' and providers' perspectives on what is helpful. *Journal of Consulting and Clinical Psychology, 54*, 438–446.

LEHMAN, D. R., & HEMPHILL, K. J. (1990). Recipients' perceptions of support attempts and attributions for support attempts that fail. *Journal of Social and Personal Relationships, 7*, 563–574.

LONG, E. C. J., & ANDREWS, D. W. (1990). Perspective taking as a predictor of marital adjustment. *Journal of Personality and Social Psychology, 59*, 126–131.

MCCAFFREY, R. J., & FISHER, J. M. (1987). Cognitive, behavioral and psychosocial sequelae of cerebrovascular accidents and closed head injuries in older adults. In L. L. Carstensen & B. A. Edelstein (Eds.), *Handbook of clinical gerontology* (pp. 277–288). New York: Pergamon.

NORRIS, V. K., STEPHENS, M. A. P., & KINNEY, J. M. (1990). The impact of family interactions on recovery from stroke: Help or hindrance? *The Gerontologist, 30*, 535–542.
PAGEL, M. D., ERDLY, W. W., & BECKER, J. (1987). Social networks: We get by with (and in spite of) a little help from our friends. *Journal of Personality and Social Psychology, 53*, 793–804.
PARSONS, T. (1964). *Social structure and personality*. London: Collier-Macmillan.
PRIMONO, J., YATES, B. C., & WOODS, N. F. (1990). Social support for women during chronic illness: The relationship among sources and types of adjustment. *Research in Nursing and Health, 13*, 153–161.
REVENSON, T. A., & MAJEROVITZ, D. (1990). Spouses' support provision to chronically ill patients. *Journal of Social and Personal Relationships, 7*, 575–586.
ROOK, K. S. (1984). The negative side of social interactions: Impact on psychological well-being. *Journal of Personality and Social Psychology, 46*, 1097–1108.
ROOK, K. S. (1987). Reciprocity of social exchange and social satisfaction among older women. *Journal of Personality and Social Psychology, 52*, 145–154.
ROOK, K. S. (1990). Stressful aspects of older adults' social relationships: Current theory and research. In M. A. P. Stephens, J. H. Crowther, S. E. Hobfoll, & D. L. Tennenbaum (Eds.), *Stress and coping in later-life families* (pp. 173–192). New York: Hemisphere.
ROOK, K., DOOLEY, D., & CATALANO, R. (1991). Stress transmission: The effects of husbands' job stressors on the emotional health of their wives. *Journal of Marriage and the Family, 53*, 165–177.
SCHULZ, R., TOMPKINS, C. A., & RAU, M. T. (1988). A longitudinal study of the psychosocial impact of stroke on primary support persons. *Psychology and Aging, 3*, 131–141.
SMITH, D. A., VIVIAN, D., & O'LEARY, K. D. (1991). The misnomer proposition: A critical reappraisal of the longitudinal status of "negativity" in marital communication. *Behavioral Assessment, 13*, 7–24.
STEPHENS, M. A. P., KINNEY, J. M., NORRIS, V. K., & RITCHIE, S. W. (1987). Social networks as assets and liabilities in recovery from stroke by geriatric patients. *Psychology and Aging, 2*, 125–129.
THOMPSON, S. C., SOBOLEW-SHUBIN, A. S., GRAHAM, M. A., & JANIGIAN, A. S. (1989). Psychosocial adjustment following a stroke. *Social Science Medicine, 28*, 239–247.
WALSTER, E., WALSTER, G. W., & BERSCHEID, E. (1978). *Equity: Theory and research*. Boston: Allyn & Bacon.

IV

Considerations of Efficacy in Coping with Chronic Stress

9

Changes in Coping with Chronic Stress
The Role of Caregivers' Appraisals of Coping Efficacy

MONIQUE A. M. GIGNAC and BENJAMIN H. GOTTLIEB

INTRODUCTION

Relatively little is known about how the coping process unfolds in chronically stressful experiences and life circumstances. This is because most research on coping focuses on the efforts individuals employ in response to acute life events. Chronic stressors, however, are presumed to be inherently different from "event" stressors. Their onset is often gradual and insidious, their occurrence is so regular that they are experienced as continuous by persons undergoing them, and their offset is typically unpredictable (Wheaton, Chapter 2, this volume). How people cope with these ongoing demands is determined, in part, by the degree of flux in the nature and requirements of the stressor over time. That is, we should expect to see both fluidity and flexibility in the coping responses of people who are dealing with chronic stress (Aldwin & Brustrom, Chapter 3, this volume).

MONIQUE A. M. GIGNAC • Arthritis Community Research and Evaluation Unit, The Wellesley Hospital Research Institute, Toronto, Ontario, Canada M4Y 1J3. BENJAMIN H. GOTTLIEB • Department of Psychology, University of Guelph, Guelph, Ontario, Canada N1G 2W1.

Coping with Chronic Stress, edited by Benjamin H. Gottlieb. Plenum Press, New York, 1997.

The process of coping also involves continuously appraising and reappraising different facets of the environment as well as the consequences of responding to it in various ways (Lazarus & Folkman, 1984). That is, people subjectively assess whether their endeavors help them achieve some degree of success in meeting their coping goals within a specific stressful context (Aldwin & Revenson, 1987). These ongoing coping appraisals are critical because they may alter the trajectory of people's coping, their feelings about their own capacity to withstand stress, and their perseverence in the face of persistent and prolonged stressful demands. Hence, the ways that a person copes will change as a function of both changing demands and changing appraisals of the effects of coping on the self, others, and the situation. Yet, there have been few studies of the appraisal process and its relation to the coping goals individuals set for themselves or to their actual coping efforts.

This chapter addresses the relationship between people's coping efforts and their appraisals of the efficacy of those efforts. We explore this relationship within the context of family members who are caring for a relative with dementia. We begin by describing the caregiving context, including the nature of the stressors typically faced by caregivers and the ways that they cope with them. Because these stressors are repetitive, persistent, and of relatively long duration, caregivers have opportunities to learn about the varied personal and environmental effects of their coping efforts, to evaluate the efficacy of those efforts, and to alter their patterns of coping to better meet their goals. We present a typology of twelve kinds of efficacy appraisals that allow caregivers to determine their progress in coping and reflect five superordinate goals that guide their coping efforts. To further elucidate the various appraisal types and as a preliminary step in determining whether they are contextually bound or more traitlike in nature, we examine the concurrent relationships between the caregivers' appraisals and their specific coping efforts as well as the relative stability of the appraisals over time. We conclude the chapter by calling on prospective data that address the impact of appraisals of coping efficacy on subsequent coping efforts. In this way, we show that coping in the context of chronic stress can be strategic and goal-oriented. That is, changes in some coping behaviors are associated with specific types of appraisals of earlier coping efforts.

COPING WITH THE CHRONIC DEMANDS OF CAREGIVING

The demands of caring for a relative afflicted with dementia form the context for our study of the relations between coping and appraisals of its efficacy. One of the most stressful of these demands revolves around the characteristics of dementia itself. In addition to suffering from confusions and memory problems, dementia patients often exhibit a range of noxious symptoms, including incessant or irrational verbalizations, outbursts of aggression, irritability, hyperactivity, or wakefulness and wandering at night (Rabins, 1989; Rubin, Morris, Storandt, & Berg, 1987). Because these symptoms are uncontrollable, occur with considerable frequency, and are relatively permanent, they are stressful for family caregivers and other household members. In addition, efforts at behavioral management may not terminate or diminish these symptoms, or they may do so only temporarily.

Caring for a demented relative also can entail actual or anticipated losses, such as giving up leisure and employment opportunities or surrendering future plans (Gottlieb, Kelloway, & Fraboni, 1994; Rakowski & Clark, 1985; Scharlach, Sobel, & Roberts, 1991; Wheaton, 1991). In our research, we asked caregivers to identify "anything that you valued or that you had looked forward to which you have had to give up." We classified responses into four types of deprivations: the loss of independence and freedom, the loss of valued activities such as employment, hobbies, or volunteering, the loss of companionship with their relative, and the loss of opportunities to socialize with other family members and friends (Gottlieb & Gignac, 1996). Psychologically, such deprivations can compromise caregivers' sense of privacy and freedom and can result in feelings of "captivity" in the caregiving role (Pearlin, Mullan, Semple, & Skaff, 1990).

A third stressful feature of caregiving is that it takes place within the context of a close relationship (Kinney & Stephens, 1989). Dementia not only brings about wholesale personality changes that detract from the relationship between the two parties, but it also fosters dependency, disrupting shared routines and familiar patterns of interaction. These changes, combined with the caregivers' knowledge that their relative will become increasingly dependent upon them, can arouse caregivers' protective impulses while challenging their ability to maintain harmonious relations with their relative. Thus, caregivers must carefully consider the interpersonal costs and benefits of responding to their relative in different ways, making coping not only problem- and emotion-focused, but also relationship-focused (Coyne & Smith, 1991; Gottlieb & Wagner, 1991).

In order to manage these largely intractable demands and to maintain their morale, caregivers must find ways of rendering their circumstances less stressful. Although not entirely consistent, the findings of a number of studies reveal that greater use of problem-focused coping is associated with less depressive affect (Haley, Levine, Brown, & Bartolucci, 1987; Vitaliano, Russo, Carr, Maiuro, & Becker, 1985), whereas wishfulness (Pruchno & Kleban, 1993; Pruchno & Resch, 1989) and avoidant coping (Vitaliano et al., 1985) are associated with more depressive mood (Pearlin et al., 1990; Quayhagen & Quayhagen, 1988). However, as Williamson and Schulz (1993) observe, virtually all of these studies treat caregiving as a unitary stressor rather than examining coping in relation to domain-specific, stressful demands, such as the demands of coping with loss, noxious symptoms, or role captivity. Empirically, Williamson and Schulz (1993) found evidence of domain specificity in coping. For example, in dealing with memory problems, caregivers who took direct action experienced more depressed affect, whereas those who employed relaxation strategies experienced less depression. However, when the stressor was the loss of the relationship with the care recipient due to the relative's gradual decline, coping through acceptance and support-seeking was related to less depressed affect, and coping through stoicism was associated with more depressed affect.

Elsewhere, we report evidence of domain specificity in coping using a context-specific coping scheme developed from content analyses of detailed narrative accounts of coping provided by 91 caregivers of persons with dementia. Specifically, we identified 53 ways of coping that we further divided into 14 classes, as shown in Table 1: making meaning, acceptance, positive framing, wishful thinking, avoidance/escape, vigilance, emotional expression and emotional inhibition, optimistic and pessimistic future expectancies, humor, help-seeking, and verbal and behavioral symptom management (Gignac & Gottlieb, 1996).

APPRAISALS OF COPING EFFICACY

Our grounded approach to coping not only yielded evidence that the ways caregivers cope with their role responsibilities depend on the demands arising from different stressor domains, but it also revealed novel information about the ways caregivers appraise the progress and efficacy of their coping efforts. That is, throughout the caregivers' accounts of their ways of coping, they made abundant evaluations of the effects of these efforts on their relative, on their relationship with their relative, and on themselves. Although many of these evaluations occurred spontaneously, the majority were elicited by two questions we posed: (1) "Do you deal with this [stressor name] or your feelings about it differently now than in the past?" and (2) "Would you say this [stressor name] used to upset you more or less than it does now, or does it upset you as much now as it ever has?" As we did for their coping efforts, all efficacy appraisals underwent a formal content analysis procedure (Gig-

Table 1. Definitions of Classes of Coping

Making meaning (1)	Caregivers remind themselves that their relative's behavior is attributable to the disease from which he/she suffers and is not a result of the type of person he/she is
Acceptance (2)	Caregivers accept or strive to accept their relative's disease/behavior and/or the necessity of their continued involvement in caregiving
Positive framing (3)	Caregivers focus on positive aspects and/or minimize the negative repercussions of caregiving
Wishful thinking	Caregivers wish the course of the disease and/or their caregiving responsibilities would change
Avoidance/escape (5)	Caregivers physically withdraw from caregiving for short periods of time and/or cognitively avoid thinking about their caregiving responsibilities
Vigilance (6)	Caregivers are continuously watchful of their relative and/or are mentally preoccupied with thoughts about their relative
Emotional expression (7)	Caregivers cope by expressing their emotions openly
Emotional inhibition (8)	Caregivers cope by inhibiting their emotions and/or admonish themselves not to express their emotions
Optimistic future expectancies (9)	Caregivers are optimistic or hopeful regarding their ability to manage their caregiving responsibilities in the future
Pessimistic future expectancies (10)	Caregivers are pessimistic regarding their ability to manage their caregiving responsibilities in the future and/or fear that they will suffer a similar fate as their relative
Humor (11)	Caregivers tease or joke with their relative when he/she exhibits dementia symptoms
Help-seeking (12)	Caregivers seek practical and/or emotional support from others
Verbal symptom management (13)	Caregivers manage their relative's behavior with a range of verbal strategies such as explanations, changing the subject, reassuring and calming their relative, making requests, and instructing their relative
Behavioral symptom management (14)	Caregivers manage their relative's behavior with a range of behavioral strategies such as assisting their relative with tasks, interrupting behavior with distracting activities, rearranging the environment, and taking over tasks and decisions

Copyright by the American Psychological Association.

Table 2. Types of Appraisals of Coping Efficacy

Appraisal type	Definition and examples
Efficacious coping outcomes (1)	Appraisals of successful coping outcomes; e.g., "I found this [letting the behavior play out] is the best thing," "I've tried everything but that [changing the subject] seems to work."
Nonefficacious coping outcomes (2)	Appraisals of unsuccessful coping outcomes; e.g., "Overnight she'll forget what we talked about and then it might start over again," "But it don't do no good. Tell her to shut up, you might as well try throwing gas on a fire. Just put[s] her in gear."
No coping options (3)	Appraisals that nothing further can be done to manage the stressor's demands; e.g., "She has the problem and there isn't anything I can do to change it," "I just give up."
Control appraisals (4)	Appraisals that respondents are exercising influence over the stressor and their emotions; e.g., "There's quite a few things that I do to, uh, control myself and that there," "I'm fortunate enough to be able to control any upset feelings."
No control appraisals (5)	Appraisals that respondents are unable to influence the stressor or control their emotions; e.g., "It's a situation that I can't control and I think that's probably what frustrates me. Most situations I can control!", "Most of the time, it's [caregiver's anger] very difficult to keep it in."
Less stressor reactivity (6)	Appraisals that the respondent is able to tolerate the stressor; e.g., "I think I'm . . . probably sensitive to a point, but now I'm so used to it that it's just water off a duck's back;" "I think it may be because I've just got up . . . and I'm feeling pretty good and I've got lots of patience."
More stressor reactivity (7)	Appraisals that the respondent is unable to tolerate the stressor; e.g., "I get more upset than I did. You think you'd get used to it, but I'm never going to get used to that," "I can't get used to a person staring out a window that was so active. It's just mind-boggling. Really, It's just like a hundred percent change in her and I just can't get used to it."
Depletion of energy (8)	Appraisals of diminished energy; e.g., "I didn't know what it was at first but . . . trying to cope with it all, it's tiring me out," "It's when I feel less equipped to deal with it, if you know what I mean. It's a struggle then, and I'm tired and I'm not able to struggle."
Improved ability to cope (9)	Appraisals of improvements in coping; e.g., "I cope much better now. In the past, I would lose my own temper. I don't do that anymore. My coping skills are better now that I'm aware of some of the symptoms that are here now or that will come in the future, "But I have discovered that I can now manage the stress of a bad mood in much more constructive a manner than I used to."

Table 2. (*Continued*)

Appraisal type	Definition and examples
Coping self-criticism (10)	Appraisals of one's shortcomings in coping; e.g., "You know you're thinking maybe you've done something wrong. You sit here and you think 'oh, geez, I should have been . . . been more sympathetic and then maybe the rest of the day would have been . . . would have had a better day myself.'"
Means/ends insights (11)	Appraisals of the relationship between coping efforts and their outcomes; e.g., "If I can get the right thing . . . changing the subject and getting on the right subject [then] he'll forget what he's doing and then he's all right," "I'd really think twice about it [expressing anger] because I might hurt his feelings. I don't want him upset."
Strategic planning (12)	Appraisals of the costs and benefits entailed in different coping efforts; e.g., regarding mother's confusion: "I remind myself to watch what I do next time in a similar circumstance . . . to not go into a lot of detail with my notes and that I talk to myself to remember," "Explain it to her or show her even though I know that she's not going to remember it. I feel a little better in that probably, that's the way of not having an outburst over something."

nac & Gottlieb, 1996) that resulted in a classification scheme containing the 12 types of appraisals of coping efficacy presented in Table 2.

In what follows we begin with a brief description of our sample, the types of appraisals of coping efficacy caregivers made, and the underlying goals of these appraisals. We then discuss the concurrent and prospective relations between these appraisals and the caregivers' coping efforts. The concurrent analyses help us distinguish between those appraisals that reflect the caregivers' evaluations of specific ways of coping and those that are more traitlike in nature. The prospective analyses inform our understanding of the influence of selected appraisals on subsequent coping.

The study participants comprised 64 female and 27 male caregivers who had been caring for their relative for an average of 29.7 months (SD = 28.0). The majority of the women (56.3%) were spouses of the care recipient, and the rest were intergenerational caregivers (43.7%), mainly daughters and daughters-in-law. Two thirds of the males in the study were spousal caregivers, and one third were intergenerational caregivers. On average, spousal caregivers were 70.7 years of age (SD = 8.4), and intergenerational caregivers were 49.4 years of age (SD = 9.0). All of the spousal and most of the intergenerational caregivers (78.4%) resided with their relative.

Turning to the appraisals of coping efficacy, the illustrative quotations in Table 2 reveal that appraisals of *efficacious coping outcomes* and *nonefficacious coping outcomes* reflect caregivers' evaluations of the impact of their coping efforts on desired outcomes, and therefore are most closely associated with problem-solving/instrumental goals. Previous research on coping efficacy has focused primarily on these goals (Aldwin & Revenson, 1987; Cummings, Davies, & Simpson, 1994; Zautra & Wrabetz, 1991). Practical, action-oriented coping efforts such as behavior and verbal symptom management and avoidance/escape are particularly likely to elicit appraisals of outcome efficacy.

Appraisals of *no coping options* and of *control* and *no control* represent caregivers' judgments of whether they are able to control the stressor or whether they are helpless, lacking options for coping with the stressor. Ultimately, these appraisals relate to the goal of protecting self-esteem since perceptions of control or helplessness may bolster or undermine the caregivers' feelings of role competence (Pearlin et al., 1990). What is not clear from the illustrations provided in Table 2 is whether these appraisals are tied to specific coping efforts or whether they represent more global evaluations that reflect stable personal dispositions. Some appraisals were clearly contextually bound, such as, "It's a situation that I can't control." Others were more ambiguous. Appraisals like, "I just give up" or, "I'm fortunate enough to be able to control any upset feelings," may actually reflect global beliefs about self-efficacy and control (Bandura, 1989). We return to this issue later, presenting data on the stability of caregivers' appraisals across two time points as a preliminary means of exploring the relevance of a state–trait distinction to the caregivers' appraisals.

Appraisals of *less/more stressor reactivity* and *depletion of energy* are especially relevant to the context of chronic stress and are related to the goal of regulating one's emotional and physiological arousal. They deal with caregivers' perceptions of their ability to maintain their stamina and to psychologically tolerate, habituate to, or withstand the stressor. Attaining some measure of progress in managing one's emotions and tolerating the stressor is critical in this chronic stress context because caregiving tends to be a full-time and prolonged responsibility that entails a high risk of emotional and physical exhaustion (Deimling & Bass, 1986; George & Gwyther, 1986; Light & Lebowitz, 1989). As such, difficulties in maintaining one's energy level and in managing one's emotions should have important implications for caregivers' subsequent coping, an issue we explore when presenting the prospective relations between caregivers' appraisals and their coping efforts.

An *improved ability to cope* and *coping self-criticism* are appraisals reflecting caregivers' awareness of changes (i.e., improvements, deterioration, limitations) in their coping skills. Both types of appraisals were mentioned by nearly half the respondents and, when combined, accounted for one quarter of all caregivers' appraisals. They indicate that, over time and with repeated exposure to the stressor, caregivers have opportunities to learn about themselves, to develop, and to gain greater self-understanding. With few exceptions (Compas & Oroson, 1993), previous goal frameworks have not included self-understanding. In other recent research, positive effects of caregiving for caregivers have been documented (Franks & Stephens, 1992; Kinney & Stephens, 1989; Lawton, Kleban, Moss, Rovine, & Glicksman, 1989), but, to our knowledge, these are the first empirical data revealing that caregivers appraise their coping experiences in terms of the self-understanding they bring.

The final two appraisal types, *means/ends insights* and *strategic planning*, are also particularly germane in chronic stress contexts. Among our caregivers, these appraisals largely revolved around the goal of regulating and shaping interactions with their relative. That is, because they wanted to manage the demands of the stressor without upsetting their relative, respondents evaluated their progress in anticipating, recognizing, and regulating the consequences of their various ways of coping in their interactions with their relative. This concern is articulated by a spousal caregiver who reported, "I'd really think twice about it [expressing anger] because I might hurt his feelings. I don't want him upset."

In sum, previous research on coping efficacy has been limited and is virtually nonexistent in the area of chronic stress. Our research suggests that five principal goals underlie caregivers' appraisals of their efficacy in coping:

1. A problem-solving/instrumental goal
2. The maintenance of self-esteem
3. The regulation of emotional and physiological arousal
4. The development of greater self-understanding
5. The preservation of harmonious relations with their relative

Past research on coping efficacy has focused almost exclusively on goals related to problem-solving and regulating emotional distress. Moreover, typically, respondents have been asked for a single, global evaluation of the efficacy of their coping efforts, such as "how well" they handled the problem or "how satisfied" they were with their coping efforts (Aldwin &

Revenson, 1987; Zautra & Wrabetz, 1991). In making a global judgment, it is possible that some people may have tried to combine or average several different goals, whereas others may have focused on only one goal. In either instance, the goals of coping upon which these efficacy appraisals were based are unknown.

We believe that two factors account for the additional goals that we have identified in our research. The first pertains to the chronic nature of the stressful context, and the second relates to the uncontrollability of the primary disease stressor. Because caregivers are repeatedly exposed to the same stressors over an extended period of time, they have the opportunity to gain instruction not only about the situational impacts of their coping efforts but also about the impacts on themselves and on their relationship with their relatives. Second, because the symptoms of dementia and its course generally are resistant to change, the fundamental challenges facing caregivers are to stay engaged, to preserve their physical and mental integrity, and to find ways of making the optimal possible meaning of their circumstances. It follows that if little can be done to improve the objective conditions of their lives—nothing will make the symptoms or the disease disappear—then the caregivers may fall back on a set of more modest and potentially achievable goals related to these latter challenges.

THE RELATIONSHIP BETWEEN COPING AND APPRAISALS OF COPING EFFICACY

What is the relationship between caregivers' coping efforts and their appraisals of the efficacy of those efforts? To what extent do these appraisals of coping efficacy reflect the caregivers' evaluations of specific ways of coping they employed, and to what extent do they reflect broader and more stable self-evaluations of their own resources, of their progress in coping, and of changes in their situational control? As mentioned earlier, some research suggests that problem-focused coping efforts and avoidance/escape efforts were associated with appraisals of outcome efficacy (Aldwin & Revenson, 1987; Gignac & Gottlieb, 1996). In contrast, appraisals of an *improved ability to cope* and *stressor reactivity* are not likely to be associated with specific ways of coping, but reflect broad self-evaluations of personal stamina, tolerance, self-control, and motivation. Finally, it is uncertain whether appraisals of *no coping options* and *control/no control* are elicited by specific ways of coping or whether they reflect dispositional characteristics of caregivers or their global beliefs about self-efficacy.

We explore the relationship between the caregivers' appraisals of efficacy and their ways of coping in two ways. First, we show that certain appraisals of efficacy are associated with specific ways of coping. We discuss this finding in terms of the goals underlying caregivers' appraisals of their coping efforts. Second, we examine the stability of caregivers' appraisals across two time points, identifying two types of relatively stable appraisals that we believe may reflect caregivers' broader evaluations of their self-efficacy.

As mentioned previously, in analyzing the appraisal data we not only tallied the frequency of mentions of each type of appraisal but also coded the presence or absence of a coping referent for each appraisal. In addition, we documented the specific type of coping mentioned in each coping referent. The results indicate that, of the 12 types of appraisals, eight were not tied to specific coping referents. Specifically, appraisals related to the goals of self-esteem (i.e., *no coping options, control*, and *no control*), emotional regulation (i.e., *more/less stressor reactivity* and *depletion of energy*), and self-understanding and development (i.e., *improved ability to cope* and *coping self-criticism*) rarely contained a referent to a particular way of coping. It is likely that these appraisals reflected caregivers' more general evaluations of their progress in dealing with the symptom they found most upsetting.

In contrast, appraisals that related to the goals of problem solving (i.e., *efficacious* and *nonefficacious coping outcomes*) and managing interactions with their relative (i.e., *means/ends insights* and *strategic planning*), referred to specific coping efforts. In fact, as Table 3 reveals, well over three quarters of each of these four appraisals was tied to a particular coping effort. Not surprisingly, *behavioral* and *verbal symptom management* were the most frequent referents for both appraisals of *efficacious* and *nonefficacious coping outcomes*. Other coping efforts that were frequently referred to in relation to these appraisals were *help-seeking* and *avoidance/escape*. Faced with the persistent, intractable needs of their relative, it is understandable that many caregivers found the support of others and temporary respite or mental distraction from their relative's demands to be particularly efficacious ways of coping.

In addition to *symptom management*, coping efforts that were frequently appraised as inefficacious included *emotional expression/inhibition* and *making meaning*. Although the caregivers frequently reported trying to inhibit their feelings of frustration and anger, their prolonged exposure to the taxing and frustrating demands of caregiving often made such efforts futile. Hence, respondents reported little success in inhibiting their emotions, and they appraised subsequent outbursts of emotional expression as nonefficacious. Finally, it is interesting that many

Table 3. Appraisal Types and Coping Referents

Appraisal type	Percent of S's (n = 91)	Total number of appraisals	Percent of appraisals with referent	Type of coping referent
Efficacious coping outcomes	51.6	89	89.9	Symptom management (50.0%) Help-seeking (18.8%) Avoidance/escape (17.5%)
Nonefficacious coping outcomes	51.6	79	84.8	Symptom management (62.7%) Emotional expression/inhibition (25.4%) Making meaning (6.0%)
Mean/ends insights	56.0	79	93.7	Emotional expression/inhibition (36.5%) Symptom management (33.8%) Avoidance/escape (16.2%)
Strategic planning	26.4	32	78.1	Emotional expression/inhibition (60.0%) Help-seeking (12.0%) Symptom management (8.0%) Avoidance/escape (8.0%)

caregivers found their attempts to *make meaning* by attributing the cause of their relative's noxious symptoms to the disease rather than to their own volition to be unhelpful. Again, chronic exposure to caregiving and persistent demands by their relative may make this way of coping difficult to employ and less effective over time.

Additional findings linking *emotional expression/inhibition* with the caregivers' goal of managing the demands of the stressor without unduly harming their relationship with their relative make this class of coping particularly noteworthy. Numerous caregivers described the effects (i.e., *means/ends insights*) and/or the costs (i.e., *strategic planning*) of their efforts to inhibit their feelings of frustration or anger with their relative's behavior. For example, in describing her frustration with her husband, who continually hid objects around their home, one caregiver noted that she no longer expressed her anger to her husband, "because it doesn't pay. If you get more angry, he gets more scared, and then . . . he gets more lost [confused]!" Another caregiver described the futility of venting his feelings, saying:

> I don't [get angry] anymore because I understand that sometimes if a child does something and you get angry with them, they can see that you're angry and they'll try to please you. With her, she'll just laugh at you. I find that getting angry with her does not change the fact, so why get angry?

Moreover, in making appraisals that addressed the goal of managing their interactions with relatives, the caregivers often reported seeking help from others and attempting to temporarily escape the caregiving situation—coping efforts that were frequently appraised as efficacious. By withdrawing from their chronically stressful circumstances, the caregivers were able to return their mood, energy, and arousal levels to baseline, a way of coping that appears to be particularly helpful in chronic stress contexts (Repetti & Wood, Chapter 7, this volume).

In sum, appraisals associated with the goals of problem-solving and regulating and shaping social interactions were consistently associated with three specific coping referents: *symptom management, avoidance/ escape,* and *help-seeking.* That is, these three classes of coping efforts were associated with appraisals that coping is effective and with appraisals that coping influences the caregivers' relationship with their relatives. Presumably, the concrete, observable nature of these coping efforts makes them relatively easy to appraise. Moreover, their varied forms provide caregivers with numerous ways to modify or tailor their efforts to better achieve their goals. At the same time, as their relative's disease progresses, some of these coping efforts will no longer continue to be helpful. In part, this may explain caregivers' mixed success with such efforts, reporting both efficacious and nonefficacious coping outcomes.

Emotional expression/inhibition was a fourth type of coping to which caregivers referred frequently when they appraised their coping as ineffective and when their appraisals touched on the goal of maintaining harmonious relations with their relative. This suggests that, as caregivers faced daily exposure to their relative's noxious behaviors, attempts to control their feelings were unsuccessful, leading to more emotional outbursts.

Of the remaining eight appraisals of efficacy, none was consistently associated with specific coping referents, but were, instead, of a more global nature. However, the fact that the remaining appraisals were not linked to specific coping efforts is not necessarily evidence that these appraisals are traitlike or dispositional. They may, in fact, be contextually bound and may demonstrate fluidity and flexibility over time, as caregivers' coping efforts or the demands of the caregiving situation change. For example, appraisals of an *improved ability to cope* may be intended by caregivers to be domain specific, despite the absence of a clear, coping referent.

THE STABILITY OF COPING APPRAISALS

By correlating the caregivers' appraisals across two time points approximately 5 months apart, we can examine the relative stability of the appraisals. For those appraisals that do not have a coping referent, evidence of stability would suggest a more traitlike or dispositionally based evaluation. Appraisals that are grounded in specific ways of coping are less likely to be dispositionally based (Zautra, Hoffman, & Reich, Chapter 10, this volume). Therefore, we would not expect these appraisals to show stability. The following analyses are based on correlational data provided by the 42 caregivers who were available at time 2 (Gignac & Gottlieb, 1996). Of the 91 caregivers who were initially interviewed, two thirds of those who did not participate in the second wave of data collection had placed their relative in a long-term care facility, and 12.6% had a relative who had died or who was too ill for the caregiver to be available for an interview. Such attrition is not uncommon in studies of respite care (Burdz, Eaton, & Bond, 1988; Lawton, Brody, & Saperstein, 1989; Montgomery & Borgatta, 1989). At time 1, there were no differences between caregivers who did and those who did not complete the time 2 interview in terms of their relationship to the care recipient, education, income, type of stressor, length of time caregiving, and perceived stress.

Of the 12 types of appraisals, only three exhibited consistency. Between time 1 and time 2, *efficacious coping outcomes* were significantly correlated ($r(41) = .32$, $p < .05$), as were *no coping options* ($r(41) = .36$, $p < .05$) and *coping self-criticism* ($r(41) = .37$, $p < .05$). Since appraisals of *efficacious coping outcomes* were frequently associated with specific coping referents, they are less likely to represent dispositionally based characteristics, or "traits," of caregivers than "state" evaluations of coping efforts. Nonetheless, future research is needed to explore this type of appraisal in order to discover whether some individuals are more likely than others to appraise their coping outcomes as successful, or whether caregivers who found that their coping efforts were successful at time 1 continued to rely upon those efforts and achieve some measure of success with them at time 2.

From a state–trait perspective, the more provocative findings come from the consistency demonstrated by appraisals of *no coping options* and *coping self-criticism*. Neither appraisal was associated with specific coping referents. *No coping options* may reflect a global sense of helplessness and ongoing difficulties in coping that impact on other areas of caregiving or caregivers' lives. In a separate analysis, these appraisals were associated with significantly lower life satisfaction from time 1 to time 2 (Gignac & Gottlieb, 1996). They may be particularly consequential in chronic stress contexts, for if appraisals that one is unable to find ways to cope persist, they may ultimately predict caregivers' withdrawal from their caregiving responsibilities and possible long-term placement of their family member. Ultimately, such appraisals may undermine caregivers' overall sense of self-efficacy in coping with stress.

The relative stability of appraisals of *coping self-criticism* also signals ongoing coping difficulties. However, rather than expressing the belief that nothing further can be done to manage the demands of the stressor, the caregivers focus on their own shortcomings in coping. Other analyses have shown that caregivers who were critical of their coping progress reported mixed success in effecting desired outcomes, difficulties in tolerating the stressor over time, and concerns about actually harming their relationship with their relative by coping in certain ways (Gignac & Gottlieb, 1996). It may be that a heightened sense of self-awareness and ongoing efforts by caregivers to monitor their thoughts, feelings, and actions may also detract from their sense of self-efficacy.

In sum, our findings suggest that caregivers' appraisals of their coping efficacy can roughly be positioned on a state–trait continuum. At one end of the continuum are appraisals serving goals related to problem solving (i.e., *efficacious* and *nonefficacious coping outcomes*) and regulating and shaping social interactions (i.e., *means/ends insights* and *strategic planning*). These appraisals appear to be contextually bound, include specific coping referents, and demonstrate little stability over time. At the other end of the continuum are two appraisals that are more traitlike in nature—*no coping options* and *coping self-criticism*. These appraisals did not have coping referents and were more global in nature and relatively stable over time. The remaining appraisal types did not reveal clear state or traitlike characteristics. They reflected caregivers' global evaluations of their progress in coping, but lacked the stability typically associated with traitlike dispositions.

It is conceivable that the lack of stability in the majority of the appraisals of coping efficacy is largely attributable to differing levels of stress or upset engendered by the caregivers' most upsetting cognitive or behavioral symptom between time 1 and time 2. However, when we correlated caregivers' upset ratings, we found that they were relatively stable over the two time points ($r(41) = .61$, $p < .001$), suggesting that changes in caregivers' coping and appraisals of efficacy were not a function of different levels of arousal.

THE IMPACT OF EFFICACY APPRAISALS ON COPING

Thus far, we have described 12 appraisals of coping efficacy and the goals they serve. In addition, as a preliminary step in determining whether they are more contextually bound or more traitlike in nature, we have examined their concurrent relations with specific coping efforts and their relative stability over time. Next, we turn to the potential impact that appraisals of coping efficacy have on caregivers' subsequent coping efforts. We do this by correlating caregivers' time 1 appraisals with their time 2 coping efforts, controlling for caregivers' time 1 coping. In this way, we show that caregivers modify their coping efforts in response to specific appraisals of the efficacy of their earlier coping efforts.

Table 4 presents the results of these analyses. Given the large number of correlations calculated and the exploratory nature of the analyses, we adopted a conservative probability level of .01 as significant. Eight of the 12 appraisal types were associated with at least one change in caregivers' subsequent coping efforts. Specifically, reports of *efficacious coping outcomes* at time 1 were associated with increased reports of coping by adopting *pessimistic future expectancies* and by *making meaning* at time 2. One interpretation of these findings is that caregivers who initially felt they could alter their relatives' behavior later realized that changes were only temporary or that new symptoms were not amenable to change. Initial success thus gave way to pessimism 5 months later. In short, caregivers reporting successful *efficacious coping outcomes* subsequently alter their future expectations to prepare for the worst and continually remind themselves that their relative has little responsibility for his or her symptoms.

Caregivers' reports of unsuccessful coping efforts (i.e., *nonefficacious coping outcomes*) at time 1 were associated with increased coping by *behavioral* techniques such as rearranging their relative's environment, taking over tasks for their relative, and interrupting noxious behavior with alternative activities in an effort to distract their relative. Recall that the results reported in Table 3 indicated that, at time 1, caregivers' frequently referred to symptom management when they made both efficacious and nonefficacious appraisals. That is, some efforts helped, at least some of the time, whereas others did not. Caregivers' mixed experi-

Table 4. Partial Correlations: Time 1 Appraisals with Time 2 Coping Classes (Controlling for Time 1 Coping)[a]

	Coping Classes						
Appraisal types	Making meaning	Wishful thinking	Emotional expression	Optimistic expectancies	Pessimistic expectancies	Behavioral symptom management	Verbal symptom management
Efficacious coping	.46*	−.06	−.16	.08	.50*	.19	.28
Nonefficacious coping	.11	−.07	.18	−.20	.05	.35*	.03
No coping options	.13	.34*	−.08	.59*	−.02	.08	.03
Control appraisals	−.07	.36*	−.14	.36*	−.08	−.31	−.10
Stressor reactivity	.38*	−.13	.06	−.11	.40*	.18	.18
Depletion of energy	−.08	−.20	.36*	−.12	.01	.23	.10
Means/ends insights	−.13	.06	−.06	−.06	−.05	−.19	−.36*
Strategic planning	.35*	−.15	.21	−.09	.19	−.16	.11

[a] Only those appraisal types with at least one significant relation to measures of coping, *p < .01, are displayed. Partial correlations control for time 1 coping.

ence with success at time 1 may be associated with increased attempts to find new ways of managing their relative's symptom or with their persevering with ways of coping that are helpful at least some of the time.

Time 1 appraisals of *no coping options* and of *control* both predicted increased reliance on *wishful thinking* and *optimistic future expectancies*. These findings are unusual because they suggest that appraisals that one is helpless or unable to cope, as well as appraisals that one is able to control some aspects of caregiving, were associated with wishing that the disease or one's caregiving would go away and with optimistic or hopeful future expectations. With regard to appraisals of *no coping options*, it may be that caregivers' perceptions that their circumstances are unmitigable leave them with few coping options as their relative's dementia progresses. As a result, they wish that their relative's disease will go away and/or console themselves with the thought that eventually their caregiving responsibilities will end. Caregivers' appraisals of *control* are related to similar changes in their coping efforts, but possibly for different reasons. The sense of efficacy that caregivers gain from perceptions of control may result in unrealistic expectations for the course of their relative's disease (e.g., it will just go away) or for their future caregiving. Although more research is needed to substantiate this explanation, it is in keeping with other coping research on illusions or unrealistic expectations held by individuals with high levels of personal control (Taylor & Brown, 1988).

Caregivers who made appraisals that signified their difficulty in habituating themselves to the stressor at time 1 (i.e., *more stressor reactivity*) were more likely to report increases in coping by finding *meaning* and expressing *pessimistic expectancies*. These findings parallel those found for *efficacious coping outcomes*. However, in this instance caregivers do not initially report success in coping with dementia. Instead, their initial appraisals of difficulty in accommodating to the stressor may intensify as the disease progresses, leading them to attribute their relative's behavior to the disease and not to his or her own volition and to expect or fear the worst for the future. Appraisals of *depleted energy* at time 1, which also touch on the goal of emotional regulation, predicted coping through outbursts of *emotional expression* at time 2. We have already discussed the importance of *emotional expression/inhibition* in this stressor context. For many individuals, the chronic demands of the caregiving situation gradually diminish their ability to psychologically tolerate and withstand the stressor. As a result, over time, caregivers' resources may be depleted and they may be unable to restrain their feelings.

Finally, initial appraisals that revolved around caregivers' efforts to manage their interactions with their relative (i.e., *means/ends insights*) were associated with decreases in the use of *verbal symptom management*. Perhaps efforts to control their relative's behavior by repeatedly making requests, commanding their relative, using rational explanations, and changing the subject are perceived as having undesirable consequences for their interactions with their relative or their relationship in general, and therefore are largely abandoned. Second, efficacy appraisals reflecting *strategic planning* at time 1 were associated with increases in *making meaning* at time 2. This suggests that caregivers who, at time 1, made evaluations of the costs to the relationship of using specific ways of coping were more likely to remind themselves that the cause of their relative's behavior was the disease from which they were suffering, not their relative's personality or volition.

On the whole, the findings from our prospective data suggest that all but two of the caregivers' appraisals of efficacy shaped their subsequent coping efforts. They also speak to the issue of coping with chronic stress in this particular stressor context. Specifically, changes in caregivers' coping largely revolved around increased use of cognitive coping efforts (i.e., *wishful thinking, making meaning, pessimistic/optimistic future expectancies*) or emotion-focused coping (i.e., *emotional expression*). Overall, there were few changes in symptom management, and even some decreased reliance upon it. The persistent, intractable nature of coping with the needs of a dementia victim may leave caregivers with coping alternatives that, over time, focus less on management of the disease's symptoms and more on dealing with one's own intrapsychic state.

It is worth noting that, although appraisals of an *improved ability to cope* and *coping self-criticism* were among the most frequent appraisals made by caregivers at time 1, they were not associated with changes in coping at time 2. Appraisals reflecting self-understanding or development may be important, but, at the same time, may not be associated with consistent changes in caregivers' coping across all caregivers. Hence, longitudinal analyses exploring intraindividual change in coping may be needed to better understand the role of appraisals that tap self-development and understanding.

SUMMARY AND CONCLUSIONS

From a theoretical standpoint, it is useful to view an individual's coping and appraisals of efficacy in terms of the goals that they serve. In our research, five superordinate coping goals were identified. However, the nature and priority of the goals that underlie coping depend on the contextual features of each chronic stressor, as well as on differences among individuals. For example, in the present stressor context, goals relating to regulating and shaping social interactions were critical. That is, because caregivers wanted to manage the demands of caring for their relatives without upsetting them, they evaluated their progress in anticipating, recognizing, and regulating the consequences of their coping on their interactions. In coping with other chronic stressors, such as unemployment or poverty, appraisals related to managing social interactions may be of a different type and may assume less importance than other goals like problem solving and managing self-esteem. Hence, future research should examine coping goals that are relevant to a variety of chronic stressors.

In previous research on acute stressors, the goals of coping have revolved largely around problem solving and, to some extent, emotional regulation (Aldwin & Revenson, 1987; Cummings, Davies, & Simpson, 1994; McCrae & Costa, 1986; Zautra & Wrabetz, 1991). In chronic stress contexts, the repetitive nature of the stressor can make problem-solving efforts futile because they do not eliminate or modify the stressor. For this reason, individuals may increasingly direct their efforts toward other goals. For example, psychological goals relating to the conservation of energy and emotional reactivity, like efforts to tolerate the stressor and renew depleted energy levels, as well as goals related to maintaining self-esteem by retaining a sense of control over one's life or one's options for coping may assume enormous significance when individuals attempt to deal with the continuous, intractable demands of a chronic stressor.

Moreover, interpersonal goals, like preserving or shaping close relationships, can also become important. In the present context, dementia gradually robs individuals of the ability to engage in the typical routines and interactions they once had with their caregivers. As mentioned earlier, other chronic stress contexts may not have such devastating effects on close relationships (Coyne & Smith, 1991). However, the persistent demands of a chronic stressor may have implications for close relationships if established patterns of interaction are interrupted, new roles need to be negotiated, or future plans need to be reconsidered (see O'Brien & DeLongis, Chapter 6, and Lepore, Chapter 5, this volume).

Finally, chronically stressful experiences can provide individuals with opportunities for critical self-reflection and self-development. That is, the relatively continuous nature of a chronic stressor allows individuals to appraise their coping skills, to learn new skills, and to broaden or refine their coping resources. It is this flexibility and fluidity of the coping process, noted by Aldwin at the outset of this chapter, that we have attempted to highlight. Although such flexibility is inherent in Lazarus and Folkman's (1984) transactional theory of stress and coping, it has not often been the subject of research on coping, which has focused instead on the different ways individuals initially appraise an event and cope with it. Moreover, when changes in coping have been explored, this has most often been in the context of acute life events (Folkman & Lazarus, 1985) rather than ongoing, stressful contexts.

From a methodological standpoint, the findings of our study suggest the use of multidimensional measures of coping effectiveness that incorporate evaluations of the ways in which coping efforts have affected the respondent's sense of control, physical stamina, psychological habituation, strategic planning, and self-understanding. For example, items could be written that ask about whether the problem upsets the respondent as much as it ever did, whether the respondent feels there has been improvement in his or her ways of handling the problem, and whether the respondent believes that he or she can anticipate the effects of alternative ways of coping. However, as mentioned previously, since the goals of coping may differ for different stressors, the dimensions of coping efficacy identified in this study may not be applicable to other stressors. Therefore, it behooves researchers to investigate the goals that underly coping in the domains under study and to generate measures of coping efficacy that are specific to these domains.

Finally, it should be emphasized that coping with chronic stress involves more than appraising a stressor, employing particular ways of coping, evaluating the efficacy of those coping efforts, and modifying or continuing with them as needed. The present research suggests that individuals' efficacy appraisals reflect the feedback that they receive from the environment (i.e., the effects of their actions and thoughts), as well as more stable, traitlike beliefs about their ability to cope with important life events efficaciously (Bandura, 1989). These appraisals of past coping efforts and more stable beliefs about coping efficacy are likely to interact in complex ways when coping with chronic stress. That is, they may shape not only the ways people cope, but also the coping goals that people set for themselves. Moreover, the enduring nature of chronic stressors may mean that, in addition to the general beliefs and dispositions individuals bring with them influencing their interpretations and reactions to stress, chronic stress contexts ultimately may shape or even alter more traitlike, global dispositions. Such complex processes present exciting and challenging avenues for future research, both theoretical and methodological, in chronic stress contexts.

ACKNOWLEDGMENTS This research was supported by CARNET: The Canadian Aging Research Network, one of 15 Networks of Centres of Excellence funded by the Government of Canada, as well as by a grant from Health Canada and by a Senior Research Fellowship award by the Ontario Mental Health Foundation to Benjamin H. Gottlieb. M. A. M. Gignac gratefully acknowledges CARNET for its support of a postdoctoral fellowship at the Gerontology Research Centre, University of Guelph. Both authors thank Barbara Morrongiello for her helpful comments on an earlier draft of this chapter, as well as Joanne Duncan-Robinson, Julia Johnson, Heather Rennie, Suzanne Wakefield, and Tracy Woodford for their help in the coding and content analysis of the data.

REFERENCES

ALDWIN, C. M., & REVENSON, T. A. (1987). Does coping help? A reexamination of the relation between coping and mental health. *Journal of Personality and Social Psychology, 53,* 337–348.

BANDURA, A. (1989). Human agency in social cognitive theory. *American Psychologist, 44,* 1175–1184.

BURDZ, M. P., EATON, W. O., & BOND, J. B., JR. (1988). Effect of respite care on dementia and nondementia patients and their caregivers. *Psychology and Aging, 3,* 38–42.

COMPAS, B. E., & OROSON, P. G. (1993). Cognitive appraisals and coping with stress. In B. C. Long & S. E. Kahn (Eds.), *Women, work, and coping* (pp. 221–237). Montreal and Kingston: McGill-Queen's University Press.

COYNE, J. C., & SMITH, D. A. (1991). Couples coping with myocardial infarction: A contextual perspective on wives' distress. *Journal of Personality and Social Psychology, 61,* 404–412.

CUMMINGS, E. M., DAVIES, P. T., & SIMPSON, K. S. (1994). Marital conflict, gender, and children's appraisals and coping efficacy as mediators of child adjustment. *Journal of Family Psychology, 8,* 141–149.

DEIMLING, G., & BASS, D. (1986). Symptoms of mental impairment among elderly adults and their effects on family caregivers. *Journal of Gerontology, 41,* 778–784.

FOLKMAN, S., & LAZARUS, R. (1985). If it changes it must be a process: Study of emotion and coping during three stages of a college examination. *Journal of Personality and Social Psychology, 48,* 150–170.

FRANKS, M. M., & STEPHENS, M. A. P. (1992). Multiple roles of middle-generation caregivers: Contextual effects and psychological mechanisms. *Journal of Gerontology, 47,* S123–129.

GEORGE, L. K., & GWYTHER, L. P. (1986). Caregiver well-being: A multi-dimensional examination of family caregivers of demented adults. *The Gerontologist, 26,* 253–259.

GIGNAC, M. A. M., & GOTTLIEB, B. H. (1996). Caregivers' appraisals of efficacy in coping with dementia. *Psychology and Aging, 11,* 214–225.

GOTTLIEB, B. H., & GIGNAC, M. A. M. (1996). Content and domain specificity of coping among family caregivers of persons with dementia. *Journal of Aging Studies, 10,* 137–155.

GOTTLIEB, B. H., KELLOWAY, E. K., & FRABONI, M. (1994). Aspects of eldercare that place employees at risk. *The Gerontologist, 34,* 815–821.

GOTTLIEB, B. H., & WAGNER, F. (1991). Stress and support processes in close relationships. In J. Eckenrode (Ed.), *The social context of coping* (pp. 165–188). New York: Plenum.

HALEY, W. E., LEVINE, E., BROWN, L., & BARTOLUCCI, A. (1987). Stress, appraisal, coping and social supports as mediators of adaptational outcome among dementia caregivers. *Psychology and Aging, 2,* 323–330.

KINNEY, J. M., & STEPHENS, M. A. P. (1989). Hassles and uplifts of giving care to a family member with dementia. *Psychology and Aging, 3,* 402–407.

LAWTON, M. P., BRODY, E. M., & SAPPERSTEIN, A. R. (1989). A controlled study of respite service for caregivers of Alzheimer's patients. *The Gerontologist, 29*, 8–16.

LAWTON, M. P., KLEBAN, M. H., MOSS, M., ROVINE, M., & GLICKSMAN, A. (1989). Measuring caregiving appraisal. *Journal of Gerontology, 44*, P61–71.

LAZARUS. R. S., & FOLKMAN, S. (1984). *Stress, appraisal, and coping.* New York: Springer.

LIGHT, E., & LEBOWITZ, B. D. (1989). *Alzheimer's disease treatment and family stress: Directions for research.* Washington, DC: U.S. Department of Health and Human Services.

MCCRAE, R. R., & COSTA, P. T., JR. (1986). Personality, coping, and coping effectiveness in an adult sample. *Journal of Personality, 54*, 385–405.

MONTGOMERY, R. V., & BORGATTA, E. F. (1989). The effects of alternative support strategies on family caregiving. *The Gerontologist, 29*, 457–464.

PEARLIN, L. I., MULLAN, J. T., SEMPLE, S. J., & SKAFF, M. M. (1990). Caregiving and the stress process: An overview of concepts and their measures. *The Gerontologist, 30*, 583–594.

PRUCHNO, R., & KLEBAN, M. H. (1993). Caring for an institutionalized parent: The role of coping strategies. *Psychology and Aging, 8*, 18–25.

PRUCHNO, R. A., & RESCH, N. L. (1989). Mental health of caregiving spouses: Coping as mediator, moderator, or main effect? *Psychology and Aging, 4*, 454–463.

QUAYHAGEN, M. P., & QUAYHAGEN, M. (1988). Alzheimer's stress: Coping with the caregiving role. *The Gerontologist, 28*, 391–396.

RABINS, P. V. (1989). Behavior problems in the demented. In E. Light & B. D. Lebowitz (Eds.), *Alzheimer's disease treatment and family stress: Directions for research* (pp. 322–339). Washington, DC: U.S. Department of Health and Human Services.

RAKOWSKI, W., & CLARK, N. (1985). Future outlook: Caregiving and care receiving in the family context. *The Gerontologist, 25*, 618–623.

RUBIN, E. H., MORRIS, J. C., STORANDT, M., & BERG, L. (1987). Behavioral changes in patients with mild senile dementia of the Alzheimer's type. *Psychiatry Research, 21*, 55–62.

SCHARLACH, A. E., SOBOL, E. L., & ROBERTS, R. E. L. (1991). Employment and caregiver strain: An integrative model. *The Gerontologist, 31*, 778–787.

TAYLOR, S. E., & BROWN, J. D. (1988). Illusion and well-being: A social psychological perspective on mental health. *Psychological Bulletin, 103*, 193–210.

VITALIANO, P. P., RUSSO, J., CARR, J. E., MAIURO, R. D., & BECKER, J. (1985). The Ways of Coping Checklist: Revision and psychometric properties. *Multivariate Behavioral Research, 20*, 3–26.

WHEATON, B. (1991, August). *Chronic stress: Models and measurement.* Paper presented at the Society for Social Problems meeting in Cincinnati, OH.

WILLIAMSON, G. M., & SCHULZ, R. (1993). Coping with specific stressors in Alzheimer's disease caregiving. *The Gerontologist, 33*, 747–755.

ZAUTRA, A. J., & WRABETZ, A. B. (1991). Coping success and its relationship to psychological distress for older adults. *Journal of Personality and Social Psychology, 61*, 801–810.

10

The Role of Two Kinds of Efficacy Beliefs in Maintaining the Well-Being of Chronically Stressed Older Adults

ALEX J. ZAUTRA, JEANNE M. HOFFMAN,
and JOHN W. REICH

The loss of autonomy that results from a disabling chronic illness is one of the most difficult and stressful experiences to cope with for an older adult. The ability lost is frequently never regained, and the older adult suffers from both the present loss and anticipation of a future of sustained and even increased confinement, both physical and psychological. As other investigators have found (see Zautra & Hempel, 1984, for a review), our research on older adults indicates that activity limitation has pervasive adverse effects on mental health (Reich & Zautra, 1988; Zautra, Guarnaccia, & Reich, 1988; Zautra, Reich, & Newsom, 1995). In comparison to those without impairment, older adults with functional loss often show more anxiety, more depression, less positive affect, and lower self-esteem (Reich & Zautra, 1988). The loss of autonomy due to chronic illness appears to lower one's sense of personal control in general. Indeed, chronically ill adults show more fatalism, more helplessness (Smith &

ALEX J. ZAUTRA, JEANNE M. HOFFMAN, and JOHN W. REICH • Department of Psychology, Arizona State University, Tempe, Arizona 85287-1104.

Coping with Chronic Stress, edited by Benjamin H. Gottlieb. Plenum Press, New York, 1997.

Wallston, 1992), and less perceived control over future events than do healthy controls (Lennon, Dohrenwend, Zautra, & Marbach, 1990).

Although the adverse effects of activity limitation are pervasive, usually they are not severe enough to provoke clinical levels of psychological upset. Most older adults are able to adjust successfully. We think that key factors in this adjustment are efficacy beliefs concerning the management of everyday life. By efficacy we mean both the extent to which older adults believe they can cope successfully with everyday stressors and the extent of their beliefs in their abilities to create positive daily life experiences. Such beliefs may be among the most important to the preservation of well-being among chronically ill persons and other older adults.

In this chapter we focus on these two efficacy beliefs. Our principal aims are to examine the antecedent conditions responsible for individual differences in efficacy beliefs and the consequences of those individual differences for the well-being of older adults at risk for chronic and disabling illness. Among our first concerns is the meaning of efficacy itself. We needed to know more about these beliefs—how they fit within the current thinking on human agency and how they relate, empirically, to similar constructs of personal control. A related issue is the stability of individuals' ratings of their own efficacy across different challenges that confront them over time. Estimates of stability define the extent to which such beliefs represent personality features, or conversely the extent to which such beliefs are specific to the situation (see also Gignac & Gottlieb, Chapter 9, this volume). We examine data from our studies of chronically ill older adults to address these questions.

Of central importance is the role of efficacy beliefs in the preservation of quality of life among those vulnerable to chronic illness and those already ill. Our longitudinal studies of older adults provide data to address this question; clinical studies of rheumatoid arthritis patients are also used to test the relationships between efficacy beliefs and clinical outcomes. Finally, we set out to identify the determinants of efficacy beliefs. We look at personality and social status as important antecedents. We also examine in detail the role of social relationships; such relationships provide us with clues about how to intervene to assist older adults in sustaining their sense of personal efficacy when coping with chronically stressful situations.

ORIGINS OF RESEARCH ON EFFICACY BELIEFS

Bandura (1992) was not the first to argue that human agency played a key role in the production of behavior, but he is among the most persuasive because he has argued from data. In his initial studies, he showed that the best predictor of approach behaviors among snake phobics, after training, was not their behavior on previous trials, but their beliefs in their ability to perform those behaviors. He used the term "self-efficacy" to define those beliefs that surround the execution of the target sequence of behaviors. These cognitions amounted to a cluster of expectations about the ability to perform the task at hand. With strong empirical evidence, Bandura (Bandura, 1992; Bandura & Adams, 1977) then argued for a reciprocal interplay between reinforcement contingencies and personal agency. In brief, both the environment and the person's cognitions are thought to influence behavior. Efficacy beliefs, in particular, represent cognitions that could shape behavior in Bandura's model. Thus, the human organism has been transformed by Bandura from a passive recipient of reinforcement contingencies to an active causal agent. The primary vehicle for this transformation for Bandura is self-efficacy beliefs.

Lazarus (1966) developed another set of ideas about human agency that has fostered an interest in efficacy beliefs. He has argued for the central role of the person in the process of the organism's adjustment to life stress. His model spotlights the response of the person as the critical determinant of adaptation to stressful events. That response has several interrelated elements, including the person's appraisal of degree of threat or challenge from the event and how he or she copes with the threat/challenge from the stressor. Coping constitutes that set of behaviors and cognitions employed to manage, master, or tolerate threats and/or challenges to the self. Two types of appraisal are identified in the model: appraisal of the threat or challenge and the person's appraisal of his or her ability to cope with the stressor successfully. This second appraisal is similar to Bandura's self-efficacy construct. Lazarus has argued, from experimental data as well as from observational studies, that the person's response to the stressors he or she faces is part of a dynamic set of person–situation transactions. The appraisals shape the person's coping response, which in turn can modify the appraisals that the person makes of the stressor.

We, among others (e.g., Revenson & Felton, 1984), have found some common ground in these two cognitive theories of behavior: efficacy beliefs in coping with both chronic and acute life stressors. Indeed, Elliott and Eisdorfer (1982) suggested that life stress transactions could be usefully partitioned into three interrelated, yet distinct, components: the stressor itself, the person's coping efforts, and the outcomes of those coping efforts. We have called the person's appraisal of those outcomes—particularly in terms of the success of their own coping efforts and their beliefs in their abilities to cope with such events in the future—

"coping efficacy" (see also Gignac & Gottlieb, Chapter 9, this volume). In this way, Bandura's human agency model may be extended into the realm of adaptation to life stressors by borrowing from Lazarus' construct of secondary appraisal and using that appraisal as a set of beliefs that arise as an outcome of coping efforts. Indeed, an evaluation of coping efficacy with regard to those chronic stressors associated with loss of autonomy resulting from the progressive worsening of a chronic illness might be especially important to understanding the quality of life of the older adult.

Thus far we have discussed one kind of efficacy, coping efficacy. Yet it was apparent from the outset of our work that coping efficacy represented only one dimension along which people differed in their expectations for their own performance. Several investigators from fields of inquiry as diverse as industrial mental health (Herzberg, 1966) and sociology (Bradburn, 1969) proposed that cognitions and emotions associated with satisfying events form a dimension of human experience that is distinct from negative and otherwise stressful experiences. Increasing evidence has accumulated from contemporary investigators broadly supporting the original concepts of Bradburn and Herzberg—that positive and negative affects provide separate templates for cognitions concerning the self and that these affective templates are phenomenologically (Watson & Clark, 1984) and neurophysiologically distinct (Lee, Loring, Dahl, & Meador, 1993).

Prior to our own investigations on efficacy, we pursued this line of reasoning. In order to examine the separate effects from both positive and negative domains of experience, we constructed measures of both positive and negative life events (Zautra & Reich, 1980) and tested individuals' causal attributions (Zautra, Guenther, & Chartier, 1985) and social relations (Finch, Okun, Barrera, Zautra, & Reich, 1989). In a series of studies we found (Zautra & Reich, 1980; Reich & Zautra, 1981; Reich, Zautra, & Hill, 1987) that beliefs in one's ability to make positive events happen played an important role in the maintenance of well-being and that such positive event efficacy may be independent in large measure from the ratings of coping efficacy made by the same individuals. That is, beliefs in one's ability to cope with adversity may do little to predict the individual's beliefs in his or her ability to produce positive life experiences. In sum, two separate affective states appear likely to underlie efficacy ratings and produce two distinct facets of self-efficacy beliefs: *coping efficacy* for handling the stresses of negative affective experiences both now and in the future and *positive event efficacy*, the degree of confidence in one's ability to produce preferred life experiences currently and in the future.

THE LIFE EVENT AND AGING PROJECT

These concepts have guided our efforts to assess life events, social relations, efficacy beliefs, and sense of well-being among clinic and community samples of older adults at risk for mental health problems. The most ambitious of our efforts to date has been the study of 244 older adults through the Life Event and Aging Project (LEAP); (Zautra, Reich, & Guarnaccia, 1990). This project has charted recovery from two major stressors: loss of autonomy through moderate to severe levels of activity limitation, which was experienced by one fourth of the sample, and recent conjugal bereavement, which occurred to another quarter of the sample. The bereaved sample was identified through the county's Vital Statistics records. The disabled were identified through telephone screening of older adults; a 26-item instrumental activities of daily living scale (Teresi, Golden, Gurland, Wilder, & Bennett, 1983) was used to estimate degree of activity limitation during screening and during follow-up interviews. Two control groups were also established for these two high-stress conditions. The controls could be neither bereaved nor show activity limitation. The age, sex, and income matching of subjects yielded a total sample of 244 that had an average age of 70 and was 78% female and 1.6% minority status.

The project staff followed the samples longitudinally, starting with 10 monthly interviews and two follow-up interviews, the last of which was conducted 4.6 years from the date of the initial interview. In addition to probes about efficacy beliefs, which we describe later, the monthly interviews contained extensive reviews of recent positive and negative events, including 350 items from lists of major and small life events tailored to an older adult population (see Zautra, Reich, & Guarnaccia, 1990). Measures of negative and positive social transactions were compiled from all reported occurrences of undesirable events from spouse, children, family, and friends subscales over all 10 months. The LEAP assessments contained measures of psychological well-being and distress derived from the Veit and Ware (1983) Mental Health Inventory and the PERI-Demoralization Composite (Dohrenwend, Shrout, Egri, & Mendelsohn, 1980). Factor analyses conducted on these scales with the LEAP data revealed two inversely correlated superordinate mental health factors: psychological distress and psychological well-being (Zautra, Guarnaccia, & Reich, 1988). In this chapter, we focus on the effects for psychological distress. That measure was composed of five subscales: depression, anxiety, helplessness/hopelessness, suicidal ideation, and confused thinking.

One of the questions we asked of these data early in our studies was the degree to which those selected because they were adapting to the life events associated with a disabling illness could be considered chronically stressed. Group differences in psychological distress were consistent with the view that disability constituted an ongoing challenge/threat to well-being. The disabled reported more distress and less well-being on all subscales in comparison to controls. On initial levels of depression and anxiety, the recently bereaved showed elevated levels comparable to the disabled. However, after 10 months, the bereaved were no longer different from controls on the mental health scales, whereas the disabled continued to show elevations in distress and lower well-being on all scales of mental health. Not all disabled older adults showed these elevations, however; many showed low levels of depression or anxiety comparable to the control samples of older adults. Could strong efficacy beliefs be a protective factor for those older adults facing a chronic disabling illness or injury?

ASSESSMENT OF EFFICACY BELIEFS FOR POSITIVE AND NEGATIVE EVENTS: DEVELOPMENT OF TWO EFFICACY MEASURES

The measurement of efficacy was designed in keeping with the dual conceptualizations of efficacy described earlier; ratings of specific events were obtained, and efficacy expectations were assessed for positive events separately from negative events. In the LEAP study, reports of events were followed by probes of up to three of the "most undesirable" and three of the "most desirable" events that had occurred in the past month. From these probes we obtained scores that made up the efficacy measures. For *positive event efficacy,* we aggregated ratings of two questions asked of each of the three desirable events: (1) the degree to which the person felt he or she was a cause of the event and (2) the degree to which the person felt he or she could cause the event to happen again in the future. For *coping efficacy,* we aggregated ratings made on two items for up to three undesirable events: (1) a rating of degree of satisfaction with his or her own efforts in coping with the event and (2) the degree of certainty expressed by the person in his or her ability to adjust to the event (or one similar to it) should it occur again in the future. In a prior study (Zautra & Wrabetz, 1991), we analyzed initial coping efficacy ratings. For the present study, we were interested in effects across the entire longitudinal study. To obtain accurate estimates of typical efficacy responses, respondents' scores were averaged across the 10 months of the study.

The average scores for the disabled as well as the nondisabled hovered around 2.0 on a 5-point scale for coping efficacy and were slightly higher for positive event efficacy. These scores designate "satisfaction" with one's own coping efforts, as well as feeling "fairly certain" of the ability to cope with such stressful events in the future and to make positive events occur again. The disabled were not different from the other older adults in the study in these efficacy beliefs, even though they reported more distress and less perceived control on global scales of mastery and internal locus of control (Reich, Zautra, & Guarnaccia, 1989). Thus, it would appear that most elders maintain their efficacy beliefs about everyday life events, even in the face of the loss of autonomy due to physical disability. This is important methodologically, as well as substantively, since it permits us to ask questions concerning how those beliefs affect mental health outcomes without the concern of confounding with disability status.

Factor Analysis of Control Beliefs

A useful distinction between efficacy ratings and other assessments of personal control is the degree to which the ratings are explicitly based on either specific transactions with the physical and social world or global self-evaluations. Beliefs in internal locus of control (e.g., Levenson, 1981), and mastery (Pearlin & Schooler, 1978) are examples of global judgments of perceived control; they are not typically thought to be grounded in actual experience. As such, they may be more susceptible to reporting biases like social desirability (Crowne & Marlowe, 1964). We expected that our transactional ratings of efficacy would provide qualitatively different information than global ratings of control such as those elicited by mastery scales.

We performed a confirmatory factor analysis of ratings of coping efficacy, positive event efficacy, and two measures of personal mastery—fatalism and personal control—taken from the Pearlin and Schooler (1978) scale. The two mastery measures were composed of smaller clusters of items from the seven-item mastery scale; they had a modest negative intercorrelation. The efficacy items were averaged across the first 3 month's ratings of up to three events each month; the mastery items were taken from ratings made in the first month of data collection.

The results of these factor analyses are reported in detail in Reich and Zautra (1991). The important findings with regard to this chapter are that the two types of efficacy ratings we are addressing here were independent of reports of mastery and were also relatively independent of one another. When we averaged efficacy ratings across all 10 months (rather than just the first 3 months), there was a modest positive correlation between positive event efficacy and coping efficacy [r (255) = .219, $p < .01$]; these measures showed modest correlations with fatalism and control ($-.19 < r < .23$). Nevertheless, the size of these correlations was small, accounting for 5% or less of the variance. In sum, the two types of efficacy we assessed proved to be largely independent of one another. Both were substantially different from global ratings of mastery and control.

Stability of Efficacy Ratings

A key question left unresolved from the analysis of types of efficacy was whether efficacy ratings were relatively stable across time or if they fluctuated month-to-month, depending upon the life event being rated. Stable processes would be considered traits, the product of stable personality and/or stable situational factors. Unstable processes would be indicative of transitory states that may be considered more dependent upon events rated and less on the person judging the events.

Since we had 10 monthly assessments of both coping efficacy and positive event efficacy in the LEAP data set, we could address this question using the methods proposed by Epstein (1979) for the examination of temporal stability. He showed that accurate estimates of stability of behavioral and physiological measures can be obtained by aggregating or averaging scores on measures over time. We developed estimates of test–retest reliability between ratings of efficacy with increasing amounts of aggregation. First, we simply computed the average of the nine correlations between efficacy ratings taken 1 month apart across the 10 months. After that, we aggregated the first two reports, the second two, and so forth, and computed the average correlation between aggregates of 2 months, and so forth. These coefficients of stability are shown in Figure 1.

Coping efficacy showed an increase in stability with increasing aggregation, consistent with the view that a traitlike consistency emerges with enough monthly reports. Positive event efficacy, on the other hand, showed only a modest increase in stability with aggregation, suggesting that this type of efficacy is more statelike and event-dependent with only 10% of its variance exhibiting traitlike stability. In sum, these analyses indicate that efficacy judgments are not easily classified as traits or state variables. Consistent with their definition as "transactional," the variables appear to contain some stable "trait" variance and sizable "state" variance.

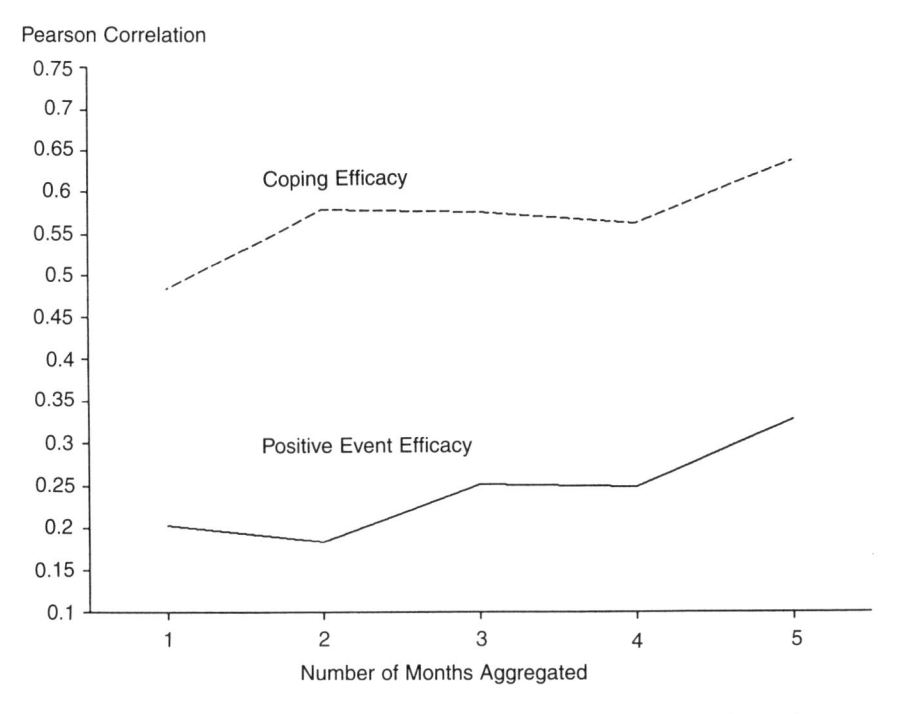

Figure 1. Correlation coefficients between efficacy ratings aggregated over time.

THE RELATIONSHIP OF EFFICACY BELIEFS TO ADJUSTMENT

A central question in the examination of efficacy beliefs is how they might preserve well-being among older adults and other groups at risk because of chronic illness. For the LEAP community sample, we first examined how the efficacy scores collected across the 10 months of LEAP interviews predicted psychological distress at the tenth month. We tested for these effects in two ways: (1) a multiple regression equation in which coping efficacy and positive event efficacy were predictors of distress at the tenth month and (2) a regression analysis in which we first controlled for initial scores on psychological distress to see whether efficacy beliefs were associated with a change in distress over time.

The analyses revealed no significant effects on psychological distress for positive event efficacy, but stable and enduring effects of coping efficacy on psychological distress for both analyses.[1] The simple correlation between coping efficacy and distress scores at month 10 was $r\,(222) = -.306$, $p < .001$. Controlling for initial distress, coping efficacy was associated with a smaller increase in distress, $r\,(220) = -.202$, $p < .005$.

Efficacy Effects on Well-Being over Time

Because we followed the older adults for 4.6 years in the LEAP study, a number of our participants became increasingly disabled over the course of the study. We decided to examine the value of efficacy beliefs assessed across the first 10 months for the maintenance of psychological well-being over the full 4.6 years of the study. We wanted to test whether efficacy beliefs would prevent a deterioration in well-being over time among those who initially showed no evidence of loss in autonomy.

Two types of well-being were assessed: Degree of change for the worse in activity limitation and degree of change for the worse in psychological distress. These variables were obtained by regressing initial levels on the follow-up data and creating a regressed change score for each measure of well-being.

There were two key findings: Positive event efficacy affected activity limitation, and coping efficacy influenced the degree of change in psychological distress. The efficacy beliefs for positive events, aggregated over the first 10 months of interviews, were associated with preservation of function. Those older adults who reported low positive event efficacy showed greater loss of autonomy as manifested by increased activity limitation over the course of the study, *beta* $(126) = .249$, $p < .005$. (This relationship was unaffected by controlling for the correlates of positive event efficacy reported later in this chapter.) Scores on positive event efficacy continued to show a significant effect on changes in activity

---

[1] In a previous paper in which we examined the correlates of coping efficacy (Zautra & Wrabetz, 1991), we found that these ratings were not always associated with less psychological distress. When we examined reports of satisfaction with coping efforts directed specifically at health problems and not future adjustment expectations, we found that individual differences in satisfaction with one's own efforts predicted less distress only for those who were actively engaged in effortful coping. While that paper also suggested that coping efficacy, when inactive, was associated with more distress, that result was not sustained in subsequent analyses across the full 10 months of the study. What was sustained in the analyses over time was the relatively greater value of coping efficacy with health problems when the person was using active coping methods. It appears that active coping potentiates efficacy ratings; if individuals are inactive, their ratings of their own efforts may be unreliable estimates of their beliefs in their own abilities to cope successfully.

limitation from the first to the last interviews, $beta = .251, p < .009$.

Over the 4.6 years, coping efficacy with everyday events played a substantial role in the prevention of psychological distress, $beta\ (124) = -.241, p < .008$. After residualizing coping efficacy by the variables that were associated with it (neuroticism, negative social interaction, marital status, income), the effects of efficacy were still significant, $beta = -.244, p < .013$. Of all predictors (which included the occurrence of stressful life events, the relative levels of neuroticism, internality, and/or levels of social support), coping efficacy showed the most consistent association with the change in psychological distress over time. These effects occurred whether the person became disabled or not during the course of the study (see Zautra, Reich, & Newsom, 1995, for further analyses of these relationships).

Thus, beliefs in one's own efficacy, gathered in response to everyday life events, are key factors in the preservation of well-being for older adults. Not only are these beliefs associated with less psychological distress, but they also predict the maintenance of autonomy and mental health over a substantial period of time. Further, it would appear that the two kinds of efficacy influence aspects of well-being in different ways. Coping efficacy appears to buffer the person from distressing aspects of life events. Positive event efficacy adds to the person's quality of life, leading to the preservation of function and autonomy in later life.

Correlates of Efficacy Beliefs with Clinical Outcomes: The Arthritis Projects

We were interested in testing further whether the findings for coping efficacy obtained on a community sample would also hold for those seeking clinical services for a chronic illness that was characterized by moderate to severe levels of physical limitation. We chose to assess outpatient clinic patients with rheumatoid arthritis (RA), a chronic autoimmune disease characterized by progressive joint damage and episodic pain from unpredictable flare-ups of the disease. We examined coping efficacy among two separate samples of RA patients. Unfortunately, positive event efficacy could not be examined because of time limitations in the assessment that took place while the patients were waiting to be seen by their physicians. These patients had an average age of approximately 55, and they were coping with moderate levels of activity limitation associated with their illness. In the first study, interviews with the patients were supplemented by blood draws from which immune cell counts were made (see Zautra, Okun, Robinson, Lee, Roth, & Em-

Table 1. Mental Health and Disease Correlates of Coping Efficacy for Everyday Events for Two Samples of Rheumatoid Arthritis Patients

	Coping efficacy[a]	
	Study 1 ($N = 32$)	Study 2 ($N = 33$)
Mental health		
Psychological distress	$-.57^b$	$-.44^c$
Psychological well-being	$.56^b$	NA
Clinician ratings of disease activity		
Global rating	NA	$-.34^d$
Joint exam	NA	$-.31^d$
Physiological changes associated with disease		
B-cell % in whole blood	$-.38^c$	NA
Prolactin	NA	$-.52^b$

[a]Measures not available for Study 1 or 2 indicated by NA.
$^b p < .01$; $^c p < .05$; $^d p \leq .10$.

manual, 1989, for a full description of the sample and procedures). In the second study, clinician ratings of disease activity were taken in addition to patient reports, and levels of prolactin were assessed from the patients' sera. In the second study, elevated prolactin was associated with greater stress reactivity and disease activity among the RA patients (see Zautra, Burleson, Matt, Roth, & Burrows, 1994).

We correlated our measure of coping efficacy with indicators of mental health, clinician ratings when available, and the physiological data on the RA patients. Table 1 shows the results. Coping efficacy had significant associations with psychological distress, physiological changes, and clinician ratings of disease activity. The direction of these relationships was consistent with our expectations: Greater coping efficacy was associated with less psychological distress and less disease activity. These findings suggest that coping efficacy is intimately involved in processes of adaptation to stresses of chronic illness, including physiological processes (see Bandura, 1992). Although in these studies we were not able to follow the patients to see if efficacy predicted changes in mental health and/or activity limitation over time, the findings do indicate substantial replication of the findings for coping efficacy among the LEAP sample of elders in the community. Indeed, the size of the associations suggest that efficacy may matter more for clinic cases than for those with mild to moderate impairments in the community.

EXAMINING THE ANTECEDENTS OF EFFICACY BELIEFS

Based on the analyses of data from older adults from the community and clinic samples of RA patients, it appears that efficacy beliefs play an important role in maintaining psychological well-being for the chronically ill. What contributes to preserving efficacy beliefs? We decided to tackle that question by attempting to account for efficacy scores with measures of traits and also with variables assessing ongoing transactions between the person and the social environment. The relatively high stability of coping efficacy suggests that personality features may play a key role in these expectations of the self. Indeed, other stable features of the person's life, most importantly level of activity limitation, could determine the extent of the person's expectations for adjustment to future stressors and beliefs in the ability to promote positive events.

To address this question we selected a wide array of measures of personality, activity limitation, social network membership, and social status taken at the beginning of the LEAP study. Our selection of variables as possible predictors was based partly on prior analyses (Zautra & Wrabetz, 1991). Since transactional measures might also play an important role in efficacy beliefs, we also included two measures averaged across reports of everyday events taken during the first 10 monthly assessments: Frequency of desirable events for which the person was likely to have some casual role and frequency of undesirable interpersonal events. We sought to predict both positive event efficacy and coping efficacy.

Table 2 shows the findings and includes all variables tested as possible predictors. First, it is of interest to note that the multiple R for the prediction of each efficacy variable was relatively modest, suggesting that a substantial portion of the ratings of efficacy was not determined by individual differences in other variables. Although the overall levels of prediction were not high, the variables that did affect efficacy beliefs are of interest, nonetheless. Among the strongest predictors of positive event efficacy was the number of desirable events over which the person had some control. A belief in personal agency and lower ratings on the belief in chance subscale from the Levenson I-E instrument (Levenson, 1981) also were associated with higher ratings of efficacy for positive events. The static measures of social network members (e.g., the number of network members who provide support and the number who are sources of stress) were unrelated to these efficacy beliefs, but a transactional indicator of social relationships was associated with efficacy beliefs. Older adults with more undesirable social interactions over the 10 monthly interviews showed less efficacy for positive events.

Table 2. Multiple Regression Predictions of Two Types of Efficacy Beliefs

	Positive event efficacy			Coping efficacy		
	b	SE	t	b	SE	t
Possible predictors						
Never married				−.892	.301	−2.96[a]
Income				.034	.011	3.24[a]
Activity limitation						
Negative social ties						
Positive social ties						
Social desirability						
Neuroticism				−.481	.165	−2.91[a]
Internality	.012	.004	2.82[a]			
Belief in chance	−.01	.003	−3.02[a]			
Desirable events	.083	.027	3.03[a]			
Undesirable interpersonal events	−.058	.025	−2.34[b]	−.075	.029	−2.61[c]
Multiple R		.38			.38	

[a] $p < .005$; [b] $p < .05$; [c] $p < .01$.

Coping efficacy for everyday events was affected in a similar manner by negative social interactions. Older adults with more negative interactions showed less coping efficacy (see also O'Brien & DeLongis, Chapter 6, this volume). Three other predictors also were significant: neuroticism, income, and marital status. Older adults with lower family incomes who had never married and who showed neurotic (labile) emotional responses also tended to have less coping efficacy. A social resource model is a useful way of understanding these relationships; those with more physical, functional, and emotional resources and fewer classic risk factors had stronger beliefs in their abilities to cope (Cozzarelli, 1993).

Social Influences on Efficacy Beliefs

The data from the LEAP study we have presented thus far are equivocal regarding the role of social relations in shaping efficacy beliefs. The number of persons in the network who provide support and the number identified as negative social ties did not predict efficacy beliefs. Coping efficacy was higher for those older adults who had been married, however, and both types of efficacy were adversely affected by many negative social interactions, as measured by everyday events.

In addition to our findings, some prior research suggested that coping efficacy would be influenced by the nature of the person's social relationships. In an earlier study of 100 female RA patients (Manne & Zautra, 1989), those who coped poorly with their illness had husbands who were more critical of them. Those who coped well reported greater satisfaction with the type of support they received from their spouses.

In a study by Manne (personal communication, 1992), the count of negative remarks was associated with poor coping, but the count of positive remarks alone was not; only perceived supportiveness was associated with adaptive coping. Coyne and Smith (1994) suggest one reason for the weak effects of positive social ties: Positive support could undermine efficacy beliefs. In a study of patients coping with myocardial infarction, they found that if the support person was overprotective, the patient felt less capable of caring for himself or herself (Coyne & Smith, 1994; O'Brien & DeLongis, Chapter 6, this volume). In light of these considerations, the LEAP findings made sense; positive aspects of the person's social relationships do not necessarily bolster efficacy beliefs.

Social Encouragement of Self-Reliance versus Dependency

This conclusion led us to examine the supportive role in more depth. We reasoned that the type of supportive message may be important to identify; Support can promote confidence to be self-reliant, but support can also promote dependence. An assessment of these two types of support messages was developed for the LEAP study by Grossman (1986).

During the tenth interview, participants provided a second detailed list of members of their social networks, as they had done at entry (see Finch et al., 1989, for a full description of the nomination procedures). From the list of names they provided, the participants identified up to five of the "most important" members and then rated each of those members of their network with three items assessing the degree of self-reliant encouragement and three items assessing the degree the network members urged the person to rely on others for support. The self-reliance items were: "[This person . . .] encouraged me to make my own decisions," "made me feel like I am in control of my future," and "encouraged me to work on my problems in my own way." The other-reliance encouragement items were: "[This person . . .] "encouraged me to let others take more responsibility for solving my problems," "made me feel like others know what's best for me," and "encouraged me to be more dependent on others." We constructed a composite scale from these inquiries based on the average ratings of self-reliance encouragement across network members minus the average ratings of other-reliance ratings. This scale provided us with the means to investigate how the social reinforcement of self-reliance beliefs would affect coping efficacy.

On the surface, one might expect a one-to-one correspondence between self-reliance encouragement and coping efficacy (e.g., Taylor, Bandura, Ewart, Miller, & DeBusk, 1985). We predicted that the relationship between beliefs about coping and the encouragement of significant others would be more complex than that, however. A person coping with life stress, particularly a chronic and disabling illness like RA, often relies on others for emotional and instrumental support. Their beliefs about their own efficacy are not based solely on their expectations for themselves but also on their beliefs concerning their access to help from members of their social networks. Self-reliance encouragement may not always communicate supportiveness of the kind needed by the person looking for a helping hand (Reich & Zautra, 1991).

For most, self-reliance support may optimize adjustment: The message encourages a focus on personal responsibility for solving problems and discourages dependency. For those with a chronic illness, a poor self-concept and lower self efficacy would seem a likely result of persistent social encouragement of dependency. Prior to the challenge to adjustment that a chronic illness brings, a social network that promotes self-reliance might be the best primary preventive resource. However, during the initial crisis of loss of autonomy, self-reliant encouragement is tantamount to telling the person to manage on their own. How supportive is that message to the older adult despairing over a recent loss of autonomy? The "lean on me" message implicit in the other-reliant encouragement may be of more benefit to those going through crises.

Thus, the fit of the supportive message to the needs of the individual at the time the support is provided may be the most crucial. In a recent paper (Zautra, Reich, & Newsom, 1995), we examined this question by relating our measures of self and other-reliance encouragement to the mental health of three different LEAP samples: our nondisabled group, a sample of initially healthy people who became disabled 6 or more months after our assessment of self-reliance versus other-reliance support, and a group that became disabled while receiving the self-reliance support.

The value of self-reliance support varied dramatically across these three conditions. Prior to disability, self-reliance encouragement from the support network was associated with better mental health. However, for those 40 older adults in the LEAP sample who became disabled during the time of assessment of the type of support, self-reliance support was associated with poorer adjustment. Thus, the *timing* of the message appears critical to its value to the processes of adaptation.

[Figure: Line graph showing Coping Efficacy (y-axis, 3 to 4.5) vs Self-Reliant Encouragement (x-axis, −1.68 to 1.68). Low Activity Limit line rises from ~3.52 to ~4.28; High Activity Limit line is nearly flat around 3.85–3.9.]

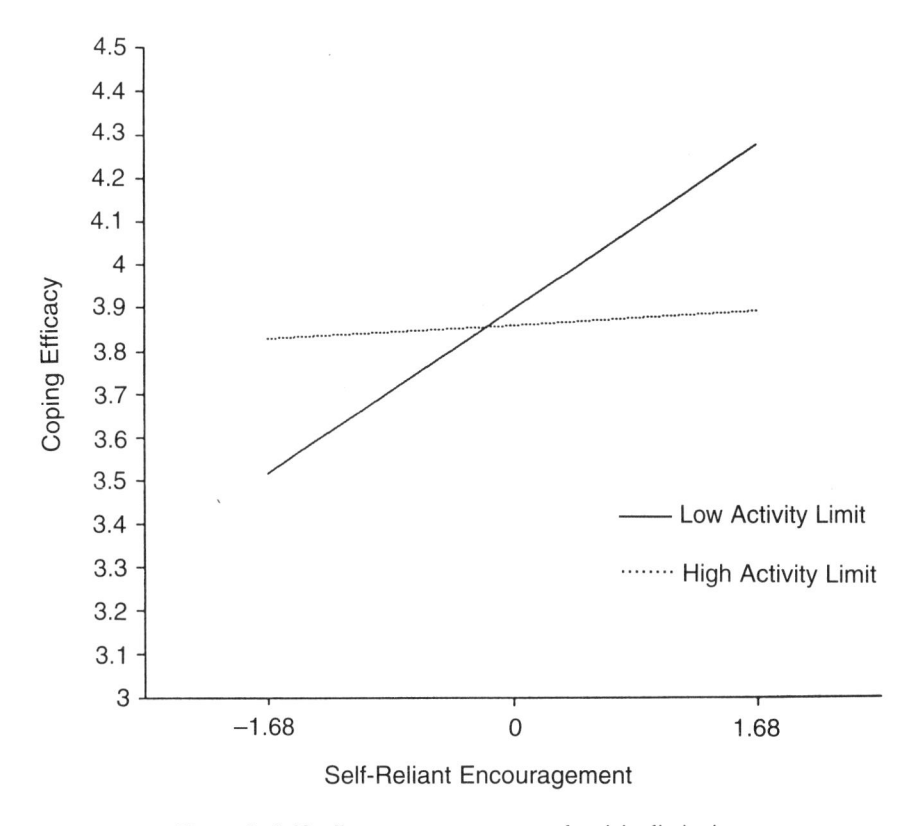

Figure 2. Self-reliant encouragement and activity limitation.

We hypothesized that the findings for self-reliance versus other-reliance encouragement were a result of their differential effects on coping efficacy. In brief, we predicted that social encouragement of self-reliance would benefit coping efficacy only for those who were healthy when they received such messages. We were able to employ the LEAP sample's data to answer this question. The findings were consistent with these predictions. For the entire sample, self-reliance support showed a modest positive and significant association with coping efficacy [$r(233) = .182, p < .01$], but these findings obscured an important interaction effect. When we assessed level of coping efficacy during the tenth month for those with little or no activity limitation at entry, those who stayed healthy through the first 10 months showed a strong relationship between self-reliance encouragement and efficacy, but those who showed an increase in activity limitation between the first and tenth monthly interview were not helped at all by self-reliance encouragement. The interaction is plotted in Figure 2.

IMPLICATIONS FOR UNDERSTANDING COPING WITH CHRONIC STRESSORS

The results of the many analyses we have discussed offer a highly differentiated view of self-efficacy. This view challenges current thinking and calls for a greater understanding of how social relations may shape self-evaluations. Our data indicate that there are fundamental differences between beliefs in one's ability to produce preferred life experiences and beliefs in one's ability to cope with negative events: One is linked to the strengthening of expectations for self-initiated satisfying outcomes, whereas the other is linked to beliefs in one's ability to overcome aversive events. What we have shown is that these two efficacy beliefs are separate "master programs" designed for the preservation of well-being. They are only tangentially related to one another through their mutual relationship to a generalized expectancy of control, although they are clearly different from such global expectancies.

Thus, it would appear that affect is an organizer of efficacy expectations in that positive and negative affective states require different efficacy beliefs. It is not an issue of primacy; both the efficacy cognitions and the affective bed from which they arise are central to the meaning of efficacy evaluations. The important point is that the affective states themselves are differentiated. As noted earlier, beliefs in one's ability to cope with adversity appear to be independent of the belief in one's ability to make positive events occur. Thus, a person has different meaning structures for self-evaluation dependent upon the underlying emotional experience.

For some stressors, it is conceivable that only one type of efficacy is important. But for the chronic stress that accompanies the loss of autonomy due to disability among older adults, both positive event efficacy and coping efficacy are critical to the maintenance of well-being. The data indicate that coping efficacy is one of the best predictors of preservation of psychological well-being. However, efficacy expectations for positive events in everyday life appear to prevent the functional loss itself. This point comes as no surprise to those social scientists who have studied the role that personal motivation plays in performance: Loss of autonomy due to functional limitation depends upon subjective estimates of ability to perform everyday tasks (Bandura, 1992). The only surprise perhaps is that so little attention has been given to efficacy-related cognitions for positive experiences as a potential resistance resource in the preservation of functioning among older adults.

A more unified theory of cognition, affect, and social events is needed to resolve the many issues raised here in our examination of efficacy beliefs. One overarching framework for the construction of such models is that of person–environment fit. Influenced by the early work of Lewin (1951), Cutrona (1990), Lawton (1982), and Kahana, Kahana, and Riley (1989) have provided an approach to understanding behavior through an evaluation of the congruence in person and environment interactions. Our research suggests that such an approach may be useful; the findings suggest that the interaction between a loss of autonomy and the person's social environment has been found to strongly influence the ability to cope (Manne & Zautra, 1989). The congruence between the type of support given and the support desired (self-reliance versus dependency) was found to be a critical issue in coping, suggesting that the supportive message must fit the needs of the individual to be helpful to him or her. We urge further work in these arenas in order to fully understand the sources and products of efficacy beliefs among older adults threatened with loss of autonomy.

Our understanding of these processes would be advanced by more longitudinal research among those coping with chronic stress. Such work would be strengthened by careful attention to cognitive and social processes involved in the preservation of positive as well as negative affective states. Personality differences are also likely to play an important role; the fit of the person to the social and affective demands of the situation may be among the most important determinants of efficacy beliefs. We would also urge the development of research tools that would allow for the examination of stress-reactivity and coping responses to naturally occurring events judged to be significantly stressful by the investigator. Such methodologies would complement the many laboratory stressors used by Bandura (1992) in his examination of efficacy beliefs, strengthening the external validity of the findings. The development of such tools would also add greater experimenter control over the study of change in efficacy and its consequences than is possible in field research such as we have presented here from the LEAP project.

The more nascent area in self-efficacy research is the integration of social relationships in the development of efficacy expectations. In this domain, we offer evidence that both types of efficacy explored here are harmed by interpersonal stress. Such stress may arise from a number of sources, but we suspect that the chronic stress of conflictual relationships causes the most harm to well-being. A reduction in interpersonal tensions would thus appear warranted in any attempt to enhance a person's self-efficacy. Such advice in itself is quite apart from the usual mastery-based training given to the person to promote a greater sense of personal efficacy. We would suggest that future research examine more thoroughly how close relationships influence efficacy beliefs and how appraisals of coping efficacy take into account coping's impact on close relationships (Gignac & Gottlieb, Chapter 9, this volume).

The push to reduce social tensions conceals a more complex issue: How does one act in order to best facilitate another person's efficacy? Our data urge a greater awareness of the needs of the person at the time the help is provided. Encouragement of self-reliance often boosts a sense of personal efficacy among those who are healthy and renews self-confidence among those who have struggled with a chronic disability for some time. Among those coping with a recent, albeit permanent, loss of functioning, however, encouragement of self-reliance may miss the mark by a wide margin. That person may need to sense the support of others close to him or her in order to maintain a belief in himself or herself.

A core set of recommendations for interventions stem from this work. Clearly, it is never too early, or too late, to attempt to change older persons' beliefs in personal efficacy for managing everyday events. Although there is some stability in these beliefs, they are only partially influenced by stable personality features, and they are quite different from dispositional control beliefs. Efficacy beliefs are alterable. Two kinds of efficacy stem from a person's involvements in everyday life, and the clinician may fail to distinguish between these separate concerns, providing help in only one or the other domain. Moreover, overconcern for how the person is adjusting to a traumatic event could obscure those sources in everyday life from which meaningful estimates of self-worth derive. The quality of life of older adults may be improved through developing the person's sense of control over everyday life problems.

There is not a single social message that strengthens efficacy beliefs. Individuals' receptivity to self-reliance encouragement appears to vary with their needs, personality, and the situational demands. Interpersonal flexibility appears to be more important to the strengthening of efficacy beliefs than is adherence to a specific schedule of social reinforcement. Based on our analyses, we would urge that these messages be delivered to the informal support networks, as well as to the professional healthcare provider. It appears that most older adults have already established a strong sense of personal efficacy, developed over years of successful coping experiences with life stressors. In times of crisis, a supportive presence is also needed to sustain efficacy beliefs and allow the older adult to adjust to threats to the self posed by a loss of autonomy.

ACKNOWLEDGMENT   This research was supported in part by grants from the National Institute on Aging (R01 AG4924).

REFERENCES

Bandura, A. (1992). Self-efficacy mechanism in psychobiologic functioning. In R. Schwarzer (Ed.), *Self-efficacy: Thought control of action* (p. 355–393). Washington DC: Hemisphere.
Bandura, A., & Adams, N. E. (1977). Analysis of self-efficacy theory of behavioral change. *Cognitive Therapy and Research, 1,* 287–310.
Bradburn, N. (1969). *The structure of psychological well-being.* Chicago: Aldine.
Coyne, J. C. & Smith, D. A. F. (1994). Couples coping with a myocardial infarction: Contextual perspective on patient self-efficacy. *Journal of Family Psychology, 8,* 43–54.
Cozzarelli, C. (1993). Personality and self-efficacy as predictors of coping with abortion. *Journal of Personality and Social Psychology, 65,* 1224–1236.
Crowne, D. P., & Marlowe, D. (1964). *The approval motive: Studies in evaluative dependence.* New York: Wiley.
Cutrona, C. E. (1990). Stress and social support—In search of optimal matching. *Journal of Social and Clinical Psychology, 9,* 3–14.
Dohrenwend, B. P., Shrout, P. E., Egri, G., & Mendelsohn, F. S. (1980). Nonspecific psychological distress and other dimensions of psychopathology. *Archives of General Psychiatry, 37,* 1229–1236.
Elliott, G. R., & Eisdorfer, C. (Eds.). (1982). *Stress and human health: Analysis and implications for research.* New York: Springer.
Epstein, S. (1979). The stability of behavior: I. On predicting most of the people much of the time. *Journal of Personality and Social Psychology, 37,* 1097–1126.
Finch, J. F., Okun, M. A., Barrera, M., Zautra, A. J., & Reich, J. W. (1989). Measurement models of positive and negative social ties: Their generalizability across elderly subgroups and their relationships to psychological distress and life satisfaction. *American Journal of Community Psychology, 17,* 585–605.
Grossman, R. M. (1986). *Attributions of responsibility and social support.* Unpublished doctoral dissertation, Arizona State University, Tempe, Arizona.
Herzberg, F. (1966). *Work and the nature of man.* New York: Thomas Y. Crowell.
Kahana, E., Kahana, B., & Riley, K. (1989). Person–environment transactions relevant to control and helplessness in institutional settings. In P. S. Fry (Ed.), *Psychological perspectives of helplessness and control in the elderly* (pp. 121–153). Amsterdam: North Holland.
Lawton, M. P. (1982). Competence, environmental press, and the adaptation of older people. In M. P. Lawton, P. G. Windley, & T. O. Byerts (Eds.), *Aging and the environment: Theoretical approaches* (pp. 35–39). New York: Springer.
Lazarus, R. S. (1966). *Psychological stress and the coping process.* New York: McGraw-Hill.
Lee, G. P., Loring, D. W., Dahl, J. L., & Meador, K. J. (1993). Hemispheric specialization for emotional expression. *Neuropsychiatry, Neuropsychology, and Behavioral Neurology, 6,* 143–148.
Lennon, M. C., Dohrenwend, B. P., Zautra, A. J., & Marbach, J. J. (1990). Coping and adaptation to facial pain in contrast to other stressful life events. *Journal of Personality and Social Psychology, 59,* 1040–1050.
Levenson, H. (1981). Differentiating among internality, powerful others and chance. In H. M. Lefcourt (Ed.), *Research with the locus of control construct: Vol. 1. assessment methods* (pp. 15–63). New York: Academic Press.
Lewin, K. (1951). Selected theoretical papers. In D. Cartwright (Ed.). *Field theory in social science.* New York: Harper & Row.
Manne, S., & Zautra, A. J. (1989). The effects of spouse critical remarks on psychological adjustment to rheumatoid arthritis. *Journal of Personality and Social Psychology, 56,* 608–617.
Pearlin, L., & Schooler, C. (1978). The structure of coping. *Journal of Health and Social Behavior, 19,* 2–21.

Reich, J., & Zautra, A. J. (1981). Life events and personal causation: Some relationships with satisfaction and distress. *Journal of Personality and Social Psychology, 41*, 1002–1012.

Reich, J. W., & Zautra, A. J. (1988). Direct and moderating effects of positive life events. In L. N. Cohen (Ed.), *Advances in research on stressful life events* (pp. 149–181). Beverly Hills, CA: Sage.

Reich, J. W., & Zautra, A. J. (1991). Experimental and measurement approaches to internal control in older adults. *Journal of Social Issues, 47*, 143–188.

Reich, J. W., Zautra, A. J., & Guarnaccia, C. A. (1989). Effects of disability and bereavement on the mental health and recovery of older adults. *Psychology and Aging, 4*, 57–65.

Reich, J. W., Zautra, A. J., & Hill, J. (1987). Activity, event transactions and quality of life of the elderly. *Psychology and Aging, 2*, 116–124.

Revenson, T. A., & Felton, B. J. (1984). Disability and coping as predictors of psychological adjustment to rheumatoid arthritis. *Journal of Consulting and Clinical Psychology, 57*, 344–348.

Smith, C. A., & Wallston, K. A. (1992). Adaptation in patients with chronic rheumatoid arthritis: Application of a general model. *Health Psychology, 11*, 151–162.

Taylor, C. B., Bandura, A., Ewart, C. K., Miller, N. H., & DeBusk, R. F. (1985). Exercise testing to enhance wives' confidence in their husbands' cardiac capabilities soon after clinically uncomplicated acute myocardial infarction. *American Journal of Cardiology, 55*, 635–638.

Teresi, J. A., Golden, R. R., Gurland, B. J., Wilder, D. E., & Bennett, R. G. (1983). Construct validity of indicator scales development from the comprehensive assessment and interview schedule. Unpublished manuscript.

Watson, D., & Clark, L. A. (1984). Negative affectivity: The disposition to experience aversive emotional states. *Psychological Bulletin, 96*, 465–490.

Zautra, A. J., Burleson, M., Matt, K., Roth, S., & Burrows, L. (1994). Interpersonal stress and disease activity in rheumatoid arthritis. *Health Psychology, 13*, 139–148.

Zautra, A. J., Guarnaccia, C., & Reich, J. W. (1988). Structure of mental health of older adults. *Journal of Consulting and Clinical Psychology, 56*, 514–519.

Zautra, A. J., Guenther, R. T., & Chartier, G. (1985). Attributions for real and hypothetical events: Their relation to self-esteem and depression. *Journal of Abnormal Psychology, 94*, 530–540.

Zautra, A. J., & Hempel, A. (1984). Subjective well-being and physical health status: A narrative review with some suggestions for future research. *International Journal of Aging and Human Development, 19*, 95–110.

Zautra, A. J., Okun, M. A., Robinson, S. E., Lee, D., Roth, S. H., & Emmanual, J. (1989). Life stress and lymphocyte alterations among rheumatoid arthritis patients. *Health Psychology, 8*, 1–14.

Zautra, A., & Reich, J. W. (1980). Positive life events and reports of well-being: Some useful distinctions. *American Journal of Community Psychology, 8*, 657–670.

Zautra, A. J., Reich, J. W., & Guarnaccia, C. A. (1990). The everyday life consequences of disability and bereavement for older adults. *Journal of Personality and Social Psychology, 59*, 550–561.

Zautra, A. J., Reich, J. W., & Newsom, J. T. (1995). Autonomy and sense of control among older adults: An examination of their effects on mental health. In L. Bond, S. Culter, & A. Grams (Eds.), *Promoting successful and productive aging*. Newbury Park, CA: Sage.

Zautra, A. J., & Wrabetz, A. (1991). Coping success and its relationship to psychological distress for older adults. *Journal of Personality and Social Psychology, 61*, 801–810.

V

Illustrations of Coping with Pervasive Life Difficulties

11

Positive Meaningful Events and Coping in the Context of HIV/AIDS

SUSAN FOLKMAN, JUDITH TEDLIE MOSKOWITZ, ELIZABETH M. OZER, and CRYSTAL L. PARK

INTRODUCTION

Most research on coping with chronic stress tends to focus inquiry on strategies that help the person manage stressor-related demands. In the case of coping with a debilitating illness, for example, the search often focuses on strategies that are related to managing the primary consequences of the illness, including disease-related limited mobility, pain, or dysphoria, and the secondary consequences of the illness, including disrupted family relationships or changes in role functioning. However, the lives of people with a debilitating illness consist of more than just their illness. They may have warm family relationships, friends with whom they talk, or work or other activities that interest them. These other aspects of people's lives may play an important role in sustaining their well-being while they are coping with their illness. Thus,

---

SUSAN FOLKMAN and JUDITH TEDLIE MOSKOWITZ • Center for AIDS Prevention Studies, University of California, San Francisco, San Francisco, California 94105.   ELIZABETH M. OZER • Division of Adolescent Medicine, University of California, San Francisco, San Francisco, California 94105.   CRYSTAL L. PARK • Department of Psychology, Miami University, Oxford, Ohio 45056.

Coping with Chronic Stress, edited by Benjamin H. Gottlieb. Plenum Press, New York, 1997.

a full understanding of the coping process in the context of chronic stress may need to take into account aspects of people's lives that at first blush do not seem to be related directly to how they cope with the chronic stress per se.

Our interest in exploring this possibility was fueled by findings from an ongoing longitudinal study of stress, coping, and adaptation among HIV+ and HIV− caregiving partners of men with AIDS and among a group of HIV+ men who are coping with their own illness. These people are in a chronically stressful situation. The caregivers' partners are dying of AIDS at a time of life when most people are building relationships. There is little that can be done to stem the tide of the disease, which becomes increasingly debilitating physically and often mentally. The demands on the caregiver are unrelenting during this period, which can last for several years (Folkman, Chesney, & Christopher-Richards, 1994; Folkman, Chesney, Cooke, Boccellari, & Collette, 1994). People who are living with HIV must cope with the tasks associated with maintaining their physical health as well as with the maintenance of their well-being while living with the knowledge that their life is likely to be cut short by a vicious disease.

Not surprisingly, the caregivers in our study reported high levels of depressive mood, assessed using the Centers for Epidemiological Studies-Depression measure (CES-D) (Radloff, 1977). Caregivers' scores averaged more than 1SD above the norm for the general population. However, as we report later, we discovered that at the same time participants were experiencing high levels of depressive mood, they also reported levels of positive morale and positive states of mind that were comparable to those reported in the general population. Similarly, participants reported levels of optimism that were comparable to those in the general population (Park & Folkman, in press).

The findings that participants reported positive psychological states while also reporting high levels of depressive mood astonished us. How did these participants, many of whom were providing care to a partner during his last months of life, sustain psychological well-being in the midst of such incredibly difficult circumstances? The caregiving literature says relatively little about the maintenance of well-being throughout the caregiving period. In two studies of family caregivers of persons with dementia, satisfaction with the caregiving role was related to positive affect but not depressive mood in spouse caregivers of elderly spouses suffering from Alzheimer's, and having larger numbers of friends and close relationships was associated with life satisfaction. (Haley, Levine, Brown, & Bartolucci, 1987; Lawton, Moss, Kleban, Glicksman, & Rovine, 1991).

Like many other studies of coping with chronic stress, our study initially focused on negative aspects of the experiences of caregivers and HIV infected men. For example, the participants in our study complete bimonthly interviews that include a section asking about the most stressful event related to caregiving or living with HIV disease that occurred during the previous week. The caregivers vividly described how they deal with the instrumental demands of providing care to a partner with AIDS and how they coped with loss, including the loss of ordinary daily routines, companionship, intimacy, and hope for a future together (Folkman, Chesney, & Christopher-Richards, 1994). The narratives of the HIV+ men coping with their own illness also described the worries and concerns that pervade their daily lives.

Shortly after the study began, however, several participants reported that by asking only about stressful events we were missing an important part of the story of how they coped with the chronic illness of their partner or their own illness. They said that we needed to ask about positive events—events that had positive meaning—as well. Our participants' comments made us realize that we may have focused our search for knowledge about how people cope with the chronic stress of caregiving, bereavement, and HIV disease too narrowly.

As a consequence, we added a section to the conclusion of the bimonthly interviews that asked participants to describe a positive meaningful event that had helped them get through the day during the previous week. In this chapter we explore the nature of these positive meaningful events, why they are a significant component of these people's coping repertoires, and their relevance to coping theory.

Positive Meaningful Events: Relevant Findings and Theoretical Issues

We define positive meaningful events as events that touch on valued beliefs and goals, are appraised as beneficial, and evoke positive emotion. We turned to the literatures on positive events, meaning, and positive emotions to suggest ways in which these events might be implicated in the maintenance of well-being under conditions of chronic stress.

Relatively little research has been conducted on the relationship between positive events and well-being under stressful conditions, and the findings of these studies are mixed. "Uplifts," positive occurrences in daily living that generate positive emotions, assessed with a checklist, were associated with reduced distress in samples of community-residing adults (Kanner, Coyne, Schaefer, & Lazarus, 1981) and adolescents (Kanner & Feldman, 1991). However, subjects in these studies were not selected for high levels of chronic stress. Uplifts had no association with distress in a sample of medical students during their first year of training, which some might characterize as a chronically stressful time (Wolf, Elston, & Kissling, 1989). In a study of recently conjugally bereaved men and women and disabled adults, desirable "small" events and major events had a variable effect on negative states (depression and anxiety) and positive states (positive affect and self-esteem), depending on the group. Bereaved subjects showed no positive effects of desirable events, whereas disabled subjects showed sizable effects (Zautra, Reich, & Guarnaccia, 1990).

These studies suggest that positive events may have a role in helping people sustain psychological well-being under conditions of stress. However, the assessments of positive events in these studies provide little information about the mechanisms through which they may have these effects. The question remains as to how positive meaningful events help people cope with chronic stress, such as the stress of caregiving or having HIV disease.

One possibility is suggested by Langston (1994), who discusses the idea of *capitalizing*, a process through which people focus on and amplify the beneficial aspects of a positive event by, for example, communicating the event to others or celebrating. His research suggests that people who engage in this process increase the impact of positive events on well-being. This finding is consistent with informal communications from several of our participants who told us that they wanted to describe a positive meaningful event to conclude their interview on an upbeat note.

Langston's notion also suggests a second possibility, namely, that the positive emotions that are experienced in positive events may have coping functions. This idea was discussed by Lazarus, Kanner, and Folkman (1980), who suggested that positive emotions can serve as breathers from stress, as sustainers of coping effort, and as restorers. Breathers, such as a vacation, a siesta, a coffee break, or a school recess, not only temporarily free the individual from a stressful experience, but also engage the person in a pleasurable diversionary activity. As sustainers, positive emotions such as excitement, challenge, or hope help motivate an individual to persist in what might be an aversive activity. Positive emotions that function as restorers facilitate the individual's recovery from harm or loss by replenishing resources or developing new ones. Pleasure at achieving a small success during a depressive period is an example of a restorative emotion. Meaningful events, which by definition are associated with positive emotions, may help people cope with chronic stress by providing a breather, by helping sustain coping efforts, or by replenishing depleted resources. All three functions are relevant to coping with chronic stress, such as caregiving, bereavement, or HIV disease.

Research on how people find positive meaning in stressful events also informs our thinking about the role of positive events. A number of authors discuss the importance of finding meaning as a way of coping with suffering and loss (e.g., Baumeister, 1991; Frankl, 1963; Klinger, 1977, 1987; Silver & Wortman, 1980). Examples include finding a redeeming value in a loss, such as when people whose loved ones have died from a disease become advocates for research on that disease; forming new or closer bonds with others because of having experienced and survived a natural disaster together; and finding that the event has clarified which goals or priorities are important and which are not.

Studies have demonstrated the relationship between finding positive meaning in a negative event and psychological adjustment in a variety of contexts, including incest (Silver, Boon, & Stones, 1983), the death of a child (McIntosh, Silver, & Wortman, 1993), heart attack (Affleck, Tennen, Croog, & Levine, 1987) and in our own study concerning providing care to a partner with AIDS (Folkman, Chesney, Collette, Boccellari, & Cooke, 1996). In the latter case, for example, caregivers indicated on Likert scales the extent to which caregiving made them feel needed, made them feel as though they had grown as a person, showed their love for their partner, and brought them closer to their partner. This measure of the positive meaning of caregiving was an important predictor of the course of depressive mood following the partner's death: the higher the score on the measure of the positive meaning of caregiving, the more rapidly depressive mood abated. Reappraisals attempting to create this type of positive meaning in a negative event are frequently assessed in a cursory manner with coping checklists such as the COPE (Carver, Scheier, & Weintraub, 1989) and the Ways of Coping (Folkman & Lazarus, 1988). We do not know whether these same appraisal mechanisms are used to create or enhance positive meaning in ordinary events that are not stressful, and if so, how this meaning might help people cope with the stressful aspects of their lives.

Goals of This Chapter

In this chapter we turn to positive meaningful events that help caregivers of men with AIDS and men who are themselves HIV+ get through their days. Our overall goal is to begin developing a theoretical framework for understanding the coping functions of these events. The first step in this process is to develop an understanding of the nature of events that are both positive and meaningful in the context of chronic stress. Are they major events, or are they ordinary occurrences? What makes them meaningful? Are they initiated by participants, or are they serendipitous? The second step is to determine how these events help people cope with chronic stress.

The participants in this analysis vary on two significant dimensions, caregiving and HIV seropositivity. A secondary goal is to examine how these dimensions may be related to differences in the nature of the events that participants find positive and meaningful. Compared to persons who are HIV−, persons who are HIV+ may be more attuned to events associated with their own health; and persons who are caregivers may be more attuned to events that are associated with their partner's well-being. In the case of HIV+ caregivers, it is not clear what their referent might be for meaningful events. For these reasons we will analyze meaningful events for the sample as a whole and, even though our sample is small, for each of the three component groups (HIV+ caregivers, HIV− caregivers, HIV+ noncaregivers).

Background: The UCSF Coping Project

The sample for this study comes from the UCSF Coping Project, which is a longitudinal study of the effects of caregiving and bereavement on the mental and physical health of gay men whose partners have AIDS. Participants are followed bimonthly for 2 years and semiannually for 3 additional years. Data collection began in April, 1990, and will continue through 1997. The data in this report were collected between 1990 and 1994.

Inclusion Criteria. To be included in the UCSF Coping Project, men had to identify themselves as gay or bisexual, be in a committed relationship and share living quarters with their partner, be willing to be tested for HIV antibodies, have no more than two symptoms of HIV disease, and not be an injection drug user. To be included in a caregiver group, the men's partners had to have a diagnosis of AIDS, need assistance with at least two instrumental tasks of daily living, and be living at home. To be included in the HIV+ noncaregiver group, the men had to test HIV+ and be in a committed relationship with healthy partners without care needs. Only one member of a couple could participate in the study.

Recruitment. We recruited participants between April 1990 and June 1992 from the San Francisco Bay area using advertisements in the gay press, public service announcements on radio and television, referrals from clinics and gay organizations, and annual mailings to residents of selected San Francisco zip codes.

Procedures. All data reported here were collected in face-to-face interviews. The interviews were conducted by individuals with clinical training and special training in the administration of the study questionnaires. Each participant was interviewed by the same interviewer over time. Participants were paid $20 for each interview.

Questions about meaningful events were inserted into the face-to-face interviews approximately 1 year after data collection began. Beginning at that time, each interview was concluded with the following prompt: "We have been talking about an event that was stressful for you. Now I want you to think back over the week and describe something that you did, or something that happened to you, that made you feel good and that was *meaningful* to you and helped you get through a day." Additional questions the interviewer asked included: "In what ways was this meaningful?" "What were you feeling?" "What else was important or significant about this event?" "Are there other ways in which this event had meaning for you?" The interviewer recorded the participant's response verbatim. Measures of positive mood (Bradburn, 1969), positive states of mind (Horowitz, Adler, & Kegeles, 1988), and depressive mood (CES-D) (Radloff, 1977) were included as part of the interviews.

Selection of Subjects for This Analysis. We selected all subjects who had provided descriptions of at least five meaningful events in interviews. These were conducted over the course of approximately 1 year at bimonthly intervals. At the time we began this analysis, which was midway through the parent study, 36 participants met our criterion. The small sample size reflected the fact that we had begun asking about meaningful events well after the study was underway. Therefore, only a small number of subjects met the inclusion criterion for this analysis.

METHOD: CODING SCHEME

The authors developed a coding scheme that evolved out of extensive discussion about the themes expressed in the meaningful events. Our coding scheme included the following major categories: the type of event, who was involved in the event, the source of meaning in each event, and whether or not the event was initiated by the participant (self-agency). Each participant's reports were coded by two judges who were blind to HIV serostatus. Multiple codes were made for source of meaning when more than one was identified in the report. The coded reports were then cross-checked to achieve inter-rater agreement. Inter-rater reliability ranged from 85% to 90%. Any discrepancies between raters were then discussed among the authors until coding agreement was reached.

Taxonomies for each category are as follows:

1. *Type of event*
   a. *Social events* included parties, weddings, and visits with family. Any event in which the participant stressed the social aspects was categorized as social.
   b. *Entertainment* events included, for example, visiting an amusement park, going to a concert, taking a walk, or enjoying the rain.
   c. *Realizations* were narratives in which the participant reported that he had gained some important knowledge about himself. For example, one participant reported:

   > Trying to find myself through sobering up and facing up to all the stress. I'm trying to stop taking the coward's way out. I've sat down and started writing a list of things that are important to me. That's been meaningful. [Response to the question: How was this meaningful?]. It's the first time I'm really trying to face all my fears, including my fears of Jimmy. It's the first time I'm trying to find out if I'm comfortable with who I am. That's why it's important—because before I can be comfortable with myself, I can't have a normal relationship with Jimmy. I have to be comfortable with myself first. [Response to the question: What were you feeling?]. I am happy and scared at the same time. That's the only way I can put it. There's almost an at-peace feeling, but I'm not at peace. It's something I haven't felt before.

   d. *Conversations* were included because some participants reported a conversation that they had over the phone or in person that was meaningful to them. Sometimes the conversation took place in the context of social events, other times the conversation was one-to-one. For example:

   > ... after dinner, we [participant, partner, and partner's parents] had a drink in a gay bar. They [partner's parents] both told us how proud they were of us. After 43 years of marriage, they know there are stressors and you have to keep communicating. They were very impressed we had been together for 8 years. To have that come from his father in a gay bar, that was like—oh.

   e. *Political events,* particularly the 1992 presidential election, were the focus of several meaningful events. For example:

   > I think probably the election. It was definitely the highlight of the week. I was kind of anxious about it even though the polls showed

Clinton leading. I went down to the Castro and watched the results in several different places. As the results started coming in it was just a real rush after waiting so long for this.

f. *Evaluations* were meaningful events that had to do with positive evaluations of work, school, or volunteer performance. For example:

> I started taking a tax course to help me get a part time job because I've been out of work for two years. I got 100% on the first quiz last night. I've been out of school for so long that I'm not used to studying, especially with all the interruptions at home now with [partner].

g. *Funerals,* although usually extremely sad and often stressful, can also be the source of meaningful events, as illustrated in the following account:

> It's been a tough week because of [partner's] funeral. I had a little speaking part and was one of the ushers. I felt in some ways that the funeral helped me release some of the grief that I felt about [partner's] death.

h. *Doctor visit/health related events* were meaningful events associated with participants' health or healthcare. For example:

> My new doctor is the best thing. I made the switch because I felt I was being dismissed and just a piece of paperwork by the other doctor.

i. *Work events* were meaningful events associated with work, excluding evaluations. For example:

> The main thing is, professionally, I feel very confident to keep my business, which is what keeps me going, emotionally and economically. Also, I'm learning how to get the best people, changing things around.

2. *Who was involved*

Events were coded as directly involving the partner, involving another or others, or not involving anyone else.

3. *Source of meaning in event*

  a. *Connection.* The events included in this category involved contact with other people who the participant felt cared about him. The connection events were often social events like parties or weddings, although sometimes they were as simple as receiving a card or a phone call.

> I went to a wedding. [partner's] cousin's son got married and it was very nice. [Response to the question: How was this meaningful to you?] Connections. The connections to the people. There was a feeling of being connected to [partner's] family and to [partner]

and to life. The fact that life goes on and significant events still happen. Since [partner's] death, I've felt very cut off and it helped that I went to the wedding.

b. *Achievement/self-esteem.* Events in which the participant accomplished something and was pleased and proud were categorized as involving achievement/self-esteem. The events were often related to work or school.

> I got my evaluation from my volunteer work at the Homeless Advocacy. It was the best written evaluation [participant's teacher] ever received on student. I thought it would be good but I didn't expect so much. I was proud and I worked hard.

> I took charge of my parents about 10 days back. I found they weren't capable of finding and purchasing a house. My father broke down in tears and said that he was so grateful for my taking charge of affairs, since they weren't able to. And I felt good again in negotiating a good deal on a house. [Response to the question: In what ways was this meaningful?] It made me feel professional and competent and needed.

c. *Affirmation/validation.* These events often centered on the theme of receiving approval and acceptance from others regarding the relationship between the participant and his partner or an activity in which the participant was involved.

> ... there was one important event at the wedding that really touched me [participant's partner's son got married]. Naturally every wedding turns into a Kodak photo opportunity. The photographer was organizing everything. Everyone got their picture taken with the happy couple. The photographer asked [partner] and [partner's ex-wife] to pose with the couple. I had never met [partner's ex-wife] before. I've never even spoken to her on the phone. [Partner's ex-wife] told the photographer to stop until I got into the picture. And she said I deserve it almost as much as the rest of us. It was something she clearly did not have to do. The affirmation of the relationship [partner] and I have ... that she expressed in doing that was very meaningful for me.

d. *Hope/reassurance.* Events that gave the participants hope, reassurance, or reason for optimism were coded for this theme.

> Our garden is right where people sit, and people can see it. That makes it special for us. We transplanted our berries, and the garden already had some other plants. . . . It was really nice. . . . Especially after going to the hospital on Friday, it was good therapy. It's a nice place to go, and when [partner] has a good day, he can walk there with the dogs. In my mind, it's [partner's] garden. . . . It's also meaningful that [partner] knows he's getting sick and he's providing this [garden] for me if he gets sicker. [Response to the question: How else has this been meaningful for you?] It's a peaceful spot,

even with the noise from the freeway. Everyone takes care of their plots. It gives a sense of spring and renewing things. We both need that right now. [Response to the question: How has this made you feel?] Hope; a sense of caring. I don't know how you describe the feelings of spring. The feeling that we're coming out of a long winter and this might bring some positive changes for [partner].

e. *Control.* If an event provided a needed sense of control over some aspect of the participant's life, it was coded for control.

> I actually got back on my bicycle after being sick for a long time. I rode it for a good 10 miles or so. No side effects. That's basically it. [Response to the question: In what ways was this meaningful?] Basically I would not let my fears of becoming ill again overtake me and cause me to become ill again. Also, it gives me the hope that I can have some control over the virus.

f. *Respite.* An event that provided the participant respite from his daily circumstances and responsibilities was coded for this theme.

> I went up the Russian River over the weekend. I went with a couple of friends and had fun. I didn't worry about taking the medication. We just had a good time. I didn't worry about anything; I left that luggage behind.

g. *Material needs.* Some of the participants reported events in which someone (friend, family member, social organization) provided some much needed financial or material assistance. These events were coded for satisfaction of material needs.

> ... we got a package, which provided a nice distraction, of homemade goodies from [partner's] mom. We got two really ugly tacky calendars that we can give to someone for Christmas. We got jars of jellies and homemade syrup, pretzels dipped in icing, and fudge and cookies. So we didn't have to buy desserts for the week. The next day his grandmother sent us $20 for Thanksgiving and we got to eat out. Getting little things from his family helped brighten things—helped us get through the week. Gave us other things to talk about. And none of our checks bounced.

h. *Emotional release.* Events that allowed participants to express pent-up emotion were coded for this theme.

> Having a good cry with [partner]. It was like knowing that we're in this together. He's not alone; I'm not alone. We're there for each other. It was very intimate. Probably the most intimate time we've shared in a while.

i. *Partner's happiness.* An underlying theme that became apparent in many of the participants' reports was having their partners be happy. Events that involved reports of participants being happy because their partner was feeling well or enjoying something were coded for this theme.

> For a couple of months, we've been planning to go to the James Taylor concert with two friends. The concert was this past Saturday night and the concert was just fantastic. It was very well performed, very well managed. [Partner] was able to sit through 3 hours of an open-air event. He was having a great time. His enjoyment—seeing one of his musical idols live—made for a very happy event for me. It was a very, very nice evening. I would like to get that kind of emotional rush every week; I'd like to bottle that.

4. *Self-agency* refers to initiation of the reported event by the participant. No self-agency indicates that the event was serendipitous or happened without any action on the part of the participant. The following illustrates an event that involved self-agency.

> The place I work puts out a quarterly newspaper. I worked on it. I did a good portion of it and was very glad when I took it to the printer. I picked it up this morning and it was nice to see the finished product. It's nice to have done this because this is a job; I'm hoping to get this job on a permanent basis. I'm very pleased and everyone else seems to be pleased with the results.

The following event, reported by the same participant in a later interview, illustrates an event that did not involve self-agency.

> It was waking up Wednesday morning and finding out the results of the election, because when I went to bed Herschensohn was ahead and 165-Yes was set, both of which are very scary to me. So it was very nice to wake up to find out they had lost.

5. *Feelings*
The participants' responses to the question, "What were you feeling?," were recorded verbatim. Within each report of a meaningful event, we coded the feelings as positive, negative, or mixed.

Coding Process

Counts within categories were then tallied, and some basic descriptive statistics were calculated. Statistical comparisons of caregivers to noncaregivers or HIV+ to HIV− were not possible due to the small sample size. However, where there appear to be differences, we report them for the purpose of discussion.

FINDINGS

Our sample included six HIV+ caregivers, 18 HIV− caregivers, and 12 HIV+ noncaregivers. With the exception of a single interview with one participant whose partner died shortly thereafter, participants were always able to report a positive meaningful event. The 36 participants reported a total of 215 events, representing an average of six events per participant, each event having been reported at a bimonthly interview.

Mood

When these participants entered the study, their scores for depressive mood as measured by the CES-D ranged from 3 to 41 with a mean of 18.11. In the general population, the average CES-D score is 9, and individuals with a score of 16 or more are considered at risk for major depression (Radloff, 1977). Thus, the depressive mood of the participants in this study was marked.

Measures of positive mood states indicated that despite experiencing depressive mood, participants were also able to experience positive mood states. The Positive States of Mind scale (Horowitz et al., 1988) asks participants to rate on a 4-point Likert scale (1 = unable to have it through 4 = have it easily) the extent to which they are able to achieve each of six satisfying states of mind. Scores for this sample ranged from 9 to 24, with a mean of 17.8. The mean item rating was approximately 3—"some trouble having it." This rating is comparable to reports by university students (Horowitz et al., 1988). Scores for this sample on a modified version of Bradburn's (1969) positive morale scale ranged from 4 to 23, with a mean of 12.6, indicating that on average participants reported feeling each of eight positive moods somewhere between once and several times during the previous week. This frequency is comparable to national norms (Bradburn, 1969).

The Context of the Meaningful Events

Across all groups, of the nine types of events, social events (35%) were the most frequently reported, followed by entertainment (18%), conversation (15%), and work-related events (12%). The frequencies with which types of event were reported by the group are shown in Table 1.

Regardless of the classification of the type of event, 75% of the meaningful events our participants described involved other people. Two thirds of the solitary meaningful events involved either work or recreation and entertainment.

Most meaningful events did not involve the participants' partners, nor were they related directly to caregiving. It is important to note, however, that many of the events would not have been meaningful or even have occurred had the participant not been involved in caregiving.

Table 1. Frequency of Ten Types of Positive Events

Type of event	Total	HIV positive caregivers	HIV negative caregivers	HIV positive noncaregivers
Social	35% (74)	49% (18)	34% (37)	28% (19)
Entertainment	18% (39)	16% (6)	25% (27)	9% (6)
Conversation	15% (32)	13% (5)	14% (15)	18% (12)
Work	12% (26)	11% (4)	12% (13)	13% (9)
Realization	5% (11)	3% (1)	4% (5)	7% (5)
Political	5% (11)	5% (2)	3% (4)	7% (5)
Project	4% (9)	0% (0)	3% (4)	7% (5)
Evaluation	3% (6)	3% (1)	2% (3)	3% (2)
Health care	2% (4)	0% (0)	0% (0)	6% (4)
Funeral	1% (2)	0% (0)	1% (1)	1% (1)
Total	100% (214)	100% (37)	100% (109)	100% (68)

For example, a participant described an event in which "people at work were supportive and concerned . . . they ask about, or are glad to hear about [partner's] improvement. . . . I was really glad to be working where I'm working, where people are comfortable with the issue." Although the event did not directly involve the partner, its meaning was dependent on the participant's commitment to his partner and to caregiving. This suggests that caregiving can provide a context for the creation of meaningful events, even though the events themselves may not be related directly to caregiving. Thus, the context of caregiving may provide caregivers with opportunities for appraising positive meaning in their lives. This may be part of what is meant by individuals who say that they have grown or benefited from adversity.

HIV+ noncaregivers gained meaningful experiences through participation in a wider variety of activities than either caregiver group. For example, HIV+ noncaregivers were the only group that mentioned exercise and health-related events and volunteer work. Their lives may be less constrained because they are not in the role of caregivers. This may also allow them more time to focus on themselves.

Source of Meaning

All events described by the participants involved at least one source of meaning, and on average, two sources. In the overall sample, two sources of meaning were the most frequently reported: feeling connected to others and having a respite or break from caregiving. Twenty

Table 2. Frequency of Types of Sources of Meaning in Positive Events

Source of meaning	Total	HIV positive caregivers	HIV negative caregivers	HIV positive noncaregivers
Connection	22% (95)	31% (21)	22% (48)	18% (26)
Respite	21% (90)	18% (12)	25% (54)	17% (24)
Achievement	17% (73)	18% (12)	12% (27)	24% (34)
Hope	13% (56)	9% (6)	13% (29)	15% (21)
Affirmation	11% (45)	12% (8)	12% (27)	7% (10)
Partner's happiness	5% (19)	4% (3)	6% (13)	2% (3)
Material needs	4% (17)	1% (1)	3% (7)	6% (8)
Control	4% (16)	3% (2)	2% (5)	7 (10)
Emotional release	3% (14)	3% (2)	3% (7)	3% (5)
Total	100% (425)	100% (67)	100% (217)	100% (141)

two percent of the total sources of meaning that were reported related to a sense of connection and feeling cared about, and 21% referred to an opportunity to be distracted from everyday cares. The next most frequently mentioned sources of meaning were achievement/self-esteem (17%), hope/reassurance (13%), and affirmation/validation (11%). Other sources of meaning included feeling good for the partner or another person (5%), material needs (4%), a sense of control (4%), and emotional release (3%). The rank ordering of sources of meaning differed slightly among the three groups, as shown in Table 2.

Self-Agency

About half of the events were initiated by the participants. The other half were initiated by another person or occurred serendipitously. Events that were initiated by the participant (self-agency) included taking an extensive, cross-country trip and seeking someone out to have a serious discussion. Events that were initiated by another person included receiving a greeting card of love and appreciation, getting a pleasant phone call, and being asked to dance.

Self-Agency and Sources of Meaning. Self-agency was associated with certain sources of meaning more than others. For example, self-agency was linked to the following four sources of meaning about twice as often as non-self-agency: having a sense of control, bolstering self-esteem, having a respite, and feeling good for the partner or someone else. Four other sources of meaning were associated with self-agency less often: generating hope or reassurance, feeling connected or cared about, receiving affirmation or validation, and experiencing emotional release or tension reduction. Only one source of meaning—receiving material or monetary support—was not associated with self-agency. Participants were much more likely to report that receiving material goods was initiated by another person or just happened rather than being initiated by themselves. There were no clear differences among HIV+ caregivers, HIV− caregivers, and HIV+ noncaregivers in the relationship between self-agency and sources of meaning.

Self-Agency and Feelings. Activities that participants initiated themselves were more likely to result in positive feelings than were other activities. However, the total number of events in which negative feelings were reported is small, which limits our ability to interpret this finding.

DISCUSSION

The context of the lives of men who are providing care to a partner dying of AIDS is chronically stressful. The demands for care and emotional support by the caregiving partner increase unrelentingly as the infections and illnesses associated with HIV become more frequent and more severe in the ill partner (Folkman, Chesney, & Christopher-Richards, 1994; Folkman, Chesney, Cooke, et al., 1994). People who are infected with HIV are also faced with an ongoing threat to their own health and well-being. Depressive mood of the participants in this study was severe and persistent (Folkman et al., 1996). Nevertheless, in the face of extreme and chronic stress, these men were able to report events that were meaningful and in most cases positive. In fact, not only were they able to report the events, but they also requested that the positive aspects of their lives be included in the interviews. At the very least, the findings indicate that individuals who are experiencing chronic stress in one part of their lives can—and even appear to need to—experience positive meaning in other aspects of their lives.

The majority of positive meaningful events were ordinary events of daily life, not major life events. The events were accessible to individuals as they went through their days. Many of these events were not directly related to caregiving or to HIV illness. They involved a wide range of activities, including going to movies, giving a party, going on a trip, or being with a group. For caregivers, however, the events were meaningful because of the context created by the caregiving situation. A note from a friend, a kind word from someone at work, or the beauty of a natural setting was meaningful because of its relationship to the stressfulness of being with and caring for a partner with advanced HIV disease.

Our study involved individuals whose life circumstances differed in ways that might have influenced their positive experiences. Some of the individuals were coping with the demands of AIDS-related caregiving and bereavement, some individuals were coping with their own HIV infection, and some were coping with both. Unfortunately, our samples of individuals who were HIV+ noncaregivers and HIV+ caregivers were too small to make statistical inferences. However, for all three groups the most frequently reported type of positive event was a social event. The three groups tended to differ, however, in the most frequently reported source of meaning. For HIV+ caregivers, the most frequent source of meaning was connection; for HIV− caregivers, respite; and for HIV+ noncaregivers, achievement. Although these findings are at best tentative, they suggest that HIV serostatus and caregiving status may influence the types of events that people appraise as positive and meaningful. More generally, the circumstances of chronic stress may influence the types of positive events that individuals initiate to help bolster their resources or restore their psychological well-being. For example, people who are in jobs that involve a great many interactions with the public might find a quiet walk in the woods or involvement in a solitary hobby restorative, whereas caregivers who are housebound and isolated might seek a social interaction to help restore their sense of well-being.

Theoretical Implications

The findings about the nature of positive meaningful events suggest that they can serve the three coping functions that Lazarus et al. (1980) ascribe to positive emotions. Namely, these events can serve as breathers, sustainers, and restorers. The most frequently mentioned source of meaning was connection—feeling cared about. Connection can help restore diminished well-being, including self-esteem, thereby corresponding to the idea of a positive event as a restorer. The next most frequently mentioned source of meaning was respite, which clearly corresponds to the idea of a positive event as a breather. A breather can temporarily free individuals from their immersion in stressful experiences. The third most frequently mentioned source of meaning was achievement, which corresponds to the idea of a positive event as a sustainer in that it provides positive reinforcement for effective coping and helps motivate persistence in coping.

Virtually every magazine article or self-help book on caregiving highlights the importance of caregivers taking time for themselves to do something they enjoy as a way of bolstering their resources and preserving their own well-being. The fact that participants initiated about half the positive events they reported suggests that many may have been following this advice. This type of coping is often captured on coping checklists with items that describe distancing oneself from a stressful event by turning to another task or taking a break.

Positive events that were serendipitous, however, were not consciously initiated to help cope with a stressful event. Nevertheless, we suggest that like self-initiated events, serendipitous events not only may have had a palliative effect on mood, but they may also have served an important coping function by bolstering coping resources. This possibility is consistent with another finding from our study (Park & Folkman, in press). We examined the effects of caregiving and bereavement on variables that we defined as coping resources: optimism, religious/spiritual beliefs, perceived social support, and dyadic satisfaction. Using the cohort of 110 men mentioned here, we examined changes in coping resources within the caregiving period and within the bereavement period, and we compared the levels of these resources prebereavement and postbereavement. The analysis covered up to 10 months prebereavement and 7 months postbereavement. We found that these resources were for the most part unaffected by caregiving and bereavement. Even though these same individuals were reporting high levels of distress throughout this time of the analysis, their underlying resources remained remarkably stable. This finding, coupled with our analysis of positive meaningful events, suggested to us that experiencing and remembering events that make people feel connected, cared about, and competent may help bolster underlying coping resources.

The ways in which participants in our study appraised positive meaning in events also provides more detail about the coping strategy called "positive reappraisal" that is assessed in some of the most widely used coping checklists. Positive reappraisal usually refers to ways in which people cognitively reframe a situation. Items commonly used to assess this type of coping include, "I came out of the situation better than I went in," "I developed new faith," or "I grew as a person." A number of studies show that positive reappraisal is associated with reduced distress and increased positive well-being (for a review, see Aldwin, 1994). Positive reappraisal played an especially important role in maintaining positive mood during caregiving and bereavement in our study (Moskowitz, Folkman, Collette, & Vittinghoff, 1996). In the cohort of 110 of the study participants mentioned here, we found that positive reappraisal had a generalized beneficial effect on positive mood, regardless of whether it was used to cope with the demands of caregiving or the losses that followed the partner's death. The relation of positive reappraisal to negative mood was more circumscribed; although it helped reduce negative mood during bereavement, it had no effect during caregiving. Checklist assessments of positive reappraisal might benefit from additional items. The spontaneous appraisals reported by the participants in our study suggest specific reappraisals, such as those having to do with feeling cared about and more competent as a consequence of the event, that might be added to checklist assessments.

Clinical Implications

We believe that the capacity, and perhaps even the need, to report positive meaningful events in the midst of extreme stress is clinically as well as theoretically meaningful. When clients are dealing with chronic stressors, such as illness or caregiving, the focus is often on the disease or stressful situation itself. Clients may benefit from having clinicians focus on meaningful events as well. By asking about meaningful events, clinicians can help clients recognize what is meaningful for them and how the daily circumstances of living can provide that meaning.

Others have recognized the importance of helping clients define goals or find sources of personal meaning outside of a chronic illness or stressful circumstances (e.g., Ozer, 1988; Turk & Rudy, 1992; White & Epston, 1990). Our study suggests that generating positive meaningful events may be a relatively comfortable and easy way to do this. In our sample, with one exception, all participants generated a positive event each time they were asked, regardless of their personality or life circumstances. This response was especially striking given the moderately severe depressive mood among the caregivers.

Clinicians cannot know in advance what makes ordinary events meaningful for a given client. Thus, the clinician needs to explore with clients what it is that makes events meaningful (Ozer, 1994; White & Epston, 1990). This exploration may have the added benefit of helping clients become more aware of their needs, such as feeling connected to others, having respite, and maintaining motivation. Finally, the exploration may help develop the client's capacity for identifying events that meet these needs.

The very act of generating positive meaningful events may in itself also have a palliative effect. It diverts attention from what is stressful and makes individuals more aware of the positive aspects of their lives. Outside of the clinical setting, telling another person about a positive meaningful event also creates a rewarding social interaction in that it is the type of exchange others enjoy. Finally, talking about a meaningful event may induce positive mood.

CONCLUSION

The study of positive meaningful events promises to add substantially to our knowledge of how people cope with chronic illness in particular, whether the illness is their own or a partner's, and of chronic stress more generally. Not only might such events provide people with opportunities to bolster their coping resources, gain respite, and sustain motivation, but the very act of identifying positive meaningful events in daily life may also be a way of coping in and of itself. It is significant that this form of coping would not have been captured with standard coping assessments that ask about how individuals coped with a specific stressful event.

The idea that positive events may have both theoretical and clinical implications for understanding adjustment to chronic and highly stressful conditions is consistent with the growing interest in positive functioning in the context of stressful events (e.g., Aldwin, 1994; Ryff & Essex, 1992). Ryff and her colleagues (Ryff, 1989; Ryff & Keyes, 1995) demonstrate that the measurement of psychological well-being requires an approach that differs from the measurement of negative psychological states. Well-being is more than the absence of negative states such as depression and anxiety. It includes dimensions such as personal growth, positive relations with others, and environmental mastery (Ryff & Keyes, 1995). Similarly, we argue that a full understanding of how people adjust to chronic and highly stressful conditions requires exploring the coping functions of positive events in addition to the traditional approach of exploring how people cope with the aversive aspects of their lives.

Our foray into this new area of investigation has shown that narratives of positive meaningful events are not difficult to collect. In fact, if the participants in other studies are like the participants in this study, they will welcome the opportunity to talk about something positive. We strongly encourage researchers who seek to understand how people cope with chronic stress to include meaningful events in their study protocols so that we can learn the extent to which these events help people who are coping with chronic stress get through their days and sustain their well-being.

ACKNOWLEDGMENTS The preparation of this chapter was supported by grants MH44045, MH9985, and MH52517 from the National Institute of Mental Health. We deeply appreciate the participants in this study, who have taught us so well. We thank Linda Gourlay for her valuable assistance in coding. Order of authorship is alphabetical and reflects equal contributions.

REFERENCES

AFFLECK, G., TENNEN, H., CROOG, S., & LEVINE, S. (1987). Causal attributions, perceived benefits, and morbidity after a heart attack: An 8-year study. *Journal of Consulting and Clinical Psychology, 55,* 29–35.
ALDWIN, C. (1994). *Stress, coping, and development.* New York: Guilford.
BAUMEISTER, R. F. (1991). *Meanings of life.* New York: Guilford.
BRADBURN, N. M. (1969). *The structure of psychological well-being.* Chicago: Aldine.
CARVER, C. S., SCHEIER, M. F., & WEINTRAUB, J. K. (1989). Assessing coping strategies: A theoretically-based approach. *Journal of Personality and Social Psychology, 56,* 267–283.
FOLKMAN, S., CHESNEY, M. A., & CHRISTOPHER-RICHARDS, A. (1994). Stress and coping in partners of men with AIDS. *Psychiatric Clinics of North America, 17,* 35–55.
FOLKMAN, S., CHESNEY, M. A., COLLETTE, L., BOCCELLARI, A., & COOKE, M. (1996). Post-bereavement depressive mood and its pre-bereavement predictors in HIV+ and HIV− gay men. *Journal of Personality and Social Psychology, 70,* 336–348.
FOLKMAN, S., CHESNEY, M. A., COOKE, M., BOCCELLARI, A., & COLLETTE, L. (1994). Caregiver burden in HIV+ and HIV− partners of men with AIDS. *Journal of Consulting and Clinical Psychology, 62,* 746–756.
FOLKMAN, S., & LAZARUS, R. S. (1988). *The Ways of Coping Questionnaire.* Palo Alto, CA: Consulting Psychologists Press.
FRANKL, V. E. (1963). *Man's search for meaning.* New York: Washington Square Press.
HALEY, W. E., LEVINE, E. G., BROWN, S. L., BARTOLUCCI, A. A. (1987). Stress, appraisal, coping, and social support as predictors of adaptational outcome among dementia caregivers, *Psychology and Aging, 2,* 323–330.
HOROWITZ, M., ADLER, N., & KEGELES, S. (1988). A scale for measuring the occurrence of positive states of mind: A preliminary report. *Psychosomatic Medicine, 50,* 477–483.
KANNER, A. D., COYNE, J. C., SCHAEFER, C., & LAZARUS, R. S. (1981). Comparisons for two modes of stress measurement: Daily hassles and uplifts versus major life events. *Journal of Behavioral Medicine, 4,* 1–39.
KLINGER, E. (1977). *Meaning and void: Inner experience and the incentives in people's lives.* Minneapolis, MN: University of Minnesota Press.
KLINGER, E. (1987). Current concerns and disengagement from incentives. In F. Halisch & J. Kuhl (Eds.), *Motivation, intention, and volition* (pp. 337–347). Berlin: Springer-Verlag.
LANGSTON, C. A. (1994). Capitalizing on and coping with daily-life events: Expressive responses to positive events. *Journal of Personality and Social Psychology, 67,* 1112–1125.
LAWTON, M. P., MOSS, M., KLEBAN, M. H., GLICKSMAN, A., & ROVINE, M. (1991). A Two-factor model of caregiving appraisal and psychological well-being. *Journal of Gerontology, 46,* 181–189.
LAZARUS, R. S., KANNER, A. D., & FOLKMAN, S. (1980). Emotions: A cognitive-phenomenological analysis. In R. Plutchik & H. Kellerman (Eds.). *Emotion: Theory, research and experience: Vol. 1, Theories of emotion.* New York: Academic Press.
MCINTOSH, D. N., SILVER, R., & WORTMAN, C. B. (1993). Religion's role in adjustment to a negative life event: Coping with the loss of a child. *Journal of Personality and Social Psychology, 65,* 812–821.
MOSKOWITZ, J., FOLKMAN, S., COLLETTE, L., & VITTINGHOFF, E. (1996). Coping and mood during AIDS-related caregiving and bereavement. *Annals of Behavioral Medicine, 18,* 49–57.
OZER, M. N. (1988). *The management of persons with spinal cord injury.* New York: Demos.

OZER, M. N. (1994). Character of the solution. In M. N. Ozer, R. S. Materson, & L. R. Caplan (Eds.), *Management of persons with stroke* (pp. 18–26). St. Louis: Mosby-Year Book Inc.

PARK, C., & FOLKMAN, S. (in press). Changes in psychosocial resources during caregiving and bereavement in partners of men with AIDS. *Journal of Personality*.

RADLOFF, L. S. (1977). The CES-D Scale: A self-report depression scale for research in the general population. *Applied Psychological Measurement, 1,* 385–401.

RYFF, C. D. (1989). Happiness is everything, or is it? Explorations on the meaning of psychological well-being. *Journal of Personality and Social Psychology, 57,* 1069–1081.

RYFF, C. D., & ESSEX, M. J. (1992). The interpretation of life experience and well-being: The sample case of relocation. *Psychology and Aging, 7,* 507–517.

RYFF, C. D., & KEYES, C. L. M. (1995). The structure of psychological well-being revisited. *Journal of Personality and Social Psychology, 69,* 719–727.

SILVER, R. L., BOON, C., & STONES, M. H. (1983). Searching for meaning in misfortune: Making sense of incest. *Journal of Social Issues, 39,* 81–102.

SILVER, R. L., & WORTMAN, C. (1980). Coping with undesirable life events. In J. Garber & M. E. P. Seligman (Eds.), *Human helplessness: Theory and applications* (pp. 279–340). New York: Academic Press.

TURK, D. C., & RUDY, T. E. (1992). Cognitive factors and persistent pain: A glimpse into Pandora's box. *Cognitive Therapy and Research, 16,* 99–122.

WHITE, M., & EPSTON, D. (1990). *Narrative means to therapeutic ends.* New York: W. W. Norton.

WOLF, T. M., ELSTON, R. C., & KISSLING, G. E. (1989). Relationship of hassles, uplifts, and life events to psychological well-being of freshman medical students. *Behavioral Medicine, 15,* 37–45.

ZAUTRA, A. J., REICH, J. W., & GUARNACCIA, C. A. (1990). Some everyday life consequences of disability and bereavement for older adults. *Journal of Personality and Social Psychology, 59,* 550–561.

12

A Framework for Understanding the Chronic Stress of Holocaust Survivors

BOAZ KAHANA, EVA KAHANA, ZEV HAREL, KATHY KELLY, PAM MONAGHAN, and LANI HOLLAND

Survivors of the Holocaust endured traumatic life situations that defy comprehension. The negative sequelae of this man-made disaster have been extensively documented (for reviews, see Kahana, Harel, & Kahana, 1988; Lomrantz, 1990). In particular, many survivors have been found to suffer long-lasting psychological distress. These after-effects of trauma have been generally viewed by social science researchers and clinicians as adverse reactions to a singular cataclysmic stressor that occurred in the distant past. However, the full spectrum of chronic stressors that long-term survivors of trauma had to cope with, and may continue to endure, has seldom been explored.

Initial accounts of the psychological impact of trauma were documented in eyewitness accounts of survivors of Nazi concentration camps and by psychiatrists treating survivors (Frankl, 1962; Krystal, 1968; Neiderland, 1986). Subsequently, during the 1970s, the literature was relatively silent with regard to sequelae of the Holocaust, perhaps paral-

---

BOAZ KAHANA • Department of Psychology, Cleveland State University, Cleveland, Ohio 44115. **EVA KAHANA, KATHY KELLY, PAM MONAGHAN, and LANI HOLLAND** • Department of Sociology, Case Western Reserve University, Cleveland, Ohio 44106-7124. **ZEV HAREL** • School of Social Work, Cleveland State University, Cleveland, Ohio 44115.

Coping with Chronic Stress, edited by Benjamin H. Gottlieb. Plenum Press, New York, 1997.

leling the "conspiracy of silence" reported by Holocaust survivors (Lomrantz, 1990). During the 1980s, some 40 years after this cataclysmic event, there was a great upsurge of scientific and professional interest in posttraumatic stress syndromes. The study of Holocaust survivorship and the effect of trauma moved beyond sole consideration of psychopathology and impairment to include research on coping strategies, the strengths of survivors, and their world outlook and philosophy of life (Helmreich, 1992). However, most of this research has still focused on the original trauma and its long-term social and psychological consequences, particularly in terms of psychopathology. Understanding of the full range of chronic stressors faced by long-term survivors of the Holocaust, and of their cumulative impact, has been limited. There is also little information on proactive adaptations and coping efforts that survivors made to foster the process of recovery (Kahana & Kahana, 1996).

Consideration of the temporal context is crucial to our analysis since the concept of chronic stress implies a temporally extended and lasting challenge to the individual. The specific trauma of the Holocaust, which occurred about 50 years ago, also requires a temporally anchored or historical perspective. Survivors of the Holocaust had experienced chronic stress both during the period leading up to World War II and subsequent to the Holocaust. These clusters of stressors were overshadowed by the enormity of the trauma endured during the Holocaust. Social functioning, psychological well-being, and adaptation to old age among these survivors are the consequences of complex interactions between the full array of traumatic stressors and general life stressors they experienced, as well as their coping efforts (Kahana, 1992). These very coping efforts are also likely to have been affected by the trauma experienced by survivors.

This chapter provides a framework for understanding and placing in a temporal context both trauma-related stressors and general life stressors that are encountered by elderly Holocaust survivors. We discuss both residual stressors that are directly related to trauma and general life stressors that are differentially appraised and responded to by Holocaust survivors. Whereas our focus is on the Holocaust as a cataclysmic man-made disaster that instigated a plethora of chronic stressors, our framework may also apply to the chronic stressors encountered by survivors of diverse traumas, including man-made and natural disasters, crime, and family violence. Modes of coping and adaptation are discussed that relate to different aspects of chronic stress. Empirical support for this framework is considered by examining data from our study of 168 elderly Holocaust survivors living in the United States and 180 survivors living in Israel, along with comparison groups of an approximately equal number of individuals who emigrated to the United States and Israel just prior to World War II (Kahana, Harel, & Kahana, 1988).

CHRONIC STRESSORS FACED BY ELDERLY HOLOCAUST SURVIVORS

Chronic stressors have been added relatively recently to the general stress paradigm, to complement the stressors posed by acute life events (Kahana & Kahana, 1984a). The major characteristics of chronic stressors are their enduring and ongoing (or long-term) nature (see Wheaton, Chapter 2, this volume). Chronic stressors are therefore to be clearly distinguished from one-time or episodic occurrences. In our view, chronic stressors include either continuing stressors or multiple occurrences of discrete adverse events. Thus, being a victim/survivor of a crime such as rape may be viewed as an acute stressor or life event. In contrast, continuous domestic violence constitutes a chronic stressor. Yet, the victims of an acute life event (e.g., rape) and of chronic abuse are both likely to endure posttraumatic problems that are chronic in nature. Victims of both types of stressors may have long-term intrusive memories of trauma and may be stigmatized because of their experiences. In fact, a distinguishing feature of their trauma is the strong probability that it will lead to long-term or chronic stress.

In the traumatic stress literature, a major controversy revolves around the distinction between traumatic stressors and general stressors. The most widely accepted approach has been to define an event or a series of events as traumatic based on their ability to produce a posttraumatic stress disorder (PTSD). This definition has been criticized for its circularity since the traumatic event is defined by its outcome (Green, 1993). The framework we present suggests that traumatic stress may be defined, at least in part, by the chronic posttraumatic stressors that result from the initial trauma as well as by the unique coping efforts that the trauma and the chronic stressors elicit.

Accordingly, trauma constitutes a constellation of environmental assaults that have ripple effects in creating further enduring chronic stressors. Some of the chronic internalized stressors that continue to affect the lives of survivors have traditionally been defined as outcomes of the trauma constituting the PTSD symptom cluster (i.e., intrusive thoughts and nightmares). However, the present conceptualization describes the ways these intrusive symptoms can produce further stressful experiences. The adaptive tasks of survivorship include the challenges of maintaining good social and psychological functioning in the face of these chronic stressors.

Long-term survivors of trauma are expected to deal with clusters of stressors that are temporally organized around the traumatic event. Independent of the traumatic events endured, the survivors are also likely to face normative stressors throughout their life course. Most of the normative stress clusters are time-limited and are resolved after the period of time has elapsed. However, the greatest continuing challenge faced by survivors is posed by the stress cluster that we term "chronic posttraumatic stressors." These are residual internalized stressors that originate from the trauma and continue to afflict survivors on an indefinite basis.

Chronic posttraumatic stressors elicit unique coping efforts. They may also interact with normative stressors of the life course, such as retirement, and may result in reinterpreting or reappraising those stressors within a posttraumatic context. Figure 1 depicts our framework for considering the spectrum of life crises and chronic stressors faced by elderly Holocaust survivors. Stressors clustered around the historical event of the Holocaust may be classified temporally as pre-war stressors, Holocaust traumatic stressors, and post-war stressors. Normative chronic life stressors may be categorized as childhood, adult, and old age-related stressors. These two distinct though interrelated groups of stressors ultimately impinge on the late life well-being of the elderly survivor. We will briefly outline key characteristics of each of these clusters of stressors, and then discuss the chronic posttraumatic stressors resulting from Holocaust trauma. Additionally, we will highlight the ways survivors cope with these stressors. We begin with an overview of our sample and methods.

SAMPLE AND METHODS

Respondents in this research included a survivor group and a comparison group in two countries: the United States and Israel. Participants in the United States sample included a group of 168 survivors of the Holocaust who immigrated between the end of World War II and 1965 and a group of 155 immigrants who arrived in the United States several years prior to World War II. The U.S. sample was selected from community census listings of the Jewish Federation in a large American city. The Israeli sample included a group of 180 survivors of the Holocaust who immigrated to Israel after World War II and 160 persons from

Temporal Dimension:　　　　　　　　　　　　　　　　　　　Temporal Dimension:
Historical Events　　　　　　　　　　　　　　　　　　　　　　Life Course

Trauma Related Stressors
1. Prewar Stressors
2. Holocaust Traumatic Stressors
3. Postwar Stressors

Normative Chronic Life Stressors
1. Childhood Life Stressors
2. Adult Life Stressors
   a. Immigration & Acculturation Stressors
   b. Older adult life stressors
3. Stressors of Aging

Chronic Posttraumatic Stressors
A. Intrusive memories of trauma
B. Living with fear & mistrust
C. Isolation (social & psychological)
D. Living with stigma

Quality of Life for Elderly Survivor

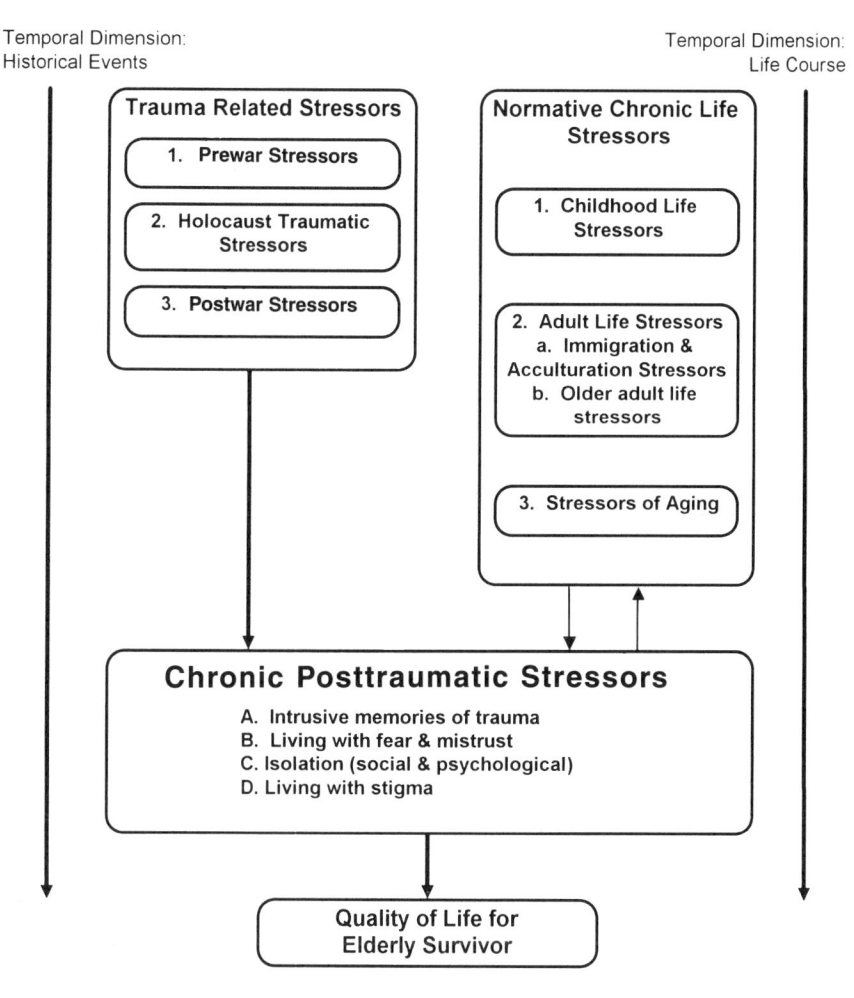

Figure 1. Spectrum of life crises and chronic stressors facing elderly Holocaust survivors.

similar Eastern European countries who immigrated to Israel just prior to the onset of World War II. The Israeli sample was selected using respondent lists from community surveys in three major cities in Israel, which included questions about residential background during World War II and date of arrival in Israel. Respondents in both groups were from countries that were under the occupation of Nazi Germany during World War II. All respondents were individually interviewed in their own homes by trained interviewers. At the time of the study (1982), respondents ranged in age from 45 to 90, with the survivors being somewhat younger than respondents in the comparison groups. Women (55%) outnumbered men slightly, and a somewhat higher percentage of survivors were married relative to the comparison group (82% versus 69%). The highest percentage of respondents originated from Poland (57%), followed by lower percentages from Czechoslovakia (13%), Germany (9%), and Hungary (8%).

There are several important reasons for inclusion of both U.S. and Israeli subsamples in the study. Consideration of data from the two very different cultures enables social scientists to integrate disparate research findings in the United States and Israel and to add important information to existing data where gaps in knowledge have been identified. There are also major differences between the post-Holocaust experiences of survivors in the United States and survivors in Israel that could have important theoretical implications for their adaptation. In contrast to the relatively peaceful existence of U.S. survivors, Israeli survivors experienced three additional wars after the Holocaust, thereby adding substantially to the cumulative stress they experienced. Furthermore, in contrast to the denial or avoidance of the memories of the Holocaust in the United States, Israeli society strongly emphasized the Holocaust experience. Thus, it may be argued that survivors in Israel were more likely to find meaning in survivorship and integrate this part of their life into an existential whole. The research design of our study enabled us to compare survivors who migrated to the United States with those who migrated to Israel on all important study variables.

Data were obtained from individual interviews with respondents (Holocaust survivors and comparison groups) using a questionnaire containing both closed-ended and open-ended questions. A wide variety of measures and scales were used in our large study (Kahana, Harel, & Kahana, 1988) to answer questions regarding differences and similarities in physical health, mental health, social supports, community involvement, and Jewish identification of survivors and comparison groups.

Details of research instruments and questions relevant to the present discussion of chronic stress among traumatized and nontraumatized respondents are provided in the following sections. Open-ended questions were asked about diverse stressful life situations encountered by our respondents from early childhood through the present time, with special attention to events preceding the Holocaust, events occurring during the Holocaust, and events occurring during the immediate and later post-war periods. Coping was measured by the Elderly Care Research Center (ECRC) Coping Scale (Kahana, Fairchild, & Kahana,

1982). This 23-item scale elicits three major factors: instrumental, affective, and intrapsychic coping strategies. This measure has been used in a variety of studies of aged populations (Kahana, Kahana, & Young, 1987; Kahana & Kahana, 1996). Chronbach's alpha is .65 for this scale. Additional questions in our interview that are related to coping include queries about self-disclosure to significant others, social participation, and social support.

The revised Philadelphia Geriatric Center Morale Scale was used as a measure of psychological well-being (Lawton, 1975). This 17-item scale is a revision of an earlier 22-item version of the scale. This scale has been used in many studies involving both community and institutionalized older persons. It has a split-half reliability of .79 and a Chronbach's alpha of .81. Items selected from the Symptom Checklist 90 (SCL 90) (Derogatis, 1977) were used to form subscales to measure PTSD.

TRAUMA-RELATED STRESSORS

Prewar Stressors

In considering the chronic nature of the trauma of the Holocaust, it is important to note that there was an extended period of threat and discrimination endured by many survivors even prior to the escalation of persecution that culminated in the Holocaust. In narratives of their life experiences, elderly survivors as well as our comparison groups of prewar refugees, both in the United States and Israel, often referred to these periods of prewar stress when they were subjected to prejudice and discrimination. For instance, many were unable to complete their education because of policies restricting entry by Jewish students to universities in their homelands. Economic discrimination against Jews, destruction of property, and threat to personal safety also characterized respondents' life experiences during this period.

Holocaust Traumatic Stressors

Holocaust traumatic stressors relate to the events of the trauma itself. This period of traumatization was cataclysmic for survivors of the Holocaust, as acute and chronic stressors enveloped their very existence. Stresses of the Holocaust included "cumulative effects of prolonged physical abuse, degradation, hunger, exposure to unbearable weather, lethal labor, repeated losses, and above all, the constant threat of extermination and death;—all in the absence of normative civilized laws and principles" (Lomranz, 1990). Thus, the original trauma of the Holocaust may be described as chronic, based on its all encompassing quality and its duration.

Much of the voluminous literature on the Holocaust focuses on stressors of the original trauma. It may be argued that the efforts marshaled by survivors to cope with this original trauma will largely determine the extent of their ultimate recovery from the trauma and their late life well-being. Our framework suggests that the original traumatization is the source of the trauma-related secondary stressors and impacts on both appraisals and modes of coping in dealing with other chronic life stressors during the post-Holocaust period.

Postwar Stressors

Reports from Holocaust survivors in our study reveal that the immediate postwar period was also fraught with many acute and chronic stressors, creating further trauma for survivors. Content analyses of our interviews with Holocaust survivors in the United States reveal a series of general postwar stressors, including the need to face perpetrators and bystanders, searching for relatives, and searching for a new country to call home. Postwar deprivations were reflected in illness and lack of food, clothing, and shelter. In addition, stressors unique to certain survivor groups included living in displaced persons (DP) camps, under Communist persecution, or in war-torn Israel. Since most survivors became refugees after the Holocaust, they faced the continuing challenges of establishing a new life in a new land.

COPING WITH CHRONIC POSTTRAUMATIC STRESSORS

Chronic stressors that are directly related to the trauma experienced during the Holocaust represent the major focus of our discussion here. In our model (see Figure 1) these stressors are identified as "chronic posttraumatic stressors" that are distinct outcomes of the original traumatic stress. The traumatic Holocaust event is now over and the threat of its recurrence is remote. Hence, the chronic stressors of Holocaust trauma may be most profitably viewed as residual stressors (both internal and external) left by the original trauma. For survivors of the Holocaust, there are four important ongoing stressors: intrusive memories of trauma, living with fear and mistrust, social and psychological isolation, and living with stigma. The first two represent internalized stressors reflected in cognitive or emotional states, whereas the third and fourth are primarily social stressors, with both internal and external components. We now turn to a more extensive discussion of each of these types of chronic stressors because they comprise the major focus of our post-traumatic chronic stress framework.

Coping with Intrusive Memories of Trauma

Intrusive memories constitute a major class of chronic stressors for survivors of extreme trauma such as the Holocaust. These memories are ongoing internalized reminders of the trauma. It has been argued that such intrusive imagery is a major mechanism by which trauma translates into chronic distress (Baum, Cohen, & Hall, 1993). Persistent thoughts or recollections of such trauma have been reported among diverse traumatized populations and have been found to be associated with distress and performance deficits. (Nolen-Hoeksema, Morrow, & Fredrickson, 1993). Based on a series of research projects focusing on war veterans and survivors of natural disaster, Baum (1990) indicates that the longer the time since the trauma, the greater the likelihood that more intrusive memories will predict adverse psychological and physical health outcomes.

Intrusive memories cause survivors to continuously relive traumatic experiences. Traumatic memories may be triggered by adverse and often unpredictable stimuli ranging from sensory experiences to anniversaries or media reports reminiscent of the type of trauma endured (McCann & Pearlman, 1990). There is extensive documentation in the field of traumatic stress studies that such memories of trauma persist. These memories are used as one of several criteria for establishing a diagnosis of posttraumatic stress disorder.

Our study provided an opportunity for a deeper exploration of the nature of memories among survivors. Among survivors in our study, 61% reported that they think daily or several times a week about the Holocaust even 40 years after their original traumatic experiences. A smaller group, ranging between 5% and 20%, endorsed experiencing other symptoms of psychological distress that could be viewed as related to PTSD. Thus, our data reveal that intrusive memories of trauma are normative rather than exceptional occurrences, even among survivors who do not exhibit the other symptoms of PTSD. Survivors of the Holocaust in both the United States and Israel reported significantly more intrusive thoughts than the comparison group in response to a subscale we created based on the Symptom Checklist 90 (Derogatis, 1977). The intrusive memories subscale displays a Chronbach's alpha of .60 and includes items such as having frightening thoughts and images.

Traumatic memories are likely to emerge as intrusive images that disrupt the psychological and social functioning of the trauma survivor (Paivio, 1986). To explore this phenomenon we compared survivors' accounts of traumatic Holocaust experiences with accounts of nontraumatic events experienced by survivors. Memories of events related to the Holocaust were described in significantly more vivid terms, using more visual imagery, than were memories of events that occurred immediately prior or subsequent to the Holocaust ($p < .01$). These findings support suggestions by Horowitz and colleagues (1975, 1982) that memories of trauma impose themselves on the mind and frequently enter into awareness as visual images. We also found that intrusive memories of trauma reported by Holocaust survivors are significantly correlated with poor morale as measured by the Lawton Morale Scale (Lawton, 1975). Thus, among survivors living in Israel, a correlation of $-.59$ ($p < .001$) was reported between intrusive memories and morale. Among survivors living in the United States, the correlation was $-.61$ ($p < .001$).

Such experiences of chronic stress through intrusive memories are exemplified in the following remarks by some of our respondents. For instance, a 58-year-old man stated, "I think about [Holocaust] when I have to throw out food, or in my dreams. I think about it quite often." Another man, age 84, stated, "We are more depressed. Others have not had our experiences; they have no depressing thoughts." A 57-year-old woman survivor reported, "You can't wipe the memories away; I have a bad feeling, maybe not having done enough for my brother." A survivor who was a child during the Holocaust reflected, "I think that people who were not in the Holocaust are healthier people; they don't have these types of memories to cope with. Bad memories don't help your emotional mentality." Another survivor who spent much of the Holocaust in a German labor camp responded, "Can't wash away, in back of my mind the Holocaust, no matter how much fun I'm having or how much I'm enjoying myself." These comments illustrate both the persistence of intrusive memories of trauma and the survivors' recognition that these memories contribute to their psychological distress long after the original trauma occurred.

Which coping strategies can survivors employ to deal with such stress? We believe that to answer this question fully one must consider a full repertoire of behaviors in addition to those typically included in conventional coping scales. The clinical literature focusing on treatment of trauma survivors points to the value of such volitional efforts as the disclosure of traumatic experiences (Jucovy, 1988). This may not only be cathartic, but depending on those involved in self-disclosure, it can also be an important way of marshaling social support (Gottlieb, 1988). Disclosure of accounts of survival also facilitates processing of traumatic memories and may help create meaning by organizing jumbled and incomprehensible experiences. In turn, the listener is likely to respond by providing social support to the trauma survivor. These dual processes then become part of a successful coping process that in turn helps reduce intrusive memories. In a relevant study of coping with the chronic stress of widowhood, Pennebaker, Barger, and Tiebout (1989) found that self-disclosure of the stressful events can reduce the incidence of intrusive thoughts and memories.

Clinical experiences in working with trauma survivors suggest that self-disclosure is seldom spontaneous. Typically, survivors must be asked directly and repeatedly about their experiences to elicit even partial self-disclosure. This is an example of the ways modes of coping by the survivor interact with behaviors of significant others. Accordingly, little self-disclosure was possible for Holocaust survivors during periods marked by a conspiracy of silence, because no one expressed interest or solicited information about their traumatic experience (McCann & Pearlman, 1990). American and Israeli Holocaust survivors in our study also faced difficulties in disclosing their Holocaust experiences. Our data suggest a bimodal distribution of self-disclosure regarding the Holocaust: 54.7% of survivors reported never discussing the Holocaust with their spouse, whereas 34% report talking about it all the time. Interestingly, only 11.3% reported the intermediate position of talking sometimes with their spouse about the Holocaust. In future research it would be valuable to explore the nature of such disclosures in greater detail (Baum, 1990).

Since memories serve as internalized representations of trauma, instrumental or problem-focused strategies cannot be readily applied to such chronic stress. Cognitive or intrapsychic efforts such as acceptance, reframing, denial, and positive comparisons appear to be better suited for coping with this stress. Horowitz (1982) suggests that traumatized persons may oscillate between states of denial and intrusion as they attempt to cope with the stress of the strong feelings generated by the intrusive memories. For example, in our study, more survivors in the United States and Israel used "acceptance" as a coping style than the comparison groups (37% and 35% for survivors and 26% and 29% for comparison groups in the United States and Israel, respectively). Such cognitive coping efforts may contribute to diminishing both the frequency and intensity of further intrusive memories and of negative feelings generated by them. In a study of Vietnam veterans interviewed 12 years after their war experience, Green (1993) found that cognitive coping efforts could reduce the impact of traumatic memories. Furthermore, in her disquisition on adult development, Neugarten (1969) suggests that adults reinterpret, select, and shape their memories in a search for coherence. In this way traumatic events may become "rationalized and interwoven into a context of explanation" (p. 126).

Coping with Fear and Mistrust

A second enduring internalized stressor that is experienced by Holocaust survivors is the pervasive sense of victimization, which may cause them to mistrust strangers, those in authority, or even anyone different from themselves. Survivors may see dangers lurking in their environment and find it hard to distinguish possible mishaps from probable ones (Kahana, Kahana, Harel, & Rosner, 1988). The experience of uncontrollable and non-normative events during the Holocaust conditioned a view of living in an uncontrollable world and resulted in maintaining a vigilant posture toward all possible future adversity. Based on this continuing sense of vulnerability, the physical and social environment may be experienced as chronically threatening. This appraisal-based experience of chronic stress is consistent with the cognitive stress paradigm proposed by Lazarus and Folkman (1984).

To determine the degree to which fear and mistrust of the social environment represent a continuing problem for survivors, a five-item scale was generated using relevant items from the Symptom Checklist 90. The mistrust subscale yielded a Chronbach's alpha of .62. Items include statements such as, "Most people can't be trusted," and "Others watch or talk about you." Survivors in Israel reported significantly higher mean scores on the fear and mistrust scale than did members of their comparison group. In contrast, survivors living in the United States did not appear to experience greater fears and mistrust relative to their comparison group.

Additionally, we found mistrust to have a greater negative correlation with morale for U.S. than for Israeli survivors. Speculatively, these findings suggest that those survivors living as part of an ethnic majority in their own homeland are less likely to experience the fear and victimization or to be negatively affected by it. This finding exemplifies the way contextual factors shape appraisals of threat. Although citizens of Israel continue to live in a social and physical environment where war and terrorism are rampant, Israeli society somehow offers survivors a psychologically safe and reassuring milieu (Solomon, 1995).

Experiences of living with fear and mistrust were frequently depicted by our U.S. survivors as they described their aging and how they differ from others who did not experience the trauma of the Holocaust. Thus, 34% of survivors reported being afraid of many things, compared to 12% of those in the comparison group.

The following statements in response to attitudes about one's aging illustrate the chronic stress of living with fear and mistrust. A 69-year-old woman survivor responded, "I live an older life, worry more, live with fear—the dreams make you crazy." Another woman, age 72, stated, "I am reserved about trusting people, we were betrayed many times." A 67-year-old woman reflected, "I am always afraid something happens to me because I worry so much of the time. I worry about my children's future because I would like to see more peace in the world, because all of a sudden anything can go wrong." Another woman, age 59, stated, "We are concerned about the family, always wondering. God knows what tomorrow will bring." Another respondent, who arrived home one day to find the German SS officers had taken away her mother, observed, "I get more frightened for my children that another war should come." It is noteworthy that these statements of fear and mistrust relate to society at large or to generalized others rather than to specific individuals. Also, they clearly reflect fear of a repetition of some great trauma akin to the Holocaust.

Survivors may not fully recognize or acknowledge the internalized aspects of chronic stressors posed by living with fear and mistrust and cannot find a direct referent for their fears. Hence, they may not be able to marshal appropriate coping strategies. This pattern contrasts with their general awareness of the chronic stressors represented by intrusive memories, which result in more deliberate coping efforts involving disclosure.

Feelings of vulnerability and perceived threats of victimization may lead to automatic coping responses of vigilance on the one hand and avoidance or withdrawal from potentially threatening situations on the other (Wilson, 1989). Vigilant persons exhibit hyperalertness to environmental threats, whereas avoidant individuals are prone to denying threats or denying feelings (i.e., numbing) that are normally elicited by threat. In our study, over one half (54%) of Israeli survivors and 42% of U.S. survivors reported using avoidance as a coping style. Both of these coping responses have been associated with poor mental health and low morale (Kahana, Kahana, & Young, 1987). however, there may also be some positive aspects of vigilant as well as avoidant orientations. Concerns about life and safety may enhance health-promoting behaviors or the seeking of medical advice in illness situations. Avoidance of stress has also been shown to have protective value (Breznitz, 1983). Accordingly, those Holocaust survivors who have minimal interaction with unfamiliar persons may do so to cope with the chronic stress of living with fear and mistrust.

There is little information available about the relationship between the sense of vulnerability to feelings of victimization and the use of different coping strategies (Kahana et al., 1988). However, in the clinical literature there are indications that learning to trust again represents an important adaptive task for survivors. To the extent that they can begin to trust again, for survivors, this particular source of chronic stress would diminish and the need for special coping strategies would be reduced (Rosenbloom, 1985).

Coping with the Chronic Stress of Social and Psychological Isolation

The Holocaust-related chronic stressors discussed thus far, including intrusive memories of trauma and feelings of vulnerability to victimization, reflect the internalization of components of the original trauma. The survivor thus becomes both the subject and the source of stress. In the case of the chronic stress of isolation, the stress has both internalized and externalized social environmental components. In fact, there are two distinct chronic stressors, one involving the absence of kin and actual social isolation, and the other internalized or psychological sense of isolation. In terms of the former, survivors lost the majority of their families of orientation, including parents, aunts, uncles, and siblings. Although most survivors endeavored to marry or remarry and reconstitute their families, the experience of being alone and bereft of family is a recurrent chronic stressor reported by survivors.

In addition to the absence of social supports and connectedness, social isolation also appears to be intertwined with a more internalized sense of psychological isolation noted by other Holocaust scholars. Survivors often report a sense of loneliness that borders on desolation (Helmreich, 1992). Psychological isolation also includes the sense of not being understood and accepted and of being set apart from others. Part of this feeling may be based on the perception that one's traumatic experiences set one apart (Kahana, 1987).

A four-item social and psychological isolation subscale was constructed using selected Symptom Checklist 90 items, such as: "feeling lonely when with others" and "never feeling close to others." The Cronbach's alpha for this scale is .61. Significant differences in reported feelings of isolation were found between survivors and the comparison group in both the United States and Israel. It is noteworthy that 41% of U.S. survivors in our study report feeling lonely a lot, whereas only 22% of the comparison group indicate experiencing frequent loneliness.

Feelings of social and psychological isolation are exemplified by the following comments made by our study respondents. A 68-year-old woman survivor stated, "I'm envious of everybody who has a nice, good, big family. We have only one son and he lives in California—I had such a beautiful family before the war. We don't have a big family, and we are lonely." A 63-year-old man felt, "There is a missing link some place, I can't describe it. I'm missing my family. It's on my mind all the time." Another woman survivor, age 69, who had lost her mother and father and all of her 11 siblings during the Holocaust stated, "I always think of home, I get nostalgic feelings—I miss the closeness from my family. A lot of times I feel nobody knows me." These statements reveal the interconnected experiences of enduring social and psychological isolation among survivors of the Holocaust living in the United States. It is noteworthy that these feelings even applied to their families of procreation.

Coping with social isolation includes instrumental behaviors to establish and maintain close ties with one's family of procreation. In fact, 99% of survivors in our sample were currently or previously married. Only 2% reported being divorced or separated, and 17% reported being widowed at the time of the interview. This pattern was consistent with that portrayed by the comparison group of Jewish older adults who immigrated to the United States prior to the Holocaust. It is interesting to note that significantly fewer survivors in either country (7%) than those in the comparison group (12%) reported being childless. This may attest to the value survivors placed on creating families. At the same time, survivors in both countries were also significantly more likely to have smaller families (1 or 2 children versus 3 or more) than members of the comparison group.

Communication with and expression of emotional closeness to children represent further indications of survivors' efforts to combat isolation. Thus, more survivors in Israel and in the United States reported discussing everyday problems with their children than did members of the comparison group (31% of U.S. survivors and 51% of Israeli survivors, compared with 24% of Americans and 46% of Israelis in the comparison groups). Additionally, Israeli survivors were significantly more likely to discuss financial and other important matters with their children than were the American survivors (75% of Israeli survivors and 32% of U.S. survivors). These data suggest that reluctance to discuss Holocaust experiences with family members should not be interpreted as a more general withdrawal from close interpersonal interactions.

In terms of more general coping strategies, seeking social integration may protect survivors from a psychological sense of isolation. Our data reveal no significant differences between U.S. and Israeli survivors and those in the comparison group in terms of using social integration as a coping strategy. As part of their responses to the ECRC Coping Scale (Kahana, Kahana, & Young, 1987), 32% of survivors reported that they are very likely to get together with others when facing a problem, compared to 30% of the comparison group. One can also consider social integration on a more lifestyle-oriented, behavioral level by considering patterns of voluntary associations and other forms of participation such as synagogue attendance. Once again, survivors showed no more or less involvement in these efforts than the comparison group. The lack of differences indicates that the survivors cope in social ways much like the comparison group. However, coping efforts did not appear to be fully successful in compensating for the stress of enduring isolation reported by many survivors. Survivors could only succeed in achieving connectedness through associating with other survivors. Responses of many of our U.S. survivors affirmed continuous feelings of isolation and suggest that their social ways of coping do not always succeed in counteracting their sense of isolation. They could never make up for the loss of their original families, nor could they feel fully connected to society at large.

Coping with Stigma

The clinical and scientific literature on survivors of the Holocaust convincingly demonstrates the intensely felt stigma associated with survivorship (Solomon, 1995). Survivors are widely depicted as "damaged goods," or persons whose suffering has irreparably affected their psychological well-being and social functioning (Kahana, Harel, & Kahana, 1988). The very propensity of clinicians to define traumatization based on the likelihood of developing PTSD suggests that those individuals who endured victimization will receive a psychiatric diagnosis (Green, 1993). Furthermore, the psychiatric illness label constitutes an additional chronic stressor (Goffman, 1963).

During the first three decades following the Holocaust, professionals painted a bleak picture of survivors, and the public at large turned a deaf ear to their experiences. In response to accounts of atrocities during the Holocaust, Americans often drew parallels to the Great Depression and admonished survivors not to feel sorry for themselves. In Israel there was also negative labeling of survivors (Solomon, 1995). It was often suggested that the survivors' inability to fight back may have contributed to their fate (Hass, 1995). The tendency of the larger society to trivialize the horrendous experiences of survivors resulted in survivors being deprived of the opportunity to communicate about their experiences. In this sense, social stigma placed constraints on the coping repertoire of survivors.

In order to ascertain whether living with stigma is recognized as a special problem by Holocaust survivors, a Living with Stigma Subscale was developed on the basis of four relevant Symptom Checklist 90 items. The scale included statements such as, "Others do not understand me or are unsympathetic" and "Others do not share my ideas and beliefs." The Chronbach's alpha was .61 for this subscale. Our findings follow the pattern observed for other chronic stressors, with significantly greater stigmatization reported by U.S. survivors than by the U.S. comparison group. No significant differences were observed between the two Israeli samples. It should be noted that rates of reported stigmatization were very low for all groups. In response to open-ended questions, survivors in our sample did not spontaneously refer to their stigmatized status. Nevertheless, some expressions of concern about the survivor label were noted. This is exemplified by one survivor, age 72, who stated, "I don't want to be labeled as a survivor."

The modal approach to coping with social stigma among survivors was an attempt to distance themselves from their past and employ instrumental behaviors that permitted them to behave like other citizens in the surrounding culture. Based on in-depth interviews with survivors, Hass (1995) suggests that "for the initial forty years of their post-war life, most survivors escaped the brunt of their past calamities by working, by doing, by not thinking, by not feeling" (p. 21).

Rather than distancing themselves from social stigma by not identifying with the survivor label, some survivors internalized the social stigma and developed negative self-perceptions through self-labeling. For this group, social stigma resulted in internalized chronic stress (Martin, 1986). Our data reveal significant differences in reporting feelings of worthlessness, with survivors in both the U.S. and Israel at least twice as likely to report such feelings as members of the comparison groups. In considering the salience of the chronic stress of social stigma for all traumatized populations, it is noteworthy that references to this aspect of the aftermath of trauma are almost completely absent in the traumatic stress literature. Consistent with these data, the posttraumatic stress literature provides little empirical support for clinical observations of guilt and shame among trauma survivors (McCann & Pearlman, 1990). It is also important to note that those who took extreme measures to avoid being identified as survivors may be least likely to participate in research on survivors. Consequently, studies of survivors, such as our own, may underrepresent those survivors who suffered most from the chronic stress of social stigma.

NORMATIVE CHRONIC LIFE STRESSORS: CHARACTERISTICS AND COPING EFFORTS

In addition to the chronic internal and external stressors that may be directly attributable to the experiences of traumatic stress, survivors of trauma must also deal with other stressors that may be indirectly related or unrelated to the trauma. We classify these in Figure 1 as (1) childhood life stressors; (2) adult life stressors, including immigration and acculturation and older adult life stressors; and (3) stressors of aging.

Traumatic stress always occurs in the context of the individual's prior life history. Some Holocaust survivors who were young adults at the time of the trauma (World War II) may have had stressful childhood experiences. Survivors may have grown up in poverty or may have been raised by distant relatives after losing a parent in early childhood. Such pretraumatic chronic life stressors may have been incorporated into the personalities and coping dispositions of survivors. These dispositions predate the trauma and comprise the background against which chronic stressors produced by trauma and other later chronic life stressors must be considered.

Adult life crises also occur throughout an individual's adult years and include such challenges and stressors as immigration and acculturation, changes in social and economic circumstances, and family problems. During late life, survivors and other older adults must also cope with chronic normative stressors of aging such as illness, losses, and lack of person–environment fit (Kahana & Kahana, 1996). In addition, older adults face chronic stressors caused by aging and ageism (Butler, 1975). Although these stressors are not unique to survivors of the Holocaust, their appraisals, along with modes of coping with such stressors, are likely to be altered by survivorship (as indicated by the dotted arrows in Figure 1).

Having discussed both the unique and enduring stressors that result from extreme trauma, we now turn to a discussion of coping with normative chronic life stressors that are experienced by survivors of the Holocaust. Stressors during childhood will be noted only briefly since for most survivors, and especially those in our study, they occurred prior to the Holocaust. Most of these survivors were young adults when the

Holocaust took place. Our focus will therefore be on adult life stressors, including those related to immigration and acculturation, to other life events of adulthood, and finally, to issues related to aging. We will now consider how the traumatic experience of the Holocaust subsequently shaped appraisals and responses to normative life stressors and how those appraisals and responses may influence well-being and quality of life for trauma survivors.

Childhood Life Stressors

Childhood life events are experiences that occur early in the life span. Due to the timing of these events, often during the formative years of personality development, they have potential long-lasting effects. Childhood life crises, such as living in poverty or losing a parent, brother, or sister, may have occurred prior to the onset of the war.

The enduring impact of childhood life stressors has been demonstrated in studies of late life subjective well-being (or happiness). Ragan and McGlashan (1986) found that states of negative affect experienced by a child when a parent dies can resurface during adulthood, leading to negative emotional states in later life. Our recent work demonstrates that adverse home conditions and loss of a parent have long-term effects on both physical and psychological well being well into later life (Kahana, Oakes, Slotterback, Kahana, & Kercher, 1995). Additionally, other researchers have found similar negative effects in adulthood when children have suffered the loss of a sibling during childhood (Krell & Rabkin, 1979; Mufson, 1985). It may be suggested that survivors of the Holocaust would experience enduring pain from the combination of childhood life stressors and Holocaust-related atrocities.

Adult Life Stressors

Immigration and Acculturation Stressors. Survivors, as well as the prewar immigrants who constitute our comparison group, faced many obstacles as they attempted to establish themselves in a trade or profession and earn a living in their adoptive countries—the United States or Israel. Additionally, many survivors experienced multiple relocations until they finally settled in a permanent locale. Learning the language and culture of their new country introduced additional challenges. For many, these stressors resolved themselves as they adapted to their new homeland after the initial 5–20 years. For others, these stressors continued well into old age (Kahana, Harel, & Kahana, 1988). Chronic stressors of immigration include a broad array of variables ranging from economic hardships to social marginality. Portes and Rombaut (1990) suggest that one major cause of this immigration stress is based on the surrendering of old roots before new ones can be established. For Holocaust survivors, surrendering old roots was not a voluntary process, but occurred as a result of turmoil and instability. Acculturation can be traumatic because the immigrants are simultaneously distancing themselves from the culture in which they grew up and embracing a new and foreign one in its place. In the case of survivors of the Holocaust, this picture gets even more complex, since survivors are products of three different cultures. Thus, survivors may have been socialized during childhood into Hungarian or Polish culture in their country of origin and subsequently immigrated to the United States or Israel. In addition, for most survivors, their basic identity is their Jewish religious, cultural, and ethnic heritage.

We did not anticipate many differences in immigration and acculturation stressors faced by survivors and by the comparison groups who were also immigrants. Issues pertaining to learning a new language, obtaining work, and learning new customs were shared by both groups. Among open-ended responses of survivors about major problems faced after arrival in the United States, 41% spontaneously cited language problems, 47% cited problems with finding work, and 9% cited problems with getting used to customs in their new locale. Nevertheless, the added vulnerability of survivors based on the trauma they endured may have exacerbated the stress of being an immigrant.

In response to open-ended questions about post-war experiences and challenges, survivors' comments reflect the long-term stress of being immigrants and of being different. A woman, age 80, responded, "We started a new life in so many countries. It was too much. I love America, but it was too much starting new all the time." A man, age 72, reflected, "It changed a lot of things; I would be more respected if I was still home, here I am a little man, a plain person. Here you are not born, you don't have the language." A woman, age 70, stated, "Being with different kinds of people. It took me too long to adjust to this way of living. It's different. But I'm very happy to be here. I appreciate more everything I have. Here [in America] people take things for granted." Another survivor, now living in the United States, responded "I had a big future when I was young and I would have had a different kind of living, a better life, financially and emotionally feeling better. I wouldn't have been a painter."

The very strategies in which Holocaust survivors engaged to help them overcome chronic posttraumatic stressors (such as intrusive memories, fear and mistrust, social isolation, and stigma) were also highly functional in helping them overcome many of the chronic stressors posed by their immigrant status. Nevertheless, it is noteworthy that the social stigma of survivorship may continue to interact with the stigma of immigrant status. Accordingly, survivors were readily identified by their accents even after assuming the social characteristics of successful natives in their adoptive countries. However, Portes and Rombaut (1990) suggest that immigrants who are successful have a sense of mastery and increased self-confidence when they believe that they have successfully integrated into their new culture. One coping strategy that appears to be important is to maintain a network of kin and friends, which gives immigrants the ability to retain their ethnic and cultural orientation while still trying to become acculturated into a new society.

Other Adult Life Stressors. The complexities of understanding and assessing coping with chronic stressors that are direct consequences of the Holocaust have been discussed. Yet, the survivor must also adapt to chronic (as well as to acute) stressors unrelated to the Holocaust or indirectly related to it. Survivorship may shape appraisals of other stressors because it affects the survivor's entire worldview. Since the full range of chronic stressors faced by older adults is extremely broad, our discussion of the special challenges posed by these stressors is illustrative rather than exhaustive. We borrow from the general stress literature and focus on those normative life events that typically represent chronic stressors for older adults. These involve interpersonal losses, including widowhood, loss of friends and other family members, health deterioration, and problems with adult children (Kahana & Kahana, 1984a). Although these stressors are unrelated to the trauma and affect both survivors and other adults in the general population, the earlier traumatic experiences of survivors are likely to affect appraisals of these stressors, modes of coping with them, and ultimate outcomes.

Based on the extreme trauma that survivors experienced earlier in their lives, many appraise general chronic stressors in later life as less significant. For instance, a woman, age 69, responded, "When [other] people have problems, I find no such problems. If you are healthy and together, that's all I want, the rest are not really problems for me." A woman, age 72, reflected, "When I was working without shoes or food and every single day being so near to death, when someone here has no food for a while or when they get old in their body and mind, for sure it is not the same [not nearly as bad]." A man, age 62, who spent time in a labor camp, concentration camp, and jail during the Holocaust and who lost his mother and father and four siblings stated, "I don't know if I am as sensitive as other people, in some ways [I am] more callous and in some ways more sensitive. [I am] less tolerant of things affecting other people, of people's complaints of minor problems."

In contrast to survivors' tendency to minimize personal problems, they exhibited great concern about stressors in specific areas, such as perceived threats to family and potential or actual illness. This was illustrated by the comments cited earlier about living with fear and mistrust and by major threats reported by survivors concerning the safety of their children. Problems concerning children's welfare assume particular importance for Holocaust survivors, more so than for our comparison groups. Even in situations in which their children are highly achieving and generally doing well, survivors' concerns over potential threats to children's health and well-being represent major chronic stressors for this group.

Our data illustrate the fact that survivors show significantly greater concern about health, safety, and well-being of their offspring than do members of the comparison group. Such excessive fears about children's welfare represent chronic stressors for survivors in both the United States and Israel. Within the United States, fully twice as many survivors (53%) as members of the comparison group (26%) stated that they worry about their children's driving safety ($p < .001$). Significant differences were also found among Israeli samples; 49% of survivors report excessive worrying versus 38% of the Israeli comparison group. Almost identical patterns of differences were obtained in considering worrying about children's physical health. Interestingly, in spite of fewer dangers facing adult children in the United States, concern was more prevalent among survivors in the United States than in Israel. These findings fit with Aldwin's (1992) observations about the salience of "non-egocentric stressors," which are stressors experienced by significant others that assume greater importance as part of the generativity needs of older persons.

It has been documented (Helmreich, 1992) that medical symptoms are particularly threatening to survivors of the Holocaust because concentration camp inmates who became ill or exhibited any symptoms of ill health during the Holocaust were put to death. Furthermore, mistrust of the medical establishment and medical regimes have also been found to characterize survivors (Krystal, 1968). Survivors in our study gave voice to these threatening appraisals of the chronic stress of ill health. A 68-year-old man stated, "I was never ill in my life before. I've had serious illness. It affected my heart. I don't know how [it affected me] mentally. I'm pretty sore. It affected my arthritis . . . sleeping naked on a cement floor, to be outside, not to be able to sit down, being punished."

To the extent that the experiences of trauma shaped ways of coping with stressors, the survivors may bring to bear these coping responses to deal with all chronic stressors (McCann & Pearlman, 1990). Our qualitative data and some quantitative findings shed light on these issues. Our data on responses to the ECRC Coping Scale suggest that survivors are just as likely as members of the comparison group to engage in instrumental coping strategies in solving problems that are amenable to instrumental solutions (Harel, Kahana, & Kahana, 1988). Instrumental problem-solving strategies, which are not readily applicable to internalized chronic stressors, are better suited to dealing with more general problems in living. Indeed, self-perceptions of survivors often emphasize this propensity toward instrumental mastery. Their examples of such adaptations reflect a belief and pride in their own resilience and toughness. A woman survivor, age 72, responded, "I know more how to fight than others. I'm prepared to fight anything that comes my way." A 69-year-old man reflected, "It gives me a lot of strength. The thought that I was lucky to survive and I feel free physically and emotionally that I can master my fate."

Other survivors commented on their difficulties in coping with stress and feeling vulnerable because of their prior victimization. A 66-year-old woman survivor, who lost her parents, nine siblings, two grandparents, and a fiancée, stated, "I have less patience, because my nerves are destroyed. It's harder for a survivor and more painful. Because we already lost so much in the concentration camp." Another woman survivor, age 59, responded, "That's why I am such a terrible worrier, because you have no family left from home. I am very nervous because of what I went through."

We know little about ways of survivors' coping with ill health that might reduce the adverse effects of this stress. Thus, for example, choosing medical personnel who are personally known to the survivor may serve to alleviate chronic stress posed by illness. Other stressors, such as the death of loved ones, may reawaken memories of Holocaust-related interpersonal loss. In addition, the bereaved survivor has diminished opportunities for self-disclosure to trusted others. Thus, the ability to self-disclose to nonrelatives and trust them enough to marshal their support may constitute particularly important coping challenges for survivors confronting late life losses.

Chronic Stressors of Aging

The stress of confronting ageism and one's own fear of aging is a central theme of gerontological research and inquiry (Butler, 1975). Interestingly, for at least some Holocaust survivors, this source of chronic stress appears to be minimal. Data from our research indicate that 45% of all our respondents who were survivors felt that dealing with their own aging was rendered more difficult because of their traumatic experiences, whereas 29% felt their experiences did not make a difference. The remaining 26% felt that dealing with aging was actually made easier by being a survivor of the Holocaust. Members of this latter group suggested that becoming old represents a triumph of survival and success in reaching a normal lifespan. Some older survivors expressed surprise that aging could be perceived negatively when, for them, it reflected extended living and longevity. They experienced relative deprivation in their youth and yet derived enjoyment from their attainments in later life. In contrast, those survivors who felt that aging was difficult tended to cite illness, fear of dependency, and lack of social support rather than problems of old age per se as the major stressors.

Coping with aging poses special challenges to Holocaust survivors. The special vulnerability of survivors to loss and illness has been documented. In addition, it is noteworthy that survivors lack role models for aging, as they did not have the opportunity to see their own parents, aunts, or uncles grow old (Rosenbloom, 1985). Furthermore, retirement removes an important and useful coping strategy of working, which had helped survivors escape intrusive memories of the trauma by keeping busy (Cohen, 1991).

A significant difference was found between survivors and the comparison group in reported degree of success in settling into retirement, with 34% of the survivors, compared to 53% of the comparison group in the United States, reporting that they were "very well settled." The divided responses of survivors to threats of aging and untimely death are noted here. Many survivors voice special concerns and fears of aging based on the trauma they endured. They feel ill and prematurely aged. A woman survivor, age 62, who had severe stomach problems and rated her health as fair, stated, "We got older without years, without dates. Our bodies were abused. Others get older because of the years. We all look older." A man, age 68, responded, "Going through all that [Holocaust] probably cost. I got too old and my health deteriorated too early."

There are also those who felt that experiencing the Holocaust did not make a difference in their experience of aging as a stressor, and some reported that survivorship had actually made aging easier. A 73-year-old woman survivor responded, "The people who were not in the Holocaust have better nerves; they don't get those bad dreams. Otherwise, getting old is the same. They get sick, too; they lose their husbands, too." Another woman, age 64, stated, "You have a lifetime 70 years. I spent 1 year in a camp. My life is not shaped by just my experiences in the Holocaust." A man, age 68, felt, "I assume that we survivors—we do not fear death as much as other people. We are able to adjust to any type of situation because we went through so much that we can easily adjust."

CONCLUSION

Major trauma has a powerful influence on the subsequent chronic stressors to which survivors are exposed. It also impacts on their appraisals of normative or more general life stressors. Furthermore, it affects both the availability and employment of coping strategies for the survivor. It should be noted that acute stressors, chronic stressors, coping efforts, and outcomes of distress versus recovery are difficult to separate and are seldom orthogonal. Nevertheless, focusing on the role of chronic stressors in the broader context of traumatic stress should clarify components of the complex process of human adaptation to trauma.

Our discussion has stopped short of presenting a formal scheme for classifying diverse coping efforts relevant to each chronic stressor. In fact, survivors were not always aware of internalized chronic stressors or of the coping responses they employed to deal with them. Nevertheless, our results suggest that it is useful to move beyond conventional categorizations such as problem-focused or emotion-focused coping by identifying behaviors and cognitive efforts that are particularly relevant to trauma-related chronic stressors. Accordingly, our discussion noted the importance of self-disclosure and cognitive reframing in dealing with intrusive memories of trauma. Social integration represents the most relevant coping response in dealing with the chronic stress of isolation. It is also important to note that the coping strategies reported by our respondents may not reflect the full range of coping responses manifested by survivors. Thus, even though vigilance and withdrawal may alternate as ways of dealing with fear and mistrust, these responses may not be subject to awareness, and are therefore less likely to be reported.

Nor do we have sufficient information on the effectiveness of specific ways of coping with trauma-related chronic stressors. In future research, the outcomes of coping with chronic stressors, particularly adaptive outcomes, should be examined more closely. Is successful coping with trauma-related chronic stressors manifested in positive psychological well-being or in other important social outcomes? Are there ways of coping that facilitate healing by permitting survivors to attach positive meaning to the trauma? In the case of internalized trauma-related stressors, it may be argued that diminishing the stress or eliminating it is the ultimate desirable outcome.

According to Raphael (1986), regardless of premorbid states, it is the reaction to severe trauma and the ability to integrate the traumatic experience that account for ultimate outcomes. Similarly, Rosenbloom (1985) comments on the need to identify those adaptive and interpretive forces that assisted survivors in their rebirth and social integration. The ultimate challenge to survivors is to maintain or restore ego integrity in later life by learning to trust again and to accept the entirety of their lives in spite of their horrendous life experiences.

REFERENCES

ALDWIN, C. M. (1992). Aging, coping, and efficacy: A theoretical framework for examining coping in a life-span developmental context. In M. Wykle, E. Kahana, & J. Kowal (Eds.), *Stress and health among the elderly* (pp. 96–113). New York: Springer.

BAUM, A. (1990). Stress, intrusive imagery, and chronic distress. *Health Psychology, 9,* 653–675.

BAUM, A., COHEN, L., & HALL, M. (1993). Control and intrusive memories as possible determinants of chronic stress. *Psychosomatic Medicine, 55,* 274–286.

BREZNITZ, S. (1983). *The denial of stress.* New York: International Universities Press.

BUTLER, R. (1975). *Why survive? Being old in America.* New York: Harper & Row.

COHEN, B. B. (1991). Holocaust survivors and the crisis of aging. *The Journal of Contemporary Human Services, 72*(4), 226–232.

DEROGOTIS, L. (1977). Confirmation of the dimensional structure of the SCL-90: A study in construct validation. *Journal of Clinical Psychology, 33*(4), 981–989.

FRANKL, V. (1962). *Man's search for meaning, An introduction to logotherapy.* Boston: Beacon.

GOFFMAN, E. (1963). *Stigma: Notes on the management of spoiled identity.* New York: Simon & Schuster.

GOTTLIEB, B. H. (Ed.). (1988). *Marshaling social support.* Newbury Park, CA: Sage.

GREEN, B. (1993). Identifying survivors at risk: Trauma and stressors across events. In J. P. Wilson & B. Raphael (Eds.), *International handbook of traumatic stress syndromes* (pp. 135–144). New York: Plenum.

HAREL, Z., KAHANA, B., & KAHANA, E. (1988). Psychological well-being among Holocaust survivors and immigrants in Israel. *Journal of Traumatic Stress Studies, 1*(4), 413–428.

HASS, A. (1995). *The aftermath: Living with the Holocaust.* New York: Cambridge University Press.

HELMREICH, W. (1992). *Against all odds.* New York: Simon & Schuster.

HOROWITZ, M. J. (1975). Intrusive and repetitive thoughts after experimental stresses: A summary. *Archives of General Psychiatry, 32,* 1457–1463.

HOROWITZ, M. J. (1982). Stress response syndromes and their treatment. In L. Goldberger & S. Breznitz (Eds.), *Handbook of stress: Theoretical and clinical aspects* (pp. 711–732). New York: Free Press.

JUCOVY, M. E. (1988). Therapeutic work with survivors and their children: Recurrent themes and problems. In P. Marcus & A. Rosenberg (Eds.), *Healing their wounds: psychotherapy with Holocaust survivors and their families* (pp. 51–66). New York: Praeger.

KAHANA, B. (1987). Isolation. In G. Maddox (Ed.), *The encyclopedia of aging* (pp. 369–370). New York: Springer.

KAHANA, B., HAREL, Z., & KAHANA, E. (1988). Predictors of psychological well-being among survivors of the Holocaust. In J. P. Wilson, Z. Harel, & B. Kahana (Eds.), *Human adaptation to extreme stress: From the Holocaust to Vietnam* (pp. 171–194). New York: Plenum.

KAHANA, B., & KAHANA, E. (1984a). Stress reactions. In P. Lewhinsohn & L. Teri (Eds.), *Clinical geropsychology* (pp. 139–169). New York: Pergamon.

Kahana, B., Oakes, M., Slotterback, C., Kahana, E., & Kercher, K. (1995). *Crises throughout the life course: Effects on physical and mental health in late life.* Paper presented at annual meeting of the Gerontological Society of America, November, Los Angeles, CA.
Kahana, E. (1992). Epilogue: Stress research and aging: Complexities, ambiguities, paradoxes and promise. In M. Wykle, E. Kahana, & J. Kowal (Eds.), *Stress and health among the elderly* (pp. 239–245). New York: Springer.
Kahana, E., Fairchild, T., & Kahana, B. (1982). Adaptation. In D. J. Mangen & W. Peterson (Eds.), *Research instruments in social gerontology: Clinical and social psychology* (149–159). Minneapolis, MN: University of Minnesota Press.
Kahana, E., & Kahana, B. (1984). The elderly Jews. In E. Palmore (Ed.), *Handbook on the aged in the United States.* Westport, CT: Greenwood.
Kahana, E., & Kahana, B. (1996). Conceptual and empirical advances in understanding aging well through proactive adaptation. In V. Bengtson (Ed.), *Adulthood and Aging: Research on continuities and discontinuities* (pp. 18–41). New York: Springer.
Kahana, E., Kahana, B., Harel, Z., & Rosner, T. (1988). Coping with extreme trauma. In J. P. Wilson, Z. Harel, & B. Kahana (Eds.), *Human adaptation to extreme stress: From the Holocaust to Vietnam* (pp. 55–79). New York: Plenum.
Kahana, E., Kahana, B., & Young, R. (1987). Strategies of coping and institutional outcomes. *Research on Aging, 9,* 182–189.
Krell, R., & Rabkin, L. (1979). The effects of sibling death on the surviving child: A family perspective. *Family Process, 18,* 471–477.
Krystal, H. (1968). Studies of concentration camp survivors. In H. Krystal (Ed.), *Massive psychic trauma* (pp. 23–46). New York: International Universities Press.
Laufer, R. S. (1988). The serial self: War trauma, identity, and adult development. In J. P. Wilson, Z. Harel, & B. Kahana (Eds.), *Human adaptation to extreme stress: From the Holocaust to Vietnam* (pp. 33–53). New York: Plenum.
Lawton, M. P. (1975). The Philadelphia Geriatric Center Morale Scale: a revision. *Journal of Gerontology, 30,* 85–89.
Lazarus, R. S., & Folkman, S. (1984). *Stress, appraisal and coping.* New York: Springer.
Lomranz, R. J. (1990). Long-term adaptation to traumatic stress in light of adult development and aging perspectives. In M. A. P. Stephens, J. H. Crowther, S. E. Hobfoll, & D. L. Tennenbaum (Eds.), *Stress and coping in later life families* (pp. 99–118). Washington, DC: Hemisphere.
Martin, L. (1986). A social learning perspective. In S. Ainlay, G. Becker, & L. Coleman (Eds.), *The dilemma of difference* (pp. 145–160). New York: Plenum.
McCann, L., & Pearlman, L. (1990). *Psychological trauma and the adult survivor.* New York: Brunner/Mazel.
Mufson, T. (1985). Issues surrounding sibling death during adolescence. *Child and Adolescent Social Work, 2*(4), 204–218.
Niederland, W. (1968). The psychiatric evaluations of emotional problems in survivors of Nazi persecution. In H. Krystal (Ed.), *Massive psychic trauma* (pp. 8–22). New York: International Universities Press.
Neugarten, B. L. (1969). Continuities and discontinuities of psychological issues into adult life. *Human Development, 12,* 121–130.
Nolen-Hoeksema, S., Morrow, J., & Fredrickson, B. L. (1993). Response style and the duration of episodes of depressed mood. *Journal of Abnormal Psychology, 102,* 20–28.
Paivio, A. (1986). *Mental representation: A dual coding approach.* New York: Oxford University Press.
Pennebaker, J. W., Barger, S. D., & Tiebout, J. (1989). Disclosure of trauma and health among Holocaust survivors. *Psychosomatic Medicine, 51,* 577–589.
Portes, A., & Rumbaut, R. G. (1990). *Immigration America: A portrait.* Berkeley, CA: University of California Press.
Ragan, P. V., & McGlashan, T. H. (1986). Childhood parental death and adult psychopathology. *Child and Adolescent Social Work, 143,* 155–157.

RAPHAEL, B. (1986). *When disaster strikes: How individuals and communities cope with catastrophe.* New York: Basic Books.
ROSENBLOOM, M. (1985). The holocaust survivor in late life. *Journal of Gerontological Social Work, 8,* 181–191.
SOLOMON, Z. (1995). From denial to recognition: Attitudes towards Holocaust survivors from WW II to the present. *Journal of Traumatic Stress, 8*(2), 2–15.
WILSON, J. P. (1989). *Trauma, transformation and healing.* New York: Brunner/Mazel.

13

Coping with Chronic Work Stress

C. GAIL HEPBURN, CATHERINE A. LOUGHLIN, and JULIAN BARLING

INTRODUCTION

Most people spend much of their waking lives involved in paid employment. Therefore, work is a context that demands our collective attention. For some time we have recognized that many individuals experience stress while engaging in paid employment. Kahn, Wolfe, Quinn, Snoek, and Rosenthal (1964) estimated that at any point in time, one third of the working population experience chronic stress, and there is no reason to suspect that any reduction in this number of people has taken place.

This chapter provides an overview of the literatures on chronic work stressors and how individuals cope with work stress. There is a disturbing lack of connection between the study of these two intuitively linked topics. The manner with which individuals cope with work stress is rarely tied to any *specific* workplace stressor. Studies examining coping with work stress typically ignore the source of workplace stress, instead focusing on how coping efforts to deal with general "difficulties" at work alleviate worker strain. Therefore, we divide this chapter into several sections, beginning with an introduction to chronic work stressors. A

C. GAIL HEPBURN and CATHERINE A. LOUGHLIN • Department of Psychology, Queen's University, Kingston, Ontario, Canada K7L 3N6. **JULIAN BARLING** • School of Business, Queen's University, Kingston, Ontario, Canada K7L 3N6.

Coping with Chronic Stress, edited by Benjamin H. Gottlieb. Plenum Press, New York, 1997.

section on coping with work stress follows, which includes a discussion of the recent literature attempting to incorporate the measurement of stressors, coping, and strain in a single study. These studies examine coping as a "moderator" of stressor–strain relationships. Finally, although the work context has the potential to contribute to positive mental health (Broadbent, 1985), it frequently fails to do so. Consequently, this chapter concludes with an examination of the literature on organizational efforts to alleviate the potentially harmful effects of chronic work stress. We argue that organizational interventions should focus not only on helping employees cope with existing workplace stressors, but also on taking steps toward the elimination of workplace stressors themselves.

CHRONIC WORK STRESSORS

In this chapter, *stressors* are defined as objective environmental characteristics or events that are quantifiable and objectively verifiable (Pratt & Barling, 1988). *Stress* reflects the subjective interpretation or experience of stressors. That is, different people experiencing the same event will interpret or perceive it in different ways. *Strain* refers to the outcome of stress (e.g., psychosomatic complaints, depression, anxiety). Further, *chronic stressors* are of no fixed duration but are relatively enduring or repetitive in nature, and it is usually difficult to specify the exact time of their onset (e.g., Pratt & Barling, 1988). Chronic stressors can be distinguished from daily (common) and acute (uncommon) stressors, both of which begin at a specific time and last for a short period of time.

Sources of Chronic Stress in the Workplace

Several influential models or descriptions of the sources of stress in the workplace have appeared (e.g., Kahn et al., 1964; Karasek & Theorell, 1990; Sauter, Murphy, & Hurrell, 1990; Warr, 1987). Although not focusing on work stress specifically, Hackman and Oldham's (1980) Job Characteristics Model also provides information about workplace conditions that can undermine well-being. Despite differences between these models, there is sufficient similarity in the workplace conditions identified to extract the core components of work stress from them. For the sake of simplicity, rather than suggesting the superiority of any one approach, we use the model provided by Sauter et al. (1990) as our framework for discussing sources of chronic stress in the workplace.

Sauter et al. (1990) list six workplace factors most likely to affect workers' mental and physical health: work scheduling, role stressors, career security factors, interpersonal relationships at work, and job content and autonomy. We will discuss each of these factors in turn.

Work Scheduling. Two aspects related to work scheduling can be experienced as stressful and result in strain. First, the pace at which work takes place must be considered. Second, the scheduling of work must be considered: As noted elsewhere, if working unusual shifts (e.g., "graveyard shifts") was not potentially harmful, why would additional compensation be offered (Barling, 1990)? When rotating shifts are necessary, stable, predictable, and forward rotating (day-to-night) shifts are the most beneficial (Sauter et al., 1990).

Role Stressors. Role stress theory (Kahn et al., 1964) is probably the earliest attempt at an approach to occupational stress. There are several types of role stressors. Role ambiguity refers to a lack of adequate guidelines (e.g., job description) to provide sufficient knowledge of what is expected for adequate performance at work. Role conflict emanates from incompatible job-related demands, such as conflicting demands and expectations from different superiors. Role overload refers to having too much to do or not enough time to complete otherwise reasonable assignments. Role overload can be either quantitative (the amount) or qualitative (the difficulty) in nature. Finally, role underload, which arises from not having enough to do or not being challenged by one's work, can also be experienced as stressful.

Career Security. Two components related to one's career are potentially stressful: Insecurity about one's current job can be a major stressor and has been linked to important outcomes (e.g., Barling, 1990), and from a more long-term perspective, individuals want to know that they have a career path within an organization (Sauter et al., 1990).

Interpersonal Relationships. People go to work for more than just financial reasons, and the potential benefits of the quality of interpersonal relationships at work can emanate from interactions with subordinates, peers, customers/clients, or supervisors. The social context in which work takes place can provide meaning to work. Indeed, Jackson (1988) has shown that the loss of the social contacts and support available at work is one of the factors associated with the negative effects of unemployment. Sauter et al. (1990) state that work relationships can either buffer or exacerbate the adverse effects of exposure to job risk factors.

Job Content. According to Hackman and Oldham (1980), three critical psychological states must be present in order for a person's work to be motivating and satisfying:

1. A feeling of personal responsibility for one's work that emanates from autonomy concerning work pace and procedures
2. Experiencing one's work as meaningful, stemming from opportunities for skill variety and task identity and from believing that the work affects other people
3. Having knowledge of the results of one's performance through feedback from the job itself, supervisors, and peers

Warr (1987) extends this model and suggests that there are nine principal job features related to personal and occupational mental health. While Hackman and Oldham (1980) only deal with intrinsic characteristics (i.e., relating to the job itself), Warr (1987) adds four extrinsic factors that affect work outcomes: pay level and pay equity, physical security (i.e., workplace health and safety), social contact (which offers support), and holding a valued social position.

Autonomy. Perhaps the most influential theory concerning autonomy is the Job Strain Model (Karasek & Theorell, 1990). According to this model, the influence of work demands on health are moderated by the degree of control individuals have over their work. Job-decision latitude reflects the degree to which a job provides substantial freedom, independence, and discretion to employees in scheduling their work and in determining the procedures used to carry it out. It is only when *high* work demands are combined with *low* decision latitude or control over one's work that health and well-being are threatened. Sauter et al. (1990) suggest that personal control is the determining factor in generating any health consequences of work demands.

Although this section has illustrated chronic work stressors, it should be kept in mind that many of the factors listed here can be experienced as daily or acute stressors under certain conditions, an issue to which we will return later.

Contemporary Sources of Chronic Work Stress

In addition to these core workplace stressors, there are also workplace stressors that are unique to current economic and social conditions. Hartley (1995) argues that people and organizations are currently dealing with unprecedented levels of change in the workplace. For example, there have been large changes recently in the types of jobs, job conditions, job holders, and relations between employer and employee that exist at work. Four contemporary workplace stressors may affect employees' physical and mental health: uncertainty, technological advances, the distribution of work, and current unemployment levels.

Uncertainty. Changes in the economic environment suggest that organizations and employees will be living with much higher levels of uncertainty than in the recent past. In fact, the Secretary of Labor for the United States, Robert Reich, calls this an "insecure age" for workers (McNamee, 1994). Research has only recently begun to address many of these issues, and currently little is known about the consequences of these changes for individuals, organizations, and employment relations (Hartley, 1995). Although it seems reasonable that these changes and high levels of uncertainty in the workplace are likely to affect individual well-being (e.g., psychological and physical) as well as employee–organizational linkages, the precise effects of change and uncertainty have yet to be determined.

Technological Advances. The introduction of computers into the work environment on a large scale has also changed the way work is conducted and monitored (Schein, 1980). Anyone who touches a keyboard can now potentially be monitored. A computer can monitor every worker every second without the disruptive or expensive need of a supervisor. The frequency and constancy of this monitoring has been associated with stress and strain (e.g., Lund, 1992).

Distribution of Work. With the push for North American firms to be more competitive in a global marketplace (Appelbaum, 1992), two trends concerning the distribution of work are emerging, and both can be stressful for workers. First, part-time employment has expanded dramatically in recent years. It is estimated that more than 30% of Canadians now work in the contingent labor force (Gibb-Clark, 1992), and "involuntary" part-time workers (those wanting full-time hours) account for most of the growth in part-time work in the United States since 1970 (Tilly, 1992). In Canada, it is estimated that one in three part-time workers is involuntarily employed on a part-time basis (Jackson, 1993). Thus, the status of one's job can be a chronic stressor in some cases. Also, many part-timers are exposed to poor quality (e.g., routine) jobs in the service sector, an area where workers are already considered to be at increased risk for psychological disorders (Sauter et al., 1990).

Second, involuntary employment extends to full-time or overtime employment. In the auto sector in Canada, workers are currently "working near-record amounts of overtime" (Daly, 1994, p. 36). Some companies choose to work their existing staff longer hours (an additional 8 hours per week) to control for cyclical fluctuations in work demands and to avoid increased payroll taxes (Daly, 1994; Hancock, 1995). Depending on whether workers are *involuntarily* employed on a part-time, full-time, or overtime basis, there are potential adverse consequences for both the worker and the organization.

Unemployment. Current unemployment rates in North America can also be a source of chronic work stress for many people. Although the effects of unemployment have been known for some time (e.g., Jahoda, Lazarsfeld, & Zeisel, 1933), we are only now beginning to see the effects of others' unemployment on the "survivors" work-related attitudes. For example, Brockner (1988) documents the stress in a postlayoff work environment, where workers are uncertain about their own job security and where the anger associated with many layoffs can be a significant chronic stressor. In turn, the onset of stress typically leads to numerous significant changes in work attitudes and behaviors.

Perceptions of Workplace Stressors

In recent years it has increasingly been recognized that different rules may apply within the same organization, depending on employee demographics. For example, employment conditions for women and minorities in North America have typically been quantitatively and qualitatively inferior to those of white males. These differences are often unrelated to individual skill or ability. Many female clerical workers and minorities in blue collar jobs are plagued by low promotion rates, short job ladders, and low ceilings in their job categories. Even for employees who do manage to rise above clerical or blue collar ranks, their past positions and present skills may make them suitable for the job currently held, but do not constitute adequate preparation for future jobs (Kanter, 1977). Women may also face unique discrimination in terms of promotional policies and possibilities (Swimmer, 1990). For example, pregnant women can suffer unique discrimination and stress in the workplace (Halpert, Wilson, & Hickman, 1993). To the extent that these types of environmental barriers exist in a given organization, they are likely to constitute critical chronic work stressors for certain groups of individuals.

In addition to this it should be noted that the chronic stressors in a given organization are not always readily apparent. For example, in a study of an all-male sample of police officers, the potential for physical injury was not the major stressor (Kroes, Margolis, & Hurrell, 1974). Instead, organizational and bureaucratic problems (e.g., court leniency) were the most salient stressors for these officers. Thus, in researching the sources of chronic work stress it is critical to recognize the variety of stressors individuals may perceive to be present in their environment.

Outcomes of Workplace Stressors

The effects of chronic workplace stressors can be serious. Numerous sources document that these stressors are associated with detrimental psychological, psychosomatic, and organizational outcomes. For example, lack of autonomy or input into decision making concerning one's job has been found to result in emotional strain, lowered self-esteem, job dissatisfaction, increased tension, anxiety, depression, irritation, and somatic complaints (Sauter et al., 1990; Wall, Corbett, Martin, Clegg, & Jackson, 1990). Nord (1977) states that worker alienation is another result of jobs lacking autonomy, and low job-decision latitude has even been implicated in increased mortality among workers (Astrand, Hanson, & Isacsson, 1989; Theorell, Perski, Orth-Gomer, Hamsten, & de Faire, 1991). In contrast, increasing worker control over their jobs has been found to improve work motivation, performance, job satisfaction, and mental health, as well as reduce employee turnover (e.g., Wall & Clegg, 1981; Wall et al., 1990).

Role conflict, role ambiguity, and role overload have also been identified as three key factors contributing to job stress (Kahn, 1980; Kahn et al., 1964). All three role stressors are clearly associated with symptoms of psychological and physiological strain. Some of the consequences of the three role stressors include increased job-related tension, decreased job satisfaction, less organizational confidence, decreased satisfaction with work relationships, decreased self-esteem, and increased anxiety and depression (Kahn, 1980). Role ambiguity and role conflict are also negatively related to commitment and involvement among workers (Fisher & Gitelson, 1983). Chronic stressors have also been related to serious physical outcomes. For example, workplace violence has been linked to severe job insecurity, poor interpersonal relations, and poor supervision (e.g., Thompson, 1994), and it has long been believed that suicide is far more likely for those in stressful occupations (Blaghly, Osterud, & Josslin, 1963; Rose & Rosow, 1973). Interestingly, interpersonal relationships may either buffer or exacerbate adverse effects from exposure to job risk factors (Sauter et al., 1990). In terms of other contemporary stressors, the outcomes are equally serious. Garson (1989) notes that "monitored clerical workers have the highest rate of stress diseases:

heart attacks, high blood pressure, muscle strain" (p. 113). Further, Garson documents cases where the implementation of computer technology and the increased control it allows caused increases in absenteeism and tardiness, "stress-related" illnesses (as indicated on medical reports), resignations, and early retirement. Thus, advances in the "information age" can also exact a high cost to workers in some cases.

The preceding list of outcomes of chronic workplace stressors is not meant to be exhaustive, but rather to give the reader a sense of how numerous and varied such outcomes can be. Finally, before leaving this issue it should be noted that the potential for negative outcomes from job stressors can occur in any occupation; the preceding outcomes are not limited to jobs where such stressors are more apparent. For example, research has found that although police ranked third among 130 occupations in suicide rates, they were behind laborers and house painters in this respect (Fell, Richard, & Wallace, 1980). Thus, it must be acknowledged that not only those working in "dramatic" jobs can suffer from the effects of chronic work stress.

Methodological Problems in Connecting Chronic Stressors to Specific Effects

Specific problems in studying the nature and consequences of chronic work stress exist; for example, when does an acute stressor actually become a chronic stressor? *The Diagnostic and Statistical Manual of Mental Disorders* Third Edition, Revised (DSM-III-R) defines an acute stressor as any event continuing for 6 months or less (American Psychiatric Association, 1987). There are suggestions, however, that acute stressors have a far shorter duration than this (e.g., Pratt & Barling, 1988). Thus, the point in time after which acute stressors should be viewed as chronic remains unclear. Only through simultaneously considering all three dimensions alluded to earlier (the duration of the stressor, the specific time of onset of the stressor, and the likelihood of recurrence of the stressor) can acute and chronic workplace stressors be differentiated. Another difficulty lies in the fact that the same event can be a chronic work stressor in one context but may be an acute stressor in another context (Barling, 1990). For example, commuting to work could be a chronic stressor for those who commute daily, but it could be an acute stressor for those who commute only occasionally.

A second challenge associated with tying particular outcomes to particular chronic work stressors lies in the difficulty associated with choosing the appropriate temporal lag between measuring the stressor and the strain associated with it (Barling, 1990). For example, daily stressors (those with short duration, specific time of onset, and high likelihood of recurrence) have been found to have same-day effects on individuals. In contrast, psychological strain following a chronic stressor has been found to last as long as several years (Barling, 1990). If it is not clear whether a workplace stressor is acute or chronic, then the prediction of how and when the strain will occur, as well as how long it will last, is complicated. In addition, it is possible that different coping techniques will be differentially effective with acute and chronic stressors. Another difficulty in identifying adverse outcomes from particular chronic job stressors lies in the fact that we are still unclear as to whether and how different types of stressors interact (Barling, 1990). For example, commuting problems could exacerbate ongoing conflict with one's spouse, as well as being inherently stressful.

COPING WITH CHRONIC WORK STRESS

The previous section provides evidence of the variety of stressors to which individuals are exposed in the workplace. Individuals have developed many ways to deal with these stressors. However, as indicated in the introduction, the literature examining coping with workplace stressors rarely links coping strategies to specific workplace stressors. In fact, usually respondents are asked to report how they handle general "difficulties" at work or to think of a specific stressful event and report how they "coped" with it. That is, when listing the coping strategies they used, individuals could be thinking of very different aspects of their workplace, as little effort is made to ensure that all individuals are focusing on the same specific type of work stressors. Studies measuring coping in this manner typically proceed to explore the impact of reported coping on measures of strain or work satisfaction.

The Measurement of Coping

In this chapter, *coping* is defined as the cognitive and behavioral efforts individuals undertake to manage those internal and external demands that tax or exceed their personal resources (Lazarus & Folkman, 1984). Perhaps the best way to introduce the variety of different coping strategies is to discuss first how coping with work stress has been measured. Coping as a function of personality traits such as type A personality or personality hardiness will not be examined. Cox and Ferguson (1991) and Parkes (1994) review the results of studies that explore the effects of personality on coping with work stress.

Researchers have measured coping efforts in a number of ways, most frequently using items that reflect Lazarus and his colleagues' widely acknowledged problem- and emotion-focused coping dichotomy. Problem-focused coping refers to efforts to act on stressful situations by altering behaviors or the environment. Emotion-focused coping refers to strategies individuals use when they seek to manage emotions resulting from stressful incidents. A third factor, appraisal-focused coping, involves cognitive strategies such as denial or redefinition of the situation (Moos & Billings, 1982). In the organizational literature, there is some concern that such global classifications of coping are insufficient or too broad, because subdimensions of these categories have been found (see reviews by Cox & Ferguson, 1991; Dewe, Cox, & Ferguson, 1993; Latack & Havlovic, 1992). For example, existing measures of coping have been analyzed using factor analytic techniques to extract additional coping dimensions. The widely used Ways of Coping Checklist (Folkman & Lazarus, 1985) contains eight factors: confrontative coping, distancing, self-control, seeking social support, accepting responsibility, escape–avoidance, planful problem solving, and positive reappraisal (Folkman, Lazarus, Dunkel-Schetter, DeLongis, & Gruen, 1986).

Amirkhan (1990), Endler and Parker (1990), and Latack (1986) have developed new, theoretically based measures of coping that have three underlying factors (Dewe et al., 1993; Newton, 1989). Consistent with previous theory, two of the three factors were problem-focused, or direct action, approaches and emotion-focused strategies. The third factor contained avoidance or escape strategies such as withdrawal or ignoring the situation.

Studies that do not rely on previous theory to develop coping dimensions are less common. For example, Dewe and Guest (1990) asked several occupational groups to answer open-ended questions about how they coped with an incident they regarded as stressful. Content analysis of the responses revealed five coping components consistent across the different occupations: rational task-oriented behavior, emotional release, distraction, passive rationalization, and social support. Similarly, Newton and Keenan (1985) asked recently employed engineering graduates how they had "handled" a recent stressful situation. Content analysis resulted in five classes of coping: talking to others, direct action, preparatory action, withdrawal, and the expression of helplessness or feelings of resentment. These studies try to align themselves with previous research by placing, perhaps forcing, their coping factors into an existing framework such as problem- or emotion-focused coping categories (Dewe et al., 1993).

In summary, research efforts have created different coping measures that contain an assortment of different coping strategies. Problem- and emotion-focused strategies remain dominant, and strategies involving escape from or avoidance of stressful situations are also commonly reported. Latack and Havlovic's (1992) framework to categorize coping measures helps to illustrate these tendencies. Following convention, strategies are first identified as either problem- or emotion-focused, and then categorized as either cognitive or behavioral. Cognitive and behavioral distinctions are further classified as being control- or escape-oriented. Finally, cognitive strategies imply a solitary approach, but behavioral strategies can be additionally identified as social or solitary.

Despite the qualification made earlier, some studies do include a measure of work stressors and attempt to relate the stressor or stress level to the coping strategies that are employed. Our discussion of coping with work stress briefly reviews these studies, and then examines the more typical approach that focuses on the relationship between coping strategies and strain outcomes.

Workplace Stressors and Coping

When do individuals use specific coping strategies? As indicated, research rarely links specific coping efforts to specific workplace stressors. It is more common for studies to focus on general work stress and to report such findings as the use of more emotion-focused coping (Bhagat, Allie, & Ford, 1991) and wishful thinking (McDonald & Korabik, 1991) among those who report high levels of such general work stress than among those reporting low levels. The two groups do not differ in their use of problem-focused strategies. One of the few studies examining coping responses to specific chronic work stressors found that greater role conflict was associated with more escapist coping strategies, whereas more role ambiguity was associated with a decline in coping strategies involving direct action (Havlovic & Keenan, 1991). These studies highlight a trend revealing that individuals in high-stress environments use emotion-focused or distancing coping strategies more than do those in low-stress environments. Additionally, greater stress may reduce the use of problem-solving activities (Havlovic & Keenan, 1991). Perhaps greater stress makes individuals have "more reason to wish the stressful situations would go away" (McDonald & Korabik, 1991, p. 196), or individual efforts may simply not be enough to resolve occupational problems (Menaghan & Merves, 1984).

Research examining how people cope with work stressors has also measured perceptions or appraisals of the stressor rather than measuring the stressors per se. The impact of this appraisal on the choice of coping strategy is then studied. For example, Dewe (1989) found that, when asked to describe a stressful event, participants were able to appraise the event's intensity, frequency, and meaning (impact). These types of appraisals have been found to contribute to an individual's choice of coping strategy (Dewe, 1989; Newton & Keenan, 1985; Schwartz & Stone, 1993). Schwartz and Stone (1993) showed that appraisal of an event's severity was a significant predictor of the use of four coping strategies: catharsis, social support, relaxation, and direct action. An event's severity rating involved the event's degree of undesirability and meaningfulness, as well as the degree to which it would change/stabilize one's lifestyle. Readers interested in individuals' appraisals of work stressors should refer to a series of studies conducted by Dewe (1991, 1992a, 1992b, 1993). Dewe has developed scales designed to measure Lazarus and colleagues' concepts of primary and secondary appraisal in a work environment.

The question remains as to whether or not any one coping strategy is more successful in reducing the negative effects of stress. Are the emotion-focused strategies used in high-stress environments appropriate? Next we consider several studies that have examined the effects of coping strategies on employee strain.

Strain and Coping

Decker and Borgen (1993) investigated coping strategies in a group of university employees. After statistically accounting for the effects of work stressors on individual strain, they found that a general increase in coping involving recreation, self-care, social support, and rational/cognitive strategies significantly reduced the amount of perceived strain. Therefore, the more coping strategies they used, the less strain these employees experienced. However, Menaghan and Merves (1984) studied how a large panel of employed Chicago area adults dealt with work "difficulties" and found that the use of the emotion-focused strategies of restricting one's expectations of work satisfaction and viewing one's work situation pessimistically was associated with greater feelings of job strain. Here, an emotion-focused coping strategy increased rather than decreased strain. Thus, the relationship between different coping strategies and strain is not clear-cut.

In another study, newly employed engineering graduates were asked to think of a recent stressful experience at work and describe how they "handled" it (Newton & Keenan, 1985). The graduates' feelings of job-related anger and frustration were reduced by the use of such preparatory actions as getting information or seeking an alternative approach, whereas increases in these feelings were associated with the use of coping strategies involving acceptance of the situation or expressing resentment. In the case of the young engineers, problem-focused coping strategies reduced strain, but more palliative strategies increased strain. Similarly, greater use of active problem solving at work by nurses was related to fewer health complaints and greater job satisfaction, whereas greater use of palliative coping strategies was associated with reporting of more health complaints (Boumans & Landeweerd, 1992). Further, problem-focused coping strategies used by teachers to deal with "difficulties" at work was related to job satisfaction and feelings of accomplishment (Bhagat et al., 1991).

Violanti (1992) studied the coping strategies of police recruits undergoing training. He found that lower levels of strain were associated with using planful problem solving as a coping strategy, as well as distancing strategies. Higher levels of strain were related to escape/avoidance strategies, but were also associated with the use of self-control strategies. Thus, in the case of police recruits the choice of coping strategy is not a simple one. Problem- and emotion-focused coping strategies can either increase or decrease strain. Violanti explains these findings in terms of the situation. Recruits are in a very controlled environment. If planful problem solving is not possible, the use of a distancing strategy may aid the recruit in dealing with the stress engendered by a highly controlling environment without physically removing the recruit from the situation he/she must face. This would not be the case with escape/avoidance strategies. The use of self-control as a strategy may also be counterproductive because recruits could isolate themselves from their peers and thus contravene the norm that they should work cooperatively. When control is possible for police recruits, problem-focused approaches reduce strain, but when control is not possible, emotion-focused distancing reduces strain (Violanti, 1992).

Similarly, Palmer (1983) studied emergency medical technicians who are constantly in contact with people who are injured and/or dying. This offers an extreme example of people in occupations where control is frequently lost. Palmer found that the technicians had developed unique and apparently functional coping strategies. For example, humor was used as an escape or safety valve, whereas psychological distancing was accomplished through technical language (e.g., death becomes a signal 27) and rationalizations such as "you lose a few, but without us none would survive."

It should now be evident that few judgments can be made about the general effectiveness of any single coping strategy. Specific occupations and/or organizational situations are likely to dictate the most effective coping strategy for employees. Violanti's (1992) study suggests that problem-focused approaches are the most effective coping strategies in environments where individuals have control. Perhaps the evidence that high-stress environments lead to greater use of emotion-focused coping reveals more about the lack of control individuals have over their environment than their ability to cope. If individuals cannot change the stressors in their environments via problem-focused coping, they must attempt to manage their perceptions of it via emotion-focused coping. The question that remains is how long such strategies will keep strain at a minimum and employees productive.

Coping as a Moderator

Several researchers have recently attempted to investigate stressors, coping, and strain in the same study. These studies of the moderating effects of coping on the stressor–strain relationship examine how various coping strategies alter the effect a stressor has on an individual's reported strain. However, as is the case for most of the previously described studies, the majority of examples adopt a general measure of work stress, asking respondents to describe how they deal with "difficulties," or "problems," at work. Typically, these moderator studies find only a few of the possible moderating relationships to be significant, and there are numerous variations in the coping strategies and strain outcome variables. For example, Bhagat et al. (1991) studied general organizational stress in teachers. Organizational stress involved ratings of the stress associated with events such as excessive responsibility for students, equipment shortages, and discipline. The study found that problem-focused coping strategies directed at work "difficulties" moderated the relationship between organizational stress and illness, as well as organizational stress and burnout. That is, those individuals using problem-focused coping strategies experienced less adverse effects of occupational stress. Emotion-focused strategies moderated the relationship between organizational stress and depersonalization. Those using emotion-focused coping strategies to combat organizational stress experienced greater depersonalization. However, many more possible moderating relationships were not found to be significant.

Greenglass and Burke (1991) examined the moderating effects of coping among school board employees. During "times of work stress," the coping strategies of internal control and preventive coping (e.g., plan/prepare for the future) moderated or buffered the impact of overall work stress on both anxiety and depression. As was the case in Bhagat et al. (1991) study, these are only two of a large number of moderating relationships that were examined.

Other researchers have found no significant moderating effects of coping efforts on the relationship between general work stress and strain. Frone, Russell, and Cooper (1991) asked a random sample of household residents about their active coping styles. They found that the use of active coping when approaching problems did not moderate the relationship between a general measure of job stress and both depression and somatic symptoms. Professional human service workers were asked to report how they coped with the "stress and strain of their jobs" (Shinn, Rosario, Morch, & Chestnut, 1984). Neither problem- nor emotion-focused coping consistently moderated the relationship between work stress and strain.

These examples exemplify the variety of coping strategies and outcome variables used in such studies, as well as the few moderating relationships found to be statistically significant. Therefore, generalization and practical application of the results of these studies are premature. Greater precision in these studies, with *specific* coping strategies being tied to *specific* stressor–strain relationships, has been called for (Parkes, 1994). For example, Boumans and Landeweerd (1992) found that the use of active problem solving by nurses moderated the relationship between the specific stressor of work complexity/difficulty and job satisfaction. Social support from people at work buffered the relationship of job satisfaction with each of the specific stressors—work pressure, lack of autonomy, and lack of promotion. Social support also buffered the relationship between lack of autonomy and health complaints. Future research must attend to specific stressor–strain relationships before any practical use can be made of these studies.

Further Methodological Problems in the Study of Coping

Several other conceptual and methodological issues need to be addressed before it is possible to apply the results of research on coping with chronic work stress. First, the difference between a coping style and a coping strategy must be recognized. Second, coping and its effectiveness must be gauged separately.

Coping *styles* are dispositional in nature. A coping style addresses the typical coping patterns of individuals or what they usually do in response to stress. Dewe and Guest (1990) assessed coping style when they asked, "If, like most people, you occasionally get particularly fed up with your job and feel tense and frustrated, how do you cope?" (p. 139). In contrast, coping *strategies* are situation-specific. Typically, respondents are asked to record an event they found stressful and then indicate how they reacted to that specific event.

The distinction between coping styles and coping strategies is well recognized (Dewe et al., 1993; Latack & Havlovic, 1992; Newton, 1989; Parkes, 1994). This distinction is critical in the study of chronic work stress because measures of coping styles may address chronic work stressors better than measures of coping strategies. Newton (1989) believes that individuals give greater consideration to ongoing chronic stressors when reporting their coping style. For example, when people are asked about how they coped with general difficulties at work, they will first consider more "typical" workplace stressors rather than an isolated incident. Measures of coping strategies, where individuals choose a specific single event they found stressful, may better reflect an isolated incident. Consequently, these strategies are more likely to address acute workplace stressors. Thus, researchers investigating how people cope with chronic or acute workplace stressors have an urgent need to make the distinction between coping styles and coping strategies, but this need is driven by the way researchers measure coping. They often do not know to what stressors participants are recording their reactions. If researchers phrased their questions more directly, the issue of how coping styles or strategies reflect chronic and acute stressors will be moot. For example, as we have suggested, participants should be asked how they reacted to specific stressors, such as role conflict or job insecurity. The issue would then be whether or not role conflict or job insecurity is a chronic or acute stressor in a given work environment. Of course, this issue has its own methodological problems, as indicated in the previous section on chronic work stressors.

Finally, coping per se and coping effectiveness are often confounded in the coping literature (Dewe et al., 1993). Latack and Havlovic (1992) noted that "Job-related coping items should allow for independent assessment of coping and coping effectiveness" (p. 493). Researchers asking individuals what has been "useful" in dealing with stressful work situations (Burke & Belcourt, 1974) or how they "coped" may invoke only effective strategies. Coping measures asking what respondents "did to try to feel better or handle the problem" (Schwartz & Stone, 1993, p. 50) or how they "reacted" to a stressful situation at work (Havlovic & Keenan, 1991; Latack, 1986) do not confound coping and its effectiveness.

WORKPLACE INTERVENTIONS FOR CHRONIC WORK STRESS

What are organizations actually doing to alleviate the negative outcomes of stress in the workplace? Typically, the intervention research focuses either on the stressor or on individuals' coping efforts. Research that focuses on the stressor supports the notion that work stress can be avoided or prevented by eliminating the source of stress. Such primary prevention makes individual coping efforts unnecessary. Research that focuses on individual coping strategies includes secondary preventive intervention, i.e., educating individuals about how to cope with workplace stressors. Tertiary preventive intervention provides assistance to those individuals who have not been able to effectively cope with a stressor and are therefore suffering from strain. Secondary and tertiary preventive interventions are the most frequently practiced interventions (Cooper & Cartwright, 1994; Murphy, 1992). Drawing on Murphy's (1992) description of these types of preventive interventions in organizations, we argue that the best approach to combat the effects of stress in the workplace combines all three strategies.

Tertiary Preventive Interventions

Organizations use tertiary interventions (e.g., employee assistance programs) to help those individuals who have not been able to effectively cope with workplace stressors and are suffering from worker strain (Murphy, 1992). The original intent of such programs was to help employees combat drinking problems. In recent years, a wider range of employee difficulties have been addressed in employee assistance programs, such as drug abuse and family violence (Murphy, 1992). Irrespective of whether employee assistance programs are provided by outside sources or are "in house," most large companies now have them in some form. However, their growth seems to be slowing and they are scarce in smaller businesses (Berridge & Cooper, 1993). Employee assistance programs should be regarded as invaluable sources of information regarding workplace stressors. However, this knowledge and its potential uses are often overlooked (Berridge & Cooper, 1993; Murphy, 1992). For example, employee assistance programs could be used to provide feedback about the effectiveness of programs designed to reduce stressors.

The question remains as to whether or not employee assistance programs are effective in alleviating employee strain. General Motors has claimed their programs have saved $37 million dollars annually (Feldman, 1991). However, employee assistance programs are often not subjected to controlled scientific evaluation, and debate continues about the best way to evaluate such programs.

Secondary Preventive Interventions

Secondary-level preventive interventions (e.g., individual stress management training) teach employees to recognize workplace stressors and early signs of their health effects. Employees are taught how to identify and cope with workplace stressors and are trained in ways to reduce arousal (e.g., biofeedback, relaxation techniques). Programs are typically restricted to white collar occupations and to volunteers. They are not targeted to workers identified with stress difficulties (e.g., Murphy, 1992; Murphy & Sorensen, 1988). Evaluations of the effectiveness of stress management programs are plagued with problems. For example, because the effects of the training may not last (Ganster, Mayes, Sime, & Tharp, 1982; Hurrell, 1995), short-term follow-up is insufficient (Ivancevich, Matteson, Freedman, & Phillips, 1990; Murphy, 1992).

Primary Prevention

Primary prevention in the workplace involves the reduction or elimination of the actual stressors. A concurrent decline or elimination of employee strain should also result. Unfortunately, the popularity of stress management programs suggests that organizations are more inclined to teach employees to cope with stress than to remove the sources of employee stress (Cooper & Cartwright, 1994). Due to the difficulties and expense involved, employees rather than the organization itself are the preferred targets of change.

However, a study by Theorell et al. (1991) dramatically demonstrates the need for primary prevention on the job. For 5 years they followed 79 men who had suffered a heart attack before the age of 45; 49 survived with no further cardiac complications, 17 survived another attack or had corrective bypass surgery, and 13 died as a result of ischaemic heart disease. After controlling for cardiovascular health, it was found that the 13 participants who died had all returned to a work environment that had not changed in terms of the demands placed on the workers *or* the opportunity for worker control over these demands. These data dramatically testify to the need for primary prevention involving organizational change.

Reviews of the literature on primary prevention (Burke, 1993; Murphy, 1992) suggest that it is effective. Specifically, controlled outcome studies that have brought about changes in job design show beneficial effects. Individuals with greater participation in decision making experienced less role conflict and role ambiguity than those with less decision latitude (Jackson, 1983). Schaubroeck, Ganster, Sime, and Ditman (1993) demonstrated empirically that when supervisors are trained to clarify their subordinates' roles, role ambiguity is decreased significantly. A job redesign study that increased worker autonomy reduced employee strain as long as 18 months after the study (Wall & Clegg, 1981). Wall et al. (1990) showed that giving workers greater control resulted in increased performance and psychological well-being. Campion and McClelland (1991) found that enlarged jobs, where two jobs are combined into one, resulted in greater job satisfaction and less mental underload. In addition, in a long-term follow-up, Campion and McClelland (1993) discovered that it is only when the combined jobs resulted in knowledge enlargement, not merely task enlargement, that the benefits continue. Increased control over work schedules with flexitime was studied by Pierce and Newstrom (1983). A positive relationship was found between aspects of work schedule flexibility and employee behavior variables such as employee performance and absenteeism. However, the relationship was not as simple for employee attitude variables. Employees' perceptions of control over their schedules mediated the positive relationships between aspects of work schedule flexibility and employees' attitude variables, such as intrinsic and extrinsic job satisfaction and organizational commitment.

Although primary prevention holds the greatest promise for combating work stress, some workplace stressors cannot be altered (e.g., involvement in a hospital emergency ward), and therefore not all employees can benefit from such initiatives. Thus, attempts to facilitate coping with chronic work stressors should allow employees access to primary, secondary, *and* tertiary interventions. This is consistent with Ganster et al.'s (1982) suggestion that primary preventive interventions should be supplemented with secondary preventive interventions such as stress management programs. Also, suggestions of conducting stress audits to determine where the problems are before any intervention is undertaken should be heeded (Cooper & Cartwright, 1994).

CONCLUSION

Our review of research on coping with work stress reveals that the work stressor itself is often unspecified, the major focus being on the relationship between individual coping efforts and resulting strain. Before practical use can be made of this body of work, researchers must attend to specific stressor–strain relationships and examine the moderating effects of individual coping strategies. In addition, because coping strategies are assumed to ultimately affect the stressors themselves, studies examining the impact of coping efforts on the original stressful situation are necessary (Edwards, 1992a,b). In general, longitudinal approaches, with stressors, measured at two points in time, are needed.

We have also observed that some individual efforts to cope with workplace stressors are not helpful in reducing strain. Indeed, some coping strategies have the reverse effect. For example, many emotion-focused and avoidance coping strategies are associated with greater strain. Also, as Violanti (1992) found in his study of police recruits, even strategies involving self-control can be associated with greater strain. The limitations of individual coping efforts are further reinforced by the fact that secondary and tertiary preventive interventions may not be effective in the long term.

In terms of future research, it is necessary to restate a critical difference between primary, secondary, and tertiary preventive interventions. Secondary and tertiary preventive interventions implicitly assume that the problem resides at the individual employee level (see Hurrell, 1995): If only we could help employees be more hardy, ruggedly individualistic, or even religious (Beehr, Johnson, & Nieva, 1995), the problem would "go away." Preselection (more accurately pre-exclusion) or individual counseling would help employees avoid chronic work stress. By itself this approach is practically and ethically questionable. A more desirable approach would be to use primary prevention to help employees change their work environments. Initial findings suggest such an approach is likely to be more successful (Hurrell, 1995). Further, an approach combining all three preventive interventions should be used.

Finally, any research examining chronic work stressors or coping with work stress must attempt to overcome, or at the very least acknowledge, certain methodological problems. We have identified a host of methodological issues, many regarding the actual measurement of chronic stressors and coping strategies. Issues as simple as how one asks individuals to report their experiences of work stressors or how they "coped" can have serious implications. The duration of a workplace stressor, its time of onset, and the likelihood of its recurrence must all be taken into account before a stressor can be defined as acute or chronic. This is critical because the same stressor can be acute in one workplace but chronic in another. Researchers must also be cautious not to confuse a coping strategy with its effectiveness. Asking individuals how they coped or what was useful may yield only those coping efforts people found effective. Instead, researchers should ask for individuals' reactions to stressful situations or what they did to try to feel better.

In conclusion, there is much room for future research examining workplace stressors and coping with work stress. Future researchers must attempt to unite the two literatures as well as evaluate organizational preventive interventions incorporating primary prevention with secondary and tertiary preventive efforts.

ACKNOWLEDGMENTS The writing of this chapter was supported by grants from the Social Sciences and Humanities Research Council of

Canada to Catherine Loughlin (752-94-1414) and Julian Barling (341-605), and from the School of Business, Queen's University, to Julian Barling.

REFERENCES

American Psychiatric Association. (1987). *Diagnostic and statistical manual of mental disorders* (3rd ed.). Washington, DC: Author.

Amirkhan, J. H. (1990). A factor analytically derived measure of coping: The coping strategy indicator. *Journal of Personality and Social Psychology, 59*, 1066–1074.

Appelbaum, E. (1992). Structural change and the growth of part-time and temporary employment. In V. L. DuRivage (Ed.), *New policies for the part-time and contingent workforce* (pp. 1–13). New York: M. E. Sharpe.

Astrand, N. E., Hanson, B. S., & Isacsson, S. O. (1989). Job demands, job decision latitude, job support and social network factors as predictors of mortality in a Swedish pulp and paper company. *British Journal of Industrial Medicine, 46*, 334–340.

Barling, J. (1990). *Employment, stress and family functioning*. Toronto: Wiley.

Beehr, T. A., Johnson, L. B., & Nieva, R. (1995). Occupational stress: Coping of police and their spouses. *Journal of Organizational Behavior, 16*, 3–25.

Berridge, J., & Cooper, C. L. (1993). Stress and coping in US organizations: The role of the Employee Assistance Programme. *Work and Stress, 7*, 77–87.

Bhagat, R. S., Allie, S. M., & Ford, D. L., Jr. (1991). Organizational stress, personal life stress and symptoms of life strains: An inquiry into the moderating role of styles of coping. *Journal of Social Behavior and Personality, 6*(7), 163–184.

Blaghly, P. H., Osterud, M. D., & Josslin, R. (1963). Suicide in professional groups. *The New England Journal of Medicine, 268*, 1278–1282.

Boumans, N. P. G., & Landeweerd, J. A. (1992). The role of social support and coping behaviour in nursing work: Main or buffering effect? *Work and Stress, 6*, 191–202.

Broadbent, D. E. (1985). The clinical impact of job design. *British Journal of Clinical Psychology, 24*, 33–44.

Brockner, J. (1988). The effects of work layoffs on survivors: Research, theory, and practise. *Research in Organizational Behavior, 10*, 213–255.

Burke, R. J. (1993). Organizational-level interventions to reduce occupational stressors. *Work and Stress, 7*, 77–87.

Burke, R. J., & Belcourt, M. L. (1974). Managerial role strain and coping responses. *Journal of Business Administration, 5*(2), 55–68.

Campion, M. A., & McClelland, C. L. (1991). Interdisciplinary examination of the costs and benefits of enlarged jobs. *Journal of Applied Psychology, 76*, 186–198.

Campion, M. A., & McClelland, C. L. (1993). Follow-up and extension of the interdisciplinary costs and benefits of enlarged jobs. *Journal of Applied Psychology, 78*, 339–351.

Cooper, C. L., & Cartwright, S. (1994). Healthy mind, healthy organization—A proactive approach to occupational stress. *Human Relations, 47*(4), 455–471.

Cox, T., & Ferguson, E. (1991). Individual difference, stress and coping. In C. L. Cooper & R. Payne (Eds.), *Personality and stress: Individual differences in the stress process* (pp. 7–30). Chichester, England: Wiley.

Daly, J. (1994, March 14). The four-day week. *Maclean's*, 36–38.

Decker, P. J., & Borgen, F. H. (1993). Dimensions of work appraisal: Stress, strain, coping, job satisfaction, and negative affectivity. *Journal of Counselling Psychology, 40*, 470–478.

Dewe, P. (1989). Examining the nature of work stress: Individual evaluations of stressful experiences and coping. *Human Relations, 42*, 993–1013.

Dewe, P. (1991). Primary appraisal, secondary appraisal and coping: Their role in stressful work encounters. *Journal of Occupational Psychology, 64*, 331–351.

Dewe, P. J. (1992a). Applying the concept of appraisal to work stressors: Some exploratory analysis. *Human Relations, 45*, 143–164.

Dewe, P. (1992b). The appraisal process: Exploring the role of meaning, importance, control and coping in work stress. *Anxiety, Stress and Coping, 5,* 95–109.

Dewe, P. (1993). Measuring primary appraisal: Scale construction and directions for future research. *Journal of Social Behavior and Personality, 8,* 673–685.

Dewe, P., Cox, T., & Ferguson, E. (1993). Individual strategies for coping with stress at work: A review. Coping with stress at work. *Work and Stress, 7,* 5–15.

Dewe, P. J., & Guest, D. E. (1990). Methods of coping with stress at work: A conceptual analysis and empirical study of measurement issues. *Journal of Organizational Behavior, 11,* 135–150.

Edwards, J. R. (1992a). A cybernetic theory of stress, coping, and well-being in organizations. *Academy of Management Review, 17*(2), 238–274.

Edwards, J. R. (1992b). The determinants and consequences of coping with stress. In C. L. Cooper and R. Payne (Eds.), *Causes, coping and consequences of stress at work* (2nd ed., pp. 233–263). Chichester, England: Wiley.

Endler, N. S., & Parker, J. D. A. (1990). Multidimensional assessment of coping: A critical evaluation. *Journal of Personality and Social Psychology, 58,* 844–854.

Feldman, S. (1991). Today's EAPs, make the grade. *Personnel, 68,* 3–40.

Fell, R. D., Richard, W. C., & Wallace, W. L. (1980). Psychological job stress and the police officer. *Journal of Police Science and Administration, 8,* 139–144.

Fisher, C. D., & Gitelson, R. (1983). A meta-analysis of the correlates of role conflict and ambiguity. *Journal of Applied Psychology, 68,* 320–333.

Folkman, S., & Lazarus, R. S. (1985). If it changes it must be a process: Study of emotion and coping during three stages of a college examination. *Journal of Personality and Social Psychology, 48,* 150–170.

Folkman, S., Lazarus, R. S., Dunkel-Schetter, C., DeLongis, A., & Gruen, R. J. (1986). Dynamics of a stressful encounter: Cognitive appraisal, coping, and encounter outcomes. *Journal of Personality and Social Psychology, 50,* 992–1003.

Frone, M. R., Russell, M., & Cooper, M. L. (1991). Relationship of work and family stressors to psychological distress: The independent moderating influence of social support, mastery, active coping, and self-focused attention. *Journal of Social Behavior and Personality, 6*(7), 227–250.

Ganster, D. C., Mayes, B. T., Sime, W. E., & Tharp, G. D. (1982). Managing occupational stress: A field experiment. *Journal of Applied Psychology, 67,* 533–542.

Garson, B. (1989). *The electronic sweatshop: How computers are transforming the office of the future into the factory of the past.* New York: Penguin.

Gibb-Clark, M. (March 16, 1992). Lawyers, literati, and buffoons. *Globe and Mail,* p. B6.

Greenglass, E. R., & Burke, R. J. (1991). The relationship between stress and coping among Type As. *Journal of Social Behavior and Personality, 6,* 361–373.

Hackman, J. R., & Oldham, G. R. (1980). *Work redesign.* Reading, MA: Addison-Wesley.

Halpert, J. A., Wilson, M. L., & Hickman, J. L. (1993). Pregnancy as a source of bias in performance appraisals. *Journal of Organizational Behavior, 14,* 649–663.

Hancock, L. (March 6, 1995). Breaking point. *Newsweek,* pp. 56–61.

Hartley, J. (1995). Challenge and change in employment relations: Issues for psychology, trade unions and managers. In L. Tetrick & J. Barling (Eds.), *Changing employment relations: Behavioral and social perspectives.* Washington, DC: American Psychological Association.

Havlovic, S. J., & Keenan, J. P. (1991). Coping with work stress: The influence of individual differences. *Journal of Social Behavior and Personality, 6*(7), 199–212.

Hurrell, J. J. (1995). Police work, occupational stress and individual coping. *Journal of Organizational Behavior, 16,* 27–28.

Ivancevich, J. M., Matteson, M. T., Freedman, S. M., & Phillips, J. S. (1990). Worksite stress management interventions. *American Psychologist, 45,* 252–261.

Jackson, A. (July 24, 1993). Drive to part-time work overestimated. *Globe and Mail,* p. D7.

Jackson, P. R. (1988). Personal networks, social mobilization and unemployment. *Psychological Medicine, 18,* 397–404.

JACKSON, S. E. (1983). Participation in decision making as a strategy for reducing job-related strain. *Journal of Applied Psychology, 68,* 3–19.
JAHODA, M., LAZARSFELD, P. F., & ZEISEL, H. (1933). *Marienthal: The sociography of an unemployed community.* London: Tavistock.
KAHN, R. L. (1980). Conflict, ambiguity and overload: Three elements in job stress. In D. Katz, R. L. Kahn, & J. S. Adams (Eds.), *The study of organizations: Findings from field and laboratory* (pp. 418–428). San Francisco: Jossey-Bass.
KAHN, R. L., WOLFE, D. M., QUINN, R. P., SNOEK, J. D., & ROSENTHAL, R. A. (1964). *Role stress: Studies in role conflict and ambiguity.* New York: Wiley.
KANTER, R. M. (1977). *Men and women of the corporation.* New York: Basic books.
KARASEK, R. A., & THEORELL, T. (1990). *Healthy work: Stress, productivity and the reconstruction of working life.* New York: Basic Books.
KROES, W. H., MARGOLIS, B. L., & HURRELL, J. J. (1974). Job stress in policemen. *Journal of Police Science and Administration, 2,* 145–155.
LATACK, J. C. (1986). Coping with job stress: Measures and future direction for scale development. *Journal of Applied Psychology, 71,* 377–385.
LATACK, J. C., & HAVLOVIC, S. J. (1992). Coping with job stress: A conceptual evaluation framework for coping measures. *Journal of Organizational Behavior, 13,* 479–508.
LAZARUS, R., & FOLKMAN, S. (1984). *Stress, appraisal and coping.* New York: Springer.
LUND, J. (1992). Electronic performance monitoring: A review of research issues. *Applied Ergonomics, 23,* 54–58.
MCDONALD, L. M., & KORABIK, K. (1991). Sources of stress and ways of coping among male and female managers. *Journal of Social Behavior and Personality, 6*(7), 185–198.
MCNAMEE, M. (1994, January 24). Robert's rules of reorder. *Business Week,* 74–75.
MENAGHAN, E. G., & MERVES, E. S. (1984). Coping with occupational problems: The limits of individual efforts. *Journal of Health and Social Behavior, 25,* 406–423.
MOOS, R., & BILLINGS, A. (1982). Conceptualizing and measuring coping resources and processes. In L. Goldberger & S. Breznitz (Eds.), *Handbook of stress: Theoretical and clinical aspects.* New York: Free Press.
MURPHY, L. R. (1992). Workplace interventions for stress reduction and prevention. In C. L. Cooper & R. Payne (Eds.), *Causes, coping and consequences of stress at work* (2nd ed., pp. 301–339). Chichester, England: Wiley.
MURPHY, L. R., & SORENSEN, S. (1988). Employee behaviors before and after stress management. *Journal of Organizational Behavior, 9,* 173–182.
NEWTON, T. J. (1989). Occupational stress and coping with stress: A critique. *Human Relations, 42,* 441–461.
NEWTON, T. J., & KEENAN, A. (1985). Coping with work-related stress. *Human Relations, 38,* 107–126.
NORD, W. R. (1977). Job satisfaction reconsidered. *American Psychologist, 32,* 1026–1035.
PALMER, C. E. (1983). A note about paramedics' strategies for dealing with death and dying. *Journal of Occupational Psychology, 56,* 83–86.
PARKES, K. R. (1994). Personality and coping as moderators of work stress processes: Models, methods and measures. *Work and Stress, 8*(2), 110–129.
PIERCE, J. L., & NEWSTROM, J. W. (1983). The design of flexible work schedules and employee responses: Relationships and processes. *Journal of Occupational Behavior, 4,* 247–262.
PRATT, L. I., & BARLING, J. (1988). Differentiating between daily events, acute, and chronic stressors: A framework and its implications. In J. R. Hurrell, L. R. Murphy, S. L. Sauter, & C. L. Cooper (Eds.), *Occupational stress: Issues and developments in research* (pp. 41–53). London: Taylor and Francis.
ROSE, K. D., & ROSOW, I. (1973). Physicians who kill themselves. *Archives of General Psychiatry, 29,* 800–806.
SAUTER, S. L., MURPHY, L. R., & HURRELL, J. J. (1990). Prevention of work-related psychological disorders: A national strategy proposed by the National Institute for Occupational Safety and Health (NIOSH). *American Psychologist, 45,* 1146–1158.

SCHAUBROECK, J., GANSTER, D. C., SIME, W. E., & DITMAN, D. (1993). A field experiment testing supervisory role clarification. *Personnel Psychology, 46,* 1–25.
SCHEIN, E. H. (1980). *Organizational Psychology.* Englewood Cliffs, NJ: Prentice-Hall.
SCHWARTZ, J. E., & STONE, A. A. (1993). Coping with daily work problems: Contributions of problem content, appraisals, and person factors. *Work and Stress, 7,* 47–62.
SHINN, M., ROSARIO, M., MORCH, H., & CHESTNUT, D. E. (1984). Coping with job stress and burnout in the human services. *Journal of Personality and Social Psychology, 46,* 864–876.
SWIMMER, G. (1990). Gender based differences in promotions of clerical workers. *Relations Industrielles, 45*(2), 300–310.
THEORELL, T., PERSKI, A., ORTH-GOMER, K., HAMSTEN, A., & DE FAIRE, U. (1991). The effects of the strain of returning to work on the risk of cardiac death after a first myocardial infarction before the age of 45. *International Journal of Cardiology, 30,* 61–67.
THOMPSON, M. (1994, May 23). The living room war. *Time,* 36–37.
TILLY, C. (1992). Short hours, short shrift: The causes and consequences of part-time employment. In V. L. DuRivage (Ed.), *New policies for the part-time and contingent workforce* (pp. 15–44). New York: M. E. Sharpe.
VIOLANTI, J. M. (1992). Coping strategies among police recruits in a high-stress training environment. *The Journal of Social Psychology, 132,* 717–729.
WALL, T. D., & CLEGG, C. W. (1981). A longitudinal study of group work redesign. *Journal of Occupational Behavior, 2,* 31–49.
WALL, T. D., CORBETT, J. M., MARTIN, R., CLEGG, C. W., & JACKSON, P. R. (1990). Advanced manufacturing technology, work design and performance: A change study. *Journal of Applied Psychology, 75,* 691–697.
WARR, P. (1987). *Work, unemployment and mental health.* Oxford: Oxford University Press.

Index

Acculturation, 333-335
Acquired Immune Deficiency Syndrome (AIDS), 293-312
Air traffic controllers, 195-196, 197, 211
Agency
 in relationships, 163, 166-168
 stressful threat to, 164

Bereavement, 145, 169, 273

Caregivers, 221-240, 293-312
 coping among, 85, 178, 179-180, 245-265, 249, 293-312
 coping efficacy among, 250-265
 coping outcomes among, 88, 134, 144, 147, 169-170
 role demands of, 7, 164, 222, 246-247
Childhood stressors, 333
Chronic illness
 among children, 165-166
 among older adults, 269-288
 demands of, 83-84
 determinants of coping with, 85-87
 disability and, 277-280
 stages of, 86
 types of
  AIDS, 293-312
  cancer, 105-106, 122, 143
  dementia, 7, 85, 134, 144, 164, 178, 179-180, 245-265
  myocardial infarction, 165, 360
  rheumatoid arthritis, 169-170, 279-286
  stroke, 221-240
 ways of coping with, 85-90

Chronic stress
 aging and, 337-339
 assessment instrument, 56-57, 69-71
 classification of, 5-6, 56-65, 134
  acculturation, 333-335
  complexity, 61-62
  conflict, 63
  demands, 58-59
  excess social stimulation, 134, 136-137, 142, 145-147
  immigration, 134, 139-140, 333-335
  interpersonal tensions, 162-164
  "invisible," 211
  loneliness, 134, 135-136, 328
  resource deprivation, 64-65
  restriction of choice, 63-64
  stigma, 134, 139, 330-332
  structural constraints, 59-60
  threats, 57-58
  uncertainty, 62-63, 347
  underreward, 60-61
 cognitive mechanisms in, 107, 122-123, 331
 contextual features of, 143
 coping efficacy and, 245-265, 274-281
 definition of, 4, 53-57
 effects on social behavior, 194-198, 150-154
 engineering model of, 32, 49-52
 family accommodation and, 211-213
 interpersonal relationships and, 7-8, 18, 133-156, 161-185
 involuntary coping processes and, 105-128, 191-218

367

Chronic stress (*cont.*)
  measurement issues, 65–68
    subjective versus objective, 66–68
  mediation of, 150–154
  models of coping with, 81–84
  moderation of, 141–149, 154
  normative chronic life stressors, 317, 319, 332–339
  parent-child interactions and, 195
  psychological strain and, 49–52, 135, 144–147, 349–350
  role strain and, 55–57, 82–83, 134, 137–138, 349
  stressful life events and, 6–10, 52–55, 107–109, 127, 134, 137, 152–153, 332–339, 350
  temporal changes in, 16–19
Cognitive appraisal, 85–86, 89, 90, 147, 326, 353–354
Communion
  in relationships, 163, 166–168
  stressful threats to, 164
Coping
  age differences in, 86
  assessment
    conceptual issues, 10–14
    everyday life routines and, 12–14
    measures, 352–353
    methodological issues, 12–16, 80–81, 91, 109–110, 213–215
    techniques for daily coping, 14
  control and, 147, 262
  costs of, 147
  cultural influences on, 87
  domain specificity of, 85, 248, 357
  dyadic, 164–185, 198–208, 221–240
  efficacy, 29–32, 79, 121, 165, 245–265, 269–288, 358
    as state or trait, 258–260, 275–277
    determinants of, 270, 281–285
    impact on adjustment, 277–280
    temporal stability of, 258–260, 276
    theoretical perspectives on, 270–271
  effort, 86, 109–110
  effortful versus involuntary, 106–128, 192
    adjustment to chronic stress and, 121–126
    definitions of, 110–115
    model of, 117–121
  empathic, 174–183

Coping (*cont.*)
  engagement versus disengagement, 106–128
    adjustment to chronic stress and, 121–126
    definitions of, 106, 115–116, 351
    targets of, 118
  environmental influences on, 17
  goals, 29–30, 110, 119–120, 253–254
  involuntary, 15, 110–115, 118–119
    negative affect and, 111–113
  older adults and, 92–95, 269–288, 315–339
  outcomes of, 87–90, 277–280, 339, 354–356
    methodological issues concerning, 90–91
    positive effects, 97
  costs, especially interpersonal, 164–169, 171–173, 183, 184
  patterns of, 79
  personality and, 175, 181–182
  relationship-focused, 162, 165–185, 247
    active engagement, 183
    protective buffering and, 166, 183
  resource deterioration and, 17
  routinized, 12–14, 16, 93
  social influences on, 16–17, 169–171, 192–208
  socioeconomic factors and, 96
  strategies compared to styles, 357–358
  temporal changes in, 16–19, 86–87, 88–89, 209–210, 215
  theoretical models of
    coping styles, 77–78, 357–358
    deviation amplification, 95–98
    psychodynamic, 76–77
    transactional, 11, 78–80, 109, 173, 213, 264–265, 271, 326
  types of, 249
    acceptance, 27, 94
    anticipatory, 97–98
    cognitive reinterpretation, 25–27
    confrontive, 172–173
    defense mechanisms, 76
    disclosure, 324–325
    distancing, 331
    distraction, 15, 114–115, 116–117, 120, 125, 127
    escape, 181
    instrumental, 28–29, 337

INDEX 369

Coping (*cont.*)
  types of (*cont.*)
    intrusive thoughts and imagery, 15, 22, 122–124, 145–146
    making meaning, 25–27, 83, 93–94, 98, 297
    optimism/pessimism, 24–25
    positive reappraisal, 310–311
    relaxation, 24
    religiosity, 27–28
    resignation, 27
    rumination, 116–117, 170
    social withdrawal, 23–24, 125, 136–137, 184, 195–196, 197, 199, 201–205, 210–211, 216, 327
    suppression, 113–115
    vigilance, 20–22, 139, 218, 327
    wishful thinking, 169, 170
    worry, 111–112
Crowding, 136–137, 142, 145–147

Daily stress, 196
Depression, cognitive processes in, 112–113, 114, 144
Diary studies, 185
Diathesis-stress theory, 7
Disasters, 152
Divorce, 137

Efficacy
  coping, 245–265, 269–288
  for positive events, 272–288
  theoretical perspectives on, 270–271
Emergency workers, 355
Emotional overinvolvement, 167
Empathy, 174–175
Employee assistance program (EAP), 359
Equity theory, 225, 237

Gender roles, 138
General adaptation syndrome (GAS), 46, 51, 97

Holocaust survivors, 315–340

Immigration, 333–335
Immunity, 134, 136, 143
Intrusive memories and images, 323–326

Job Characteristics Model, 344
Job Strain Model, 346
Just world hypothesis, 150

Loneliness, 135–136

Maternal daily stress and coping, 198–208
Model of selective optimization, 92–95

Observational coding, 199–200
Occupational stress, 138, 195, 197, 199, 211, 343–362
  impact on adjustment, 350–351
  prevention of, 358–361
  types of, 345–348

Police, 355
Positive meaningful events, 295–312
  types of, 300–304
Posttraumatic stress disorder (PTSD), 21–22, 317
Posttraumatic stressors, 319, 322–332
Poverty, 216–218
Preschool children's coping, 198–208
Primary prevention, 360–361

Role theory, 137

Secondary prevention, 359–360
Sick role, 236
Social disorganization, 140
Social integration, 135
  mortality and morbidity and, 135
Social isolation, 328–330
Social support, 7–8, 16–18, 84, 89, 94, 141–144, 192, 222–240, 329–330
  communication of, 228–235
  contingent nature of, 142, 169–170
  deterioration of, 142–143, 147, 150–152
  effect on self-reliance versus dependency, 283–285
  efficacy beliefs and, 282–285
  miscarried, 151, 178, 224, 226–227
  reciprocity of, 225–227, 232–235, 236–239
  seeking of, 163
Stepfamilies, 170, 177
Stress
  amplification, 144–148, 155,
  buffer or moderator, 141–144, 150, 154, 356–357
  defined, 44–52
  management, 360
  mediator, 150–154
  modifier, 141–149
  spillover and, 9, 195

Stressors, defined, 46–48
Sudden Infant Death Syndrome (SIDS), 145
Systems theory, 95–96, 197

Teachers, 356
Tertiary prevention, 359

Traumatic stressors, 319–322
Trust, 326–328

Uplifts, 295–296

Victimization, 150–151, 326
Violence, 216–218